THE FLOUR WAR

The
FLOUR WAR

Gender, Class, and Community
in Late Ancien Régime French Society

CYNTHIA A. BOUTON

THE PENNSYLVANIA STATE UNIVERSITY PRESS
University Park, Pennsylvania

Library of Congress Cataloging-in-Publication Data

Bouton, Cynthia A.
    The flour war : gender, class, and community in late Ancien Régime
    French society / Cynthia A. Bouton.

        p.   cm.
    Includes bibliographical references and index.
    ISBN 0-271-01053-3.—ISBN 0-271-01055-X (pbk.)
    1. Crowds—France—History—18th century. 2. Riots—France—
    History—18th century. 3. Food prices—France—History—18th
    century. 4. Wheat trade—France—History—18th century. 5. France—
    History—Revolution, 1789–1799—Causes. 6. France—History—
    Revolution, 1789–1799—Economic aspects. I. Title.
    HM283.B68   1993
    306'.0944'09033—dc20   93-20349
                                                                          CIP

Published by The Pennsylvania State University Press, Barbara Building, Suite C,
University Park, PA 16802-1003

CONTENTS

LIST OF TABLES AND MAPS

Tables

Maps

ACKNOWLEDGMENTS

Like all historians, I hesitate to declare unequivocally the origins of anything, but the long trail that led to this book had its proximate beginnings
years ago in Colgate University's Study Abroad program and gained direction through the friendly persuasions of Professor Harry Payne, then a
member of Colgate's History Department.

The history faculty at the State University of New York at Binghamton
welcomed me, French literature degree and all, into its doctoral program.
At Binghamton I benefited from the kindness and patience of the late
Thadd Hall and the unwavering support and inspiring example of W. Warren
Wagar, a teacher who brings to his classroom stunning abilities and tireless
commitment. In my final years at Binghamton, Elizabeth Fox-Genovese
joined the faculty, at once became a source of wisdom and encouragement,
and has remained such ever since.

In France I have found everywhere people who belie the American image
of the French as sullen, arrogant, and hostile to strangers generally and to
Americans in particular. In Paris and outside it, librarians and archivists
everywhere have lent a hand. French scholars—Arlette Farge, Florence
Gauthier, Jean-Marc Moriceau, Jean Nicolas, and others—have generously
shared their insights and information. I owe a debt that I cannot adequately
describe, let alone pay, to two dedicated scholars of Ancien Régime France.

The late René Samson, for whom the study of Beauvais and the Beauvaisis was a lifelong labor of love, opened for me not only his knowledge of the region's history, much of it as a running commentary as we drove through villages and lanes where Flour War rioters once rambled, but also his home. I hope that M. and Mme. Samson may somehow know how well and how gratefully their "petite jeune fille américaine" remembers.

I have enjoyed the same generosity and kindness from Guy-Robert and Lucette Ikni, who have provided an infallibly warm welcome in France, despite the pressures of family, business, and scholarship. Guy proved time and time again to be a generous colleague and friend.

Many people have taken the time to read the manuscript in whole or in part and to share their comments with me. These include John Bohstedt, Nancy Fitch, Robert Forster, Ted Koditschek, Darline Gay Levy, David Lux, John Markoff, Judith Miller, Robert Resch, James Rosenheim, Dan Thorp, Louise Tilly, Peter Wallenstein, and LeeAnn Whites. I have also had helpful interaction with Robert Schneider, Julius Ruff, and the members of the James Allen Vann Seminar at Emory University.

Over the years I have had crucial financial support in the form of a year fellowship from SUNY Binghamton, a College of Charleston Research Grant, a Research Fellowship at Virginia Polytechnic Institute and State University, a Texas A&M University International Enhancement Grant, and a grant from the Council for European Studies. I would like to thank the Bibliothèque Nationale, Paris, for allowing me to reproduce the figures that appear at the beginning of each chapter. I have also enjoyed unwavering support from the department heads I have served: Clarence Davis at the College of Charleston, Mariann Whelchel at Antioch, and Larry Hill at Texas A&M. For Larry Hill I feel a special appreciation for the good fortune of having had for six years as department head the fairest, most patient, and principled colleague I have known.

At Penn State Press, Peter Potter acted with exemplary speed, courtesy, and professionalism to shepherd the manuscript through the review process. Peggy Hoover's copy editing has made it a better book.

I want to make a special note of appreciation for Al Hamscher of Kansas State University, who reached out a helping hand when I needed one and has never withdrawn it.

Other people have helped in less tangible but still important ways. I thank, especially, Darlene Allison, David Jones, Laura P. Livesay, Rebecca Martinez, Stephen Raich, Kathy Raich, Jocelyn Wills, and Nan Woodruff.

My family has provided support whenever I needed it. My parents may have thought a business degree a safer course, but they warmed to the idea of history when I showed myself to be as stubborn as they raised me to be. My son, Kevin, has grown up with this book, and although we sometimes clashed over priorities, he has provided me with the best diversions and rewards possible. For my husband, Harold Livesay, I lack the words to express my gratitude for all the ways he has supported me over the years. I can only hope he senses how much it has all meant. I dedicate this book to him.

WEIGHTS, MEASUREMENTS, AND MONEY

It is impossible to give a complete list of the diverse measures used in the region where the Flour War erupted. Measures cited in this study are provided for approximate (and local) comparison only. General guidelines are noted below. For more detailed data, see Ronald E. Zupko, *French Weights and Measures Before the Revolution: A Dictionary of Provincial and Local Units* (Bloomington, Ind., 1978).

Land (area)

The *arpent* was the principal land measurement throughout France. However, there were three national standards and many regional variations. The most common measurement in the Paris Basin was the *arpent de Paris*.

> 1 arpent (de Paris) = 0.342 hectares = 0.84 acres
> 1 arpent (de Paris) = 100 perches
> 1 charrue = 120 arpents (de Paris)

In the provinces, the arpent varied widely: 1.4 acres (Aisne), between 1.3 and 0.83 acres (Seine-et-Marne), and 1.4 and 0.98 acres (Seine-et-Oise).

Volume

The *setier* was a general measure of capacity for grain in the Paris Basin. The most common measurements were:

> 1 setier = 156.1 liters = 4.43 bushels
> 12 boisseaux = 1 setier
> 2 mines = 4 minots = 1 setier
> 1 muid = 12 setiers

Local variations could be significant. For example, the setier could measure 1.6 bushels (in Noyon), 2.7 bushels (Soissons), and 10.8 bushels (Troyes). Moreover, measurements differed depending on the type of grain negotiated. Thus, a setier of oats measured 8.9 bushels.

Weights

The principal measurement for weighing grain, flour, and bread was the *livre*.

> 1 livre = 498.5 grams = 1.1 lb.

There were, of course, also local variations.

Money

> 1 livre = 20 sols (sous)
> 12 deniers = 1 sol (sou)
> 20 sols (sous) = 4 liards

Distance

Also subject to variation, the *lieue* served as the main measure of distance. The *lieue de Paris* was the most common measure for roads in the Paris Basin.

> 1 lieue = 3898.08 meters = 4262.9 yards = 2.4 miles

ABBREVIATIONS

AD   Archives départementales
AHR   *American Historical Review*
AHRF   *Annales historiques de la Révolution française*
AN   *Archives nationales*
AESC   *Annales Economies Sociétés Civilisations*
BA   Bibliothèque de l'Arsenal
BM   Bibliothèque municipale
BN   Bibliothèque nationale
FHS   *French Historical Studies*
JEH   *Journal of Economic History*
JIH   *Journal of Interdisciplinary History*
JMH   *Journal of Modern History*
JSH   *Journal of Social History*
RHM   *Revue d'histoire moderne*
RHMC   *Revue d'histoire moderne et contemporaine*

INTRODUCTION

France in 1775 had enjoyed six decades free of widespread, death-dealing hunger. None could have known it at the time, but the kingdom had survived the last winnowing by starvation it would ever have to endure. Though human follies such as war, and such natural vagaries as drought, continued to inflict localized misery from time to time, by the late eighteenth century France had mastered the most fundamental problem of human existence: the problem of subsistence. It had become a society that could, year after year, decade after decade, feed its people, all its people, including those who produced food and those who did not, whether they lived in the country, in the towns and villages, or, as more and more of them did, in the cities.

By keeping general famine at bay, France achieved one of the essentials of a stable society and demonstrated one of the qualities of a viable nation-state. It did not, however, thereby guarantee continued tranquillity in society and government, for the common people, having no way to foresee the future, remained haunted by the lingering specter of famine. That they had not starved for decades did not mean they had not endured hunger; most were hungry most of the time, and the dreams and myths and legends of the poor revolved around cornucopias of food, feasts unending, and ever-flowing casks of wine. Reality centered on bread, truly the staff of life on which the common people leaned.

Over centuries, the people and their rulers had evolved a complex understanding on the subject of provisioning, the process by which the people obtained their daily bread—or the flour or grain from which to make it. To the ordinary folk this meant that they had a *right* to fairly priced provisions, that authorities had the *responsibility* to guarantee that right, and that failure in either area justified a public uprising to force the sale of provisions at a "just price." This process of forcing transactions at a price set by some popularly held sense of equity rather than a price determined by the market has manifested itself in a multitude of times and places as disparate as the villages of seventeenth-century France and the Yukon River of twentieth-century Alaska. British historian E. P. Thompson dubbed the phenomenon "the moral economy of the crowd," while the French called their version the *taxation populaire*. By 1775, the *taxation populaire* had a long history of use in the complex process that fed the people of France and had become one of the traditional components of the subsistence relationship between the people and those who governed them.

History presents a plethora of such arrangements between people and rulers, some of them enduring one way or another through the twentieth century. Usually a skein of formal legislation, decrees, and regulatory standards interwoven with strands of informal understandings sanctified by long-established practices, these complex undertakings have the advantage, for governments, of maintaining domestic stability by ensuring that the people will have their bread. Such advantages, however, rarely come without a stiff price, and by ensuring cheap bread, governments create a tiger hard to dismount, as rulers from imperiled ancient Rome to the collapsing Soviet Union have learned. Nothing so converts an improved condition into a "traditional right" as continued access to it; few things outrage a people so much as a decline in what they can expect—particularly if those expectations attach to a cherished tradition, and most emphatically if that tradition involves the right to subsistence.

France in 1775 remained a society in many ways traditional, while simultaneously undergoing fundamental changes. Ultimately these changes transformed a rural, agrarian, economically insecure society governed by a hereditary monarch into an urban, industrial, prosperous democracy. To the common people, however, the changes they could perceive held far more threat than promise. As part of a swelling population that had grown by one-third over a century, many of them in cities swarming with ever more mouths to feed while producing little with which to feed them, they observed with apprehension a multitude of shifts in the ways of trade, commerce, manufacture, and agriculture. Taken together, these seemed certain to make the rich and powerful more rich and powerful yet, to reduce the poor to even baser levels of destitution, and to push those in the strata between, toward, and perhaps across the fragile line that separated sufficiency and self-respect from poverty and shame.

In the fall of 1774, an event occurred that seemed to many a harbinger of just such ominous changes. The government of the newly crowned King Louis XVI declared in effect that it would henceforth allow the free circulation of grain within the kingdom. The people, whose spirits had risen with the arrival of the new king in the wake of the late departed and much-despised Louis XV, thus found their expectations doubly diminished. In such an atmosphere, many perceived this "freeing" of the grain trade as a negation of the state's traditional responsibility to protect their subsistence. Such violations had in the past often been followed by the people's traditional response, and so too this time: in the following spring—that worst of times, when the last harvest is long past and the next long to wait—the disturbances that came to be known as "The Flour War" erupted in Paris, Versailles, and the towns and countrysides of neighboring provinces at the end of April and the first weeks of May.

The Flour War began on Thursday, 27 April, when a riot erupted in the market town of Beaumont-sur-Oise. This event ignited an explosion of rioting throughout the Paris Basin. In the next twenty-two days, more than 300 riots broke out. From the first eruption at Beaumont, there followed disturbances throughout the pays de France, the Beauvaisis, the Brie, the Vexin, and, even farther away, in the provinces of Normandy, Picardy, and Champagne.[1] Major riots rocked market towns crucial to the Paris provisioning system: Pontoise on 29 April, Magny-en-Vexin on 1 May, Gonesse on 4 May, Brie-Comte-Robert and Nanteuil-le-Haudouin on 5 May. Riots wracked Versailles on 2 May and Paris itself on 3 May. In the days that followed, smaller market towns more distant from Paris also endured the forceful seizure and sale of provisions: Gaillefontaine on 5 May and 12 May, Montdidier on 6 May, Braine on 7 May, Roye on 8 May, Fismes and Auffay on 13 May, and Dieppe on 18 May. Altogether, eighty-two market towns experienced some form of disturbance.

1. For the location of these regions within the Paris Basin, see Map 1.

Trouble did not confine itself to the marketplace, however. Rioters descended on overland routes and waterways to intercept and seize the cargoes of grain convoys headed for Paris or other regional centers. Twelve such episodes occurred on the roads to Paris: at Epinay-sur-Seine (2 May), Chaumes-en-Brie (6 May), and along the rivers—on the Seine at La Roche-Guyon (2 May) and Stors (28 April), on the Oise at Pontoise (29 April). Riots also erupted at the farms of large-scale cultivators throughout the Paris Basin. Some 203 villages experienced invasions into farms by people demanding their grain. Rioters occasionally assailed a rural monastery, such as the one at Saint-Leu-d'Esserent (30 April), or a resident seigneur, such as Nicolas Deshuissards at Saint-Martin-lès-Voulangis (6 May).

As the disorder spread throughout the Paris Basin, the government took increasingly emphatic action. Unwilling to trust entirely the insufficiently numerous and problematically loyal local police and authorities, it dispatched on 4 May two armies to patrol the countryside and regional markets. For example, a detachment of *chevaux légers* (lightly armed cavalry) and two detachments from the infantry regiment of Penthièvre kept the peace in Etrépagny after the initial eruption on 2 May.[2] Other troops guarded Paris itself. Altogether, 25,000 troops were deployed in the field.[3]

This martial atmosphere, coupled with the increasing importance of flour in the subsistence trade, gave the movement its name: Lieutenant General of Police Jean-Charles-Pierre Lenoir observed that the public called it *la guerre des farines* (the flour war).[4] The Maréchal Duc de Biron commanded the troops, and Parisian society dubbed him *général des farines* (the flour general), or even "Jean Farine." Biron also became the butt of a song sung to a popular tune:

2. "Lettre de M. de Pommery à M. Crosne (10 mai)," AD Seine-Maritime, C 108, fol. 108.

3. Mousquetaires Noirs were stationed along the banks of the Marne, the Mousquetaires Gris along the lower Seine, the Gendarmes and Chevau-Légers along the upper Seine, and the Suisses, Gardes Françaises, and Invalides in the Paris *faubourgs* and in front of Parisian bakers' shops. Gustave Schelle, ed., *Oeuvres de Turgot et documents le concernant* (Glashutten im Taunus, 1972), 4:49, n. 2; Edgar Faure, *La Disgrâce de Turgot* (Paris, 1961), pp. 268–79; "Emeute arrivée à Paris part raport au prix du bled et du pain, le 3 mai 1775 et différentes pièces rélatives à cet événement," AN, H2* 1876 and AN, K 1022.

4. See Jean-Louis Soulavie, *Mémoires historiques et politiques sur le règne de Louis XVI* (Paris, 1827), 2:297; Abbé J.-F. de Georgel, *Mémoires pour servir à l'histoire des événements de la fin du dix-huitième siècle* (Paris, 1817–18), 1:424; Robert Darnton, ed., "Essai sur la guerre des farines: Le Lieutenant de police J.-P. Lenoir, la guerre des farines et l'approvisionnement de Paris à la veille de la Révolution," *RHMC* 16 (Oct.–Dec. 1969): 617.

Biron, tes glorieux travaux,
En dépit des cabales,
Te font passer pour un héros
Sous les pilliers des halles;
De rue en rue, au petit trot,
Tu chasses la famine:
Général digne de Turgot,
Tu n'es qu'un Jean Farine.[5]

Which translates approximately as:

Biron, your glorious works,
Pushed on despite the cabals,
Make you pass for a hero
In the fight for the market stalls.
From street to street at a trot,
You chase hunger from scene to scene.
General, Turgot deserves you;
You are only a "Jean Farine."

By mid-May 1775 this forceful response, tempered by occasional conces-
sions, had restored order, at least on the surface.

Brief as it was, the Flour War provides a unique window on the society of
France in the late eighteenth century. An examination of the Flour War in
detail—those who protested and those whom the protesters targeted, the
context in which they lived together, and the relationship between that
context and their protests—tells us what the protesters and the protested
did, who they were, and why they reacted the way they did, and sets this
episode of violent popular protest within the larger scope of pre-Revolutionary French subsistence movements in general.

Although historians began studying these long-forgotten people more
than thirty years ago,[6] we can refine our knowledge of Early Modern French
food rioters and their world further in at least two ways.

5. See *Mémoires de l'abbé Terray, contrôleur-général de finance avec une relation de l'émeute arrivée à Paris en 1775*, ed. J.-B.-L. Coquereau (London, 1776), p. 266. Unless otherwise noted, the translation (below) of this song, and all other translations in this book, are my own.

6. The point of departure for all students of the Flour War is the work of George Rudé: "La Taxation populaire de mai 1775 à Paris et dans la région parisienne," *AHRF* 143 (Apr.–June 1956): 139–79, and "La Taxation populaire de mai 1775 en Picardie, en Normandie et dans le Beauvaisis,"

First, although historians have correctly located the heyday of the food riot within a particular historical period—the late seventeenth to the mid-nineteenth century—and rightly noted the greater sophistication of rioter behavior and demands that developed over time, they have tended to assume that all such riots were alike, on the basis of obvious similarities among subsistence movements during this period. However, all subsistence riots were not alike. Common concerns about access to food may have shaped them, but the riots also exhibited considerable variety.

Rioters responded to specific local conditions, to shifts in royal policy, and to broader, long-term difficulties inflicted on them by the processes of uneven development (the uneven integration of disparate parts of French society into regional, national, and even international markets). Indeed, uneven development and its consequences played at least as great a role in shaping popular protest as government policies on the grain trade in France. I therefore propose to analyze how and why behavior, participation, and the choice of targets related to the impact of different rhythms and forms of development in French society.

My second and related purpose is to examine the dynamics of food riots. Such riots revealed the nature of contemporary communities, many of them obscured to history in normal times. The rioters and those who opposed them did not act out of ideals or emotions unique to them as individuals, but rather out of assumptions held in common with others. The Flour War exposed the tensions felt by people who had allegiances to several communities that found themselves in conflict with one another. It also revealed that the changes under way in the late eighteenth century had strengthened some traditional groups, weakened others, and fertilized embryonic clusters whose primacy lay yet in the future. In terms of issues, while subsistence movements involved a primary battle over the control of food, they also embodied conflict over power, not just in the classic "high" political sphere, but also in the realms of economic, social, gendered, cultural, local, and historically specific power, where they had greater impact.

This study deals with the disturbances in the towns, villages, and

---

AHRF 165 (July–Sept. 1961): 305–29. Rudé provides a summary in his *Crowd in History: A Study of Popular Disturbances in France and England, 1730–1848* (1964; rev. ed., London, 1981), pp. 23–31. Other studies include Faure, *Disgrâce*, pp. 195–318; Vladimir S. Ljublinski, *La Guerre des Farines. Contribution à l'histoire de la lutte des classes en France à la veille de la Révolution*, trans. F. Adiba and J. Radiquet (Grenoble, 1979); Guy-Robert Ikni, "La Guerre de farines: Mise au point et nouvelles recherches," *Bulletin de la Commission d'histoire économique et sociale de la Révolution française*, 1980–81, pp. 57–84. Other works that address the Flour War within more general contexts are cited below.

countryside outside Paris. I began my research in the Parisian archives, hoping to find ways in which the common people of Paris were caught up in the debates over the interrelated matters of political economy and the subsistence issue, as well as confrontations over political legitimacy and control. I had expected that because Paris was proximate to the locus of state power it would provide a specific case of political interaction involving people, the Parlement, the king and his ministers, and other important notables, but extensive research uncovered little evidence to support that. In fact, though rioting occurred throughout much of Paris, nowhere did rioters invoke or engage royal authority. Aside from the rare assertion that the king had lowered the price of bread (and similar things had been said before, outside Paris as well as within it), the common people never addressed or challenged authority beyond the level of the police. I found no evidence of a connection between the proximity of rioting communities to national power and the forging of particular relationships or transformations in popular political consciousness. As I shall show below, the case of Versailles demonstrates this point even more clearly.

I did perceive, however, the inherent merits of a study that focused not on the capital but on the provinces, not on the larger urban centers (with all allowances for the nuances of "urban" for this period), such as Paris, or even Saint-Germain-en-Laye and Versailles, but on the smaller ones and the rural areas. These places lent themselves more readily to the exploration and explication of the processes at work within late eighteenth-century France: uneven economic, social, and political development and their impact on French society. Furthermore, while historians have not ignored the Flour War, they have largely neglected its local conflicts, particularly those in villages and countryside, which constituted a vital dimension of the episode to the people and the state at the time. For this reason, this study largely excludes Paris, Saint-Germain, and Versailles from its scope.

Indeed, only through detailed examination of the Flour War in its *local* variations can the complexity of its origins, permutations, and above all its implications become part of our appreciation and understanding of the complex fabric that was Ancien Régime France. In the areas outside Paris we find not just urban consumers and those immediately concerned with supplying them, but also the whole apparatus of production and consumption: the land and those who controlled and worked it; the produce and those who processed it, transported it, sold and bought it. These elements, and the varied combinations in which they existed regionally, played a dynamic role throughout the French economy and society, a role most effectively exposed through an examination of the Flour War outside Paris.

George Rudé and E. P. Thompson have contributed the most to our current understanding of food rioting. My study builds on their work, but diverges from it in several ways. Rudé's work on crowd action in general, and food rioting and the Flour War in particular, encouraged historians to identify the faces in the crowds and to seek motives and beliefs in patterns of behavior. His work served as a point of departure for my own, from which I have moved on to a more contextualized study of food rioting, a more nuanced analysis of social recruitment, a more diachronic interpretation of the evolution of rioting, a vision of food rioters more as active participants in shaping their lives than as passive reactors to circumstances, a portrait of food rioting as a political, albeit not high-political, act, and a history of rioting in which gender as well as class plays an important role. Moreover, Rudé ignores the continued importance of seigneurialism in Ancien Régime France and the role it played in subsistence movements like the Flour War, a gap that I have tried at least partially to fill. With his work on the moral economy, E. P. Thompson provided historians with a powerful conceptual umbrella under which we can locate popular attitudes about subsistence and its allocation. However, not all food riots were alike, and we must look under the umbrella of the moral economy to explain significant differences in recruitment, behavior, and scope across time and place.

I have employed many of the types of sources now familiar to social historians: criminal and civil records, tax rolls, various types of *états* (status reports) compiled by royal and local administrators, and a wide range of administrative correspondence. A project such as this also relies heavily on the work of other historians. In this case, in particular, I have drawn from the wealth of local and regional histories—demographic, socioeconomic, administrative, and cultural—that generations of historians have generated about the Paris Basin and beyond. I have also depended on the strong foundation of works, descriptive as well as theoretical, already established for the study of popular movements in France and in England and beyond.

My study thus links a detailed analysis of the Flour War to this already vast and growing literature on subsistence rioting. Chapter 1 discusses and assesses the state of our knowledge of subsistence movements. Chapter 2 provides an analysis of the long-term and short-term factors that intersected in the Paris Basin to construct the historical context in which the Flour War erupted. Chapter 3 tells the story, begun thirty years ago by George Rudé, of the 1775 subsistence crisis and the Flour War that erupted in its midst, outlines its general characteristics, and attempts to refine further our understanding of participation. Chapter 4 offers a typology of the theaters of action, behavior, and participation for the Flour War. Chapter 5 analyzes the nature of the values and social relations that subsistence crises invoked to generate collective action. Chapter 6 compares certain features of the Flour War with previous movements and suggests linkages with the movements of the Revolutionary period. The Conclusion offers a more general analysis of the implications of subsistence rioting in the context of the question of politics and the early Revolutionary experience.

The main purpose of this study is thus to examine the role of uneven development in shaping subsistence riots, using the Flour War as the major example. It is not intended as a day-by-day account of the Flour War itself, although it examines some facets of it in close detail. It deals with high politics and the politics of liberalization by analyzing the consequences of the changing patterns of distribution they fostered—that is, as they manifested themselves in anxious common folk and those who confronted them in town and country, mill and market, highway and byway, not in terms of contests among ministers or in struggles between king and the Parlements played out in châteaus and drawing rooms.

Although the study focuses heavily on the period of the Flour War, it is also grounded in a larger, comparative context that includes food riots in France before and after the Flour War, as well as subsistence movements that occurred elsewhere, such as in England. I make no claims for the absolute uniqueness of the Flour War, but I do believe that those who participated in it manifested both creativity and historically specific characteristics, while simultaneously drawing from long traditions of assumptions and responses. Moreover, as George Rudé observed, "while the Flour War fits clearly into the tradition of the great popular revolts . . . of the Ancien Régime, . . . there are also elements that announce the social movements of the Revolution."[7] In addition, though certainly not the only popular uprising in the last half of the eighteenth century, this revolt was one of the most extensive, and the last major eruption before the Great Fear of 1789.

Whenever possible, I let the people speak for themselves and let their specific actions serve as examples for broader historical generalizations. Among the common people, one finds, unfortunately, too few historical "characters" like the stormy Pierre Hamelin and Madeline Pochet, who briefly emerged from obscurity to lead bands of rioters and about whom the

7. "La Taxation populaire . . . région parisienne," p. 177.

sources reveal enough to add them to a cast headed by such exalted and well-documented figures as the king himself and his controller general, Anne-Robert-Jacques Turgot de Brucort. I have tried to make the most of this kind of evidence whenever I could find it. And the past does sometimes divulge images, however fleeting, of the lives of ordinary folk. These images reveal a people struggling to maintain a foothold on the slippery slope of a traditional society reshaped by forces of change.

Chapter 1

EARLY MODERN FOOD RIOTS

We set the stage by establishing two broader contexts: (1) the historical understanding of these movements and (2) the broader context of the times, the processes of uneven development under way in late eighteenth-century France, particularly in the Paris Basin. The research of the last three decades has vastly expanded our knowledge of the Flour War and similar movements.[1] This chapter surveys the state of this knowledge by focusing on five

1. Historian George Rudé served as a veritable pioneer in "crowd" studies of Early Modern and

basic areas of research on subsistence movements—the classic what, who, where, when, and why of historical inquiry—then looks at the relationship between food riots and the nature of the preindustrial community, considers the debate over the relationship between the food riots and the political sphere in pre-Revolutionary, preindustrial France, and finally analyzes other approaches to understanding food riots, which subsequent chapters will explore.

The classic contours of such preindustrial food riots as the Flour War of 1775 are now well known. Faced with the threat of scarcity and rising prices (usually of grain and bread), a "crowd" composed largely of vulnerable consumers assembled to demand affordable, accessible subsistence. The people thus assembled then confronted those who controlled this vital necessity—bakers, merchants, millers, cultivators, and local authorities—and took what provisions they needed, forcing sales at a price that was below the "market" (or asking) price but that the rioters deemed "just." This price-fixing behavior forms the outline of what French observers often called the *taxation populaire* and closely corresponds to events of the Flour War as well.

Food riots thus manifested similar characteristics. Rioters sought grain, flour, or bread wherever they thought it could be found. Sometimes they literally pillaged what they found; more often they paid at least something, even if the price they offered fell considerably below the market price. Food rioters occasionally roughed up uncooperative local officials or suspicious

---

Revolutionary Europe. His work on the Flour War has already been noted, but his books, *The Crowd in the French Revolution* (Oxford, 1959) and, more important, *The Crowd in History, 1730–1848* (1964), became methodological textbooks for a whole generation of historians who sought to dissect and understand preindustrial crowd behavior. For a list of Rudé's works to date, see "George Rudé: A Bibliography," in *History from Below: Studies in Popular Protest and Popular Ideology*, ed. F. Krantz (London, 1988), pp. 343–48. For British historians, the work of E. P. Thompson rivals that of Rudé for its conceptual and methodological influence. See esp. Thompson, "The Moral Economy of the English Crowd in the Eighteenth Century," *Past and Present* 50 (1971): 76–136. For years Thompson's work was largely unknown to many French scholars. It has only recently been translated: "L'Économie morale de la foule dans l'Angelterre du XVIIIe siècle," in *La Guerre du blé au XVIIIe siècle. La Critique populaire contre le libéralisme économique au XVIIIe siècle*, ed. F. Gauthier and G.-R. Ikni (Montreuil, 1988), pp. 31–92.

British historians have concerned themselves with the preindustrial food riot as avidly as French historians, and the result is an impressive accumulation of important conceptualizations on both sides of the English Channel. Although there is always a danger in crossing state frontiers, and the pages that follow remain sensitive to French differences, it is still fruitful to bring a comparative dimension to a project such as this. Thus, I draw not only from British history but also from other histories and other disciplines to complement understanding of the French experience. Many other important works followed Thompson's, and those contributions are credited in the pages and footnotes that follow.

merchants, but more frequently they broke down bakery or granary doors, damaging property not people.

The discovery of similarities in behavior during subsistence riots separated by time and place has led historians to survey the repertory of traditions and practices from which food rioters may have drawn their strategies. In the "paternalist" actions and regulations of seigneurs and local authorities, monarchy and church, in the concrete usages of mutual aid practiced in their own village communities and neighborhoods, and in rituals associated with traditional festival celebrations, such as carnival,[2] there emerged a diverse arsenal of weapons to address subsistence crises: price-fixing, food-requisitioning, alms-giving, marketing regulations, collective rights, carnivalesque inversions, transvestism, and so on. Past experiences and strategies—many dating from the Middle Ages—accumulated in the collective memory, were then transmitted via oral traditions and networks of sociability and thus served as a fund or "mobilizing myth"[3] from which the common people could draw and adapt to respond to present crises.

Historians have identified the faces in the crowd, mainly by analyzing the occupational, or socioeconomic characteristics of rioters.[4] Contrary to the assertions of some contemporary observers and the historians who echoed them in the nineteenth century, food rioters came neither from the uprooted dregs of French society—the vagabonds and criminals—nor from the ranks of clients of the various machinating court factions, those seemingly ubiquitous but slippery conspirators accused of lurking behind any opposition to Crown policy. They came overwhelmingly from the *menu peuple*—the common people—which included the families of artisans, journeymen, shopkeepers, day-laborers, small peasants, and vine-growers.

That the common people should have comprised such an impressive proportion of participants in a food riot is not surprising. They had to purchase all or part of their food, a diet that consisted overwhelmingly of

2. On sources of behavior, see, e.g., Yves-Marie Bercé, *Fête et Révolte. Des Mentalités populaires du XVIe au XVIIIe siècle* (Paris, 1976); idem, *Revolt and Revolution in Early Modern Europe: An Essay on the History of Political Violence,* trans. J. Bergin (New York, 1987); Natalie Davis, *Society and Culture in Early Modern France* (Stanford, Calif., 1965); E. P. Thompson, " 'Rough Music': Le Charivari anglais," *AESC* 27 (1972): 285–312; Charles Tilly, *The Contentious French: Four Centuries of Popular Struggle* (Cambridge, Mass., 1986), esp. p. 116.

3. Phrase used by Terence Ranger, "Peasant Consciousness: Culture and Conflict in Zimbabwe," in *Peasants and Peasant Societies: Selected Readings,* 2nd ed., ed. T. Shanin (Oxford, 1987), p. 313.

4. This was probably Rudé's most important methodological contribution. His chapter "Faces in the Crowd" in *Crowd in History* became obligatory reading for graduate students in social history everywhere.

bread. Securing regular sustenance constituted a preoccupation among most of the common people.[5] During normal years, these families managed, sometimes only through complex strategies in which all members played an integral part, to stay on the "right side of the line between poverty and indigence."[6] During crisis years, however, disjunctures among prices, wages, and other expenses could threaten the very survival of the family unit. Then, these ordinary people turned in defense of their families to an "economy of expedients" or "makeshifts" that included rioting.[7]

Historians have further uncovered a gendered dimension to food riots, a dimension contemporaries knew well and often noted. Women of the common people participated massively in these movements, often assuming crucial roles as instigators and leaders.[8] Indeed, Olwen Hufton has argued that women, in their roles as wives, mothers, and daughters, whose tasks as purveyors of food and supplies for their families drew them frequently into the marketplace, helped define the marketplace as a female space. Women's linchpin provisioning role thus rendered the food riot—the final and most extreme option in a wide range of strategies designed to defend the family economy against destitution, dismemberment, or destruction—a predominantly "female, or rather maternal terrain."[9]

    5. The literature on this is immense: Michel Morineau's "Budgets populaires en France au dix-huitième siècle," *Revue d'histoire économique et sociale* 50 (1972): 203–36, 449–81, is a classic.
    6. Olwen Hufton, "Women in Revolution, 1789–1796," *Past and Present* 53 (Nov. 1971): 94.
    7. Olwen Hufton, *The Poor of Eighteenth-Century France, 1750–1789* (Oxford, 1974), p. 24.
    8. The literature on women in subsistence movements is growing. Female participation is well documented for riots in both France and England. See, e.g., Olwen Hufton, "Women and the Family Economy in Eighteenth-Century France," *FHS* 9 (Spring 1975): 19; Nicole Castan, "La Criminalité familiale dans la ressort du parlement de Toulouse, 1690–1730," in *Crimes et criminalité en France sous l'Ancien Régime, 17e–18e siècles,* ed. François Billaçois (Paris, 1971), pp. 91–108; Darline Gay Levy and Harriet B. Applewhite, "Women of the Popular Classes in Revolutionary Paris, 1789–1795," in *Women, War, and Revolution,* ed. C. R. Berkin and C. M. Lovett (New York, 1980), pp. 10–12; Cynthia A. Bouton, "Gendered Behavior in Subsistence Riots: The French Flour War of 1775," *JSH* 23 (June 1990): 735–54; Malcolm I. Thomis and Jennifer Grimmett, *Women in Protest, 1800–1850* (London, 1982), esp. chap. 2, among many others noted below.
    9. "Women in Revolution," p. 94. Dominique Godineau makes a similar claim when she notes that "a special connection between women and subsistence does exist, based on women's social function of nurturer." See Godineau, "Masculine and Feminine Political Practice During the French Revolution, 1793—Year III," in *Women and Politics in the Age of Democratic Revolution,* ed. H. B. Applewhite and D. G. Levy (Ann Arbor, Mich., 1990), p. 65. British historian John Bohstedt has challenged this assessment of food riots as a predominantly female activity, claiming that men rioted at least as frequently as women during the period 1790–1810. See Bohstedt, "Gender, Household, and Community Politics: Women in English Riots, 1790–1810," *Past and Present* 120 (August 1988): 88–122, and his "The Myth of the Feminine Food Riot: Women as Proto-Citizens in English Community Politics, 1790–1810," in *Women and Politics in the Age of Democratic Revolution,* pp. 21–60. For more on this argument, see below and Chapters 3, 4, and 5.

We have also detected an important yet ambiguous role played by local authorities and notables during subsistence movements. Standing between hostile camps of consumers and merchants and producers, local authorities became pivotal figures in confrontations that revolved around subsistence crises. Although preserving order constituted a primary duty—a duty that included arresting and punishing those who disturbed the public order—village, municipal, and even royal authorities frequently sympathized with the plight of distraught consumers and sometimes actually actively collaborated with rioters, even when protests engendered violence. For example, we find them turning a blind eye to crowds that stopped merchants from moving supplies, assisting in the price-fixing and distribution of grain obtained by popular force or threats, joining and sometimes leading rioting crowds, and protecting individuals accused of violent actions.[10]

French food riots erupted from the Channel to the Mediterranean and from the eastern frontier to the Atlantic. Although bad harvests could occur anywhere and food riots could and did erupt in a wide variety of contexts, certain conditions rendered some regions particularly vulnerable. The most likely environments for trouble included regions that contained any one or combination of such characteristics as numerous vulnerable consumers who bought their food rather than grew it; provisioning networks that extended beyond local consumers and producers; and susceptibility to bad harvests or disrupted circulation.[11] Regions that generated a strong and growing purchasing power, such as the capital, major provincial centers, or areas experiencing industrial growth, disturbed established patterns of trade and increased the possibilities for unrest in the zones on which they relied for supplies.[12]

Within this broad geographical context, the theaters of action varied with the complexities of the production and provisioning system itself. Although public markets constituted the most common site of subsistence

10. See Rudé, Crowd in History, pp. 31, 204–5; E. P. Thompson, "Moral Economy," pp. 120–26; Steven Kaplan, Bread, Politics, and Political Economy in the Reign of Louis XV, 2 vols. (The Hague, 1976); Cynthia A. Bouton, "National Policy and Response to the Guerre des Farines," in Proceedings of the Fifth George Rudé Seminar in French History, Wellington, 1986 (Wellington, N.Z., 1986), pp. 282–97; Judith Miller, "The Pragmatic Economy: Liberal Reforms and the Grain Trade in Upper Normandy, 1750–1789" (Ph.D. diss., Duke University, 1987).

11. For the best descriptions of the geographical distribution of food riots, see Kaplan, Bread, 1:189; Tilly, Contentious French, p. 190; Olwen Hufton, "Social Conflict and the Grain Supply in Eighteenth-Century France," JIH 15 (Autumn 1983): 301–8.

12. Andrew Charlesworth, An Atlas of Rural Protest in Britain, 1548–1900, ed. A. Charlesworth (Philadelphia, 1983), p. 64; Manfred Gailus, "Food Riots in Germany in the Late 1840s," Past and Present (forthcoming).

riots, crowds also raided bakeries, grain in transit on carts and barges, mills, public granaries, private storage rooms, and individual farms, including those of seigneurs, monasteries, and large-scale cultivators. People frequently assembled before the town hall (hôtel de ville) to demand support from local authorities, and they protested outside homes of individuals known for their association with the grain trade.[13]

Although food-related riots in these and other forms have had very long histories, the particular behavior associated with the taxation populaire occurred with greatest frequency in France from the middle of the seventeenth century. Food riots occurred in the 1630s in Caen in Normandy, in Pertuis and Reillane in Provence, and in Angers in the Anjou.[14] The Caen episode presented a clear example of the taxation populaire, involving popular price-fixing rather than what contemporaries loosely and unhelpfully called "pillaging." Food rioting flourished during the eighteenth century and the Revolutionary period, so much so that historians have often observed that food riots were the most classic form of popular protest during that period.[15] Indeed, a computer-assisted analysis of popular movements currently under way in France indicates that food riots had become a general feature of the popular experience. Guy Lemarchand recently reported that while the period 1690–1720 experienced 182 such disturbances, the period 1760–89 totaled 652, almost four times as many.[16] Their incidence faded only after the mid-nineteenth century in France.[17]

13. Bercé, Fête et Révolte, provides the most systematic examinations of festival and seditious spaces. The most interesting work on spaces of popular action focuses on Paris. See, e.g., Arlette Farge and André Zysberg, "Les Théâtres de la violence à Paris au XVIIIe siècle," AESC 5 (Sept.–Oct. 1979): 984–1015.

14. On Caen, Michel Caillard, "Recherches sur les soulèvements populaires en Basse Normandie (1620–1640) et spécialement sur la révoltes de Nu-Pieds," in M. Caillard et al., A Travers la Normandie des XVIIe et XVIIIe siècles (Caen, 1963), pp. 38–39, and the discussion in Louise Tilly, "The Food Riot as a Form of Political Conflict in France," JIH 2 (1971): 48, n. 49. On riots in Provence, René Pillorget, "Essai d'une typologie des mouvements insurrectionnels ruraux survenus en Provence de 1596 à 1715," in Actes du 92e Congrès national des sociétés savantes, Strasbourg, 1967 (Paris, 1970), p. 379; on Angers, François Lebrun, "Les Soulèvements populaires à Angers aux XVIIe et XVIIIe siècles," in Actes du 90e Congrès national des sociétés savantes, Nice, 1965 (Paris, 1966), p. 126.

15. L. Tilly, "Food Riot," pp. 24–25.

16. "Troubles populaires au XVIIIe siècle et conscience de classe. Une Préface à la Révolution française," AHRF 279 (Jan.–Mar. 1990): 34.

17. Subsistence riots disappeared only with increased productivity, the development of modern communication and transportation networks, and the renegotiation of access to food for those previously made vulnerable during the nineteenth century. See Louise Tilly's contribution to this subject, "The Decline and Disappearance of the Classical Food Riot in France," New School for

Food riots could and did erupt at any time during the year, but the period between Easter and Michaelmas (March to September) offered conditions most conducive to subsistence disturbances.[18] By this point in the agricultural cycle, subsistence-level peasants—who had sold much of their harvest in the fall to pay taxes, tithes, and dues—had eaten far into their carefully coveted stocks and often joined artisans, shopkeepers, and day-laborers buying the family's bread, and sometimes replacement seed for the next year's harvest, at the market stalls.[19] At this point as well, large-scale merchants and producers entered the market to move grain supplies held in storage until demand, and hopefully prices, began to rise.[20] The months of April and May, and those of August and September, generated the largest numbers of riots. During this first, springtime period, small producers calculated from their winter stocks how much seed they could sow and sometimes had to go into debt to make up any shortfall between stocks and planting needs. Moreover, the big merchants in the grain trade might try to generate artificially high prices by manipulating the balance between demand and supply and playing on uncertainties about the next year's harvest. During the second period, the gap between supplies from the last year's harvest and the unnerving wait for the current year's harvest—what contemporaries called the *soudure*—could produce real dearth and distress. Between the planting and the harvest, people waited tensely, hoping that nature might not bring disasters, such as hail or drought, and that the previous year's supplies would last long enough to sustain them until the next crop.

Understanding the "when" of subsistence riots means not simply locating them in chronological space but also placing them in the context of evolving historical phenomena. And, in fact, we have learned a great deal more about the context in which subsistence movements erupted. The frequent eruption of food riots coincided with and related directly to the massive but uneven transformations wrought by the development of capitalism, the centralization of the state and its intervention in economic affairs, and, after the mid-eighteenth century, shifting demographic behavior and a

Social Research, Working Paper No. 147, 1992. Although there is no precise count of food riots in France, incomplete totals demonstrate a strikingly widespread phenomenon. I have undertaken a count for the period from 1614 to 1789 (see Chapter 6). Teams under the direction of Jean Nicolas are working on compiling a more definitive analysis for France: Nicolas, "Les Emotions dans l'ordinateur, table ronde," in *Troubles populaires en France aux XVIIe et XVIIIe siècles* (forthcoming).

18. On this, see esp. Hufton, "Social Conflict," pp. 320–24.

19. On this, see esp. Jean Meuvret, *Le Problème des subsistances à l'époque Louis XIV*, vol. 2, *La Production des céréales et la société rurale* (Paris, 1987), pp. 55–57.

20. On what follows, see Hufton, "Social Conflict," pp. 322–26.

growing crisis in the mechanisms of traditional charity. In short, changes taking place in the distribution and production of food, in social structure, and in entitlements to food were major factors in the timing of food riots.[21]

The centralizing monarchy, struggling to extract more and more taxes from its subjects, came to recognize that economic growth held the key to treasury replenishment. As the eighteenth century unfolded, it therefore threw its support, if sometimes indirectly and ambiguously and often erratically, behind expanding markets of regional, national, and even international extent, urbanization, the commercialization of agriculture, and a greater division of labor with its attendant proletarianization. These developments had the multiple effect of producing an ever-growing number of people dependent on purchasing their food (and therefore especially vulnerable to shifts in the accessibility and price of grain and its products), a distribution network that favored urban markets over rural ones, more diverse and more powerful producers and merchants who mobilized to take advantage of expanding marketing channels, and a change in official position on entitlements.

Perceptions of grain as a limited and common good had long prevailed in Medieval and Early Modern Europe, a position generally characterized by the belief that food, like land, was in limited, not expandable supply, and by the general assumption that everyone deserved access to enough of this "primary necessity," as contemporaries called it, to ensure survival. This did not imply any commitment by European elites to an egalitarian society. Rather, it entailed a more general assumption that one was entitled to a living from village resources, that prices should be kept within everyone's reach, and that assistance should be rendered to those in true distress. As medievalist Raymond de Roover observed long ago, this so-called just price "was simply the current market price, with this important reservation: in cases of collusion or emergency, the public authorities retained the right to interfere and to impose a fair price."[22] Jean Meuvret has argued that "the

---

21. For specifics on these developments, see Chapter 2. The literature on these general problems for France alone is far too numerous to cite here. For some of the more central pieces, in addition to the works noted above, see, e.g., Louise Tilly, "Food Entitlement, Famine, and Conflict," *JIH* 14 (1983): 333–49; Charles Tilly, *From Mobilization to Revolution* (Reading, Mass., 1978); idem, "Food Supply and Public Order in Modern Europe," in *The Formation of National States in Western Europe*, ed. C. Tilly (Princeton, 1975), pp. 380–455.

22. "The Concept of the Just Price: Theory and Economic Politics," *JEH* 18 (Dec. 1958): 421. See also G. M. Foster, "The Peasants and the Image of Limited Good," *American Anthropologist* 67 (1965): 293–315.

common people and many elites were committed to stable prices" above all.[23]

Moreover, experience had taught local authorities that dearth could bring not only starvation and related disease, but also unrest among the suffering. Such unrest threatened the public order. Experience also taught that subsistence crises resulted as much if not more from human as from natural causes: people could starve not only from absolute shortage (such as that produced by bad harvests) but amid inaccessible plenty, as well. High prices thus constituted as great an obstacle to survival as empty markets and bakeries.[24] Hence, in order to combat the combined evils of killing shortages, high prices that made food inaccessible not only to the poor but also to a wider swathe of the vulnerable common people and sometimes even richer groups, and to dampen the consequent threats to public order, there had emerged a congeries of strategies designed to facilitate access, or to provide "subsistence insurance."[25] These strategies have often been classified as "paternalist" in nature. Paternalism in this context emphasized a particular relationship between local or monarchical authority and the people. A term that cast authority in the role of father and people as children, it assumed a "family model of authority."[26] Paternalism implied that "the father is conscious of duties and responsibilities towards his son" and that "the son is acquiescent or actively complaisant in his filial stations."[27] On subsistence issues, paternalist authority claimed concern for and commitment to feed its child-subjects. The child-subjects had the right to appeal for assistance to the father but, most important, owed loyalty and obedience. Dearth triggered this relationship in complex ways. English historians John Walter and Keith Wrightson have argued, with specific reference to seventeenth-century England, that "while 'dearth' could undoubtedly contribute

23. *Le Problème des subsistances à l'époque de Louis XIV,* vol. 1, *La Production des céréales dans la France du XVIIe et du XVIIIe siècle* (Paris, 1977), p. 39, and ibid., vol. 3, *Le Commerce des grains et la conjoncture,* p. 155.

24. The most interesting analysis of this problem deals with twentieth-century subsistence crises: Amartya Sen, *Poverty and Famines: An Essay on Entitlement and Deprivation* (Oxford, 1981). See Louise Tilly's review of Sen's book: "Food Entitlement."

25. The term is James Scott's. See his *Moral Economy of the Peasant: Rebellion and Subsistence in Southeast Asia* (New Haven, 1976).

26. Sarah Hanley, *Le Lit de Justice of the Kings of France: Constitutional Ideology in Legend, Ritual, and Discourse* (Princeton, 1983); idem, "Engendering the State: Family Formation and State Building in Early Modern France," *FHS* 16 (Spring 1989): 4–27.

27. E. P. Thompson, "Eighteenth-Century English Society: Class Struggle Without Class?" *Social History* 3 (May 1978): 136.

to social disorder, . . . [it] could also serve as an active element in the maintenance of social stability." In other words, the dearth drove vulnerable consumers into the arms of the authorities for protection and occupied them with concerns other than more serious forms of rebellion.[28]

Since the Middle Ages, public authorities had installed a series of regulations that governed the grain trade and the traders themselves.[29] These included three basic types of regulations: controls on who could participate in the trade, regulation of business transactions in the grain markets, and regulation of intermarket commerce. Although specific policies might vary from place to place as well as over time, the general outlines differed very little until after the mid-eighteenth century in France. Most places installed regulations that specifically excluded certain categories of people from trading. These regulations usually prohibited cultivators from doing any trading other than selling their own produce for fear that they might take undue advantage of their already powerful control over food. All officials who participated in policing the grain trade were also barred for fear of corruption. Millers could sell grain they often received as payment for milling, but could not buy any; bakers could buy enough to produce bread, but none for resale. Regulations also prescribed behavior for all other traders on how, when, and where they could transact business, and required that all potential traders register with local administrators who could then police their activities. Other regulations empowered officials to search for and requisition supplies during periods of dearth. Moreover, regulations required that all transactions (except for a few privileged exceptions) take place publicly in the grain market. All grain for sale had to be available to all legitimate customers and to be measured accurately by an official measurer. An established price could not be altered, and grain left unsold at the end of one market day had to be offered for sale on the next. Families buying for their own consumption had first access to grain when markets opened, and only after those sales could merchants, bakers, and institutions make their purchases.

These subsistence regulations and practices were usually subsumed under

28. "Dearth and the Social Order in Early Modern England," *Past and Present* 71 (May 1976): 22–42.

29. These regulations have been examined carefully elsewhere. See, e.g., Pierre Binet, *La Réglementation du marché du blé en France au XVIIIe siècle et à l'époque contemporaine* (Paris, 1939); Leon Biollay, *Etudes économiques sur le XVIIIe siècle. Le Pacte de famine. L'Administration du commerce* (Paris, 1885), pp. 1–22; Abbott Usher, *The History of the Grain Trade in France, 1400–1710* (Cambridge, Mass., 1913); and, most recent, Kaplan, *Bread*, vol. 1, chap. 2, "Regulations and Regulators," pp. 52–96.

what contemporaries called *la police des grains* or *la police de subsistance.* Thus, police and people interacted in complex ways in subsistence crises. During a dearth, if authorities hesitated or flatly refused to use their powers to maintain a supply of grain, flour, and bread at a fair price, the common people often took the law into their own hands. By invoking particular administrative acts or by appropriating and manipulating the regulation apparatus, the people themselves in effect supplied, however briefly, the *police.*[30] In fact, the *police de subsistance* may have had popular rather than elite origins. Indeed, John Bohstedt has made a provocative suggestion about the origins of such paternalist behavior in Great Britain and the relationship between people and authorities on the subsistence issue: "It seems more likely that ancient paternalistic regulation of markets derived from popular price-fixing traditions than vice-versa."[31]

Although never entirely successful in steadying food prices and supply, these regulatory policies served, on one level, to mitigate some of the worst effects of wildly fluctuating prices, to supply empty markets caused by the human element (hoarding and speculation), or to halt the departure of grain to other markets (usually referred to as exportation, even if the destination was not far from the point of departure). On another level, they indicated political commitment and sensitivity to local welfare. In general, then, paternalists focused on problems of local supply, were consumer oriented (or at least concerned about consumer violence in the context of subsistence crises), were deeply suspicious of producers and merchants alike, and saw agricultural productivity as essentially immutable, subject only to the short-term vagaries of climatic conditions or unethical business practices.

Initially, these practices developed and were administered locally.[32] With monarchical centralization, the royal government gradually intruded on local regulations and local supervision with royal policy and royal officials.[33] As Meuvret has explained, during the reign of Louis XIV there emerged a "political economy on which the welfare (*bonheur*) of the people depended" that replaced more localistic and pragmatic conceptions of the problem of

30. For more on how this interaction took place, specifically and in the context of the Flour War, see Chapters 3 and 5.

31. See his *Riots and Community Politics in England and Wales, 1790–1810* (Cambridge, Mass., 1983), p. 66, n. 160. Abbot Usher suggests this as well in his *History of the Grain Trade*, pp. 239–44.

32. Usher, *History of the Grain Trade*, pp. 240–67; Meuvret, *Problèmes*, 1:22–23.

33. Usher, *History of the Grain Trade*, pp. 223–40, 295–345; Meuvret, *Problèmes*, 1:22–23; C. Tilly, "Food Supply," pp. 392–98, 409–12, 428–37; L. Tilly, "Food Riot," pp. 27–35; and Kaplan, *Bread*, 1:1–8, among others, have observed this phenomenon.

subsistence.[34] The paternalist king thus gradually acquired the attributes of
"The Baker"—for there was nothing immutable about paternalism—as the
women marchers to Versailles called him in October 1789. In quintessentially Early Modern French royal style, however, royal administration and
regulation did not involve the abolition of either local administration or
local regulation, or even its neutralization. Indeed, the local level of
authorities and regulations usually remained in place and continued to play
vigorous roles while a generous topping of royal officials and royal policies
emerged to overlay the concoction, thereby complicating interactions with
the people and the grain trade itself.[35]

Ultimately, changing and expanding market relations and the French
Crown's determination to encourage economic growth via physiocratic
models of a market economy altered commitment to regulation.[36] Although
administrators had always enforced subsistence regulations selectively,[37] and
producers and traders continually experimented with more efficient but
legally ambiguous business practices, overt political commitment to free
trade (or liberalization, as French historians have come to call it) signaled a
sea-change in attitudes. During the era of paternalist administration, the
people could normally expect enforcement, even if reluctant, of at least
some traditional regulations during crises. Free trade threatened to alter this
relationship considerably, prohibiting public authorities from intervening
even to mitigate the worst effects of high prices and shortages. From 1763
to 1770, and again from 1774 to 1776, the French government abandoned

34. Meuvret, Problèmes, 1:24.
35. As Kaplan has observed, "the leading figures in the police of any given community are easy
to identify, but the cast of characters, the attribution of function, and the system of recruitment
vary from place to place" (Bread, 1:28).
36. In the second half of the eighteenth century, the assertions of the proponents of a market
economy that free trade would encourage economic expansion made it an option attractive to the
state. Increased productivity promised greater revenues, and greater revenues meant increased
taxable resources for the Crown. It is not the objective of this study to discuss the philosophical
underpinnings and debates of paternalist regulationism or Physiocracy. For this, see the various
contributions of Georges Weulersse, La Physiocratie à la fin du règne de Louis XV (1770–1774) (Paris,
1959), esp. chap. 2, "Le Programme agricole"; idem, Physiocratie sous les ministères de Turgot et de
Necker (1774–1781) (Paris, 1950), pp. ix–232; R. L. Meek, The Economics of Physiocracy (Cambridge, Mass., 1963); André Bourde, Agronomie et agronomes en France au XVIIIe siècle, 3 vols.
(Paris, 1967); Elizabeth Fox-Genovese, The Origins of Physiocracy: Economic Revolution and Social
Order in Eighteenth-Century France (Ithaca, N.Y., 1976); idem, "The Many Faces of Moral Economy:
A Contribution to a Debate," Past and Present 58 (Feb. 1973): 161–68; Kaplan, Bread, esp.
introduction and conclusion.
37. Miller's "Pragmatic Economy" provides useful evidence of the eclectic practices of subsistence administrators at the local level.

almost completely its regulatory posture and freed the grain trade from regulation, thus consigning the subsistence question, at least in theory, to the play of the free market. The royal judgments that announced this new regime encouraged everyone to participate in the grain trade, permitted transactions everywhere, and allowed every sort of business practice.[38] Between 1771 and 1774 Abbé Terray reinstated subsistence regulations, but he never completely returned the French grain trade to the pre-1763 period.[39] Then, from 1776 until 1787, at least partially as a result of the Flour War, the Crown again renewed its commitment to regulation in the style of the 1771–74 period.[40]

After mid-century the combined effects of a rising population and the gradual breakdown in the traditional system of poor relief exacerbated social stresses.[41] Despite the absence of an English-style agricultural revolution in

38. Despite the spirit of the free-trade edicts, the grain trade was never entirely free. Technological difficulties (such as inefficient information-gathering and transportation networks) aside, impediments continued to confront traders—for example, tolls, various marketplace dues (droits de marché), monopolies (banalités), and other local practices that governed when certain categories of people could enter the market went largely unchallenged. Moreover, a few restrictions remained in place (see below and Chapter 2).

39. Although he required everyone intending to engage in the grain and flour trade to register, he countenanced freedom of commerce within the kingdom and retained the open qualification policy of the liberal period. On this see, Kaplan, Bread, 1:287, 2:557–58; Georges Lefebvre, Etudes Orléanais, 2 vols. (Paris, 1962), 1:248; Faure, Disgrâce, p. 215. Violations of Terray's regimes were numerous. See, e.g., Charles Desmarest, Le Commerce des grains dans la généralité de Rouen à la fin de l'Ancien Régime (Paris, 1926), p. 186.

40. This 1776–87 period is a much underresearched segment of French history with regard to the grain trade. Kaplan ends his massive study (Bread) with the end of Louis XV's reign, and his Provisioning Paris (Ithaca, N.Y., 1985) continues the analysis, but from a different angle; Judith Miller's "Pragmatic Economy" surveys the period from the angle of Normandy; and Weurlersse's 1950 work, Physiocratie sous les ministères de Turgot et de Necker, stands largely alone.

41. The "demographic revolution" of the second half of the eighteenth century is the subject of considerable study. See, e.g., Pierre Goubert, "Révolution démographique au 18e siècle," in Histoire économique et sociale de la France, vol. 2, 1660–1789, ed. F. Braudel and E. Labrousse (Paris, 1970), pp. 66–76; Jacques Dupâquier, La Population française au XVIIe et XVIIIe siècles (Paris, 1976); idem, "Les caractères originaux de l'histoire démographique française au XVIIIe siècle," RHMC 33 (1976): 193–202. See also John E. Post, Food Shortage, Climatic Variability, and Epidemic Disease in Preindustrial Europe: The Mortality Peak in the Early 1740s (Ithaca, N.Y., 1985). Historians of poverty and poor relief agree generally that the existing systems of poor relief did not work effectively. Thus, population pressure accelerated pauperization (but not widespread starvation). See, among others, Camille Bloch, L'Assistance et l'Etat en France à la veille de la Révolution (Paris, 1908); Jean-Pierre Gutton, La Société et les pauvres. L'Exemple de la généralité de Lyon, 1534–1789 (Paris, 1970); Cissie Fairchilds, Poverty and Charity in Aix-en-Provence, 1640–1789 (Baltimore, 1976); Olwen Hufton, The Poor; Alan Forrest, The French Revolution and the Poor (New York, 1981); Colin Jones, Charity and "Bienfaisance": The Treatment of the Poor in the Montpellier Region, 1740–1815 (Cambridge, 1982); Robert Schwartz, Policing the Poor in Eighteenth-Century France (Chapel Hill, N.C., 1988);

the eighteenth century,[42] French production and distribution had responded to mounting demand enough to prevent the starvation that was widespread during earlier periods. Now, however, French society experienced mounting pauperization, though not a widespread crisis of mortality caused directly by starvation. Fear of destitution haunted most French people, and—at least for significant periods of time—actual indigence regularly confronted one in five of the population.[43] The institutions of charity and repression proved unable to meet the challenge despite efforts to reform them throughout the century.[44]

These circumstances—the structural changes associated with the development of capitalism, the interplay of royal policy, demographic pressure, and a weakening of already insufficient mechanisms for support—had dramatic implications for those who had to buy grain to survive. Indeed, the areas of France that experienced these developments most intensively were most susceptible to food riots. This particular conjuncture created a window of vulnerability. In effect, French society erupted repeatedly into a battle over the control of and entitlement to food.

In terms of what happened, who participated, and where and when riots took place, the Flour War had much in common with the general patterns just discussed, although, as subsequent chapters will show, it also embodied crucial variations in detail that may help us to refine our understanding of these questions. In terms of why food riots erupted, how rioters mobilized, and the significance of these movements, the issues become more complex, and considerable historical debate has emerged. The Flour War can be seen to fit many of the patterns cited—in fact, it provided some of the evidence used to construct many of them—but it also raises issues explored in detail in later chapters.

In this context, we can discuss the fifth contribution historians have made to our understanding of subsistence movements: the question of motives. The *taxation populaire* of the late seventeenth century to the mid-nineteenth

---

Thomas M. Adams, *Bureaucrats and Beggars: French Social Policy in the Age of Enlightenment* (New York, 1990). For more on this, see Chapter 2.

42. See Michel Morineau, *Les Faux-Semblants d'un démarrage économique. Agriculture et démographie en France au XVIIIe siècle* (Paris, 1970), and the critique of much recent work in James L. Goldsmith, "The Agrarian History of Preindustrial France: Where Do We Go from Here?" *Journal of European Economic History* 13 (Spring 1984): 175–200. See also Chapter 2.

43. See the summary in Forrest, *Poor*, pp. 2–3.

44. On the efforts at repression rather than charity or poor relief, see Hufton, *Poor*; Schwartz, *Policing*; Iain Cameron, *Crime and Repression in the Auvergne and the Guyenne, 1720–1790* (Cambridge, 1981), pp. 101–32, 161–78.

century was, we have learned, no simple visceral or "spasmodic" reaction to hunger.[45] Although people were still dying from starvation at the turn of the eighteenth century, and more subtle demographic reverberations from subsistence crises (for example, disease brought on by malnutrition and a decline in the birth rate) continued throughout the period considered here, we cannot accept uncritically the simple equation of hunger equals riot. Of course, subsistence riots correlate with short-term price rises, and we should not underestimate the continuing power of the "subsistence mentality" or "psychosis of scarcity"[46] that dominated daily life for so many French people. Not all price rises, however, nor even the most dramatic price rises, were accompanied by rioting.[47] Consequently, historians have searched for more comprehensive causalities.

The origins of and the animus behind the *taxation populaire* lay beyond the short-term fluctuations resulting from or pointing to shortages: rioters were responding to the larger structural and political changes at work within their communities. In the collective memory of past crises and past responses, and in community bargaining over control of food, the people had elaborated a model of how the subsistence question should be addressed. This popular "moral economy," as E. P. Thompson has taught us to call it, was grounded in adherence to the perception of grain and its products as a "common good" and enshrined guidelines for protecting consumers that drew on images of past paternalist practices. As markets expanded and changed, as merchants and producers developed new marketing techniques, as the number of potentially vulnerable consumers increased, as administrators hesitated to enforce subsistence regulations, or as the monarchy attempted to dismantle the regulations altogether, the people invoked the *taxation populaire* to force the government to act. Should officials refuse,

45. The description of popular behavior as "spasmodic" is the definition attributed by E. P. Thompson to the cluster of English-speaking writers who explained food riots as "elementary—instinctive—[reactions to] hunger" when "one spasm led to another: the outcome was 'plunder' " (Thompson, "Moral Economy," p. 77). See Rudé's analysis of several similar French interpretations from the nineteenth century in *Crowd in History*, pp. 7–8. See also the description of late nineteenth-century crowd in Susanna Barrows, *Distorting Mirrors: Visions of the Crowd in Late Nineteenth-Century France* (New Haven, 1981).

46. The phrase "subsistence mentality" belongs to Kaplan (*Bread*, 1:200, 2:542). The phrase "psychosis of scarcity" is Bercé's (*Revolt*, p. 102). For more on the problem of need, see Chapters 5 and 6.

47. On the relationship between hunger and rioting in England, see Dale E. Williams, "Were 'Hunger' Rioters Really Hungry? Some Demographic Evidence," *Past and Present* 71 (May 1976): 70–75. Williams argues that rioters in the 1760s really were hungry but that hunger in itself does not explain why some communities rioted and others did not.

equivocate, or respond with insufficient vigor, the people stood ready to take action themselves.

When the monarchy slowly, hesitatingly, and unevenly withdrew its support for subsistence regulation in the grain trade in favor of the physiocratic vision of laissez-faire economics, the common people sharpened and contrasted their own position, a position opposed in almost every way to the direction of change in the Ancien Régime. Against an expanding market servicing distant needs, the common people envisioned a tightly limited market defined by local needs;[48] against the development of large-scale commercial agriculture, the people envisioned a peasant economy governed by subsistence needs and sensitive to local problems of supply;[49] against the free-trade position articulated by the Physiocrats and embraced by greater numbers of ministers and administrators (not to mention many merchants and producers), the people demanded the continuation and furthered sensitivity of paternalist practice. The issues were, first and foremost, control of and entitlement to food, and the people demonstrated clear positions, by rioting if necessary. They viewed property in food as "contingent," not "absolute"; they believed that real limitations existed on the disposition of food, limitations defined by public welfare. As Steven Kaplan put it, "Private property had public obligations."[50] One was entitled to food whether or not

48. Steven Kaplan, *Provisioning Paris: Merchants and Millers in the Grain and Flour Trade During the Eighteenth Century* (Ithaca, N.Y., 1984), distinguishes between the "market principle" and the "marketplace" as organizing assumptions (p. 27), which corresponds in general to Thompson's market economy and moral economy and is a way around some of the objections to Thompson's choice. Thompson's term "moral economy" has come under attack on several occasions. In all cases, protestors have objected to the notion that classical free-market economics, cast in these terms, is assumed to be less moral. They point out that morality is in the eye of the beholder: consumer or producer, urban or rural resident, etc. See, e.g., A. W. Coats, "Contrary Moralities: Plebs, Paternalists, and Political Economists," *Past and Present* 54 (Feb. 1972): 130–33; Fox-Genovese, "The Many Faces," pp. 161–68; and, most recent, Hilton Root, "Politiques frumentaires et violence collective en Europe moderne," *AESC* 45 (Jan.–Feb. 1990): 167–89.

49. See, e.g., Florence Gauthier's description of peasant visions in her *La Voie paysanne dans la Révolution française. L'Exemple picard* (Paris, 1977), pp. 95–144, 205–19.

50. *Bread*, 1:194. See also William H. Sewell, *Work and Revolution in France: The Language of Labor from the Old Regime to 1848* (Cambridge, 1980), chap. 6. John Bohstedt claims that the "ethical ambiguity" that suffused preindustrial notions of property (and especially food) created the conditions for debate of the subsistence issue (*Riots*, pp. 25–26). For other statements on the ethical ambiguities residing in the subsistence question, see Thompson, "Moral Economy," pp. 76–136; Douglas Hay, "Property, Authority, and the Criminal Law," in *Albion's Fatal Tree: Crime and Society in Eighteenth-Century England*, ed. D. Hay et al. (New York, 1975), pp. 17–64. Compare this with Philip Roeder's description of peasant attitudes toward property, especially land, as "contingent" and "bounded": "Legitimacy and Peasant Revolution: An Alternative to the Moral Economy," *Peasant Studies* 11 (Spring 1984): 153, 159–60.

one could afford it at the market price. Protesters believed they were defending their long-established legitimate rights against dangerous innovations. They also believed that the government should defend those rights.

This vision of a different kind of economy articulated by protesters hostile to the one they saw developing around them has helped historians explain better the timing and the nature of participation, behavior, and theaters of action during the *taxation populaire* of the late seventeenth century through the mid-nineteenth century. Riots were most frequently triggered by what rioters saw as evidence of improper behavior in the grain trade, behavior that threatened their entitlements to food. Rising prices and empty markets certainly operated as the most obvious evidence, but so too did signs of grain-exporting, hoarding, bidding wars over available supplies, sales outside public spaces, changes in milling and baking procedures, and breakdowns in the traditional patronage system that provided charity.[51]

Locating food riots in the context of the "moral economy" has also helped to explain more fully the gendered character of these movements. Women of the common people occupied the marketplace as a logical extension of their roles in the family economy: providing food and supplies for their households.[52] Their linchpin roles in family survival made them especially sensitive to variations in prices and the availability of basic necessities. Women thus took positive and often violent actions to rectify intolerable conditions that threatened family and community stability. They became guardians of the community's norms, and as such sometimes invoked the *taxation populaire* as the last recourse.[53]

Moreover, female (as opposed to male) participation in rioting was a wise strategy, given the usual local and official responses. Women often emerged

51. Compare the descriptions of triggers of food riots in England in Thompson, "The Moral Economy," pp. 85–88, 98–107; Dale E. Williams, "Morals, Markets, and the English Crowd in 1766," *Past and Present* 104 (Aug. 1984): 69–70; Bohstedt, *Riots*, pp. 22–23.

52. The creation of the marketplace as quintessentially female space may have been furthered by the ordering of the male workday, especially in urban areas. As Mark Harrison has argued for eighteenth-century Bristol, England, "the regular working week was a characteristic of the urban environment" even before the work-discipline of the factory ("The Ordering of the Urban Environment: Time, Work, and the Occurrence of Crowds, 1790–1835," *Past and Present* 110 [1986]: 134–68, quote on p. 167). However, the eighteenth-century French workday as described by Michael Sonenscher (*Work and Wages: Natural Law, Politics, and the Eighteenth-Century French Trades* [Cambridge, 1989]) appears much less orderly than that portrayed by Harrison.

53. Related is Dominique Godineau's argument that women during the Revolutionary period had a "distinctive role . . . that they assumed fully and that the entire society recognized, [which] was that of firebrands, those who use words to incite action" ("Masculine and Feminine Political Practice," p. 76). Of course, this role extended far beyond subsistence rioting.

less severely punished than their male counterparts. Police and then judges conducted the arrest and punishment of women rioters with more leniency.[54] Of course, the authorities' relatively benevolent posture toward women stemmed from a different attitude toward female behavior and roles as compared with that of males. This attitude comprised several traditional assumptions about women that included identifying them exclusively with their familial roles, and more specifically with their maternal roles, perceiving them as politically powerless and therefore less politically dangerous, and believing them naturally unruly and uncontrollable.[55] It was precisely the woman's maternal role that, in the eyes of authorities, legitimized her recourse to desperate expedients when the family economy was threatened. Politically, socially, and culturally restricted to the private sphere, a woman's actions were perceived as a statement of private distress. Similarly, the image of the disorderly woman unable to control her unruly and irrational impulses served to exonerate her when her strategies burst from the legal to the illegal realm.

Perhaps ironically, women's perceived powerlessness in the public sphere and the nature of common assumptions about female character and behavior gave them a kind of real power during subsistence crises. In the food riot, women's power thus lay in their turning the assumptions of the traditional gender system into weapons to defend community and family against bakers, producers, merchants, millers, and even authorities who failed to respond sympathetically to the crisis, and into legitimizing shields to protect them from retribution. The combination of female activity in food riots and the conservative assumptions about women may have muted the political threat embodied in the taxation populaire and frequently enabled them to emerge relatively unscathed, and sometimes even victorious, even if victory meant only a few days of cheap but plentiful bread for their families and neighbors.

Recently, however, John Bohstedt has challenged this understanding of the food riot as a female sphere of activity in late eighteenth- and early nineteenth-century Great Britain. He has argued that while women were visible and significant participants in subsistence movements, they shared this terrain with men. Women appeared in fewer than half of the English food riots between 1790 and 1810. While the food riot was indeed their domain, compared with other types of popular unrest (enclosure move-

54. This appears not to have been the case in England. See Bohstedt, "Gender," pp. 119–20.
55. On what follows, compare Hufton, "Women and the Family Economy," p. 19, and her "Women in Revolution," p. 94; Natalie Zemon Davis, "Women on Top," in Society and Culture, pp. 124–46; Nicole Castan, "Criminalité," pp. 91–108.

ments, labor strikes, etc.), they in no way dominated the subsistence riot. He claims that "male mobs of colliers and tinmen and construction workers and militiamen were more numerous than female mobs."[56] Moreover, he warns us not to assume that the "food market was a woman's province" and suggests that men as well as women participated in provisioning their families. In crises, therefore, Bohstedt argues, "men were expected to defend their families' living standard as much as women."[57] Female presence in food riots is best understood, he continues, in the context in which "women and men and children . . . acted together in household production."[58] Women bread-rioters should thus be seen "as proto-citizens and constituents of the local polity and economy, nearly coequal to men in claiming their rights to affordable bread."[59]

Bohstedt's work sounds an important cautionary note to assumptions about gender roles and hierarchies in preindustrial societies. However, his arguments also reside in what may constitute a fundamental developmental difference between an increasingly industrial (and certainly protoindustrial) British economy and society and a more agrarian and peasant (with all the nuances for this term understood) French society and economy.[60] Certainly, men had never been excluded from food riots, and we have striking examples of male-dominated and even exclusively male disturbances that date from the seventeenth century.[61] And, when men did riot in France they were often the proletarianized or semiproletarianized wage-earners of the general type described by Bohstedt.[62] But the scale and rate of development differed in France in the eighteenth century. Larger numbers of peasants and peasant family economies, larger numbers of only semiproletarianized wage-earners who also controlled some small amounts of land, and a more developed seigneurial system persisted for much longer in France, and all this had an impact on the construction of family roles.[63] Moreover, Bohstedt's work

56. "Gender," p. 93.

57. Ibid., p. 88, and his "Myth," p. 32.

58. "Gender," p. 93.

59. Ibid., p. 98.

60. According to a recent account, the yeomanry of England held no more than 10 percent of the land at the end of the eighteenth century, while French peasant households held 33 percent (Peter Jones, *The Peasantry in the French Revolution* [Cambridge, 1988], p. 7).

61. See Chapter 6 esp.

62. Moreover, when significant numbers of wage-earning men rioted during the Flour War, they did so under particular circumstances and in particular spheres (see Chapter 4).

63. These are important issues. A comparative study of family structures and roles would be useful. Could French families have been more patriarchal than English families, or could roles have been allocated differently in French families? On women's roles in Ancien Régime peasant families, see James B. Collins, "The Economic Role of Women in Seventeenth-Century France," *FHS* 16

covers a relatively limited (and late) chronological period, making it difficult
to tell what, if anything, was changing in English gender roles.

Bohstedt argues that protoindustrialization modified patriarchal authority.
This modification resulted in a rise in female status that enabled women to
claim a share of the family political voice in such arenas as subsistence.[64]
Bohstedt relies on the important work of such historians as John Gillis[65] to
support his argument for rising female status, but a considerable body of
literature suggests that the growing lack of differentiation between gender
roles in the family economy, while indeed modifying patriarchal authority,
did so because it constituted more of a decline in male status than a rise in
female status.[66] Of course, the status of both women and men may have
been changing and thereby converging. Because this problem leads ultimately to the question of motives, it deserves attention. The chapters that
follow address this debate further. Certainly, women were visible and
important participants in subsistence movements, even if they did not
occupy that space alone. Moreover, as we shall see below, subjecting
subsistence riots to a more nuanced analysis that distinguishes between
market riots and rioting that involved raids on the farms of large-scale
cultivators exposes important differences in male and female participation.

A wide spectrum of French society shared this sense of outrage in the face
of what protesters denounced as illegitimate dealings. Thus, for example,
understanding motivation grounded in the moral economy also helps us to
understand why local authorities and the propertied occasionally endorsed
popular demands and collaborated with protesters during subsistence crises.
Confronted with such evidence of elite participation in food riots, Rudé had
earlier concluded that most authorities had been coerced.[67] However,
Thompson and especially Steven Kaplan have emphasized a different, more

---

(Fall 1989): 436–70. Collins describes women in the marketplace as sellers of goods they produced—
fruits, garden crops, poultry, butter, etc.—to provide income for the family, but he does not discuss
the issue of men and women as buyers.

64. "Gender," p. 96.

65. "Peasant, Plebeian, and Proletarian Marriages in Britain, 1600–1900," in *Proletarianization
and Family History*, ed. David Levine (Orlando, 1984), pp. 87–128.

66. See, e.g., Ulrich Pfister, "Work Roles and Family Structure in Proto-Industrial Zurich,"
JIH 20 (Summer 1989): 83–105; idem, "The Proto-Industrial Household Economy: Toward a Formal
Analysis" (Paper presented to the Conference on the European Peasant Family and Economy,
Minneapolis, 1988); Gay Gullickson, *Spinners and Weavers of Auffay: Rural Industry and the Sexual
Division of Labor in a French Village, 1750–1850* (Cambridge, 1986); Bouton, "Gendered Behavior,"
JSH 23 (Summer 1990): 735–54.

67. Rudé was unable to accept the possibility that we could "charge magistrates with complicity
in the riots" (*Crowd in History*, p. 29).

multiplex, and more convincing explanation. Both historians have suggested that while rioters may have coerced some local notables, many shared with the common people a position on the subsistence issue, although not always for the same reasons. Local authorities traditionally included among their responsibilities regulating the grain trade (a function to which they clung fiercely). Moreover, their assumption of paternalist roles sensitive to the plight of poor consumers often inclined them to support popular protests during subsistence crises. On occasion, of course, magistrates simply concluded that concession to the will of the protesters constituted the wisest course.[68] In many places, protesters proved adept at manipulating these traditions to their advantage[69] and the crowd knitted a diverse collectivity into one that shared strategies about how to address the subsistence question.

Participation in the *taxation populaire*—the Flour War included—makes more sense when we recognize that the invocation and emulation, if in more extreme form, of the previous paternalist model and practice rooted in its perceived legitimacy among diverse groups. Moreover, the spaces in which rioters acted related more directly to areas where distribution problems accompanied expanding markets, where the people discovered examples of what they challenged as illegitimate production and marketing practices, and where previous practices designed to mitigate the worst effects of subsistence crises were breaking down (from alms-giving to enforcing subsistence regulations), than to those in which prices rose fastest. Food riots erupted most frequently in public marketplaces, but others were the work of rioters who invaded private property: mills, bakeries, and merchant or producer granaries. These actions reflected popular assumptions about the public nature of food, wherever it was found, that overrode considerations of private ownership and control.

68. Thompson, "Moral Economy," pp. 121–24. The most significant work in this area is that of Steven Kaplan, who has contributed greatly to our understanding of behavior of local authorities, or the subsistence police. See esp. Kaplan, "Regulations and the Regulators," *Bread*, 1:52–96. See also Walter and Wrightson ("Dearth," pp. 40–42), who argue that in seventeenth-century England there was a significant consensus between rulers and ruled on the regulation of the marketplace and paternal responsibilities. Compare with Bohstedt, who speaks of the local authorities and elites as "allies" of the crowd who might be motivated by "humanitarianism, a desire for social peace, or self interest" (*Riots*, pp. 22–23) during the period 1790–1810.

69. E. P. Thompson, "Folklore, Anthropology, and Social History," *Indian Historical Review* 3 (Jan. 1978): 247–66, reprinted as a Studies in Labor History pamphlet (Sussex, 1979), pp. 13, 21. James Scott provides useful analyses of how the peasantry could manipulate elite notions of paternalism to its advantage: *Weapons of the Weak: Everyday Forms of Peasant Resistance* (New Haven, 1985), pp. 306–7, 309–11.

Thus, most historians have agreed that the food riot was the product of and rooted in a collectivity or community that shared similar values, conceptual frames of reference, and dense social ties.[70] The "moral economy" reflected a consensus that was communal both in the geographical or organizational sense (village, neighborhood, kinship, patronage, friendship, gender, workplace, and class networks, for example) and in the normative sense. It often crossed social and economic, political and cultural, as well as gender boundaries, thus linking common people and elites, men and women, rulers and ruled. The early modern community constituted the preexisting organization that shaped collective action such as food riots, and the food riots, in turn, shaped community. It defined social obligations— collective responsibilities—for its members and thus ordered behavior.

While, as Colin Lucas has observed, "this all-embracing form of community was subject to considerable stress and defection by the time of the later *ancien régime* . . . the divorce between popular community and elite community was not complete."[71] In fact, this process of separation (if ever the community was "all-embracing" or if separation ever occurred completely) created the context for food rioting. The common people appealed to producers, to merchants, and to local officials who had been lured away by the potential of the free market, by asking them to rejoin the community, embrace the moral economy, and celebrate this reconciliation by distributing food publicly at just prices. The people demanded that defectors stand accountable to the community by bearing the collective responsibilities to provide collective goods. When appeals fell on deaf ears, the community invoked the *taxation populaire* and even sanctioned violence. Community

70. Lucas, "The Crowd and Politics Between Ancien Régime and Revolution in France," *JMH* 60 (Sept. 1988): 426, 429–30; Thompson, "Moral Economy," p. 78; William Reddy, "The Textile Trade and the Language of the Crowd at Rouen, 1752–1871," *Past and Present* 74 (Feb. 1977): 82–83; Bohstedt, *Riots*, p. 23; Lefebvre, "Revolutionary Crowds," pp. 175, 179–81. On this, see also C. J. Calhoun, "History, Anthropology, and the Study of Communities: Some Problems in Macfarlane's Proposal," *Social History* (Oct. 1978): 363–74; idem, "Community: Toward a Variable Conceptualization for Comparative Research," *Social History* 5 (Jan. 1980): 105–30; idem, *The Question of Class Struggle: Social Foundations of Popular Radicalism During the Industrial Revolution* (Chicago, 1982), pp. 213, 226, 234; Suzanne Desan, "Crowds, Community, and Ritual in the Work of E. P. Thompson and Natalie Davis," in *The New Cultural History*, ed. Lynn Hunt (Berkeley and Los Angeles, 1989), 47–71. For a more general analysis of the dimensions of eighteenth-century French community, see, e.g., David Garrioch, *Neighborhood and Community in Paris, 1740–1790* (Cambridge, 1986), esp. chaps. 1 and 6; Jean-Pierre Gutton, *La Sociabilité villageoise dans l'ancienne France* (Paris, 1979).

71. Lucas, "Crowd and Politics," p. 430. Bohstedt speaks of the mobilization of "horizontal" and "vertical" community relations (*Riots*, p. 23).

members were transformed into food rioters. Thus, those who denied these core values, for whatever reason, opted out of the community and opened themselves up to sanctions destined for outsiders.

Recently, several historians have challenged this emphasis on communal consensus.[72] They have asked, first, whether those who joined rioters or supported their efforts actually shared the same assumptions. Did women and men, elites and common people, urban and rural folk, authorities and people, join in food riots for the same reasons? These historians point out that we have "reified" the crowd[73] and assumed that "being there" was evidence enough of shared motives. This assumption does not adequately account for the presence of individuals or groups pursuing other goals within the framework of collective action. Indeed, Clark McPhail suggests not only that "members of gatherings [are] engaged in ongoing sequences of individual behavior" but also that it is "not uncommon for several separate sequences of collective behavior to occur simultaneously within a large gathering."[74] Some of these authors go on to suggest that norms were not culturally determined, but rather "malleable, renegotiated and shifting according to considerations of power and strategic interaction among individuals."[75] Even if we accept the notion that virtually all the common people and even some elites did share similar assumptions about the proper resolution of subsistence issues, what, then, differentiated those who rioted from those who did not? In some cases, entire villages erupted into riot; in other cases, only some smaller number of people participated; in still others, entire villages remained calm while others nearby exploded into violence.

Second, such an emphasis on a communal consensus, these authors argue, has led us to overlook such issues as "potential power struggles within the crowd itself."[76] They remind historians that they confront and must explain an apparent paradox. How do we explain the reality of a socially

72. See, e.g., Robert Woods, "Individuals in the Rioting Crowd: A New Approach," *JIH* 14 (1983): 1–24; Tim Harris, *London Crowds in the Reign of Charles II: Propaganda and Politics from the Restoration Until the Exclusion Crisis* (Cambridge, 1987), esp. pp. 8–13; Desan, "Crowds," pp. 47–71; Root, "Politique frumentaire," pp. 169–72. For a broader view, see Samuel L. Popkin, *The Rational Peasant: The Political Economy of Rural Society in Vietnam* (Berkeley and Los Angeles, 1979).

73. Harris, *London Crowds*, p. 6. Clark McPhail claims: "It is a long-standing misconception—when collective behavior occurs, every member of the gathering is involved" (*The Myth of the Madding Crowd* [New York, 1991], pp. 153, 162).

74. *Myth*, pp. 153, 159.

75. Popkin, *Rational Peasant*, p. 22.

76. Desan, "Crowds," p. 61.

differentiated and stratified Early Modern society even at the level of the village community that had always existed in some form[77] with this image of a communal consensus on the subsistence issue? They dispute that such a community could find consensus on the subsistence issue, an issue that engages the question of property. We should not confuse the historical community itself with the image of community that functioned as a mobilizing myth (embodied in the moral economy) to rally crowd action. Indeed, we are exhorted to abandon these latter concepts of community as too vague and romanticized—grounded, for example, in Tönnies's *Gemeinschaft/Gesellschaft* dichotomy, in Redfield's "folk community," or in Turner's "communitas"—to carry much explanatory power.[78]

Third, we are asked to consider what dynamics might catalyze a preserving crowd (which was both shaped by and reinforcer of the communal status quo) into a transforming crowd (which attempted to change the community). We are asked to consider the presence and ramifications of competing social interests and power struggles within any community. Food riots might, for example, serve the interests of women against men, some local authorities against others, some producers or merchants against others. Riots opened arenas for competition and provided opportunities for transforming power relations.[79]

These observations await refinement, and the section below, Chapter 5, and a Conclusion will address some of these issues. So far, and by way of a partial response to these objections, the communal consensus proponents have always maintained that what is striking (and still in need of elaboration) about food riots is how successfully they rallied public collective agreement (whatever private interests might be) in the face of changing structures within preindustrial society. The basic contours of the food riot remained in place for more than a century in England and France, and even longer in other parts of Europe.[80] True, frequency dropped, defection from the ranks of supporters occurred, and the *taxation populaire* underwent

77. The most extreme statement on this score is that of Alan Macfarlane on Medieval and Early Modern England: *The Origins of English Individualism: The Family, Property, and Social Transition* (Oxford, 1978).

78. Ferdinand Tönnies, *Community and Society*, trans. J. Samples (New Brunswick, N.J., 1988, 1957, 1887); R. Redfield, *The Little Community: Peasant Society and Culture* (Chicago, 1960); V. Turner, *The Ritual Process: Structure and Anti-Structure* (Ithaca, N.Y., 1977).

79. Desan, "Crowd," pp. 58–60; Root, "Politique frumentaire," pp. 168–72.

80. In Germany, the food riot is most common in the period from the 1790s to the middle of the nineteenth century (Gailus, "Food Riots," p. 3).

internal transformations, and all this demands analysis. Nevertheless, the century and a half that witnessed the heyday of the subsistence riot also experienced tremendous structural changes. Although food riots are frequently cited as evidence of tension, they are also evidence of cooperation, of solidarity, of community.

These historians have also noted how such riots could exert a transformative force as rioters and their opponents squared off against each other over such issues as rights to property (such as food) and social welfare (such as the allocation of collective goods). Food rioters could produce change. Rioters attempted to apply traditional tools (which were themselves creations of previous attempts to cope with change) to continually changing circumstances. In the attempt to reassemble the community, to recall outliers to their collective responsibilities, they changed their world. Thompson has argued that new consciousness arises out of new experiences as actors apply past practices to their present. When they fail to fulfill expectations (and sometimes even when they succeed), they trigger transformation. On the one hand, food rioters may be driven to refine and reevaluate their own assumptions in the wake of failure; on the other hand, they may, by their success or threatening stance, further accelerate the defection of producers, merchants, and authorities from the community.[81]

Another contribution to our understanding of pre-Revolutionary subsistence riots lies in a debate over their political significance. Here one finds a spectrum of approaches. At one end, historians as diverse as Yves-Marie Bercé and George Rudé have largely refused to grant political significance to food rioters' behavior. Bercé asserts that they were merely "banal" economic "struggles for survival" "bereft of political implications." He distinguishes two types of outbreaks of popular violence: struggles for survival and struggles for power. He classifies food riots among the first type, and uses the food riot as his prototype for struggles for survival.[82] Rudé makes this distinction even

---

81. This position is most clearly stated in Thompson, "The Poverty of Theory; or, An Orrery of Errors," in *The Poverty of Theory and Other Essays* (London, 1978), pp. 1–210, esp. pp. 7–9. Similarly, Marshall Sahlins argues that transformation is in effect the product of failed reproduction as people learn that previous practices fail to produce the customary or expected results (Sahlins, *Historical Metaphors and Mythical Realities: Structure in the Early History of the Sandwich Islands Kingdom* [Ann Arbor, Mich. 1981], esp. 67–72). Dale Williams argues that food riots should also be considered important episodes in the development of middle-class consciousness ("Morals, Markets," pp. 56–73).

82. *Revolt*, pp. 100, 108. He was less inclined to this position in his earlier work, where he states that the "bread riots assumed the character of an assertion of morality, a defense of the established order against social climbers" (Yves-Marie Bercé, *History of Peasant Revolts: The Social*

clearer when he differentiates between political movements and food riots.[83] In a specific reference to the Flour War of 1775, he asserts that "there was no question of overthrowing the government or established order, of putting forward new solutions, or even of seeking redress of grievances by political action." The riots of 1775 constitute, for him, the "eighteenth century food riot in its undiluted form," and he emphasizes their "political innocence."[84] Like Bercé, Rudé refuses to see these riots (and others like them) as a manifestation of political concerns and, if compared with the antitax rebellions of the seventeenth century and the Revolutionary *journées*, the food riot does indeed pale considerably.[85]

At the other end, a cluster of historians—such as E. P. Thompson, Louise Tilly, and Florence Gauthier and Guy-Robert Ikni—have argued for a more political content to rioter behavior during subsistence crises. Thompson's "moral economy of the poor" is, in essence, a political as well as an economic and social vision, carrying images not simply of a different construction of the economy and of a different role for government, but, more profoundly, of a different type of society that could embody this vision. For Thompson, the cultural traditions embodied in the popular "moral economy" mediated between experience, on the one hand, and responses to that experience, on the other hand. This interaction worked to define and refine political consciousness among the plebeians.[86] Looking at the

---

Origins of Rebellion in Early Modern France, trans. A. Whitmore [Ithaca, N.Y., 1990], p. 178, which is a translation of his earlier *Histoire des Croquants* [Paris, 1974]).

83. This posture is most apparent in Rudé's examination of the French Revolution, *Crowd in History*, where he divides crowd action into three parts: "The Political Riot," "The Food Riot," and "The Labor Dispute."

84. Ibid., p. 31. Rudé takes as evidence of political content "animosity toward the court and the nobility" and, finding no overt statements of such hostility, concludes that they were "conservative and traditional" (p. 118).

85. This perception of subsistence riots is shared by historians of diverse political perspectives. René Pillorget provided a typology for popular protest from the sixteenth to the eighteenth centuries in Provence. He distinguished between movements against authority—ecclesiastical authority, seigneurial authority, judicial authority, military authority—and "pure subsistence riots" ("Essai d'un typologie des mouvements insurrectionnels ruraux survenus en Provence de 1596 à 1715," *Actes du 92e Congrès national des sociétés savantes, Strasbourg, 1967* [Paris, 1970], pp. 359–82). Jeffry Kaplow also tends to see popular behavior as "prepolitical" (*The Names of Kings: The Parisian Laboring Poor in the Eighteenth-Century* [New York, 1972], pp. 153–70); Steven Kaplan described them as constituting a "primitive political gesture" (*Bread*, 1:194). J. F. Bosher has reasserted a more extreme version of this position and extended it to the Revolutionary period, where most historians are inclined to see a more "political" common person: "hunger and fear of hunger, not political ideas, were the strongest forces moving the populace." See Bosher, *The French Revolution* (New York, 1988), p. 33. For more on this, see below.

86. See Thompson, "The Moral Economy," pp. 131–36; idem, "Patrician Society, Plebeian Culture," *JSH* 7 (Summer 1974): 382–405; idem, "Eighteenth-Century English Society," 133–65.

French situation, Louise Tilly argues at least as forcefully for an increasingly politicized food riot, one that accompanied the "shift of subsistence policy to the national arena." She asserts that the food riot was "the political tool of a powerless people" that, over time, "sharpened" their "political consciousness." The subsistence riot thus served as a kind of political training ground for the common people as they struggled to assert their vision of economic organization in a society increasingly dominated by a national market and a centralizing nation-state.[87]

All historians have located the subsistence riot in the context of emerging capitalism and associated theories of classical economics. This context certainly appears to fit the British situation, even if historians dispute the exact nature of the relationship and the timing.[88] Locating France's food riots within the context of emerging capitalist production and marketing practices provides only a part of the situation. There tends to be an almost universal neglect of the fact that, in France, the emerging market economy and the centralizing state were developing within the context of a still dynamic feudal/seigneurial society.[89] Gauthier and Ikni largely stand alone when they assign broader political import and increasing political sophistication to the pre-Revolutionary food riot by placing it in the context not only of emerging capitalist relations but also of feudal relations within France. Production and marketing continued to be shaped and constrained by a panoply of privileged interests that even liberalization of the grain trade did little to undermine during the eighteenth century.[90] The authors

---

See also Thompson's argument in his various books and esp. *Customs in Common* (London, 1991). This search for the origins of working-class consciousness constitutes the overriding theme in his work. On Thompson's thought, see Richard Johnson, "Thompson, Genovese, and Social Humanist History," *History Workshop* 6 (1978): 79–100; Ellen Trimberger, "E. P. Thompson: Understanding the Process of History," in *Vision and Method in Historical Sociology*, ed. Theda Skocpol (Cambridge, 1984), pp. 211–43; Desan, "Crowds," pp. 47–71.

87. L. Tilly, "Food Riot," pp. 56–57; idem, "Food Entitlement," pp. 333–49.

88. Most historians agree that by the eighteenth century England was already a capitalist, but not yet industrial, society. For a summary of this argument, see Fox-Genovese, "Many Faces," pp. 162–64. See also J. Stevenson, "The 'Moral Economy' of the English Crowd: Myth and Reality," in *Order and Disorder in Early Modern England*, ed. A. Fletcher and J. Stevenson (Cambridge, 1985), pp. 218–38.

89. The most extreme example of this position is Charles Tilly, who defines food riots as "reactive" or "defensive collective reactions" against capitalism (*Mobilization*, p. 148). See also C. Tilly, L. Tilly, and R. Tilly, *The Rebellious Century, 1830–1930* (Cambridge, Mass., 1975), pp. 49–55; C. Tilly, "Proletarianization and Rural Collective Action in East Anglia and Elsewhere, 1500–1900," *Peasant Studies* 10 (Fall 1982): 13. See the most recent commentary on Tilly's work by Lynn Hunt, "Charles Tilly's Collective Action," in *Vision and Method*, pp. 244–75.

90. Rudé, Lemarchand, and Goujard, for example, argue that while food rioters may have had the indirect—indeed unintended—effect of attacking the seigneurial regime, there was no direct

emphasize the elaboration of an "essentially egalitarian program" among the peasantry "which resided in the refusal of feudalism as well as in the opposition to the process of the development of capitalist social relations," a program that was increasingly visible in the subsistence movements of the late eighteenth century.[91] This popular, or, more specifically, peasant program belonged to neither bourgeois nor feudal elites but was independently constructed and emphatically political.

Furthermore, all, with the partial exception of Gauthier and Ikni, appear to agree that subsistence riots were essentially conservative, rooted in a "backward looking" vision of an ideal society governed by custom and tradition, and this imperfectly articulated. This vision was derived from official paternalist culture and embedded in popular culture. It was adapted to the particularities of popular experience, then lodged in popular memory and passed on through oral and ritual traditions. Called the "traditional ideology of the common people" by Rudé and "a popular consensus" by Thompson, it looked to some golden past.[92] Rioters demanded that officials implement time-honored subsistence regulations when prices rose, markets emptied, and merchants and producers engaged in innovative business practices. The legitimizing notions that animated rioters to invoke the *taxation populaire* were rooted in a vision of a previous system of economic behavior and mutual social responsibility.

Rudé argues further that this "inherent ideology" of the common people "can carry protesters into strikes, food riots, peasant rebellions, and even into a state of awareness of the need for radical change, but evidently it cannot bring them all the way to revolution."[93] E. P. Thompson explains

antiseigneurial content. See, e.g., Rudé, *Crowd in History*, p. 31; Lemarchand, "Troubles," p. 413; Philippe Goujard, *L'Abolition de la "Féodalité" dans le pays de Bray* (Paris, 1979), pp. 78–79. Moreover, this is clearly a major reason why Rudé denies that food riots have any political significance: they were not overtly antiaristocratic, or antiseigneurial. Lemarchand, however, argues that food riots contributed to the development of political consciousness among the people (pp. 426–27).

91. "Le mouvement paysan en Picardie: Meneurs, pratiques, maturation et signification historique d'un programme (1775–1794)," in *Mouvements populaires et conscience sociale* (Paris, 1985), reprinted in *Guerre du blé*, pp. 187–204; see also Gauthier and Ikni's introduction to that volume (pp. 7–30). Georges Lefebvre also attributed strong antiseigneurial positions to the common people, positions that were grounded in a "very old popular tradition . . . as old as feudalism itself." See Lefebvre, "Foules révolutionnaries," in *Etudes sur la Révolution française* (Paris, 1954), pp. 271–87 (translated as "Revolutionary Crowds" in *New Perspectives on the French Revolution*, ed. J. Kaplow [New York, 1965], pp. 173–90; quotation from the translation, p. 181).

92. Rudé, *Ideology*, p. 10; Thompson, "Moral Economy," p. 179.

93. *Ideology*, p. 32. He also calls this "naive, traditional ideology" (p. 10) generated by the common people "mother's milk ideology"(p. 28).

why: this popular consensus was also wrought in and drew on elite culture. Thus, he argues, "cultural hegemony induces a state of mind in which the established structures of authority and even modes of exploitation appear to be in the very course of nature."[94]

The very social heterogeneity of the common people itself further complicated this problem. Diversity among the common people—from petty production to wage labor, from the urban trades to the peasantry—made the articulation of any coherent political program highly unlikely. Most historians of the pre-Revolutionary, and especially of the preindustrial crowd, agree that positive political class consciousness could not emanate from a crowd in which the people who comprised it did not constitute a class in any formal sense. On the one hand, only the forge of revolutionary experience transformed the common people into the politically radical *sans-culottes* (the urban rank-and-file of the Revolution) of the 1790s (and therefore positive but still somewhat contradictory political consciousness) as the monarchy vacated the public sphere and the people were propelled onto the political stage during the struggles for power that followed.[95] On the other hand, only industrialization could produce a proletariat that could then generate positive uncontradictory political class consciousness. Thus, Thompson warned of the English counterparts of the common people, "if we insist on looking at the eighteenth century only through the lens of the nineteenth-century labour movement, we will see only the immature, pre-political, the infancy of class."[96]

94. "Patrician Society," p. 288. The influence of Gramsci's work on cultural hegemony on both Rudé and Thompson is obvious. Bourdieu refers to this as a state of "doxa," where there is a "quasi-perfect correspondence between the objective order and the subjective principles of organization [and] the natural and social world appears self-evident." In class societies, Bourdieu continues, "dominant classes have an interest in defending the integrity of doxa or, short of this, of establishing in its place the necessarily imperfect substitute, orthodoxy" (*Outline of a Theory of Practice* [Cambridge, 1977], pp. 164, 169).

95. The literature on the making of the *sans-culottes* had grown immensely and focused significant debate. The classics are Albert Soboul, *Les Sans-Culottes parisiens en l'an II. Mouvement populaire et gouvernement révolutionnaire* (Paris, 1958), abridged and translated as *The Parisian Sans-Culottes and the French Revolution, 1793–1794* (Oxford, 1964); George Rudé, *Crowd in the French Revolution*; R. B. Rose, *The Making of the Sans-Culottes: Democratic Ideas and Institutions in Paris, 1789–1792* (Manchester, 1983). See also Richard Cobb, *The Police and the People: French Popular Protest, 1789–1820* (Oxford, 1970), esp. pp. 85–214; François Furet's contribution to "Les Sans-Culottes et la Révolution française," *AESC* 18 (1963): 1098–127; George Comninel, "The Political Context of the Popular Movement in the French Revolution," in *History from Below*, pp. 115–40; Sonenscher, *Work and Wages*, pp. 328–62. On the peasantry, see David Hunt, "Peasant Politics in the French Revolution," *Social History* 9 (Oct. 1984): 277–300; Peter Jones, *The Peasantry*.

96. "Patrician Society," p. 398.

During the pre-Revolutionary, preindustrial period, the common people who shared interests as consumers gradually developed a popular social consciousness that emerged both from this concern with affordable access to subsistence and from new experiences (such as the emerging market economy and the centralizing state) that demanded revised responses and conceptualizations. At best, this social consciousness was nebulously political, or as Thompson described it, neither "political in any advanced sense" nor "unpolitical either."[97]

Moreover, the gendered character of food riots appears to reinforce perceptions of apolitical subsistence movements. Bercé argues that "riots most closely connected to survival and the most bereft of political implications were those in which women played the leading roles."[98] He observes that the "flocking of women to the riots at the price of bread is a reminder of the almost biological nature of this kind of episode."[99] Rudé, while at antipodes from Bercé politically, shares with Bercé the same unavowed view of women as passive emblems: women involved themselves in "bread and butter" questions, while men acted in overtly political movements.[100] Although other historians note significant female involvement in food riots, they frequently appear to associate apolitical behavior with female participation.[101] As Joan Scott observes about many recent investigations of the working class, "one is struck not by the absence of women in the narrative, but by the awkward way in which they figure there."[102] Historians appear compelled to explain why women (as opposed to men) participated in food riots and lodge that explanation in the female association with the family economy and its subsistence needs. Locating women politically, socially, and culturally within the private/domestic sphere, historians have largely echoed assumptions articulated by eighteenth-century elite culture,[103] that women's actions were a statement of private/familial distress. Thus, as Scott argues, historians frequently conclude that "women's activities have less

97. "Moral Economy," p. 79.
98. *Revolt*, pp. 100, 108.
99. *Peasant Revolts*, p. 174.
100. Rudé, *Crowd in History*, pp. 207–8.
101. See Joan Scott's discussion of the "working class" in the work of E. P. Thompson: "Women in *The Making of the English Working Class*," in Joan Scott, *Gender and the Politics of History* (New York, 1988).
102. Ibid., p. 71.
103. See the analysis of changing assumptions about women in the eighteenth century: Joan Landes, *Women and the Public Sphere in the Age of the French Revolution* (Ithaca, N.Y., 1988), esp. part 1.

weight," for the domestic sphere "is a place from which politics cannot emanate because it does not provide the experience of exploitation."[104] Indeed, historians have far more frequently associated women with their roles as reproducers of society and socializers to the status quo than as revolutionaries. Thus, the women's protests are not political, and the political is not generated from women's protests. If the food riot was largely female terrain, then it was not political.[105]

Three other approaches to the problem of subsistence movements and the political sphere merit particular attention: the first developed by British historian John Bohstedt, the second and third generated by French historians William Reddy and Colin Lucas. Based on his analysis of the frequent eruptions of subsistence riots in England and Wales between 1790 and 1810, Bohstedt proposed that we view food riots as "local" or "community" politics,[106] a form of "bargaining by riot."[107] He argued that food riots constituted "a kind of informal give and take that shared several characteristics of institutional politics . . . [which] tested rioters' and magistrates' resources of force and persuasion, affected the policies of local authorities and the distribution of goods and social burdens and took place within calculable conventions."[108] Bohstedt asserted that riots "were direct contests of coercion" that helped determine "the local physiology of power and conflict."[109] While they "did not normally challenge the arrangement of local power," they did modify "the property rights of farmers and food dealers."[110] As communal politics (grounded in face-to-face communication, patronage relations, and dense horizontal and vertical social ties) broke down under the multiple assault of commercial and industrial capitalism, urbanization, and intensified repression, food riots ceased to fulfill their political function, degenerated into undisciplined violence, and then halted altogether.[111]

104. Scott, "Women in *The Making of the English Working Class,*" p. 74.

105. Bohstedt's challenge to this assumption of the food riot as exclusively female terrain has the benefit of returning the political significance to subsistence riots. It achieves this, however, by returning men to center stage and granting women an important but shared spotlight. See his articles "Gender" and "Myth."

106. Bohstedt, *Riots.*

107. Ibid., p. 68.

108. Ibid., p. 4.

109. Ibid., p. 5.

110. Ibid., pp. 61, 221.

111. Compare this argument with Craig Calhoun, *The Question of Class Struggle,* who argues (p. 226) that the "mutuality of experience in a closely knit community is a much more likely and solid foundation for collective action."

William Reddy, in a perceptive article that attempted to bridge the gap between preindustrial and mature industrial labor movements, warned against attempts to distinguish between the economically and the politically motivated aspects of crowd behavior in the eighteenth century.[112] He argued, "We shall always remain hopelessly confused if we attempt to impose alien categories such as 'economic' or 'political' motives on people who did not neatly separate out such dimensions in their own experience and behavior."[113] Furthermore, he noted that invocations of "primitive" or "traditional" mentalities constituted "labels too often used in lieu of explanation."[114] Reddy observed further that "the tie between kingship and grain was an unquestioned assumption of the age. . . . In the people's world, . . . bread was the fruit of a properly working, divinely ordained hierarchy."[115] In essence, since subsistence symbolized the political, subsistence issues were thus political issues.

A more recent article by Colin Lucas reminds us again about the dangers of ahistorical applications of the term "political" to the Ancien Régime, in which we use "the politics of the Revolution as the touchstone" for defining the political sphere. He notes that this assumption is especially problematic when studying the popular political sphere in the pre-Revolutionary period.[116] Most historians of the crowd, he argues, come perilously close to denying political consciousness to the common people because they seek and cannot find in popular behavior an overt understanding of, commentary on, or response to "high" politics. As Rudé's own work demonstrated, the historian would be hard-pressed to find revolutionary political content in pre-Revolutionary food riots if the politics of the Revolution and afterward are taken as the definitional point of departure. Nowhere do we find overt demands for a change of government, for example.

Lucas proceeds to offer what he claims will be a more historically appropriate analysis of the political nature of pre-Revolutionary food riots. Classifying subsistence riots as one form of what he calls a "purposive crowd," defined as a crowd assembled for a specific purpose, he argues that such crowds were, in the contexts of the Ancien Régime, political. The purposive crowd acted as a representative of a community (an informal

112. Reddy, "The Textile Trade," pp. 62–89.
113. Ibid., p. 71.
114. Ibid., p. 62.
115. Ibid., pp. 72–73.
116. Lucas, "Crowd and Politics," pp. 421–57.

corporate entity), as both a topographical construct and as an embodiment of shared assumptions.[117] When this representative crowd acted, as it almost always did, in a public space (such as the marketplace) or in a place declared public (such as merchant or farmer granaries)—which in the Ancien Régime meant the political space of the state—it carried political meanings.

Food riots—were they apolitical manifestations of economic distress, training grounds for the creation of partial political consciousness among the common people, local community politics at work, the concrete embodiment of assumptions about the correct functioning political sphere, the representative of an Ancien Régime corporate entity, among myriad others? Depending on one's point of departure, all these conclusions contain merit. At work in all of these approaches is some general assumption about the political and the common people. Is there, these historians ask, such a thing as popular or peasant politics in the Ancien Régime? Have the common people developed a political consciousness, or can they develop one? Can we interpret the food riot as a manifestation of popular politics? The answers to these questions rest on one's understanding of what the very terms "political" and "popular politics" mean.[118]

Although none of these contemporary historians would accept definitions of the political that centered exclusively on "high politics" or the state, most have embraced quite modern (post-Revolutionary and industrial) definitions as measurements against which to gauge popular behavior. In general, for different reasons and with differing degrees of subtlety, they have associated the political with overt attempts to conquer or alter the official machinery of power and with the (often related and primary) class struggle. When the (principally male) common people assailed châteaus as in part of the Ancien Régime antiaristocratic/antifeudal struggle, when they challenged the institutions and authorities of local and royal government as

---

117. See discussion of such assumptions as the moral economy above.

118. These questions formed the core around which much of the International Conference on Popular Movements was organized in Paris in 1984. See, e.g., Jean Nicolas, "Un Chantier toujours neuf"; Raymond Huard, "Existe-t-il une politique populaire?" *Mouvements populaires et conscience sociale, XVIe et XIXe siècles*, ed. Jean Nicolas (Paris, 1985), pp. 13–21, 57–68. This issue has been of considerable anthropological interest. See, e.g., the work of Georges Balandier, *Political Anthropology*, trans. A. M. Sheridan Smith (New York, 1970; French ed., Paris, 1967); Pierre Bourdieu, *Outline*; Maurice Godelier, *The Mental and the Material: Thought, Economy, and Society* (London, 1986; French ed., Paris, 1984); Bertrand Hervieu, " 'Le Pouvoir au Village': Difficultés et perspectives d'une recherche," *Etudes rurales* 63–64 (1976): 15–30. Unfortunately, most of these anthropologists focus either on "primitive" or lineage societies or on societies caught up in the forces of imperialism.

in assaults on tax collectors or installations of revolutionary municipal governments, or when as workers they invoked strikes or attacked employers as in the Reveillon riots of 1789, and when they evolved new forms of behavior to address these issues, the common people acted politically and progressively. When the (principally female) common people lashed out as consumers in the marketplaces, when they focused on "bread and butter" issues, and when they drew on traditional forms of behavior, they acted apolitically or prepolitically and looked backward. The more abstract the conceptualizations, the more proletarianized the labor force, the more clear the agenda, the more the movement was political.

For those who adhere to this particular trajectory of the political, the food riot poses difficulties. Their approach, which encourages viewing preindustrial, pre-Revolutionary popular behavior as something incomplete, emerges as a common weakness in the work of Rudé, for example. The more useful way of understanding popular behavior emphasizes the political as a process, not a product—that is, food riots reflect the process of creating a more coherent political consciousness among the common people, a per-spective common to Thompson, L. Tilly, and Gauthier and Ikni. I develop this distinction more below and in subsequent chapters. For the moment, it is important to note that the emphasis within all these works continues to rest on the assumption that the truly political lies yet in the future.

Bohstedt, Reddy, and Lucas offer other ways of defining popular behavior in food riots as political. Bohstedt analyzes food riots as one form of bargaining within the local community; Reddy demands that we expand the political to include the economic and thus view food riots as political manifestations of popular protest over economic issues because the people themselves made these sorts of associations; and Lucas calls on us to recognize that both the Crown and the people viewed the food riot as the political act of a purposive crowd that was prepared to intrude into public / political space to invoke responses to its demands. These approaches get us much closer to generating a more historically appropriate perception of the relationship between food riots and the political. Yet each focuses on one aspect or a small congeries of facets of this relationship. We need to study further the kinds of changes that occur over time in the nature of participa-tion, behavior, spheres of action, and even motives within food riots.

There are two additional points of departure to further exploration of the political nature of food riots such as the Flour War. First, we need to move beyond the important first steps of discovering and emphasizing the general similarities among subsistence movements that erupted across time and place. We now need more specific analyses of the role that uneven develop-ment played in creating both the disparate historically specific contexts that shaped local behavior, and the variety of specific popular responses that ensued. As Peter Jones has recently observed with reference to the peasantry, "rural history is perforce local history."[119] Neither Jones nor I intend a demand for a return to isolated village studies that claim to resist larger generalizations. Rather, more comparative works are needed that will hopefully distinguish the nature and impact of different modalities of development within the larger changes at work within French society during the Ancien Régime. We need to recognize more clearly that popular actions and the legitimizing notions behind them were, like the forces to which they were responding, historically constructed and constantly reshaped.

This observation leads to my second point. Food riots were more than collective defensive protests of a powerless people over issues of survival in a period of transition, although they were certainly that as well. We need to move beyond the assertion that the mobilizing notions behind popular behavior were rooted in conservative and traditional notions of ancient rights or primordial beliefs. Indeed, anthropologist William Roseberry has recently suggested that "the moral economy need not have existed in the past; it may be perceived in the past from the perspective of a disorderly present. . . . The images of moral economy may be a meaningful image even if 'what actually happened' was less idyllic."[120] In other words, food riots called into play the present complex relations of power that had developed within urban and rural communities. This involved the power exercised by the state, but also the economic, social, cultural, and gendered relations of domination and subordination within Ancien Régime society, which in-cludes relations involving informal power.[121] These forms of power were fought over on many different levels and in many different spaces. Food riots constituted one important arena of struggle.

119. *Peasantry*, p. 1.
120. *Anthropologies and Histories: Essays in Culture, History, and Political Economy* (New Bruns-wick, N.J., 1989), p. 57.
121. Historians and anthropologists who study women have worked at the forefront of the study of the problem of informal power. See, e.g., Natalie Z. Davis, "Women on Top," pp. 124–46; Susan Rogers, "Female Forms of Power and the Myth of Male Dominance: A Model of Female/Male Interaction in Peasant Society," *American Ethnologist* 2 (Nov. 1975): 727–56; idem, "Women's Place: A Critical Review of Anthropological Theory," *Comparative Studies in Society and History* 20 (Jan. 1978): 123–62; Ernestine Friedl, "The Position of Women: Appearance and Reality," *Anthropological Quarterly* 40 (July 1967): 97–108; Diane R. Margolis, "Considering Women's Experience: A Reformulation of Power Theory," *Theory and Society* 18 (1989): 387–416.

Food riots were struggles to preserve or alter relations of power, not necessarily on the level of high politics nor always on the level of changes in local governments or administrators, but always demanding changes in policies and attitudes and thus calling for changes in economic and social relations. Rioters attempted to renegotiate proprietorship, realign paternalist obligations, and reshape relations of domination and subordination in their many forms. They demanded changes in attitudes and perceptions; they attempted to bridge the growing gaps between popular and elite cultures, to bring elite culture back in touch with popular culture. All subsistence riots also manifested gendered struggles for power; subsistence crises empowered women, allowing them to turn the assumptions of the traditional gender system into weapons that enabled them to invade the public/political sphere and, conversely, demonstrate male weakness in this context. All these contests for power were political.

The common people did not win and did not even expect to win every such struggle. In some cases the power-holders ruthlessly suppressed their challengers. Yet the food rioters achieved something—they showed that relations of power rested on a tenuous base, potentially vulnerable to assault from those subordinated to it. In so doing, they demonstrated an important historical verity: no one is ever entirely powerless. As we look at events in the Paris Basin in the spring of 1775, therefore, we see the people searching for an adequate and appropriate response to the changing circumstances that confronted them.

Chapter 2

THE CONTEXT:
UNEVEN DEVELOPMENT

The Paris Basin, the area in which the Flour War took place, formed then, as now, the core of France—economically, administratively, culturally. The drainage basin of the river Seine roughly defines the region geographically. In the eighteenth century—and until the coming of the railroad in the nineteenth—the Seine, together with its manifold tributaries, bound together the region's villages, towns, cities, and rural districts. Over this riverian network, goods and news traveled in an era when shallow-draft

boats represented the most practical way to ship bulky commodities such as
grain and flour. At the center of the basin and its network lay Paris, the
capital, which provided at once a focus and a dynamic heart, pulsing with
the vitality of a diverse population, throbbing with the appetite of a
multitude that consumed much but grew little. A big city to feed, Paris in
1775—indeed, the biggest in France—but by no means the only one, even
in its own region.

The Paris Basin, so easily defined as a geographic entity, presents a starkly
different picture when viewed in terms of its economic activities, together
with the latticework of privilege and local government within which those
activities took place. Within the Basin a wide range of pursuits coexisted,
and an equivalent variety of people engaged in them. Agriculture produced
grapes and vegetables, grain and cattle; processing yielded wine and flour,
meat and cheese. Nascent industry turned out thread, cloth, lace. Within
the population coexisted rich and poor, those who owned land and those
who didn't, people who worked for themselves and people who worked for
others, skilled craftsmen and unskilled laborers. This diversity of activities—
far more complicated and diverse than suggested here—played a causal role
in the events of the Flour War and thus merits close consideration.

At the time of the Flour War, the Paris Basin constituted one of the most
advanced—if still unevenly developed—regions of Early Modern France.
Proximity to the capital and to other nearby urban markets—Orléans,
Rouen, Reims, and Troyes—created a dynamic thrust for development in
the region. Increasingly the region's products reached national and even
international markets. This expansion of commercial agriculture, vigorous
industries, and a far-flung, bustling marketing network—the cumulative
work of centuries—impressed many observers, such as Arthur Young, who
only twelve years after the Flour War sang the praises of the area's economic
progress. Administrative centralization had advanced furthest in the Paris
Basin as well. Long before Colbert and well after Turgot, royal ministers
worked to strengthen the authority of the Crown by reducing or weakening
(but never eliminating) the impediments—privileged interests and local
autonomy, for example—to its reach and exercise. When the Flour War
erupted, then, it was small wonder that from its flash point it quickly flared
across the expanse of the Basin, while its ferocity waned as the distance
from Paris increased.

The presence of a widespread variety of developmental activities reflected
rather than contradicted the heterogeneity of the Paris Basin. In fact, the
area consisted of several distinct countrysides, or *pays*, each defined by its

particular mixture of crops, industry (if any), commercial networks, proprietorship and landholding patterns, social structures and power relations. At the same time, the Parisian and other regional urban markets for food and other goods and services exerted both a unifying and a divisive force on the towns and villages of the Basin. The particularities of behavior that subsequent chapters will examine reflect in large part the distinct character of local economic, social, and political development. But to understand the context in which the Flour War, as well as other subsistence movements, erupted, we need to develop broader categories of analysis that can support explanations involving both long-term and short-term processes and are able to accommodate diversity of historical development amid shared developmental features.

Fortunately, the underlying, omnipresent problem of subsistence created two historically valid and analytically useful categories into which these diverse "pays" can be classified, for all of them either exported or imported grain.[1] And in those days of the "subsistence mentality," those who controlled the means of subsistence (grain, flour, and bread) via production, marketing, custom, and/or coercion, or the means to attain it (wages, charity, or administrative fiat) wielded power. Within each of these two categories of regions, similar socioeconomic and political patterns emerge that transcended geographic separations and myriad superficial differences in customs and topography.

This chapter examines the long-term and short-term developments within these two categories—grain-exporting versus grain-importing regions—that affected the evolution of subsistence movements. It also explores implications of the seigneurial system and the pivotal role of town and village administration. My purpose is not to explain how these particular structures developed in the first place, but to demonstrate the relationship between these forms of development and the reactions of food rioters. Fortunately, a great deal of work has already been done on various areas in the Paris Basin in the eighteenth century and for the first part of this chapter I rely heavily on this very helpful literature. My own work with tax records and other regional materials from many of the towns and villages in the region in which the Flour War erupted has also proved helpful. Subsequent chapters provide more detailed analysis of individual locales and their relationship to these developments during the Flour War.

---

1. In the Paris Basin, only a small cluster of regions, if any, could be said to be self-supporting isolated enclaves without links to the marketing network.

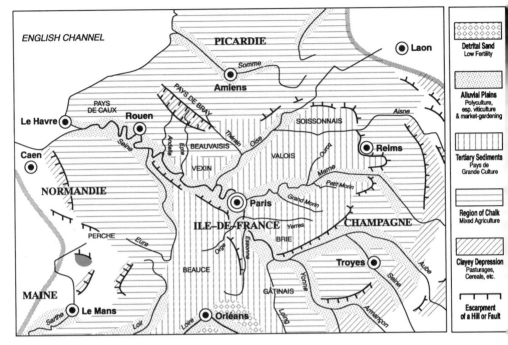

Map 1.   Regions of the Flour War

Grain-Exporting Regions:
Long-Term Developments

The lands of the grain-exporting type comprised the fertile, grain-producing plains of the *pays de grande culture*, which included the Beauce, western Brie, the pays de France, the Multien, the Soissonnais, the Vexin normand and français, and the more distant Picard plain (Map 1). This region served as the granary of northern France, for its surplus fed Paris and other centers—Rouen, Caen, Amiens, Orléans, Reims, and Troyes.[2] In the last

---

2. There is an ever-growing literature examining the lands of the *pays de grande culture*. See, e.g., Pierre Goubert, *Beauvais et le Beauvaisis de 1600 à 1730. Contribution à l'histoire social du XVIIe siècle* (Paris, 1960); Jean Ganiage, *Le Beauvaisis au XVIIIe siècle. La Campagne* (Paris, 1988); Pierre Brunet, *Structure agraire et économie rurale des plateaux tertiaires entre la Seine et l'Oise* (Caen, 1960); Marc Bloch, *The Ile-de-France: The Country Around Paris*, trans. J. E. Anderson (Ithaca, N.Y., 1966); J. Loutchisky, "Régime agraire et populations agricoles dans les environs de Paris à la veille de la Révolution," *RHM* 7 (1933): 97–142; Jean Jacquart, *La Crise rural en Ile-de-France (1550–*

three centuries of the Ancien Régime, the entire *pays de grande culture* underwent a transformation in agricultural, social, and commercial organization. Its exceptionally fertile, mostly loam, soils encouraged early and increased specialization in the production of grains for the seemingly insatiable Parisian market.[3] Of course, other urban markets grew too, and exerted their influence. The region came to specialize not only in grain production but specifically in the production of *froment*, wheat that enjoyed an increasingly wider market during the eighteenth century. The social characteristics of this transformation included the development of a highly polarized social structure in the countryside. There had emerged a small but highly visible number of powerful landholders at one extreme, and a growing proletarianized mass of largely underemployed rural day-laborers at the other. Between the two stood a small but persistent number of medium-sized landholders and artisans.

Over these last three centuries of the Ancien Régime, the map of landowning and landholding had changed considerably in this region. A struggle for control of the highly profitable grain-producing lands drove these developments. Traditionally, the upper nobility and the great ecclesiastical institutions had predominated, carving out fiefs and estates. Indeed,

---

1670) (Paris, 1974); Jules Sion, *Les Paysans de la Normandie orientale. Pays de Caux, Bray, Vexin normand, Vallée de la Seine* (Paris, 1909); M. Venard, *Bourgeois et paysans au XVIIe siècle. Recherche sur le rôle des bourgeois parisiens dans la vie agricole au sud de Paris au XVIIe siècle* (Paris, 1957); Jacques Dupâquier, *La Propriété et l'exploitation foncière à la fin de l'Ancien Régime dans le Gâtinais septentrional* (Paris, 1959); Michel Vovelle, *Ville et campagne au 18e siècle. Chartres et la Beauce* (Paris, 1980); Albert Demangeon, *La Picardie et les régions voisines: Artois, Cambrésis, Beauvaisis*, 4th ed. (Paris, 1974); Florence Gauthier, *La Voie paysanne dans la Révolution française. L'Exemple picard* (Paris, 1977); Michel Philipponneau, *La Vie rurale de la banlieue parisienne. Étude de géographie humaine* (Paris, 1956); Gilles Postel-Vinay, *La Rente foncière dans le capitalisme agricole. L'Exemple du Soissonnais* (Paris, 1974); Emile Mireaux, *Une Province française au temps du Grand Roi: La Brie* (Paris, 1979); Gérard Béaur, *Le Marché foncier à la veille de la Révolution. Les Mouvements de propriété beaucerons dans les régions de Maintenon et de Janville de 1761 à 1790* (Paris, 1984); J. Ricommard, *La Lieutenance général de police à Troyes au XVIIIe siècle* (Paris, 1934); A. Defresne and F. Evrard, *Les Subsistances dans le district de Versailles de 1788 à l'An V*, 2 vols. (Rennes, 1921); Jean Meuvret, *Le Problème des subsistances à l'époque de Louis XIV*, 3 vols. (Paris, 1977, 1988); Steven Kaplan, *Provisioning Paris* (Ithaca, N.Y., 1984). Other works appear in the footnotes that follow. I also consulted administrative surveys and tax records for many of the places touched by the Flour War. Other important sources are mentioned in subsequent notes.

3. For the latest and most thorough analysis of the Parisian market and its development, see Kaplan, *Provisioning Paris*, pp. 80–121; Jean-Marc Moriceau and Gilles Postel-Vinay (*Ferme, Entreprise, Famille. Grande Exploitation et changements agricoles, XVIIe–XIXe siècles* [Paris, 1922]) claim that within a circle of thirty kilometers around Paris, producers could meet from one-fifth to one-quarter of Paris' grain needs.

such important families as Condé or the Conti near Paris, the Montmoren-
cys in Normandy, and the Rochefoucaulds in the Beauvaisis persisted as
large proprietors at the end of the Ancien Régime.[4] So too, of course, did
such ecclesiastical institutions as the Abbaye de Saint-Denis near Paris and
the Cathedral Chapter of Chartres in the Beauce.[5] Despite this continuity,
however, by the 1720s to 1730s much land had passed into the hands of the
urban bourgeoisie, royal officeholders, and the robe nobility of Paris and
other regional centers. Spurred by the status of country proprietorship and
the life of the *rentier*, living off revenues, they purchased seigneuries (both
land and dues) from the old nobility and church while collecting smaller
parcels from peasant proprietors. By the early eighteenth century, rich
commoners and the newly ennobled controlled much of the land in the *pays
de grande culture*.[6]

No matter who owned the land, however, the owners rarely cultivated it
themselves. Predominantly absentee proprietors, they typically chose to live
in Paris, Rouen, Beauvais, Meaux, Troyes, and other towns, rather than
engage directly in the management of their lands. They entrusted their
lands and other sources of income (such as seigneurial dues [*droits*], tithes,
and the exploitation of their monopolies) to the management of *fermiers*.
Fermiers and the system of landholding in which they participated called
fermage, appeared either simultaneously or singly in three forms: (1) A
fermier might lease a small piece of land (*ferme*) from a peasant proprietor
and exploit it himself with the assistance of his family. (2) A large proprietor
might lease all his land (sometimes called a *corps de ferme*), or a portion of

4. On the Condé and Conti and other important proprietors near Paris, see Loutchisky,
"Régime agraire," p. 107; Eugene Darras, *Les Seigneurs-Châtelains de l'Isle-Adam, 1014–1814*
(Persan, 1939). The Duc de Montmorency figures significantly during the Flour War at Gournay-
en-Bray. On the Rochefoucaulds, see Guy-Robert Ikni and J. D. de La Rochefoucauld, *Le Duc de la
Rochefoucauld-Liancourt* (Paris, 1980).

5. Loutchisky, "Régime agraire," p. 107; Vovelle, *Ville et campagne*, pp. 177–91.

6. On these developments, see, e.g., Braudel and Labrousse, eds., *Histoire économique et sociale
de la France*, vol. 2, *1660–1789* (Paris, 1970), esp. part 3; Jacquart, *La Crise rurale*, p. 731; Sion,
Normandie orientale, pp. 261, 271; Goubert, *Beauvais*, p. 214; P. Brunet, *Structure agraire*, p. 416;
Mark Venard, "Une Classe rurale puissante au XVIIe siècle. Les Laboureurs au sud de Paris," *AESC*
10 (1955): 521; idem, *Bourgeois et paysans*; Claude Brunet, *Une Communauté rurale au XVIIIe siècle:
Le Plessis-Gassot (Seine-et-Oise)* (Paris, 1964), p. 36; Pierre Deyon, "Quelques remarques sur
l'évolution du régime seigneuriale en Picardie (XVIe–XVIIIe siècles)," *RHMC* 8 (Oct.-Dec. 1961):
277; François Bluche, *Les Magistrats du Parlement de Paris au XVIIIe siècle*, rev. ed. (Paris, 1986), pp.
139–58. Jacques Dupâquier claims that on the eve of the Revolution in the Vexin français the
nobility and clergy owned more than half the lands: *Ainsi commença la Révolution . . . Campagne
électorale et cahiers de doléances de 1789 dans les bailliages du Chaumont-en-Vexin et Magny-en-Vexin*
(Pontoise, 1989), p. 52.

it, to a single tenant, also usually called a fermier. This tenant then managed the farm, directed production and the marketing of the produce, hired labor, supplied the movable capital—horses, furniture, tools, and so on—and paid a theoretically fixed rent. Leases varied from three to twelve years, but nine-year leases were the most common in the Paris Basin. (3) The proprietor, if he was a seigneur, might lease his rights to collect seigneurial dues or the tithe, or to exploit any *banalités* (monopolies of such activities as baking, milling, and wine-pressing), to a fermier, who was often then also called a *receveur*. Large proprietors might lease the rights to manage their lands to a general overseer, sometimes called a *fermier général*, who then leased portions of the land out to smaller fermiers.[7] This form of land management offered considerable advantages to proprietors, large and small. As Robert Forster observed, "by having dues collected and land managed by a *fermier*, the absentee landlord could avoid the oscillations of the market, count on a regular money income, and plan a budget."[8] Everytime the lease expired, terms could be renegotiated. Such prospects of a rationalized management of lands encouraged proprietors to unite more and more of their lands under the management of one fermier, whose activities could be watched carefully and whose lease could be controlled rigorously. In fact, during the seventeenth and eighteenth centuries, the tendency was toward leasing larger and larger landholdings *(grosses fermes)* to a single tenant. Some holdings eventually reached well over 200–500 arpents (approximately 160–420 acres).[9] The same period also witnessed the growth of fermage of small properties.

Fermage was a risky business for the fermier, whose entire enterprise was extremely sensitive to grain price fluctuations. On the one hand, when grain prices exceeded rents there was ample opportunity for profit. As manipulators of considerable quantities of grain, fermiers could benefit greatly from moderate shortages that raised grain prices without dramatically affecting

---

7. Fermage is becoming the subject of ever more studies. See, e.g., Georges Lefebvre, *Questions agraires au temps de la Terreur* (La Roche-sur-Yon, 1954); Robert Forster, "Obstacles to Agricultural Growth in Eighteenth Century France," *AHR* 75 (Oct. 1970): 1606–7; Pierre Goubert, "Le Paysan et la terre: Seigneurie, tenure, exploitation," in Braudel and Labrousse, *Histoire économique*, pp. 144–46; Micheline Baulant, "Groupes mobiles dans une société sédentaire. La Société rurale autour de Meaux au XVII et XVIIIe siècles," in *Les Marginaux et les exclus dans l'histoire*, ed. B. Vincent (Paris, 1979); Jean-Pierre Jessenne, "Le Pouvoir des fermiers dans les villages d'Artois (1770–1848)," *AESC* 38 (May–June 1983): 702–34; idem, *Pouvoir au village et Révolution: Artois, 1760–1848* (Lille, 1987); Postel-Vinay, *La Rente foncière*; Jean Meuvret, *Le Problème*, 2:98–99, 136; Moriceau and Postel-Vinay, *Ferme*, p. 320.

8. "Obstacles," p. 1608. See also Lefebvre, *Questions*, p. 91.

9. Dupâquier, *Gâtinais*, pp. 261–62; Venard, *Bourgeois*, p. 51; Mireaux, *Brie*, pp. 75–78, 104–6.

production. They were, of course, frequently—and often justly—accused of causing dearth by withholding grain from market until prices rose to their liking.[10] Moreover, since leases tended to be short, fermiers were not tied to one exploitation. Such mobility not only provided the option to leave one exploitation for another when the lease expired, but also permitted the accumulation of more than one ferme.

On the other hand, what might be an advantage in good times could prove troublesome in bad times. Short leases permitted the readjustment of rents upward—a fairly frequent occurrence during the late seventeenth century to the early eighteenth, and again, from the 1770s onward. Fermiers' fortunes moved in cycles. Until the 1720s, rents for land in fermage were in some places suffocatingly high, causing a high rate of tenant farmer failure. Some proprietors had trouble finding tenants for their *corps de ferme*. The early eighteenth century witnessed struggles between proprietors and fermiers over control of the land and its products. From the 1720s to the 1760s/1770s, fermiers benefited from relatively lower rents, but then proprietors waged a new offensive.[11] Furthermore, the plethora of bothersome regulations that governed "rites of passage" from one farm to another, the weighty additional demands (*pots-de-vin*, for example) that could be exacted above and beyond basic lease arrangements, and the uncertainties of remaining in place for the duration of the lease itself made fermage a problematic arrangement. A fall in grain prices, a dearth that undercut possible profits from shortage, or an increase in rent could spell disaster for the fermier, threatening him with seizure of his capital and expulsion from his farm.[12]

Despite the risks involved, there had emerged in most parishes of the *pays de grande culture* in the eighteenth century at least one and sometimes two or three *gros fermiers*.[13] Their incomes and exploitations towered above those

10. The best description of the socioeconomic patterns of grain sales is that of Olwen Hufton, "Social Conflict," pp. 320–22. Moriceau and Postel-Vinay argue that such speculation was rare in the seventeenth century but increasingly common in the eighteenth (*Ferme*, pp. 224–33).

11. Baulant, "Groupes mobiles," pp. 84–85; Postel-Vinay, *La Rente foncière*, pp. 43–44, 79; Jonathan Dewald, *Pont-St.-Pierre, 1398–1789: Lordship, Community, and Capitalism in Early Modern France* (Berkeley and Los Angeles, 1987), pp. 49–89; Moriceau and Postel-Vinay, *Ferme*, pp. 122, 150–54.

12. Baulant has a good description of what was involved in moving from one ferme to another ("Groupes mobiles," p. 87). On the *pots-de-vin*, see Postel-Vinay, *La Rente foncière*, p. 47; Mireaux, *Brie*, p. 112, n. 2. On the vulnerability of the fermier, see Forster, "Obstacles," pp. 1610–13. This was a particular problem at the end of the reign of Louis XIV, when a high percentage of fermiers failed. See Venard, "Classe rurale," pp. 521–24; idem, *Bourgeois*, p. 100; Postel-Vinay, *La Rente foncière*, pp. 43–44, 79.

13. Historians have debated their status. For example, Georges Lefebvre called them "rural bourgeois" (*Les Paysans du Nord pendant la Révolution française*, new ed. [Paris, 1972]), while A.

of other villagers, and they exercised considerable power in their communities.[14] As managers of large exploitations, they employed local labor, both permanent and seasonal, and frequently engaged local artisans and other skilled workers to perform special tasks. They thus dominated the labor market within their communities, often paying for labor in kind.[15] As collectors of seigneurial dues and tithes, or as exploiters of seigneurial monopolies, they emerged as the immediate local representatives of the seigneurs, both secular and religious. Indeed, they accumulated, from a variety of sources, various quantities of local grain. Meuvret emphasizes that while some of this grain could be marketed as commercial grain, much of it was recycled into the community as wages, charity, and loans.[16] In communities with absentee landlords, fermiers sometimes assumed patronage responsibilities.[17] Fermiers also functioned as significant local creditors, lending not only money to neighbors in need, but, and perhaps even more significant, lending stocks of grain for seed for future harvests or family subsistence.[18] They often benefited from reductions in taxes when they leased land that carried the exemptions of their privileged proprietors. As producers of large surpluses of grain, they engaged heavily in the grain trade, regularly shipping supplies to market, storing grain in their granaries for later sale, and sometimes selling directly from their storage rooms to those Parisian or Rouenais merchants (and during liberalization anyone) authorized to buy directly from producers. These *gros fermiers* thus controlled the destiny of the surplus grain supply in their neighborhoods.

Veritable dynasties of fermiers, founded on intermarriage and buttressed by familial solidarity, emerged throughout the *pays de grande culture*. Such families frequently dominated several villages for generations by colluding to control the land market against proprietors and other peasants, passing on capital to heirs, and continuously reinforcing their ranks through marriage.[19] Since they came to form an educated elite—veritable cultural

Defresne and F. Evrard called them a "peasant aristocracy" (*Subsistances*, 1:xxxiii). See also the discussion in Peter Jones, *The Peasantry in the French Revolution* (Cambridge, 1988), pp. 10–14.

14. For information on the relative size of fermier income and landholdings during the time of the Flour War, see Chapter 6.

15. Their control was even more pervasive because, despite the clear evidence of proletarianization in these regions in the eighteenth century, the labor force was rarely entirely propertyless and thus not completely mobile (see below).

16. *Problèmes*, 3:42–43.

17. See Jessene, *Pouvoir*, p. 235. Mireaux notes that fermage contracts sometimes stipulated that the fermier maintain a certain level of charitable giving within the community (*Brie*, p. 205). See also Meuvret, *Problèmes*, 3:159. More on this in Chapter 5.

18. Meuvret, *Problèmes*, 3:25, 259–63.

19. Baulant, "Groupes mobiles," pp. 85–86; Venard, "Une classe rurale," pp. 518–19; P. Brunet, *Structure agraire*, pp. 376–78. Postel-Vinay describes a range of strategies (some of them

intermediaries[20] between village and urban society—fermiers often comple-
mented their powers by controlling the political processes within their
communities. They served as *syndic* or held other village administrative
positions, frequently dominating village meetings. Where they leased the
seigneurial lands, fermiers sometimes held the post of *procureur fiscal*, the
local representative of seigneurial justice.[21]

At the other extreme in this surplus-grain-producing region, a mass of
day-laborers (*manouvriers* and *journaliers*) emerged to work for others at
unskilled regular or seasonal tasks (also referred to as wage labor). By the
eighteenth century, and in some cases even earlier, they often formed as
much as 40 to 50 percent (and occasionally more) of the working population
within a community.[22] Sometimes rural families of day-laborers owned a
house and a small garden, but frequently they rented both. Occasionally,
they owned a very small plot of land, but more often, if they exploited any
land at all, it too was rented. Moreover, it was the insufficiency of the
holdings that made them workers. For some, the status of day-laborer was

organized) employed by fermiers in the Soissonnais to combat the domination of proprietors, a
struggle he claims succeeded from the 1720s to approximately 1770, when rents rose relatively little
for fermiers (*La Rente foncière*, pp. 44–47, 51). See also Jean-Marc Moriceau, "Mariages et foyers
paysans aux XVIe et XVIIe siècles: L'Exemple des campagnes du sud de Paris," *RHMC* 28 (July
1981): 481–502; idem, "Un Système de protection sociale efficace: Exemple des vieux fermiers de
l'Ile-de-France (XVIIe–début XIXe siècle)," in *Annales de démographie historique*, 1985, pp. 127–44.
On fermiers' extensive kinship networks, see especially Moriceau and Postal-Vinay, *Ferme*.

20. On cultural intermediaries, a subject that has long drawn the attention of anthropologists
and, more recently, historians, see F. G. Bailey, "The Peasant View of the Bad Life," in *Peasants
and Peasant Societies: Selected Readings*, ed. Teodor Shanin, 2nd ed. (Oxford, 1987), pp. 286–91;
Michel Vovelle, "Les Intermédiaires culturels," in his *Idéologies et mentalités* (Paris, 1985), pp. 163–
76; Gutton, *Sociabilité villageoise*; Jessene, *Pouvoir*, p. 234.

21. Lefebvre, *Questions*, p. 69; Meuvret, *Problèmes*, 2:136–37; Jessene, *Pouvoir*, pp. 30–47;
Moriceau and Postel-Vinay, *Ferme*, p. 19.

22. Meuvet claimed that in some parts of the region day-laborers had existed in some numbers
since the Middle Ages (*Problèmes*, 1:178–79). See also J. Dupâquier, "Structures sociales et cahiers
de doléances: L'Exemple du Vexin français," *AHRF* 194 (Oct.–Dec. 1968): 438. Dupâquier claims
that they represented more than 40 percent of the population in this region. Loutchisky argues that
the *manouvriers* represented 58.4 percent of the population around Paris (where they were most
frequently called *journaliers*) ("Régime agraire," pp. 124–25). And Venard presents the case of the
village of Sainte-Geneviève-des-Bois in 1717, where out of twenty-five households (*feux*) on the
rôle de taille (main direct tax), there were five *laboureurs* (a peasant who owned the tools and plow
team necessary for cultivation as well as owned land and was thereby relatively well-off) and
fourteen journaliers ("Une Classe rurale," p. 518). This is assuming there is only one manouvrier
per family, a very doubtful situation that would depend largely on the stage in the family life-cycle.
More likely, families who depended on unskilled wage labor contained as many manouvriers as
there were employable adults (or near-adults) in the household, thus including women and older
children (more on this below). We need to know more about how the day-laboring population grew
from the Middle Ages and about the rate of this change.

temporary: children of fermiers, smaller peasant proprietors who waited to inherit more property, or families saving little by little to increase holdings through leases or purchases. For many others, their status was relatively permanent, hoping to do little more than improve their condition ever so slightly relative to other day-laborers like themselves.[23] Yet these links to the land underscore the incomplete nature of the process of proletarianization (the process by which there emerges a free, mobile wage-labor force) at work in the countryside. Access to the land functioned as a source of independence for workers who could refuse or resist certain types of work for wages because they had an alternative or supplemental source of subsistence. However, such links to the land could also deny them the mobility to seek alternative forms of work and wages elsewhere. In the Soissonais, for example, both proprietors and fermiers consciously tried various strategies to maintain potential workers' attachment to the land and thereby create an immobile, cheap labor market for themselves.[24] Moreover, unlike some other parts of France, the *pays de grande culture*[25] had attracted little textile

23. On the differences in the condition of the manouvriers in various regions, compare Loutchisky, "Régime agraire," pp. 122–26; Meuvret, *Problèmes*, 2:81, 174; Dupâquier, "Structures sociales," p. 440; P. Brunet, *Structures agraires*, pp. 386–87; Postel Vinay, *La Rente foncière*, pp. 59–73; Dewald, *Pont-St.-Pierre*, pp. 55–56. Moriceau and Postel-Vinay provide an excellent example of dramatic downward mobility from the status of fermier to that of day-laborer (*Ferme*, p. 121).

24. Postel-Vinay, *La Rente foncière*, pp. 53, 64, 70; Clay Ramsay, *Ideology of the Great Fear: The Soissonnais in 1789* (Baltimore and London, 1992), pp. 17–18. However, considerable geographical mobility did occur in Early Modern France; see esp. Baulant, "Groupes mobiles," pp. 78–121; James B. Collins, "Geographical and Social Mobility in Early Modern France," *JSH* 24 (Spring 1991): 563–77. Moriceau and Postel-Vinay, *Ferme*, pp. 230, 245–51, 319. Yet it is not clear how many small landholders were among these mobile groups. Baulant, for example, discusses mobile agricultural workers at harvest time (pp. 96–98) but has nothing to say about the rest of the year. Collins discusses an "unstable society" that included those "with a cottage and a small rented piece of land" (p. 574). There were also day-laboring families with very small pieces of property, which might have been more sedentary. There is no doubt, however, that those at the bottom of the social ladder could and did move more often than those higher up. Comparisons between the situation in the Soissonnais and the region near Paris also suggest a higher degree of mobility closer to the capital. Cf. Postel-Vinay, *La Rente foncière*, and Moriceau and Postel-Vinay, *Ferme*.

25. The notable exceptions were the Picard plain and a few regions close to provincial centers. Although the Picard plain is always included within the *pays de grande culture* because of its fertile grain-producing soil (especially wheat), it had experienced a different social evolution, in large part because there was a vigorous textile industry. This textile industry, emanating from the *fabriques* of Beauvais and Amiens, engaged widely in protoindustrial production. Thus, domestic industry contributed to the persistence of a wider distribution of land within the society. The Amienois, studied by Florence Gauthier, was the domain of the small landholding peasantry. On the one hand, there was a total absence of the very large exploitation under one proprietor or fermier, but on the other hand, only 22.3 percent of the population exploited enough land to qualify as at least self-sufficient (although 74 percent exploited some). Even in normal years, therefore, they were

or other important industry to employ rural day-laboring families and thus supplement family income.[26] There did exist, however, in the regions closest to Paris, supplementary income derived from the wet-nurse business.[27] Underemployed and sometimes unemployed, these day-laborers simultaneously fell victim to both an underdeveloped manufacturing or service sector and to incomplete proletarianization.[28]

Day-laborers and their families combined with others like them to form the majority of the population in many communities in this region. Several other occupational categories, such as the *couvriers de chaume* (roof-thatchers), *vanniers* (basket-makers), *batteurs-en-grange* (threshers), *bergers* (shepherds), and many *chartiers* (carters, wagoners) were little more than semiskilled manouvriers. Tax records show that they often fared no better economically, because their occupations engaged them at temporary tasks at low pay. Only a fortunate few found full-time employment with a fermier.[29]

Between the *gros fermier* and the mass of day-laborers, there persisted in the *pays de grande culture* during the eighteenth century a few middling peasants, frequently called *laboureurs*. These laboureurs usually combined land held as property with a small amount of land leased as fermes and the

---

consumers as well as producers of grain. In order to survive, this group relied heavily on domestic industry or a supplementary occupation, and almost all depended on the use of communal lands.

Even in Picardy, however, the lands closest to the major lines of transportation (such as the northern Clermontois close to the Oise, the Santerre, and Vermandois) demonstrated a socioeconomic organization similar to that of the rest of the *pays de grande culture*. Historians have found in these places a more polarized social structure dominated by one or several *gros fermiers* and encumbered with a majority of manouvriers. On Picardy, see the work of Gourbert, *Beauvais*, pp. 123–24; Pierre Deyon, "Le Mouvement de la production textile à Amiens au XVIIIe siècle," *Revue du Nord* 44 (Apr.–June 1962): 201–12; Demangeon, *Picardie*, pp. 244–49; Gauthier, *La Voie*, pp. 30–34; idem, "Formes d'évolution du système agraire communautaire picard (fin XVIIIe–début XIXe siècle)," *AHRF* 240 (Apr.–June 1980): 181–204.

26. A domestic industry revolving around the production of silk lace (*dentelle de blonde*) did extend into the Vexin français but was most developed in the neighboring pays de Thelle (Dupâquier, *Ainsi . . . Chaumont*, pp. 47, 54).

27. Ibid., p. 54. Moriceau and Postel-Vinay observed a heavy reliance on wetnurses by fermiers in the Ile-de-France (*Ferme*, p. 77).

28. Postel-Vinay notes the coexistence of rural unemployment and unfilled jobs in the Soissonnais (*Rente foncière*, p. 62). On this characteristic of preindustrial, unevenly developing economies, see the summary in James L. Goldsmith, "The Agrarian History of Preindustrial France: Where Do We Go from Here?" *Journal of European Economic History* 13 (Spring 1984): 190.

29. Meuvret, *Problèmes*, 2:147–48; P. Brunet, *Structure agraire*, p. 438; Goubert, *Beauvaisis*, p. 159; Dupâquier, *Ainsi . . . Chaumont*, p. 54. Moreover, Moriceau and Postel-Vinay argue that the turnover in even permanent jobs offered by fermiers was extremely high. They also point to a very low wage-scale and a tendency to reduce the numbers employed over the year (*Ferme*, pp. 245–51). However, it is not clear how these factors are related.

extent of their holdings varied considerably. They sometimes resembled most closely a predominantly landowning version of smaller fermiers and both groups often used the titles interchangeably.[30] In many cases, they were little more than subsistence-level peasants, compelled, for example, to sell their product early (and therefore cheaply) to pay taxes, rents, tithes, and dues.[31] In the Vexin français, for example, the laboureur had experienced "nonstop" decline from the seventeenth century because of parcelization stemming from inheritance divisions.[32] Moreover, during crisis years, they might not produce enough for family consumption, and they were rarely able to benefit from bad harvests, as could their *gros fermier* neighbors. They almost never leased rights to collect the tithe or seigneurial dues, they rarely exploited monopolies, and in some places, like the Soissonnais, they witnessed rents they paid for smaller parcels of land rise faster than rents demanded for the *corps de ferme*. Thus, these middling landowners and tenants continued to be something of an endangered species during the eighteenth century, as their numbers declined in the *pays de grande culture*.[33]

This *pays de grande culture* supported few full-time independent artisans. Although many villages maintained at least one blacksmith, one wheelwright, and one mason, most tasks requiring the work of a skilled craftsman were too infrequent for full-time employment. Many jobs were performed by the nearest town artisan, by a traveling craftsman, or by skilled workers employed by landed proprietors and fermiers. Even the few who managed to find enough work to permit residence in a small village had to supplement their incomes by doing other kinds of jobs or by exploiting a small parcel of land.[34]

30. This makes it very frustrating for the historian seeking to sort the one type from the other, a situation either simplified or made even more annoying by the gradual adoption of the generic term *cultivateur* from the late eighteenth century. Much that has been written about the laboureur reflects this confusion. For example, when Venard discusses the laboureur, he usually means the large-scale *fermier* (a term not much used in the region he studied). See Venard, "Une Classe rurale," pp. 517–25, and the discussion about the different kinds of fermiers in Jessenne, *Pouvoir*, pp. 160–61. Moriceau and Postel-Vinay sometimes refer to fermiers as *marchands-laboureurs* (*Ferme*, p. 20). I try to distinguish between a *fermier* (someone who *rents* the majority of the land he exploits) and the *laboureur* (someone who *owns* the majority of the land he exploits). Although this rigor is lacking in the eighteenth-century contemporary literature, it is important to distinguish between proprietorship and tenant status. On laboureurs, see Goubert, "Paysan," p. 141.

31. See, again, Hufton, "Social Conflict," p. 320.

32. Dupâquier, *Ainsi . . . Chaumont*, p. 54.

33. Dewald, *Pont-St.-Pierre*, pp. 53–54; Postel-Vinay, *La Rente foncière*, pp. 53–56; Guy-Robert Ikni, "La Terre de Lierville de 1715 à la Restauration," in *Contributions à l'histoire paysanne de la Révolution française*, ed. A. Soboul, pp. 251–82 (Paris, 1977).

34. Baulant, "Groupes mobiles," pp. 88–91; P. Brunet, *Structure agraire*, p. 387; C. Brunet, *Le Plessis-Gassot*, p. 36.

Thus, by the mid-eighteenth century a fairly advanced form of commercial agriculture specializing in grain production had developed in the Paris breadbasket. This region had a polarized social structure grounded in the control of land and its product. It had also produced a burgeoning and increasingly sophisticated marketing system that drew grain from its point of origin via collector markets, forwarded on through feeder or relay markets to urban provisioning markets.[35] The second half of the eighteenth century witnessed the accelerated development of this system, which first focused local attention and suspicion on the market towns and then intensified tensions in the countryside.

Grain-Importing Regions: Long-Term Developments

Regions in this grain-importing category fall into three basic groups, all of which share one important trait. Each group, while having to import the grain necessary for consumption, was nonetheless highly integrated into other aspects of the market economy of the eighteenth century. Whether it was grain importation itself, agricultural markets for cattle, dairy products, wine, or vegetables, or the industrial markets for textiles or other commodities, these regions manifested high but unevenly developing degrees of commercialization and division of labor.

The first of the regions in the grain-importing category, the Parisian *banlieue*, was delimited by a two-league ring around the capital. It extended west to Neuilly, south to Bourg-la-Reine, east to Montreuil, and north to Aubervilliers. By the eighteenth century, most of the *banlieue* had developed distinct agricultural and commercial structures that specialized in production for the Parisian market and had evolved complex social structures. An agricultural region heavily peopled by market-gardeners, the *banlieue* was marked by wide social differentiation and a veritable corporate identity. Powerful ecclesiastical institutions predominated as proprietors of extensive holdings, renting their large exploitations to tenants, who in turn either managed the land directly and hired wage labor, or sublet smaller parcels at

---

35. These are the terms used by Kaplan in *Provisioning*, pp. 92–93, and by Dominique Margairaz, *Foires et marchés dans la France préindustrielle* (Paris, 1988), pp. 177–81. For more on this, see below and Chapter 4.

high rents. Side by side with such important proprietors as the Collègiale Sainte-Opportune, there stood numerous small family proprietors, whose tiny exploitations remained viable because of the proximity of the Parisian market and their capacity to cultivate the soil intensively to produce vegetables, fruits, flowers, and vines for the capital. At the end of the sixteenth century, these market-gardeners (maraîchers) of the banlieue organized a corporation that resembled other urban corporations and was designed to protect their interests in the marketplace.[36] An urban society sustaining a more diversified occupational structure geared as much toward passing travelers as local demand, the banlieue had by the eighteenth century become more Parisian than provincial, more urban than rural.[37]

Next among the grain-importing category were areas that engaged in a more diversified production—part of the Clermontois, part of the southern Beauvaisis, the pays de Bray, the pays de Caux, parts of northern Brie, southeastern Brie, a part of the Gâtinais, and the region around Versailles. In general, less fertile soils, climatic conditions, hilly terrain, or the presence of forested zones militated against the exclusive cultivation of grain, despite the traditional obsession with subsistence agriculture. The proximity and attraction of growing urban markets encouraged many inhabitants willing to enter these markets to meet family consumption needs and other obligations by developing polyculture such as livestock raising, cheese and other dairy products, hemp, vines, and forest products. Some areas participated in a vigorous textile industry. Although these areas never constituted a homogeneous unit, certain general characteristics tended to unite these disparate lands.

Compared with the pays de grande culture, land was more widely distributed—sometimes as property but more frequently in ferme—among the rural population. Nowhere did exploitations equal the size of those of the grain-exporting zone. Only in the pays de Caux, where grain production met the subsistence needs of its population in normal years, did exploitations as large as 80–100 hectares (33–42 acres) exist.[38] Even these, however, could not rival the 150–300 hectare (64–125 acre) exploitations found, for example, in the Vexin.

36. See esp. Philipponneau, Banlieue parisienne, pp. 11–60.

37. All the larger towns and cities of the provinces produced similar though much smaller banlieues, all performing largely the same functions.

38. Sion, Normandie orientale, p. 274. Sion claims this was the result of the custom governing the pays de Caux that demanded primogeniture and thus favored the maintenance of larger exploitations.

Medium-sized exploitations abounded in all these regions of mixed cultivation in the eighteenth century. Relying on stock-raising on natural
pasturelands and communal lands, peasants maintained small exploitations
by trading in butter or cheese and by the sale of their stock. In some areas,
such as the Bray near Gournay, commerce emerged based on distant markets
in butter, beef, and pork.[39] In northern Brie, peasants combined hemp and
wood production with livestock-raising. Such production sufficed only for
local needs, but the Departmental Assembly of Meaux reported in 1788
that the region generated enough commerce that "there is no inhabitant
who does not have his field to work or his vine to cultivate; everyone is well-
off, but no one is rich."[40] In the southern Beauvaisis, the title *haricotier*
distinguished the middling-peasant who engaged in a variety of activities
ranging from grain production to stock-raising. Often renting as much land
as they owned, these *haricotier* families walked a thin line between subsistence and failure.[41]

In some areas, domestic industry permitted the survival of small landholdings. In the pays de Caux, for example, the cotton manufacture centered in
Rouen employed so many families that Arthur Young described it as "a
manufacturing country; the properties usually small; and farming . . . but a
secondary pursuit to the cotton fabric."[42] This industry also penetrated the
pays de Bray.[43] Other forms of protoindustry flourished in parts of the
Beauvaisis. In the pays de Thelle, rurals made lace, brushes, fans, dominoes,
and buttons; in the Clermontois, inhabitants around Mouy, as we have

39. "Etat de la subdélégation de Gournay-en-Bray (1787)," AD Seine-Maritime, C 185;
Philippe Goujard, *L'Abolition de la Féodalité dans le pays de Bray (1789–1793)* (Paris, 1979); Hugues
Neveux and Bernard Garnier, "Valeur de la terre, production agricole et marché urbain au milieu
de XVIIIe siècle: L'Exemple de la Normandie entre la baie de Seine et la baie de Veys," in *Problèmes
agraires et société rurale: Normandie et Europe du nord-ouest (XVIe–XIXe siècles)*, ed. G. Desert et al.
(Caen, 1979), pp. 77–78.

40. P. Brunet, *Structure agraire*, p. 358.

41. Goubert, *Beauvais*, pp. 163–65; Ganiage, *Beauvaisis*, pp. 7–66. On medium-sized exploitations elsewhere, see, e.g., Dupâquier, *Gâtinais*, pp. 207, 215, 255.

42. *Travels*, p. 265. Sion confirms the primary importance of this industry in the region
(*Normandie orientale*, p. 273). See esp. Gay L. Gullickson, "The Sexual Division of Labor in
Cottage Industry and Agriculture in the Pays de Caux: Auffay, 1750–1850," *FHS* 12 (Fall 1981):
177–99; idem, *Spinners and Weavers of Auffay: Rural Industry and the Sexual Division of Labor in a
French Village, 1750–1850* (Cambridge, 1986), pp. 38–68.

43. The penetration was less extensive here than in the pays de Caux, however, because of the
greater distance from the center at Rouen and the poor condition of the roads (see Sion, *Normandie
orientale*, p. 182; Goujard, *Abolition*, p. 23). Ganiage notes that the part of the pays de Bray that
usually fell within the Beauvaisis had developed from the seventeenth century a flourishing wet-
nurse business for Parisian infants (*Beauvaisis*, p. 24).

already seen, worked in the textile industry, making serge for the royal army.[44]

With the possible exception of the pays de Caux and a portion of the Clermontois in normal years, peasants in this cluster of regions generally had to purchase their grain. Smaller exploitations permitted a dense population, while the climate and soil prohibited adequate cereal production. The largest part of the rural population, therefore, had to trade in its various products in order to meet its subsistence needs. They were just as dependent on the marketplace, and on the nearby surplus-producing regions, as were the urban consumers. They were thus drawn to such market towns as Auffay in the Caux, Gournay-en-Bray, Beaumont-du-Gâtinais, Neufchâtel-en-Bray, and Mouy for their provisions. In these elementary marketplaces, grain, produced by local cultivators or collected by *blatiers* (small-scale merchants who scoured the countryside and more-distant markets for supplies), accumulated for display and sale.[45]

The final regions in the grain-importing category comprised those bordering on the rivers that traversed the Paris Basin. These regions were characterized by a dense population, an intensive polyculture, small exploitations, and widespread small proprietorship. Soil conditions varied considerably, ranging from richly fertile to marshy or extremely sandy. Inhabitants turned to crops demanding intensive cultivation. Vines constituted the most important source of income, particularly near Paris.[46] Although much of the wine produced was consumed locally, some areas managed a more far-flung trade. For example, the villages of Bennecourt, Freneuse, and Méricourt, located in the loop of the Seine below La Roche-Guyon, produced wine for the market in Rouen, and the village of Gommecourt, to the west of these villages, sold wine in Picardy.[47] In most places, however, inhabitants engaged in a variety of activities: viticulture as well as market-gardening, orchard-growing, hemp production, grain cultivation (principally oats and

44. Ganiage claims that lace-making *(dentellerie)*, conducted principally by merchants out of Chantilly, employed 3,000 women in the bailliages of Senlis, Chaumont, and Beauvais *(Beauvaisis, pp. 25–34)*.

45. See Chapter 4, below.

46. Marcel Lachiver, *Vin, vigne, et vignerons en la région parisienne du XVII au XIXe siècles* (Paris, 1982); Loutchisky, "Régime agraire." Vine-growing was also prominent along the Oise near Noyon, along the Marne between the rivers Ourcq and Grand Morin, along the Aisne in most places (P. Brunet, *Structures agraires*, p. 286), along the Essonne and Loing (Dupâquier, *Gâtinais*, pp. 28, 34–35), along the Yerres (Mireaux, *Brie*, p. 190), along the Seine north of Versailles (Defresne and Evrard, *Subsistances*, 1:xviii), and between the Seine and Magny-en-Vexin (Dupâquier, *Ainsi . . . Chaumont*, p. 47).

47. Dupâquier, *Ainsi . . . Chaumont*, p. 47.

rye), and livestock-raising.[48] Depending on location and the demands of the
market, production of one or sometimes several of these crops made small
exploitations viable.[49]

The presence of small properties and the relative absence of lands held in
ferme was the most striking feature of the lands along the slopes of the major
rivers—the Seine, Oise, Marne, and Aisne—as well as the smaller ones,
such as the Yerres, Thérain, Grand-Morin, Authonne, Loing, Esches, Epte,
and Brèches. Within the pays de vignoble (the vine-growing country)
encircling Paris, approximately 40 percent of the peasantry owned and
exploited at least some land.[50] At the end of the eighteenth century, in the
parish of Vauréal, where peasants engaged in a more diversified agriculture,
an even larger number were proprietors.[51] Along the Brèche, peasant
proprietorship reached 36 percent, a figure considerably higher than the 17
percent calculated for the Clermontois as a whole.[52]

The fact of proprietorship did not mean wealth, however, and not every
family with land owned enough to support itself. Furthermore, the shortage
of rentable lands limited the size of exploitations river-dwellers could hold.[53]
In the pays de vignoble, for example, at least 80 percent of the peasants with
land supplemented their incomes as vine-growers with another occupation.
For those with few resources, this usually meant working as a manouvrier,
although those with somewhat greater resources often doubled as publicans,
coopers, or quarry workers, and many families found work in other households.[54] Outside the pays de vignoble, inhabitants resorted to other part-time

48. Bahu, "Les Paysans de la région de Clermont de l'Oise à la fin de l'Ancien Régime," AHRF
14 (1937): 193; Sion, Normandie orientale, pp. 10, 253–58; P. Brunet, Structure agraire, pp. 359–60;
J. C. Brulé, "Trois communes de la Basse-Vallée de l'Oise: Cergy, Jouy-le-Moutier, Vauréal à la fin
de l'Ancien Régime," Mémoires de la Société historique et archéologique de Pontoise, du Val-d'Oise et du
Vexin 60 (1966): 28; Brossard de Ruville, Histoire de la ville des Andelis, et de ces dépendances, 2 vols.
(Les Andelys, 1863), 1:253; Defresne and Evrard, Subsistances, 1:xvi–xxiii; Dupâquier, Gâtinais, p.
41.

49. There were a few exceptions to the predominant aspect of small exploitations—for example,
around La Ferté-sous-Jouarre on the Marne and near the Petit Morin, large exploitations dedicated
to cereal production dominated (P. Brunet, Structures agraires, p. 86).

50. Lachiver, Vin, p. 365.

51. Brulé, "Trois Communes," p. 40. This was in 1792, after the sale of the biens nationaux.
Brulé calculated that the peasantry owned 68 percent of the land, but he argues that proprietorship
was probably quite high even before the Revolution.

52. Bahu, "Les Paysans de Clermont," pp. 194–95.

53. Large exploitations were rare, and when they did occur they usually signified a large fermier,
exploiting grain-producing lands (Brulé, "Trois communes," p. 30). See, e.g., the property held by
Bernard Delaissement in the parish of Cergy near Pontoise ("Rôle de taille, 1773," AD Yvelines, C
184, n. 85).

54. Approximately 20 percent of the vine-growers in this region were independent (Lachiver,
Vin, pp. 434–36).

occupations, such as seasonal employment as unskilled laborers in the *pays de grande culture*.[55] Proximity to rivers also offered a wide range of opportunities unavailable elsewhere. Villagers near navigable rivers often engaged in some aspect of river transport, administering the multiple tolls (*péages*) along the route, navigating barges, and repairing and building equipment necessary for river transport.[56] Fishing could also supplement family incomes, both as a source of food and for sale.

Thus, the nature of agricultural production and the multiplication of small exploitations created a consumer population along the riverbanks of the countryside in the Paris Basin. This dense population was extremely sensitive to problems of supply and price, not only in grain but also in their own produce. And of course the two were related.

Within the Paris Basin, therefore, there existed regions that had experienced different kinds of development. While some, like those lands in the fertile *pays de grande culture*, specialized in grain cultivation, others focused on different crops more suited to local conditions. Each had developed particular responses to the various pressures exerted by the Parisian market and other regional urban markets. On the one hand, rural producers supplied these urban markets with their various products, whether grain, vegetables, meat, butter, wine, or wood. On the other hand, these great urban markets competed with rural consumers, forcing the consuming countryside to vie with city consumers for their subsistence needs. By the mid-eighteenth century each region had emerged with an increasingly distinct socioeconomic organization.

Accelerations and Transformations: The Last Half of the Eighteenth Century

During the last half of the eighteenth century, several changes—demographic, economic, and political—accelerated transformations long under way in the countryside outside Paris. The population grew; agricultural productivity almost kept pace; prices rose; wages rose, but not as fast as prices; rents also rose, but not as fast as prices either. The Crown embraced,

55. P. Brunet demonstrates that a common temporary job for many riverbank dwellers was harvester (*Structures agraires*, p. 391).

56. Sion, *Normandie orientale*, p. 257; Léon Cahen, "Ce qu'enseigne un péage du XVIIIe siècle: La Seine entre Rouen et Paris, et les caractères de l'économie parisienne," *Annales d'histoire économique et sociale* 12 (Oct. 1931): 490.

then discarded, then embraced again, a version of the physiocratic dream of a grain trade free of the trammels of paternalistic regulation as part of a drive to foster agricultural productivity, economic growth, and a strong, vigorous, taxable population. These developments carried ramifications that shaped subsistence movements in the late eighteenth century.

Sometime between 1720 and 1750, the population of France began to grow.[57] The France of 20 million people during the reign of Louis XIV expanded to 27 million at the end of the eighteenth century, an increase that affected the countryside as well as the cities. Paris swelled from around 500,000 under Louis XIV to almost 700,000 under Louis XVI. By 1789 the city of Versailles held 51,000 inhabitants, while the addition of the population at the château and the troops of the Maison du Roi drove the number to just over 60,000.[58] Rouen's population topped 50,000 by the end of the century, making it one of the seven largest cities in the kingdom.[59] Despite important regional variations, however, a generally larger population percolated within the social and economic structures of the Paris Basin of eighteenth-century France described above.

To feed these growing urban populations, and thereby maintain social order, cities continued to extend their supply lines farther and farther into the countryside and to put greater pressure on grain production and the marketing system to supply them. Both cities and countryside further strained the lines of supply and disrupted market organization in several ways in the last half of the eighteenth century.[60] When Paris and other growing regional centers extended their provisioning lines ever deeper into the provinces, they did so either by sending merchants to new markets to buy grain[61] or by squeezing harder those regions already in the net. Both

57. For the Paris Basin, Pierre Goubert concludes that population growth began closer to 1750. See his "Révolution démographique au 18e siècle," in *Histoire économique et sociale de la France*, vol. 2 (Paris, 1970), pp. 66–76. See also Jacques Dupâquier, "Les Caractères originaux de l'histoire démographique française au XVIIIe siècle," *RHMC* 33 (1976): 193–202; idem, "Croissance démographique régionale dans le Bassin parisien au XVIIIe siècle," in *Sur la population française au XVIIIe et au XIXe siècles: Hommage à Marcel Reinhard* (Paris, 1975).

58. A. Defresne and F. Evrard, *Les Subsistances dans le district de Versailles de 1788 à l'An V* (Rennes, 1921), p. vii.

59. On Paris, Daniel Roche, *Le Peuple de Paris* (Paris, 1981), pp. 21–22; on Rouen, Goubert, "Révolution démographique," p. 73. Of course, the demographic history of different regions varied enormously—for example, in the Vexin français the population in 1789 was exactly that of 1712, but that of the adjacent pays de Thelle rose 22 percent (see Dupâquier, *Ainsi . . . Chaumont*, p. 39). Some demographic change was a product of migration as much as net increases or mortalities.

60. On what follows, see L. Tilly, "Food Riot"; Kaplan, *Bread*; idem, *Provisioning*, pp. 80–121. See also Chapter 4.

61. Kaplan has a description of the development of the provisioning "crowns" circling Paris (*Provisioning*, pp. 88–103).

ways upset the previous alignments established between local and more distant demand, and among the various interests that fed off the provisioning system.

Moreover, merchants, producers, and Crown adjusted forms of marketing, production, or regulation to the changing circumstances. Well before the first attempts at official liberalization, merchants developed and extended new forms of doing business, producers reorganized their productive capacity to take advantage of new market opportunities, and local authorities selectively enforced or ignored regulations.[62] The free grain trade eras of 1763–64 to 1770, and again from 1774 to 1776, legitimized (at least in the eyes of the Crown), facilitated, and accelerated processes already under way in the French economy. Reversals of policy, such as Terray's between 1770 and 1774, delegitimized many new business practices but did not eliminate or drastically curtail them.[63]

Perhaps the most telling sign of uneven development in late eighteenth-century France was the problematic relationship between the social, economic, and political context and demographic growth. How did France feed a growing population? Despite the clearing and cultivation of some new lands, the introduction of new crops in some places, and the testing of new technologies on some lands, French agriculture on the whole experienced no revolution in productivity commensurate with the growing population. We now know, of course, that no revolution in productivity is possible or necessary in certain contexts. France had plenty of untapped productive capacity, so the question was not how to produce more but how to distribute it more effectively.[64] In the *pays de grande culture*, however, increasingly convincing evidence suggests that there was indeed a significant rise in productivity at the rate of 0.3 percent between 1750 and 1774, and 1 percent between 1775 and 1789.[65] And, indeed, fewer people starved at the end of the eighteenth century than at the beginning.[66] Production and

---

62. R. B. Outhwaite argues that in eighteenth-century England "there were increasing tendencies in periods of dearth for authorities to *respond* to social disturbances by invoking old policies rather than, as happened in earlier periods, for authorities to implement such measures in order to *anticipate* such troubles" (*Dearth, Public Policy, and Social Disturbance in England, 1550–1800* [London, 1991], p. 44 [emphasis in the original]). We need to know more about this for France.

63. Kaplan, *Bread*, 1:90–96, 2:492, 532–39.

64. On this, see esp. the work of Michel Morineau, *Les Faux-Semblants d'un démarrage économique. Agriculture et démographie en France au XVIIIe siècle* (Paris, 1970), and his "Y a-t-il eu une révolution agricole en France au XVIIIe siècle?" *Revue historique* 239 (1968): 299–326. See also Meuvret, *Problèmes*, 1:203, 215; 2:213–14.

65. See the compelling work of Philip Hoffman, "Land Rents and Agricultural Productivity: The Paris Basin, 1460–1789," *JEH* 51 (Dec. 1991): 771–805. Hoffman argues that these rates of growth are comparable or even superior to the rate of growth achieved in Great Britain.

66. On the demographic implications of a subsistence crisis on this newer pattern, see the study

distribution not only managed to keep pace with population but also became more efficient during the second half of the eighteenth century, if by that we are prepared to accept pauperization rather than starvation as a sign of "keeping pace." True, few starved, but more were poor and weak. As Olwen Hufton has summarized, "periodic starvation was replaced for a possible 30 to 40 percent of the total population (perhaps 60 to 70 percent in some regions) by long-term malnutrition."[67] Historians have everywhere documented the mounting problem of poverty in the second half of the eighteenth century.[68]

Thus, this expanding population confronted competition—a potential entitlement crisis—for relatively scarce resources such as land, food, and jobs. Ernest Labrousse has shown that the second half of the eighteenth century witnessed the socially unhappy conjuncture of unevenly moving prices, rents, and wages. Food prices rose rapidly after mid-century, with grain prices rising most dramatically.[69] Wages failed to keep pace with prices.[70]

For a while, proprietors and fermiers who controlled surplus-grain-producing lands benefited strikingly from these trends. However, for the fermiers the bonanza proved short-lived, because sometime after 1765 proprietors began increasing the price of leases on their fermes faster than grain prices rose.[71] At the other extreme, wages failed to keep pace with rising prices, so

---

by Bricourt et al., "La Crise de subsistence des années 1740 dans le ressort du Parlement de Paris," in Annales de démographie historique, 1974, pp. 281–333.

67. "Social Conflict," p. 305. See also Michel Morineau, Faux-Semblants, pp. 7–95; Jacques Dupâquier, "La Situation de l'agriculture dans le Vexin français (fin du XVIIIe et début du XIXe siècle) d'après les enquêtes agricoles," in Actes du 89e Congrès national des Sociétés savantes, Lyons, 1964 (Paris, 1964), pp. 321–45.

68. The latest assessment is by Robert Schwartz, Policing the Poor in Eighteenth-Century France (Chapel Hill, N.C., 1988), pp. 132–53. See also Chapter 1.

69. Wheat prices rose 56–66 percent between 1726/41 and 1771–89; rye prices rose 60–70 percent during the same era (Ernest Labrousse, Esquisse du mouvement des prix et des revenues en France au XVIIIe siècle [Paris, 1933], pp. 104–13, 176, 183). From the early 1770s, the price of grains leveled out or even declined, with the exception of 1775, but this flattening curve carried important difficulties for grain proprietors as well. On other prices, see below.

70. Labrousse, Esquisse, pp. 147–48, 305, 365, 379, 444–46, 582–603; Morineau, Faux-Semblants, pp. 7–95.

71. G. Beaur, "Le Mouvement annuel de la rente foncière chartraine, 1760–1780," in Prestations paysannes, dîmes, rente foncière et mouvement de la production agricole à l'époque préindustrielle, 2 vols., ed. J. Goy and E. Le Roy Ladurie (Paris, 1982), 2:491–501; Postel-Vinay, Rente foncière, pp. 79, 85–95. It is also possible that experience with liberalization and the attendant high prices of the 1763–64 period directly encouraged proprietors to raise leases. At the very least, liberalization functioned as an accelerator of trends already under way or contemplated (Kaplan, Bread, 2:571–73). There is some indication that between 1770 and 1780–87 the rate of increase in grain prices leveled out (with the exception of bad years, such as 1775). If this is true, the increase

day-laborers, especially *manouvriers* and *journaliers*, faced a decline in real income. Food, particularly grain, took more and more of the family budget. A similar difficulty beset the small peasant proprietor or tenant farmer, the *paysan parcellaire*, who did not produce enough to profit from higher grain prices and had to buy at inflated prices to supplement production at home.

Throughout both regions discussed here, these movements in population, grain productivity, prices, landed income, and wages meant increasing distress for a growing majority of the people. Competition for land and subsistence intensified everywhere, threatening the social relations within communities and straining relations between rural and urban consumers. The specific local effects of this situation varied in intensity and focus according to each region's particular socioeconomic organization and agricultural orientation.

Grain-Exporting Regions: Developments After Mid-Century

In the *pays de grande culture*, the most obvious response to these circumstances was the struggle for control of the profits from grain-producing lands. From mid-century on, the battle waged—not between potential proprietors, as it had before 1730, but among the peasantry itself—over control of *fermages*.[72] Behind this struggle lay the interests of proprietors, both large and small. The large absentee landed proprietors confronted a rising cost of living in the cities where they resided; the small confronted rising prices in general. And while both had previously been content with relatively stable incomes that kept up with inflation, they recognized sometime around 1760 that they were either losing ground because of higher prices, or missing the opportunity to increase revenues. A few engaged in "physiocratic" land reforms[73] through the application of new technologies, many restructured and concentrated holdings in order to rationalize the management of their properties, but most simply raised rents.[74] Sometimes, in fact, they raised

---

in the leases on *fermes* would have been much more harmful. See Labrousse, *La Crise de l'économie française à la fin de l'Ancien Régime et au début de la Révolution* (Paris, 1944), p. x.

72. Relations between proprietors and *fermiers* deteriorated too. Postel-Vinay suggests these tensions were responsible for the alliance between peasants and *fermiers* against large landed property and feudalism during the Revolution (*La Rente foncière*, 92).

73. André Bourde, *Agronomie et agronomes en France au XVIIIe siècle*, 3 vols. (Paris, 1967), pp. 1561–96; Jacques Dupâquier, "Structures sociales," p. 449.

74. On rising rents after 1760s, see Labrousse, *Esquisse*, pp. 379–83; Dewald, *Pont-St.-Pierre*, p. 74; Postel-Vinay, *La Rente foncière*, pp. 85–95.

rents savagely. Philip Hoffman has documented rises in rents of up to 120 percent between the 1730s and 1780s.[75] The fermiers were driven to find ways to adjust.

Watching the shrinking margins between grain profits and their rents, the fermiers recaptured some of this "loss" by keeping wages low or by reorganizing the labor force. Fermiers in some places attempted to reduce their reliance on the more expensive, skilled labor (that was also more local, autonomous, and better organized) by reorganizing the labor process. Hoffman claims that by the end of the century they had succeeded in reducing the number of workers employed.[76] Many others responded by accelerating behavior adopted during the good old days: they enlarged their holdings by leasing more than one large ferme or by accumulating many small holdings, thereby increasing production to profit more from seasonal variations in prices.[77] Thus, after 1760, when the large fermiers entered the land market, seeking even small parcels to augment their lease holdings, the small peasantry suffered a blow. Most had always depended on leasing small parcels and had exploited these as well as their own small properties. In the uneven struggle with larger fermiers for access to these small holdings, the small peasantry simply could not compete in the eyes of proprietors with fermiers in status, dependability, or price. For example, in 1761 the subdelegate at Crépy-en-Valois wrote that "it is the ambition of all the *gros laboureurs* to unite to their *corps de ferme* all the properties [for lease] in a parish, to the extent that all the *hacotiers* [sic] and *menagers* find themselves devoid of all resources to subsist. . . . The *laboureur* overlooks nothing to crush the little person. . . . He offers an equal or even a higher price to the proprietor."[78] At least some of these strategies worked, for Hoffman shows

75. Hoffman, "Land Rents."

76. See Labrousse on overall wages, *Esquisse*, pp. 490–519. On the labor process, see Postel-Vinay, *La Rente foncière*, pp. 100–104; Hoffman, "Land Rents"; Moriceau and Postel-Vinay, *Ferme*, p. 151. Another symptom of the manipulations to keep wages low and diminish worker autonomy was the important increase in contests between harvest workers in the *pays de grande culture* and their employers over wages and working conditions. See Jean-Marc Moriceau, "Les 'Baccanals' au grèves des moissonneurs au nord de l'Ile-de-France (deuxième moitié du XVIIIe siècle)," in *Mouvements populaires et conscience sociale, XVIe–XIXe siècles* (Paris, 1985), pp. 420–34.

77. The fermiers had always engaged in this form of "reunion" as a means to increase profits, but this activity became more frequent after the 1760s. See P. Brunet, *Structure agraire*, pp. 288–90; Postel-Vinay, *La Rente foncière*, p. 90; Dewald, *Pont-St.-Pierre*, p. 57; Ikni, "Lierville," p. 260. Moriceau and Postel-Vinay observe that, after 1760, fermiers turned more frequently to fill out and consolidate landholdings as part of a different family strategy (*Ferme*, pp. 307, 325).

78. P. Brunet, *Structure agraire*, p. 289; Dupâquier, *Gâtinais*, p. 218; Postel-Vinay, *La Rente foncière*, p. 90; Dewald, *Pont-St.-Pierre*, p. 54; Defresne and Evrard, *Subsistances*, 1:xxxiv; Hoffman, "Land Rents."

that there was no sign of increased turnover among fermiers in the late eighteenth century despite higher rents.[79]

These strategies drove the larger fermiers into direct confrontation with the rural labor force, on the one hand, and with the smaller and middling peasantry, on the other hand. From mid-century on, the numbers of middling landholders dwindled throughout the *pays de grande culture*, while the virtually landless poor and the unemployed increased in number in the villages, and the rootless poor roamed and appeared ready to raid the countryside. In the Soissonnais from the 1760s, fermiers complained that vagabonds forced them to pay out 100, 200, and even 300 livres in forced distributions that the beggars called "charity."[80] In 1775, on the eve of the Flour War, two fermiers from the parish of Chelles painted an angry picture of tensions within their communities by listing thefts and threats that had previously been committed but had gone unpunished. They testified:

> Such violence is contrary to all law [and is] disquieting and discouraging for the laboureurs certainly in a village where impunity seems to authorize crime, where . . . thefts of all types are committed in homes, where not only is fruit stolen from enclosures and gardens but also where trees and saplings are chopped down, where foreign and unhealthy beasts are introduced into pastures, where fermiers and proprietors are menaced with fires by anonymous and circular letters so that they do not dare complain.[81]

In sum, in the *pays de grande culture* the second half of the eighteenth century witnessed the increased polarization of rural society. There had emerged an even more narrow elite of large fermiers, a smaller number of medium-sized cultivators, and an increasingly proletarianized mass of manouvriers and semiskilled laborers.[82] The fact that this elite of *gros fermiers* often leased the rights to collect seigneurial dues, the monopolies, and the tithe, enjoyed certain privileges because of their power and status, and were

79. Hoffman, "Land Rents."

80. Postel-Vinay, *Rente foncière*, p. 62. During shortages, this sort of behavior was quite frequent and often accompanied by threats to burn farms if charity was not forthcoming. See Bricourt et al., "Crise," p. 297.

81. "Lettre de Nicolas Bourgeois et Jean Vincent LaMotte (n.d.)," BN, Collection Joly de Fleury, 1159, fols. 42–44.

82. Evidence of polarized villages in these regions abounds in the tax records for this period. The results of my analysis of tax records are used in detail in Chapters 3 and 6.

heavily involved in surplus-grain production and marketing made them likely targets for expressions of hostility.

Grain-Consuming/Importing Regions: Developments After Mid-Century

Outside the *pays de grande culture,* the regions of mixed agricultural production also felt the strains of the changing late eighteenth-century environment. Demographic pressure increased fragmentation of properties.[83] Nor could inhabitants avoid the menacing impact of the various price fluctuations of this second half of the century. Forced to exchange their produce for subsistence grain at a time when grain prices rose faster than produce prices, many peasants with medium- and small-sized holdings found themselves sucked into a downward economic spiral.

For example, for those who raised livestock, the price news was not good. Meat prices rose 55 percent between 1726–41 and 1771–89—almost as fast as wheat prices, not as fast as rye prices—but fodder rose even faster.[84] Vine-growers also encountered a period of difficulty. Wine prices rose only 41 percent during the same period, with a sharp rise at the end of the 1760s and first half of the 1770s. Yet low productivity could hurt smaller producers, despite generally higher prices. Thus, although the years 1770–80 were years of high prices in the *pays de vignoble* (vine-growing country), they resulted from low production. This meant that the small vine-grower, like the small grain-producer, often failed to harvest enough to benefit from high prices.[85]

The tendency toward concentration of rental lands in the hands of one

83. Except in regions where inheritance laws favored primogeniture, such as the pays de Caux, and even here, protoindustrialization enabled tenants and owners to live on small properties (Sion, *Normandie orientale,* pp. 271–82; Gullickson, *Spinners,* pp. 44–57). In certain regions, such as the *pays de vignoble* around Paris, inhabitants responded to the threat of population growth by voluntarily limiting births, a process evident as early as 1760–70 (Lachiver, *Vin,* p. 705).

84. Labrousse, *Esquisse,* pp. 281–90, 291–303.

85. Ibid., 267–76; Lachiver, *Vin,* pp. 303–39. Changing relations between prices and productivity in the wine market took their toll on producers in other ways. As prices rose for grain and wine, consuming a larger part of many family budgets, people found cheaper substitutes, such as cider. Producers responded at the end of the eighteenth century by replacing vineyards with plantations of fruit trees for cider, particularly in eastern Normandy. But this conversion was expensive. See Lachiver, *Vin,* pp. 324–25; Demangeon, *Picardie,* pp. 257–58.

tenant emerged even in the regions of small- and medium-sized holdings, where peasants mixed proprietorship and fermage. In the Bray, for example, where grazing lands cost more than arable lands, there was a movement toward the exploitation of several fermes by one fermier. Similar concentrations were occurring in the Gâtinais.[86]

The news was not all bad before 1775, however. Protoindustrialization continued to absorb and shelter small peasant and rural wage-laboring families, probably an ever-growing number of them. In such regions as the Beauvaisis, the pays de Caux, Picardy, and growing parts of the pays de Bray, domestic industry supplemented family incomes and enabled them to weather economic difficulties before the 1780s and, although they were still subject to seasonal and short-term crises, to avoid dispossession and relocation. These families also provided the temporary and seasonal labor for the cultivators in their regions.[87]

Trading in Grain and Its Products in the Eighteenth-Century Paris Basin

The complex grain trade in the Paris Basin was structured delicately in the eighteenth century.[88] As Kaplan explains, "the market 'system' . . . turned on a slippery interplay between local and metropolitan, retail and wholesale, archaism and modernity, marketplace and market principle."[89] For consumer, merchant, and producer, this always tricky business became even

---

86. Goujard, L'Abolition, pp. 21–22; Dupâquier, Gâtinais, p. 262.

87. Only when much of the textile industry ran into difficulty in the 1780s did widespread dislocation occur. Of course, as we have already seen, wool- and cotton-processing were not the only forms of industry in the countryside, and many industries suffered short-term crises. For example, the Seven Years' War virtually ruined the industry in tableterie around Méru, but it quickly rebounded once the war had ended, and remained vigorous until the Revolution (Ganiage, Beauvaisis, p. 28).

88. Steven Kaplan's Provisioning Paris (Ithaca, N.Y., 1984) is the most important recent analysis of the Paris provisioning system. See also Abbot P. Usher, The History of the Grain Trade in France, 1400–1710 (Cambridge, Mass., 1913); Margairaz, Foires et marchés; Charles Desmarest, Le Commerce des grains dans la généralité de Rouen à la fin de l'Ancien Régime (Paris, 1926); Meuvret, Problèmes, vol. 3, Le Commerce des grains et la conjoncture (Paris, 1988); Joseph Letaconnoux, "La Question des subsistances et du commerce des grains en France au XVIIIe siècle," RHM 8 (1906–7): 409–45; George Afanassiev, Le Commerce des céréales dans France au XVIII siècle, trans. P. Boyer (Paris, 1894), among many others.

89. Kaplan, Provisioning, p. 80.

more treacherous in times of dearth. This section sketches the Paris Basin
marketing structures (Chapter 4 provides some deeper case studies drawn
from the Flour War).

The Parisian market and other regional urban markets exerted both a
unifying and a divisive force on the countryside in their provisioning zones.
On the one hand, rural producers in each region supplied these urban
markets with their various products, whether grain, vegetables, meat, butter,
or wine. On the other hand, these great urban markets competed with rural
consumers, forcing the consuming countryside to vie with city consumers
for its subsistence needs. Different types of markets emerged to link rural
consumers and producers and to couple the urban market to the countryside,
thus balancing (but only precariously) the needs of the various consumers.

As the greatest of the urban "collector markets" that drew grain for its
hungry consumers, the Parisian market exerted the most constant pressure
on the countryside of the *pays de grande culture*. Its first provisioning zone,
or "crown,"[90] included the producing lands closest to Paris: the Beauce,
Valois, Vexin, Hurepoix, and Brie. As the capital's population had grown
over the centuries, the provisioning net was flung farther and farther out
from the center to ensure adequate supply. By the eighteenth century, all
the grain-producing lands of the Basin's *pays de grande culture* had been
entwined in the net. A second "crown" included Picardy, the Soissonnais,
Champagne, the Gâtinais, and the Orléanais. During times of dearth, Paris
could and did draw from much farther away: Flanders, Burgundy, and even
abroad.

Numerous markets had emerged to concentrate grain produced in these
zones and direct it onward to Paris. First and foremost among these collector
or feeder and relay markets[91] were those along the major river routes to Paris.
Along the river Oise, for example, Pontoise, a town of 5,118 people in
1790,[92] twenty-seven kilometers from Paris, functioned as an important focal
point for grain traveling either by barge along the river or by land from the
Vexin français. In 1771 Pontoise's eight *marchand fariniers* (flour dealers)
reported that they regularly bought grain nearby and converted it to flour

90. On the provisioning crowns, see ibid., pp. 88–103.
91. Collector markets attracted local surpluses and exported to other places. Feeder and relay
markets performed the primary function of relaying grain shipped from other markets on to other
places. Of course, Ancien Régime markets were rarely specialized and thus usually provided multiple
services. For the best description of these different types of markets and their evolution in Ancien
Régime France, see Usher, *Grain Trade*, and Margairaz, *Foires et marchés*, pp. 177–87.
92. Jacques Dupâquier et al., *Paroisses et communes de France. Dictionnaire d'histoire administrative
et démographique, Région parisienne* (Paris, 1974), p. 583.

for the Parisian market.[93] Many other towns along the Oise, Seine, Aisne, and Marne, as well as some of the smaller rivers, similarly emerged as important distribution centers for grain shipped toward Paris, Versailles, and Saint-Germain-en-Laye. Along the Oise, other such towns included Noyon, which attracted grain from the Vermandois and the Santerre; Compiègne, which stood at the confluence of the Oise and the Aisne; and Pont-Sainte-Maxence. Those along the Aisne markets included Soissons and Attichy. Along the Seine there were Les Andelys, Vernon, and Meulan, in one direction, and Melun and Bray in the other. Meaux and Châlons-sur-Marne stood out among the other important markets along the Marne.

Rivers also provided opportunities for milling grain into flour. Towns such as Melun, Pontoise, and Beaumont-sur-Oise along the main rivers, and Dourdan on the Orge, Etampes on the Juine, and Lizy on the Ourcq, and other towns, became important transformation markets. These centers channeled grain and milled it for the Versailles and Paris markets.

Within the *pays de grande culture* itself, similar feeder or relay markets served the overland trade. In the Paris Basin, most of these markets were also located in zones of surplus production. Within a ten-league circle around Paris, surplus-producers were legally compelled to supply the capital themselves rather than rely on cost-increasing intermediaries. Elsewhere, grain concentrated in town markets. From there, it went either directly to Paris, as in the case of the nearby markets of Gonesse, Dammartin-en-Goële, and Brie-Comte-Robert, or to other distribution centers along the rivers. Magny-en-Vexin, a small town located between the fertile regions of the Vexin normand and the Vexin français, exemplifies this last type of market. As the subdelegate's responses to a questionnaire in 1775 indicated, Magny was the "entrepôt for grains from the Vexin normand destined for consumption in Paris, Versailles, and Saint-Germain." The laboureurs from the region owned or rented storage rooms around the covered market, or *halle*, where they deposited their grains and sold them to flour merchants from Paris.[94] These *fariniers* transported their purchases overland to Pontoise and then by land or river to the Parisian markets.[95] The town of Roye, not

93. "Registre des laboureurs dans le ressort du bailliage de Pontoise (29 août 1770–28 janvier 1771)," AD Yvelines, 12 B 720. Grain was often converted to flour for shipping because it was less bulky and because the Parisian bakers did business directly in the country. On the growing flour trade, see Kaplan, *Provisioning*, 339–494.

94. "Questionnaire de mai 1775," AD Seine-Maritime, C 109, n. 58.

95. "Lettre (1 mai)," AD Seine-Maritime, C 109, n. 43; "Registre (1770–1771)," AD Yvelines, 12 B 720.

far from the Oise in Picardy, also performed a similar function. A late eighteenth-century état reported that merchants "come here [Roye] to buy grain in order to transport it to the market at Pont-Sainte-Maxence, which serves the provisioning of Paris."[96]

Other regional centers, such as Rouen, Orléans, Reims, Troyes, and Amiens, not to mention Versailles and Saint-Germain, bought grain for their own needs as important provisioning markets—while also sometimes serving as relay markets that funneled grain on toward Paris—and exerted pressure around the edges of this Paris provisioning zone. Les Andelys, on the Seine, furnished both the Parisian and the Rouenais markets.[97] In the Beauce, Orléans and Paris vied for the commerce of certain grain-producing lands, such as those in the subdelegation of Dourdan.[98] Versailles drew its supplies first from the Beauce but then from as far away as Picardy and the Soissonnais. Grain for Versailles descended the Oise and then the Seine as far as Pecq. From there it was loaded onto carts for the final leg of the trip.[99]

In the countryside, different kinds of markets met local subsistence needs. In the *pays de grande culture*, local consumers usually purchased their grain at the same markets that supplied the great urban centers. Some rural-dwellers had long established the habit of buying what they needed directly from the farms of fermiers, who often paid for their labor from the same reserves. However, other smaller, elementary markets, such as the one at Chaumont-en-Vexin, serviced only local needs with local supplies.[100] Another type of market emerged in the zones of widespread rural consumption and underproduction of grain (the grain-importing regions). This entrepôt market brought grain from more distant surplus-producing regions and sold it locally. The market at Gournay-en-Bray, for example, distributed grain brought from Picardy and the Vexin.[101]

During the course of the eighteenth century, the impact of Paris intensified. Kaplan explains that, despite population growth, "Paris did not seek to draw new areas into its sphere of influence; instead it sought to make more efficient use of the available supply."[102] Some markets increasingly concen-

---

96. "Etat des marchés . . . dans la généralité d'Amiens (n.d.)," AD Somme, C 90. Other similar markets included Etampes, Dourdan, Montfort-l'Amaury, Crépy-en-Valois, Nanteuil-le-Haudouin, and Montdidier.

97. Brossard de Ruville, *Histoire de la ville des Andelys*, 1:284.

98. Georges Lefebvre, *Etudes Orléanais*, vol. 1, *Contributions à l'étude des structures sociales à la fin du XVIIIe siècle* (Paris, 1962), p. 243.

99. A. Defresne and F. Evrard, *Les Subsistances dans le district de Versailles de 1788 à l'An V*, 1:lxi.

100. "Lettre du subdélégué (6 mai)," AD Seine-Maritime, C 108, n. 327.

101. "Etat de la subdélégation de Gournay (1787)," AD Seine-Maritime, C 185.

102. Kaplan, *Provisioning*, p. 89.

trated supplies for Paris merchants, others transformed more and more grain into flour. Moreover, the government had long authorized some merchants and bakers from Paris to buy outside markets directly in the farms of producers.[103] This "country-buying" intensified throughout the century. Over the same period, urban consumers bought more bread than grain, and millers, and flour-traders became more substantial and influential.[104] During normal times, the system was vulnerable to stresses and full of risks: an unusually large confluence of buyers large or small, breakdowns in transportation, an uneasy balance between regulation and free trade. Any of these could swiftly turn stability into crisis. During dearths, even more things could go wrong, and often did.

Before the liberalization laws of the 1760s, markets lay tangled in a web of regulations that aimed to mitigate the worst effects of dearth and prevent such commonly assumed unfair practices as hoarding, forestalling, speculation, and doctoring grain at the people's expense.[105] However, an ad hoc crisis mentality had inspired the regulations that governed the trade, and a similar attitude attended their enforcement. During periods of high prices and shortages, authorities usually exercised their powers vigorously, collecting declarations of stocks, seizing stores, forcing producers to bring grain to market, and sometimes fixing prices. This enforcement was never applied with complete equality, even in the bleakest times. Officials tended to spare the nobility and other officers. Nevertheless, unevenly enforced as they were, the regulations served fairly well to reduce speculation and fraud, to force grain to market, and to slow price rises.[106] Where local supplies lacked, municipalities themselves made grain purchases in markets farther away and then sold the supplies in the local market. Driven by the desire to find sufficient subsistence and, if possible, to slow price rises, local officials entered the provisioning network. In such dealings, referred to by Clay Ramsay as an "institutional market," "shortages that could not be made good through local requisitioning were met through bargaining with the municipalities of other towns."[107] During good years, authorities relaxed

103. The best description of these monopolies is Usher, *History of the Grain Trade*. A great deal of the wholesale trade bypassed the markets completely, even during the era of regulation. Merchants bought on sample, or purchased grain while it still stood in the field. Historians have yet to analyze the actual extent of this trade.

104. Kaplan argues that millers and flour dealers increasingly replaced the hegemony of the grain merchant in the Paris market (*Provisioning*, p. 339).

105. On these regulations, see Chapter 1.

106. On the problems of enforcement in 1709, see Paris, "La Crise de 1709," pp. 199–222.

107. *Ideology*, p. xxix; see also pp. 32–35, 39–44. Of course, this local version was very similar to royal purchases either to prevent or to allay dearth. See Kaplan's discussion of the Malisset

their vigilance, because supply was sufficient and prices reasonable. As long as producers and merchants avoided obvious acts of speculation, hoarding, and collusion, they could be expected to operate freely.[108]

Official liberalization permitted larger numbers of people to engage openly and with impunity in new commercial activities. Producers entered the trade; merchants increasingly sold by *echantillon* (sample) or directly out of storage rooms. "Country-buying" (sales from farms) became more common. Merchants transacted business anywhere, anytime. Liberalization promised to change fundamentally the nature of the trade of grain and its products. However, the 1774 judgment (*arrêt*) left many issues unresolved or unaddressed. First, although it encouraged importation, it retained ("until conditions became more favorable") the prohibition on exportation, for exportation had been at the heart of a heated debate during the period from 1763–64 to 1771.[109] Second, it retained the special exemption for Paris and its *cercle interdit*–a ten-league circle around the capital within which any marketable grain had to be brought directly to the city by the producer, thus prohibiting intermediaries.[110] Third, it did not include the baking industry, thus leaving it open to regulation.[111] Finally, it did not attack the various privileged interests that fed off the trade: tolls, various marketplace dues (*droits de marché*), monopolies, and other local practices.

The Paris Basin thus displayed a wide variety of targets for food rioters. An elaborate market structure, land and river routes, mills, and surplus producers provided visible opportunities for attack. It also encompassed an active commercial environment. Towns held markets once or twice a week (a few like Bray held them every day), but the proliferation of markets made it possible to visit different ones every day. The Parisian trade, added to local or regional trade, made the roads and rivers veritable highways of grain

---

Company and Daniel Doumerc and Sorin de Bonne, *Famine Plot*, pp. 58, 62; *Bread*, 1:347–89, 2:616–18, 624–25, 630–49.

108. On relaxing enforcement of regulations, see Kaplan, *Bread*, p. 78; Afanassiev, *Commerce des céréales*, p. 18; Pierre Deyon, *Amiens: Capitale provinciale* (Paris, 1967), p. 141; Judith Miller, "The Pragmatic Economy: Liberal Reforms and the Grain Trade in Upper Normandy, 1750–1789" (Ph.D. diss., Duke University, 1987).

109. See Kaplan, *Bread*, 1:254–68.

110. "Lettre patentes sur la liberté du commerce des grains (2 novembre 1774)." The original judgment of the Conseil d'Etat did not contain this provision, but the *lettres patentes*, the form that actually passed before the Parlements for registration, resurrected the Paris provision that was part of the 1763 declaration.

111. See Judith Miller, "Pragmatic Economy," pp. 170–213; idem, "Politics and Urban Provisioning Crisis: Bakers, Police, and Parlements in France, 1750–1793," *JMH* 64 (June 1992): 227–62.

flowing in predictable directions. It was also tightly interwoven with the system of privilege of the Ancien Régime.

Privilege and the Paris Basin

The tensions produced by uneven movements in prices, wages, rents, by changing patterns of landholding, and by the menacing problem of pauperization occurred in the context of the complex of privilege that prevailed in the Ancien Régime in the Paris Basin. Seigneurialism may not have been the red-fanged, exploiting monster of earlier days, but, as we have already seen in the case of seigneurial fermiers, it continued to shape French society in significant ways. Although it would be a mistake to overestimate the extent of a seigneurial reaction in the Paris Basin in the second half of the century, and there were significant local and regional differences, many historians have marked a more aggressive posture on a number of fronts by the privileged orders, both secular and religious.[112] In particular, seigneurial interests in such operations as marketplace dues (*minage, mesurage,* and *hallage,* for example), monopolies (especially milling monopolies), and estate-management systems (such as fermage) contributed to the tensions, as criticisms of these practices mounted even if their actual incidence everywhere did not.

Entry dues and tolls confronted merchants and producers at the gates to market towns. Numerous interests also fed on the marketplace through the collection of various marketplace dues.[113] The proprietors of the dues—most

112. On the "seigneurial reaction" in the Paris Basin, see, e.g., Guy Lemarchand, "La Féodalité et la Révolution française: Seigneurie et communauté paysanne (1780–1799)," *AHRF* 242 (Oct.–Dec. 1980): 536–58; Goujard, *L'Abolition,* pp. 21–22; Dupâquier, *Gâtinais,* p. 262; Ikni, "Lierville," pp. 251–79; Albert Soboul, *Problèmes paysans de la révolution, 1789–1848* (Paris, 1983); Gauthier, *Voie,* pp. 51–62; Dewald, *Pont-St.-Pierre,* p. 232; R. B. Rose, "Jacquerie at Davenescourt in 1791: A Peasant Riot in the French Revolution," in *History from Below: Studies in Popular Protest and Popular Ideology,* ed. F. Krantz (Oxford, 1988): 141–58; Meuvret, *Problèmes,* 2:69.

Another approach to the problem of the seigneurial regime is that proposed by Hilton Root, "Challenging the Seigneurie," in his *Peasants and King in Burgundy: Agrarian Foundations of French Absolutism* (Berkeley and Los Angeles, 1987), and "The Rural Community and the French Revolution," in *The French Revolution and the Creation of Modern Political Culture,* vol. 1, *The Political Culture of the Old Regime,* ed. Keith Baker (Oxford, 1987), pp. 141–53. Root argues that the village, with the support and sometimes the provocation of the Crown and its officials, was becoming increasingly antiseigneurial.

113. The various names for these dues varied from place to place and have been the subject of several studies. See, e.g., George Afanassiev, *Commerce des céréales en France au XVIIIe siècle,* trans.

often the local seigneurs, but sometimes the king himself, or a municipality, or an institution such as the Hôpital-Général—almost always leased them to a fermier.[114] The case of Melun was not unusual. There some marketplace dues (minage) belonged to the Royal Treasury; another (tonlieu) belonged to the Bénédictins de Saint-Pierre; the executor of capital sentences collected a cuillerée (a scoop of ever-increasing size, if complaints can be believed) of the spring grain crop from every sack displayed; and the Hôtel-Dieu Saint-Jacques claimed the droit de minage on grains displayed in front of its entrance.[115] Although these dues usually weighed lightly on individual transactions, the aggregate dues could provide significant incomes for the proprietor and his fermier. For example, in 1775 the subdelegate at Noyon calculated from the registers of the steward of the marketplace dues owned by M. de Broglie, bishop, count, and seigneur at Noyon, that during the average year these dues amounted to a revenue of 19,200 livres.[116] More serious, is that these dues could also deter business from a market if they varied significantly from the regional norm. Indeed, the very location of a market was often the result of seigneurial interests, patronage, and power as much if not more than rational economic logic.[117] Many are the laments of local authorities who explained declining local markets by pointing a finger at high tolls and market dues. The subdelegate at Crépy-en-Valois complained in 1761 that the "due [of minage collected in kind for the Duc d'Orléans] weighed very heavily and . . . it is hoped for the public good that it can be reduced to the level of other neighboring markets where all the laboureurs prefer to go in order to avoid the due and the debates that ensue over its collection."[118] Similar accusations were leveled at other so-called "impediments" to trade in aspiring market towns, such as the seigneurial monopolies, especially the milling monopoly. At Dormans in 1775, inhabitants reported that virtual warfare had erupted between the agents of the

---

P. Boyer (Paris, 1894), pp. 27–28. In general, these included hallage or stellage (charged for the right to a place on the market), mesurage or minage (owed to the official measurer), and other diverse and sometimes local dues.

114. An inquiry was begun in 1761 by Controller General Bertin on the nature of the seigneurial dues collected in markets (see copy of this 4 July 1761 inquiry in AD Aisne, C 335); another was initiated by Turgot in 1775. Numerous responses have survived from the Paris Basin. See collections of responses in AD Aisne, C 335; AD Oise, C 295, C 331; AD Orne, C 1142.

115. Gabriel Le Roy, Les Maires de Melun et le pouvoir municipal avant 1789 (Meaux, 1875), p. 21.

116. "Lettre de 11 août," AD Oise, C 331.

117. Margairaz, Foires et marchés, p. 182.

118. "Etat des droits (26 juillet 1761)," AD Aisne, C 335. See also "Lettre du subdélégué de Sézanne à l'intendant (17 mars 1775)," AD Marne C 416.

mill holding the local monopoly and other millers and flour merchants attempting to market their goods in town. The seigneurial millers seized the "foreign" flour, claiming it violated the terms of the monopoly, a scene that resulted in a scuffle. The inhabitants lamented that, although already "reduced to misery" by dearth and high prices, the struggle over the marketing of flour in Dormans further exacerbated the "public calamity."[119]

Measurers and other dues collectors were visible characters on the marketplace, and in times of scarcity their exactions, culled publicly from sacks displayed for sale, no matter how slight, appeared far more threatening.[120] They also appeared (and in fact were) supremely placed, along with the sack-carriers (portefaix) and millers' aides, to profit from subsistence crises. Moreover, as merchants and producers evolved alternative means of transacting business that bypassed, legally or illegally, the marketplace, they provoked outcries of frustration and focused hostility from those who derived their livelihood from taxing and collecting from the marketplace transactions. In some towns, bourgeois, in the Ancien Régime sense, benefited considerably from the privilege that exempted them from paying entry tolls on their goods and permitted them to sell supplies in their homes without paying taxes assessed in the marketplace. Grain merchants sought bourgeois status to benefit from these privileges.[121]

In the countryside, seigneurial dues weighed relatively lightly in most regions of the Paris Basin, but they could still generate tensions, especially when leased (as part of revenue management schemes) to a fermier who relied on his collection for income.[122] In some areas of the Paris Basin, seigneurs did indeed revise their terriers (estate registers) and attempt with the help of feudistes (feudal experts) to squeeze greater revenues from their seigneuries.[123] Others attacked common lands by insisting on a division

119. What makes this case particularly interesting is that the struggle over the milling monopoly in 1775 forms only part of a much longer general struggle in town between the community and the seigneur, the Countess de Rouault. The inhabitants complained that in the 1750s the countess attempted to subject them improperly to a whole range of seigneurial obligations. They appealed to the Parlement and lost, and the struggle continued even past 1775. See materials on this case in AD Marne, C 408, 416, 587.

120. Meuvret, Problèmes, 3:156.

121. Ibid., p. 108.

122. Furthermore, as many historians have noted, these forms of estate management helped undermine traditional justifications in the eyes of those who had to pay them. Alexis de Tocqueville was convinced of this (The Old Regime and the French Revolution, trans. S. Gilbert [New York, 1955], pp. 121–22).

123. Goujard, L'Abolition, pp. 53–54, 61–62. Dewald speaks of the care with which the terrier was compiled from the 1740s at Pont-Saint-Pierre, where although the proportion of revenue seigneurial dues paid had declined considerably relative to earlier centuries (and due in large part to

(*triage*) that could lead to abolishing them.[124] Many dominated village assemblies by controlling seigneurial judges and officials, such as the *procureurs fiscaux*.[125] But perhaps the most salient feature of the seigneurial system in the Paris Basin was the way it became associated with the large, rationalizing landowners, who manipulated lands, fermes of all kinds, rents, and resources throughout the eighteenth century, and with greater flair and experience in the second half.[126]

Administering Towns and Villages in the Ancien Régime

The second half of the eighteenth century witnessed the persistence and intensification of two conflicting tendencies in the administration of French towns and villages.[127] On the one hand, the Crown continued its centraliz-

---

inflation), certain rights (such as the *treizièmes* on land sales and the *retrait féodal*, which assured first refusal on land offered for sale within the barony) were assured and expanded (*Pont-St.-Pierre*, pp. 232–33). Hilton Root ("Challenging") offers the example of antiseigneurial tension fostered by the centralizing administration of the intendants who encouraged village protests over seigneurial obligations. Donald Sutherland has said, "Just because it is difficult to demonstrate that peasants were experiencing unprecedented rigors from the seigneurial regime before 1789, it does not follow that they were receiving value for their money" (*France, 1789–1815: Revolution and Counterrevolution* [New York, 1986], p. 71).

124. The right of *triage* was a seigneurial claim to one-third of communal property if it were divided. *Triage* was an issue in Picardy, the pays de Bray, and parts of the Gâtinais (where they have been most thoroughly studied for the Paris Basin). On the nature of the tensions and the social dimensions to the problem, see, e.g., Gauthier, *Voie*, pp. 95–111; Goujard, *L'Abolition*, pp. 51–62; Dupâquier, *Gâtinais*, p. 262.

125. The *procureur fiscal* was a lawyer or prosecutor that handled the judicial affairs of seigneuries. Village administration was the subject of considerable interest in the second half of the eighteenth century. In the heart of the Paris Basin, the village *communauté des habitants* had suffered considerably (if it had ever been strong) in the hands of seigneurial officials, royal administrators, and fiscal mismanagement. See more on this below.

126. Meuvret discusses how seigneurial dues collected by fermiers were used: recycling as payments for labor, loans, seed for next year's harvest, and so on. He suggests that this was a way for a "relatively large number of consumers (either not producers or producers of insufficient quantities) to get access to grain without going through the market" (*Problèmes*, 3:25). But Hoffman ("Land") argues that there was no reason to believe these resources were not calculated in market terms.

127. On the administration of French towns and villages in the eighteenth century, particularly the second half of the century, see such general works as Maurice Bordes, *L'Administration provinciale et municipale en France au XVIIIe siècle* (Paris, 1972); A. Babeau, *Le Village sous l'Ancien Régime* (Paris, 1882); idem, *La Ville sous l'Ancien Régime*, 2nd ed., 2 vols. (Paris, 1884); Henry Babeau, *Les*

ing push into the administration of the realm. The elaboration of an administrative bureaucracy was a hallmark of the absolutist state during the seventeenth and eighteenth centuries. As French kings mobilized for wars seeking territory, gain, and glory, as they struggled to increase their tax base, to domesticate their "overmighty" subjects, and to maintain public order, they enlisted the support of an ever-growing network of servants to represent them and expanded their spheres of activity. Intendants elaborated an increasingly sophisticated network of subdelegates in a growing number of towns in each *généralité*, to whom they delegated authority on a range of fronts.[128] The subdelegates, in turn, mounted royal intervention at the local level: by reorganizing municipal governments, manipulating elections and nominations of town and village officers, and restricting local autonomy and independent decision-making by local officials.[129]

On the other hand, pervasive decentralization, conflicting interests, and policy vacillations also constituted divisive forces within town and village administrations, forces that threatened to negate efforts at centralization. Confusion stemmed from the diffusion of overlapping jurisdictions, divergent legitimizing principles underlying offices, and inconsistency in royal commitment to administrative reform. For example, subdelegates were often ill-equipped to handle certain problems because they were torn by conflicting loyalties, had poorly defined jurisdictions and responsibilities, and were far too few in number. Indeed, the state had also been responsible for creating

---

Assemblées générales des communautés d'habitants en France du XIII siècle à la Révolution (Paris, 1893); Nora Temple, "The Control and Exploitation of French Towns During the Ancien Regime," *History*, n.s. 51 (1966): 16–31; idem, "Municipal Elections and Municipal Oligarchies in Eighteenth-Century France," in *French Government and Society, 1500–1850: Essays in Memory of Alfred Cobban*, ed. J. F. Bosher (London, 1973), pp. 70–91; Albert Soboul, "La Communauté rurale (XVIIIe–XIXe siècles): Problèmes de base," *Revue de synthèse*, 1957, pp. 283–315; Marcel Marion, *Dictionnaire des Institutions de la France aux XVIIe et XVIIIe siècles* (1923; reprint; Paris, 1979). More specific works are noted below.

128. The literature on intendants and subdelegates is large. For a general survey, see Bordes, *L'Administration*, pp. 116–59; Jean Ricommard, "Les Subdélégués des intendants aux XVIIe et XVIII siècles," *Information historique* 24 (Sept.–Oct. 1962): 139–48; (Nov.–Dec. 1962): 190–95; 25 (Jan.–Feb. 1963): 1–8.

129. We should be wary about attributing all cases of centralization to a centralizing impulse on the part of the monarchy. Sometimes local officials and notables requested royal intervention. Suzanne Deck has suggested that royal influence on municipal administration was less a product of conscious centralization than a condition necessitated by what she calls "the decline of urban particularism" that called for royal arbitration ("Les Municipalités en Haute-Normandie," *Annales des Normandie* 12 [1961]: 230). See also Robert Schneider, *Public Life in Toulouse, 1463–1789: From Municipal Republic to Cosmopolitan City* (Ithaca, N.Y., 1989).

municipal governments with ever-greater jurisdictions, which included not simply some forms of local administration but also police powers and fiscal responsibilities.[130] After centuries of building, revising, and manipulating, the administrative structures appeared to be mired in conflicting claims to precedence, jurisdiction, and limited resources. Royal authority rested on a complex network of venal officeholders, appointed administrators of the Crown, seigneurs, and more-or-less popularly elected local representatives; it literally drew from the entire spectrum of Ancien Régime society for its staff. The traditional landed or robe nobility, the traditional or capitalist bourgeoisie, the artisan, the peasant, and even the lowly day-laborer found posts within town or village governments.

In towns, virtually all the possible types of offices and officeholders might coexist, and the possibilities for tension and even breakdown loomed constantly. A tangle of officials lay claim to at least some dimension of the *police des grains*: subdelegates, *procureurs du roi* (public or royal prosecutors), officers of the bailliage and prévôtal courts, seigneurial officials, town officials (mayors, echevins, syndics, etc.), lieutenants de police, and cavaliers of the maréchaussée.[131] When Louis XV's Controller General François de Laverdy's efforts to reform, make more uniform, and liberalize municipal governments in the 1760s failed to maintain the support of the king, Abbé Terray abrogated these efforts in 1771.[132] With abrogation came not stability but "a veritable municipal confusion in the last years of the Ancien Régime."[133] Some towns (especially those within the jurisdiction of the Parlement of Paris) reestablished their former administrations by purchasing and reuniting offices established during Laverdy's regime and by reestablishing elections. Others, such as Gournay-en-Bray and Neufchâtel-en-Bray,

130. See esp. Deck, "Les Municipalités en Haute-Normandie," *Annales de Normandie* 11 (1961): 279–300; 12 (1961): 77–92, 151–67, 213–34.

131. Steven Kaplan provides the most recent study of this congeries of officials. See esp. *Bread*, 1:28–29. See also Charles Desmarest, *Le Commerce des grains dans la généralité de Rouen à la fin de l'Ancien Régime* (Paris, 1926), pp. 28–30; André Paris, "La Crise de 1709 dans le bailliage de Montfort-l'Amaury, le marché des grains vu à travers le contrôl de l'administration royale," in *Actes du 101ère Congrès national des Sociétés savantes, Lille, 1976* (Paris, 1977); Ricommard, *Lieutenance*; Judith Miller, "The Pragmatic Economy."

132. On Laverdy's reforms, Terray's reversals, and what follows, see Bordes, *L'Administration*, pp. 254–322, and esp. idem, *La Réforme municipale du Contrôleur Général Laverdy et son application (1764–1771)* (Toulouse, 1968). Bordes claimed that Laverdy's intentions were "to break municipal oligarchies, suppress venal offices, reestablish elections, assure a better management of local finances, and give a certain uniformity to the administration of the cities of the kingdom." Laverdy also intended to reduce the level of intendant tutelage (*L'Administration*, p. 254).

133. Bordes, *Laverdy*, p. 277. We still know very little about the precise composition of many municipal governments or their attributions.

debated purchases and reunions until 1778 and 1776, respectively, while royal commissions "suppressed all elections and reserved municipal functions to the creatures of the intendants and subdelegates."[134] Still others, such as Melun and Noyon, neither held elections for some posts nor replaced officials when positions became vacant.[135] Overall, the experience of the Laverdy and post-Laverdy period significantly complicated the administration of French towns and cities and exposed conflicting interests as contenders for positions within the administrations vied for status and authority.[136]

In the villages the situation was less complex, but no less potentially explosive. The Laverdy reforms were not directed at reorganizing village administration and thus the century witnessed a fairly steady escalation of royal intervention in village affairs through the intendants and their subdelegates. They aimed principally at the office of syndic. During the eighteenth century, the syndic played a pivotal and increasingly prominent role in village life in the Paris Basin. Usually elected as a representative of the community of inhabitants (the *communauté d'habitants* or *assemblée de la communauté*) for a term of one or two years, the syndic served in a variety of legal and administrative capacities. He convoked the village general assembly, managed community affairs, and represented and supported his community in the pursuit of its legal and fiscal goals. Royal edicts and ordinances made syndics personally responsible for proper financial management. Moreover, intendants and subdelegates intervened more and more frequently in village elections. Thus, the syndic also came to serve as an agent of the Crown, acting both as a source of information on village affairs and as a mouthpiece for royal policy. This dual role as spokesman for and mediator between both people and state probably weighed on syndics little during

134. The king chose the municipal governments of both Gournay and Neufchâtel. Many towns attempted to renegotiate the costs involved in reunions. Turgot reduced the prices of offices that remained to be sold in order to facilitate their reunion (Bordes, *L'Administration*, pp. 322–23, 326, 328). The price of repurchase (*rachat*) for Gournay had to be reduced from 15,000 livres to 4,000 before the town agreed to pay it (Deck, "Municipalités," 12 [1961], pp. 217–18). Rouen completed a renegotiation in 1773 that lowered costs from 300,000 to 80,000 livres (ibid., p. 92); M. E. Le Parquier, "Un Essai d'organisation municipale à Rouen du XVIIIe siècle," *Précis analytique des travaux du l'Académie des sciences, belles lettres et arts de Rouen*, 1933, p. 137.

135. In Melun, elections were never reinstituted for the mayor, and the Conseil du Roi controlled appointments. However, at the time of the Flour War, the post was vacant (Le Roy, *Maires de Melun*, pp. 15, 26). In Noyon no new elections for municipal officers occurred between 1766 and 1777. By 1775 the mayor had resigned and the number of *echevins* had fallen below full size (Leon Mazière, "Du Gouvernement et de l'administration de la commune de Noyon. Attributions des magistrats municipaux," *Comptes rendues et mémoires du Comité archéologique et historique de Noyon* 10 [1893]: 291).

136. On this, see Bordes, *Laverdy*, pp. 274–77.

years when the community did not come into conflict with the dictates of the Crown, but when the community, or part of the community, engaged in some extraordinary action, such as a lawsuit or a subsistence riot, the syndic's post could become a fulcrum of intolerable pressures.

Contemporaries noted that finding appropriate candidates for the position of syndic proved increasingly difficult. Largely nonremunerative except for certain tax benefits in some places, the post did not always attract local notables. Although we still know too little about village syndics, evidence indicates that in some places in the Paris Basin the *communauté d'habitants* elected day-laborers to the post more frequently than fermiers and laboureurs. Contemporaries complained that syndics were illiterate and unable to sign community documents. Reforms of village administration began in 1776 in Champagne and were aimed in particular at prohibiting the accession of such lowly common people to village administration and at ensuring the dominance of the notables in the community in general.[137] As villages in the Paris Basin underwent greater socioeconomic polarization, the post of syndic reflected the tensions.[138]

This, then, was the status of local administration on the eve of the Flour War. National policy only had substance and force when it had substance and force at the local level. Without the support of local authorities, a national policy such as liberalization could not succeed. The administrative arm of the monarchy had long outgrown the possibility of direct control by the king. The Crown often had to rely on the cooperation of the same local elites who had previously handled local affairs relatively autonomously but who were now asked to function as representatives and enforcers of royal policy as well. Intervene as royal ministers might in the selection of local royal representatives and local officials, they worried endlessly that it was difficult to find suitable candidates who would "always begin by obeying."[139]

137. On village administration and the syndic, see the work of Bordes, *L'Administration*, pp. 175–98, 328–29; Babeau, *Le Village*; Auguste Rey, *Notes sur mon village: Syndics et municipalités à la fin de l'Ancien Régime* (Paris, 1891); Soboul, "La Communauté"; Jean-Pierre Gutton, *La Sociabilité villageoise dans l'ancienne France: Solidarités et voisinages du XVIe au XVIIIe siècles* (Paris, 1979); Pierre de Saint-Jacob, "La Communauté villageoise," in *Annales de Bourgogne*, 1941, pp. 169–202; and, most recent, the work of Hilton Root, *Peasants and King in Burgundy* (Berkeley and Los Angeles, 1987). I am preparing a study of Paris Basin village government.

138. Royal government also relied more and more heavily on parish priests and sometimes on seigneurial officials, but the syndic's position felt the pressure most directly.

139. Temple, "Municipal Elections," p. 84. On the general problem of loyalty and efficiency in government officials, see, e.g., Wolfram Fischer and Peter Lundgreen, "The Recruitment and Training of Administrative and Technical Personnel," in *The Formation of National States in Western Europe*, ed. C. Tilly (Princeton, 1975), pp. 456–561; Marc Raeff, "The Well-Ordered Police State

The previous attempt at liberalization had thoroughly underscored the unhappy ramifications of an uncooperative officialdom at the local level. [140] Now, in 1775, a fresh royal initiative encountered the same difficulties, intensified by changes in the intervening years.

---

and the Development of Modernity in Seventeenth- and Eighteenth-Century Europe: An Attempt at a Comparative Approach," AHR 80 (December 1975): 1221–43.

140. Kaplan, Bread, 1:194–214, 225–31.

Chapter 3

THE FLOUR WAR:
WHAT HAPPENED AND WHO DID IT

What Happened

In the spring of 1775 that wave of subsistence riots—known then and ever since as the *guerre des farines*, or Flour War—erupted. Disturbances raged in Paris, Versailles, and the towns and countryside of an area roughly centered on Paris and encompassing the Ile-de-France, eastern Normandy, southern Picardy, western Champagne, and the northern Orléanais. As the pioneer-

ing work of George Rudé has shown,[1] the proximate causes were a poor
grain harvest in 1774 and the inevitable price rise that followed, and the
dislocations produced by Controller General Turgot's judgment of 13 September 1774, establishing freedom of commerce in grain within the kingdom. The judgment represented the third time in twelve years that royal
policy on the grain trade had shifted radically. The state had proclaimed
free trade permanent in 1763, had shown it to be only temporary in 1770–
71, when Abbé Terray returned briefly to a modified paternalist regulatory
policy, and then, with the accession of Louis XVI in May 1774 and his
appointment of Turgot, had reversed its position again in September. Turgot
quashed Terray's work and ordered the reimposition of the Declaration of
1763.[2] Article I of the 1774 edict permitted "all persons of whatever quality
to sell and buy [grain and flour] anywhere within the kingdom, even outside
the *halles* and markets, to store it and ship it at will," and Article II
prohibited "anyone . . . from forcing any merchant, fermier, laboureur or
any other to bring grain or flour to the market, or to stop them from selling
anywhere."[3]

A hiatus of barely a decade separated one set of liberalization edicts from
another, and even less than that separated the periods of unrest that followed
in the wake of economic dislocation in a context of freed trade. The Paris
Basin had witnessed sporadic eruptions in market towns in 1764–66, but
the years 1767–68 were accompanied by a veritable explosion of unrest.
Such market towns as Troyes, Rouen, Châlons-sur-Marne, Darnétal, Magny-
en-Vexin, Gournay-en-Bray, and others that would detonate again in 1775,
were the sites of significant disturbances. The countryside of the Brie
experienced incursions by villagers into the farms of fermiers where they

---

1. "La Taxation populaire de mai 1775 à Paris et dans la région parisienne," *AHRF* 143 (Apr.–
June 1956): 139–79; "La Taxation populaire de mai 1775 en Picardie, en Normandie et dans le
Beauvaisis," *AHRF* 165 (July–Sept. 1961): 305–26; *The Crowd in History: A Study of Popular
Disturbances in France and England, 1730–1848*, rev. ed. (London, 1981), pp. 22–30.

2. On the 1763 attempt and on Terray's policies, see Steven Kaplan, *Bread, Politics, and Political
Economy in the Reign of Louis XV*, 2 vols. (The Hague, 1976).

3. From "Arrêt du Conseil D'Etat du Roi par lequel sa Majesté établit la liberté du commerce
des grains et farines dans l'intérieur du Royaume . . . (13 septembre 1774)." Turgot intended the
judgment as the first plank in a much broader platform that included not only further attacks on
traditional subsistence policies but also a radical redefinition of relations between state and society
and a reshaping of society that involved reforms in the labor market and fiscal policy. Thus, the Six
Edicts and the myriad of other decrees that punctuated the period between Turgot's appointment
and disgrace constituted discrete pieces of his general political economy. However, most of this
work lay in the future and had little effect on the outcome of the Flour War. See, e.g., Douglas
Dakin, *Turgot and the Ancien Régime in France* (London, 1939); Edgar Faure, *La Disgrâce de Turgot*
(Paris, 1961); Perry Shepherd, *Turgot and the Six Edicts* (New York, 1903).

sought grain. The rioting of 1767–68 was not as widespread as that of the Flour War, but was nonetheless far-reaching and memorable for common people and authorities alike.[4] Trouble continued in the north in 1770, but in 1773 there were widespread eruptions in the south—Carcassonne, Bordeaux, Aix-en-Provence, Bergerac, Montpellier, Toulouse, Libourne, Albi, Riberac, and elsewhere.[5] Neither state nor people were strangers to unrest, and even Louis XVI, who might better have preferred calm, chose as his Controller General a man committed to reestablishing free trade.

To make matters worse, amid tensions already simmering over so emotionally charged an issue as subsistence, Turgot chose a bad year to reinstitute liberalization. The harvest of 1774 was mediocre at best,[6] and prospects for supplementing the deficit with imports at reasonable prices were poor. The harvest everywhere was below average in 1774. Supplies would eventually come from Poland, a major source for importation to France, but too late to help distress at the time of the Flour War. To make matters worse, in the fall of 1774 Turgot had liquidated much of the grain supply purchased on the king's account during the previous ministries.[7] Turgot knew of the harvest deficiencies as early as the end of August 1774.[8] Nevertheless, he was unwilling to postpone the decree until more favorable times. Thus, he confronted an already volatile combination of dearth, high prices, uncertainty, and suspicion. And in the spring that followed the promulgation of the liberalization judgment, unrest began.

Even before the Flour War ignited, per se, tensions flared and violence threatened sporadically in various parts of the kingdom (in Caen, Metz, and Nevers) throughout the winter.[9] The frequency of disturbances accelerated during the months of March and April 1775, when scarcity struck and prices

4. The best information on these disturbances is in Kaplan, Bread, 1:188–92, 217–18; 2:453–54; Guy Lemarchand, "Les Troubles de subsistance dans la généralité de Rouen au XVIIIe siècle," AHRF 35 (Oct.–Dec. 1963): 401–27.

5. See, e.g., Kaplan, Bread, 2:497–504; H. Bourderon, "La Lutte contre la vie cher dans la généralité de Languedoc du XVIIIe siècle," Annales de Midi 25–28 (1954): 155–70; Julius Ruff, Crime, Justice, and Public Order in Old Regime France: The Sénéchaussées of Libourne and Bazas, 1696–1789 (London, 1984).

6. See Gustave Schelle, ed., Oeuvres de Turgot et documents le concernant, 5 vols. (Glashutten im Taunus, 1972), 4:45; Faure, Disgrâce, p. 226; Georges Weulersse, La Physiocratie sous les ministères de Turgot et de Necker, (1774–1781) (Paris, 1950), p. 186.

7. Weulersse, Turgot, p. 191; Faure, Disgrâce, pp. 220–21.

8. See his letter of 24 August to Louis XVI in Schelle, Oeuvres, 4:45.

9. In October, trouble loomed at Caen (ibid., pp. 229–31) and flared into violence at Metz (Weulersse, Turgot, p. 190). In December, riots threatened to ignite in Nevers (BN, Collection Joly de Fleury, 1159, fol. 198; also cited in Faure, Disgrâce, p. 233).

rose dramatically in many markets (Montlhéry, Pont-sur-Seine, Meaux, Reims, and elsewhere).[10] Trouble menaced on 15 March at Reims, the city that would host the traditional *sacre du roi* celebrating Louis XVI's coronation. The people appeared on the verge of "reiterat[ing] the pillages and excesses to which they had been led in July 1770." "Several individuals of the populace threatened and complained but created no public menace" and 200 people went to the Abbaye de Saint-Pierre to demand grain. The abbess sold small quantities to 100 people but refused to deliver any more. The people threatened to search the convent, reminded the abbess that they "still remembered the ways to enter the house," but failed to follow up on the threat.[11] In mid-April the situation deteriorated further. After an insufficiently supplied and high-priced market in Dijon on 15 April, an observer reported that "the women resolved to render justice." Three days later, riots exploded after a violent encounter between a group of women and the miller Carré, a man suspected of hoarding, selling bad flour, and colluding with a counsellor of the Parlement of Burgundy to raise prices. Rioters sacked Carré's mill, the home of the counsellor, and that of an unlucky *procureur*, who tried to protect the fleeing miller. During the same period, rioters stopped a grain barge at Saint-Jean-de-Losne and forced the merchants to sell their stock on the spot.[12]

Then, on Thursday, 27 April, a riot in the market town of Beaumont-sur-Oise ignited a chain of disturbances throughout the Paris Basin. In twenty-two days more than 300 riots broke out. These events constituted what contemporaries called the *guerre des farines*—the Flour War.

This initial and most familiar uprising at Beaumont-sur-Oise detonated in

10. See, e.g., prices quoted in J. Dupâquier, M. Lachiver, and J. Meuvret, *Mercuriales du pays de France et du Vexin français, (1640–1792)* (Paris, 1968), p. 211. Disturbances loomed in Montlhéry on 14 March (BN, Collection Joly de Fleury, 1159, fol. 186) and in Pont-sur-Seine five days later (fol. 222). Others threatened in Meaux (fol. 266), at Ervy (fol. 168; "Procès-verbal [14 mars]" and "Interrogatoires [28 juillet]," AD Yonne, 1 B 565), and at Méry-sur-Seine (fols. 171–72). See also Faure, *Disgrâce*, pp. 234–35; Schelle, *Oeuvres*, 4:45.

11. The subdelegate promised to thwart further possible eruptions by sending out spies (*faire répandre des mouches*) to discover the leaders. See "Lettre (16 mars)," AD Marne, C 414.

12. For a more detailed account of events at Dijon and Saint-Jean, see "Mémoire historique sur le tumulte arrivé à Dijon," in Gabriel Dumay, ed., *Une Emeute à Dijon en 1775 suivie d'une ode à Mgr. d'Apchon* (Dijon, 1886); P.-E. Girod, "Les Subsistances en Bourgogne et particulièrement à Dijon à la fin du XVIIIe siècle, 1774–1789," *Revue bourguignonne de l'enseignement supérieur* 16 (1906): i–xxiii, 1–145; Faure, *Disgrâce*, pp. 236–43. Although local and royal officials viewed events at Dijon with alarm, there appears to have been no connection between this disturbance and the rioting that would explode on and after 27 April.

response to the confluence of high prices, popular discontent with the practices associated with free trade, and administrative disorganization.[13] At the previous market on 22 April, a setier of *blé méteil* (a mixture of wheat and rye) had sold for 26 livres, a price that had made consumers grumble. Five days later the market appeared abundantly supplied, and consumers therefore expected a price decrease. Indeed, some apparently came prepared to force a discount if one was not forthcoming voluntarily. Several witnesses reported that even before the market opened on 27 April they had heard "the porters and women from the waterfront [some said "women of the people"] say that they would see whether grain would be sold as dearly as usual. . . . Starving or being killed [by the police] amounted to the same thing to them."[14] Thus, when the *blatier* Descroix imprudently demanded 32 livres for the same grain that sold for 26 livres five days before, the market erupted into violence.

Rioters carried the unhappy Descroix to the fountain, dunked him twice, then dragged him dripping before Nicolas Bailly (the local dean of notaries and procurators serving temporarily as lieutenant general of police) and demanded justice. To the plea that he "come police the market and force down the price of grain," Bailly replied that "the sale of grain was free at all times and that they should let the market continue without trouble." He then retreated back inside his house; the rioters, rebuffed by authority, returned to the market and imposed their own form of regulation. As Bailly watched from the safety of his window, the people set the price of grain at 12 livres per setier, drove the merchants from the market, ransacked their displays, and only then went home themselves.

The local administration offered no resistance. Aside from Bailly, only the "slightly simple-minded" mayor, Dubois, was present among officialdom to witness events.[15] Out of a brigade of five cavaliers of the maréchaussée,

13. On what follows, see "Extrait des minutes du Greffe au Bailliage Royale, ville et comté de Beaumont-sur-Oise (29 avril)," AD Oise B 1583; "Interrogatoire de Nicolas Bailly (11 juillet)," AN, Y 11441; "Supplique de Louis Salmon au Bailliage Royale de Beaumont (28 avril)," AD Yvelines, 3 B 173; "Lettre du substitut du procureur du roi (27 avril)," BN, Collection Joly de Fleury, 1159, fol. 11, and BA, Archives de la Bastille, MS 12,447; Rudé, "La Taxation populaire . . . région parisienne," pp. 142–46; Faure, *Disgrâce*, pp. 250–51.

14. See, e.g., "Extrait des minutes . . . , déposition de Vincent Boissel (29 avril)," AD Oise, B 1583.

15. Both Bailly and Dubois were arrested after the uprising and sent to the Bastille. Their interrogators suspected them of plotting against liberalization and encouraging the riots, but eventually concluded the two were merely incompetent. See their interrogations and attached notes in BA, Archives de la Bastille, MS 12,447.

only three patroled the market, one of them "aged 55 and an invalid." The substitute for the recently deceased *procureur du roi* was very old and "confined for the last two months with a major illness." Against a mutinous people in the market, therefore, there existed no effective counterbalance. Nor was there any means to prevent the rage from spreading.

The next day, eleven people from Beaumont traveled ten and a half miles to the town of Méru, stopped at a cabaret, and discussed the events of the previous day.[16] When the Méru market opened several hours later, witnesses reported that "suddenly, everyone rushed to pillage grain." Women brought knives and used them to "rip open sacks of grain," while other women scooped into their aprons the "gleanings" left scattered over the ground. Some paid 12 livres per setier for what they took; others paid nothing. The three official measurers, of the *droit de minage et mesurage* for the fermier, scraped up 2 setiers to serve as indemnity for what they could not collect during the riot.[17]

While people rioted in Méru, inhabitants from over seventeen neighboring villages descended on a grain barge moored at a mill at Stors along the river Oise.[18] The grain belonged to Jean Martin, a miller, grain merchant, and flour merchant. The rioters offered 18 to 20 livres per setier. Martin's wife claimed she had collected a total of 300 livres from the rioters, but the entire shipment had cost 19,400 livres. The same day, authorities reported a disturbance at Pont-Sainte-Maxence.[19]

On Saturday, 29 April, rioting spread up the river Thérain to the market at Mouy, while that at Beauvais experienced "a small tumult."[20] The uprising that ignited at Pontoise the same day appeared more threatening than earlier disturbances, because it involved larger numbers of people and because they

16. On what follows, see "Information sur la sédition à Méru (29–30 avril, 2–3 mai)," AD Oise, B 1583; "Procès-verbal (23 juin)," B 1584; "Extrait des pièces du procès, interrogatoire de Suzanne Mandart," B 1583bis; "Interrogatoire de Jean Désert," B 1583ter; "Lettre de Miromesnil à Versailles (10 juillet)," B 1584; "Lettre de Martin Houdant, receveur des droits de minage and mesurage à Méru (14 juillet)," B 1583ter.

17. The privilege belonged to the Prince de Conti, seigneur of Méru. Rioters also forced the fermier of his land near Méru, Claude Morin, to bring grain to the marketplace from his farm.

18. "Déposition de Jean Martin (n.d.)," AD Oise, B 1583ter.

19. "Lettre du procureur du roi à Senlis (1 mai)," BN, Collection Joly de Fleury, 1159, fols. 245–46.

20. On the riots at Mouy, see "Extrait des minutes du Greffe de la Prévôté du marquisât de Mouy (92 avril)" and "Information au sujet du tumulte arrivé à Mouy (2–3 mai)," AD Oise, B 1583; and "Procès-verbal des séditions à Mouy (6 mai)," B 1583ter. On the tumult at Beauvais, see "Lettre de M. Le Danse (2 mai)," BN, Collection Joly de Fleury, 1159, fol. 13; "Lettre des officiers du Présidial de Beauvais à Miromésnil (1 mai)," BM Beauvais, Collection Bucquet, 82, fol. 807.

sallied beyond the marketplace to strike targets central to the Paris distribution network.[21] When less grain than usual arrived on the market, thus
raising prices, Angelique Lefevre "led more than 100 people before the
lieutenant general of police" to demand that he lower the price of grain.[22]
Upon his refusal, "people from Pontoise and peasants from the countryside"
denuded the market, paying 12–18 livres per setier. They then turned to
intercept several grain carts, to raid two barges moored at the port, and to
sack the homes of six grain and flour merchants. Too few in number to
intervene, the cavaliers of the maréchaussée withdrew from the fray, while
other local authorities hesitated to take action and squabbled among
themselves. By the time they had resolved to mobilize the garde bourgeoise
(bourgeois militia) to impose order, the worst had passed.

Rioters expanded their range of activities in other ways. At Mours and
Presles, people from Beaumont and neighboring villages ransacked several
mills, as well as the homes of flour merchants.[23] At Mours, rioters accosted
the parish priest, looking for the grain they knew he stored. "People from
the pays and environs" invaded farms of laboureurs and fermiers at Berne,
Morancy, Bruyères, and Boran, searched their granaries, and paid a popularly fixed price for what grain they found. At Boran, rioters forced the
monastery of Saint-Martin-lès-Nonnettes to distribute its stock of grain.

On 30 April, while Pontoise still simmered,[24] 300 inhabitants of Saint-
Leu-d'Esserent and neighboring villages attacked the monastery and demanded grain at 12 livres per setier.[25] "In order to lessen the effects of the
sedition and to avoid the pillage of the granary and the house," explained
one monk, "we promised to employ village bakers to bake whatever quantity

21. On events at Pontoise, see "Procès-verbal du pillage fait tant au marché que sur le pont et
chez différents fariniers de Pontoise (29 avril)," AD Yvelines, 12 B 519; "Lettre du lieutenant
général civil et criminel (30 avril)," BN, Collection Joly de Fleury, 1159, fols. 216–17; "Lettre de
Miromesnil à Versailles (10 juillet)," AD Oise, B 1584; BA, Fonds de la Bastille, MS 12,447, fols.
132, 139, 308–13.
22. "Extrait des pièces du procès, interrogatoire d'Angelique Lefevre," AD Oise, B 1583bis.
23. On these events, see "Lettre du procureur du roi au prévôt de la maréchaussée à Beaumont
(1 et 3 mai)," AD Oise, B 1583ter; "Procès-verbal des séditions et déclarations faites à Mours (29
avril)," B 1583bis.
24. Mostly trouble brewed among the local authorities and resulted in a criminal proceeding
against the avocat du roi of the bailliage de Pontoise for reducing the price of grain on 30 April. See
"Interrogatoire de Charles Adrien DeSaffrey de Boislabbé (22 mai)," AN, Y 11441; "Lettre de Sr.
Forêt, substitut du procureur du roi (30 avril)," BN, Collection Joly de Fleury, 1159, fols. 214–5;
and pieces from BA, Archives de la Bastille, cited in note 21 above.
25. See "Extrait des minutes du greffe du Bailliage de Senlis (1 mai)," in BN, Collection Joly
de Fleury, 1159, fols. 249–50.

of bread necessary" to supply the people, and the monks agreed to sell it at a reduced price.

By Monday, 1 May, rioting had penetrated deeper into the Beauvaisis and beyond into Normandy. When consumers encountered a poorly provisioned market at Noailles, they sortied into the countryside to ransack two mills belonging to Henri Parent, a miller and flour merchant who traded with Paris.[26] At Saint-Germain-en-Laye, rioters forced merchants to sell flour at 20 sols per *boisseau* and grain at 12 livres per setier, invaded the storage rooms of flour merchants, and attacked bakeries.[27] Market riots also erupted at Gisors, Magny-en-Vexin, and elsewhere. Rioting becomes too frequent to mention in detail. What follows is a discussion of salient examples. Table 3 contains a full enumeration.[28] No longer limiting action to the market-place or the *halle*, rioters raided storage rooms of flour and grain merchants and the granaries of local laboureurs and fermiers. At Nanterre, rioters pillaged bakers' shops.

In villages throughout the southern Beauvaisis and the pays de France, inhabitants and their neighbors invaded farms, then searched and emptied granaries. For example, "a crowd of people, men as well as women, on foot or with horses" who visited the seigneurial farm at Mouchy-le-Châtel "entered the house and demanded grain at 16 livres per setier." The fermier recognized most of them as inhabitants of the nearby villages of Balagny, Cires-lès-Mello, Heilles, Mouchy-la-Ville, and Foulangues.[29]

On 2 May, attention focused on disturbances at Versailles.[30] Rumors spread that rioters numbering in the thousands and demanding cheap bread had approached the château itself. According to Métra, the king addressed the crowd from the balcony, speaking to them with "as much sympathy as good will." Métra claimed that this angry crowd barely listened to Louis XVI until he calmed them with a promise to lower the price of bread immediately. The king ordered that bakers sell bread at 2 sols per livre, for which they would be recompensed.[31] Abbé Georgel reported that when the

26. Even after many people had left for the mills, the market experienced trouble: "Many people wanted [grain], but there wasn't enough for everyone." See "Procès-verbal (1 mai)," AD Oise, B 1583.

27. "Procès-verbal (1 mai)," "Déclarations (3, 4, 6 mai)," and "Information (20 mai)," AN, Y 18692.

28. The maps in Chapter 4 offer a spatial orientation.

29. "Déposition de Nicolas Borde, fermier à Mouchy-le-Châtel (3 mai)," AD Oise, B 1583.

30. For previous studies of this disturbance, see Faure, *Disgrâce*, pp. 255–57; Schelle, *Oeuvres*, 4:46–47.

31. François Métra, *Correspondance secrète* (London, 1787–90), 1:341–43. This version was

crowd arrived at Versailles, guards closed the gates, alarm spread throughout the royal family, and the king's ministers proposed to evacuate to Choisy or Fontainebleau until military power could be brought to bear on the mob. Instead, the king ordered that the gates be opened and an announcement made that "the king, touched by the people's hardship, had heard their cries . . . and that he ordered that they not lack bread." The people cried "Vive le Roy" in response, and the crowd quickly dissipated.[32] Although, as we shall see, elements of these rumors found their way among the common people, actual events occurred much differently.

According to police reports,[33] no one approached the château. Instead, people from the region surrounding Versailles—some of whom had been to Saint-Germain the day before—and locals raided the Poids-le-Roy, the covered flour market that contained rooms for storing sacks of flour and served bakers from as far away as Paris on Mondays and Thursdays. On other days of the week, the market sold bread to local people.[34] Although 2 May was not a flour market day, rioters forced merchants to hand over sacks of flour that were stored there. The people hauled some sacks away for later distribution and cut others open to load into aprons. Of 900 setiers of flour stored at the market, more than half was pillaged or spoiled. Police arrived to save the rest. Rioters also visited some bakeries and halted several carts carrying flour and forced them to return to the Poids-le-Roy. Although there is no evidence that the king either spoke with the people or ordered a reduction in the price of bread, it is likely that the Prince de Poix, the military governor of Versailles, did announce a reduction to 2 sols per livre.[35] When rioters in other parts of the Paris Basin argued that the king had fixed the price of grain, they may have been referring to some of the rumors surrounding events at Versailles.[36]

Versailles was not the only event that day, however. Riots broke out in other town markets—Senlis and Etrépagny—and flared in many villages as well. At La Roche-Guyon, rioters threatened to invade the château belong-

---

repeated by Jean-Louis Soulavie, *Mémoires historiques et politiques sur le règne de Louis XVI* (Paris, 1801), 2:290.

32. *Mémoires pour servir à l'histoire des événemens à la fin du dix-huitième siècle* (Paris, 1817–18), 1:447–48.

33. The sources for these events include reports, testimonies, and interrogations in AD Yvelines, 1 B 219, 1 B 298, and BN, Collection Joly de Fleury, 1159, fols. 268–69.

34. On the Poids-le-Roy, see Defresne and Evrard, *Subsistance*, 1:lxxxi–lxxxii.

35. See Louis XVI's letter to Turgot in Schelle, *Oeuvres*, 4:417; discussions in Jacob-Nicholas Moreau, *Mes Souvenirs* (Paris, 1898–1901), 2:190.

36. For more on this, see Chapter 5.

ing to the Duchesse d'Enville (mother of the Duc de Rochefoucauld-Liancourt), but the appearance of a barge loaded with 1,400 sacks of flour distracted them at the last minute.[37] Soldiers were forced to drive away the people who threatened the property and life of Etienne Sauvage, a miller on the bridge of Poissy.[38] At Argenteuil, local authorities and flour merchants agreed to sell flour at a reduced price in order to avoid violence.[39] At Gournay-en-Bray, the seigneur, the Duc de Montmorency, arranged a brief truce.[40]

On 3 May, a major upheaval rocked Paris.[41] Around eight o'clock in the morning, people from villages and suburbs outside the customs barriers that controlled access to the city entered Paris to transact marketday business. Once arrived, they joined with locals on the way to grain, flour, and bread markets as well as to bakers. Authorities had just raised the price of bread from 13½ to 14 sols, and this price rise combined with news about previous events in Versailles, Saint-Germain-en-Laye, and elsewhere to catapult the people into action. They quickly denuded the stalls in the bread market of their goods and determined to do the same elsewhere. Only fast thinking by the lieutenant of police, J.-P. Lenoir, who ordered that the gates to the flour market be closed, saved that market from a similar fate. Rioters also searched and confiscated all edible merchandise in bakeries all over town. According to one report, the people stormed 1,200 to 1,300 bakeries in the center of the city and in the *faubourgs*.[42] Sometimes they paid the market price for what they took, sometimes they fixed and paid a lower price, and sometimes they paid nothing at all.

Despite news that rioting had already inflamed many markets very close to the capital, Parisian authorities had taken few precautions. On 2 May,

---

37. "Lettre du subdélégué à Magny à l'intendant Crosne (3 mai)," AD Seine-Maritime, C 107.

38. "Information (27 juin)," AN, Y 18682. Sauvage, or his heir, was "massacred" by a crowd during the uprisings of July 1789 (Defresne and Evrard, *Subsistances*, 1:cxv).

39. "Lettre du procureur fiscal (4 mai)," BN, Collection Joly de Fleury, 1159, fols. 3–4.

40. "Lettre du subdélégué (3 mai)," AD Seine-Maritime, C 109.

41. For events in Paris, see Simon-Prospère Hardy, "Mes loisirs, ou journal d'événemens tels qu'ils parviennent à ma connaissance," BN, ms. français, nos. 6680–87, III; "Emeute arrivée à Paris, par raport au prix du bled et du pain, le 3 mai 1775 et différentes pièces rélatives à cet événement," AN, H2* 1876 and K 1022; and the reports, depositions, and interrogations held in AN, Y 10558, 10626, 11016a, 11400, 11494, 11592a, 11705, 12185, 13127, 14824, 15384, 15473, 15869; "Blés-Emeute (1775)," Papiers du Président Lamoignon, BN, ms. français 6877. See also Rudé, "La Taxation populaire . . . région parisienne," pp. 150–56; Faure, *Disgrâce*, 259–63; Robert Darnton, "Le Lieutenant de police J.-P. Lenoir, la guerre des farines et l'approvisionnement de Paris à la Révolution," *RHMC* 26 (1969): 611–24.

42. "Emeute arrivée à Paris."

Lenoir had alerted the watch, the musketeers, and the principal officers of the guard, but mobilized no troops nor stationed any guards.[43] Only during the afternoon of 3 May did the forces of order begin to muster a more effective response.[44] Troops policed the marketplaces, and soldiers guarded bakery doors. The police started arresting suspects. By evening, the tumult had died down completely.

The same day, rioting spread into Picardy at the market of Bréteuil. At Vernon in Normandy, rioters assaulted an important grain and flour magazine called "La Tour de Vernonnet," located on the bridge of Vernonnet that crossed the Seine and forced authorities to sell flour at a greatly reduced price. As violence mounted, the subdelegate, Doré, ordered the clerk to close the doors and refuse further sales. When the rioters attacked the locked doors with scissors, hammers, and even sledgehammers, the police fired into the crowd, wounding four to six people. Far from scaring the rioters into retreat, this measure exacerbated the violence. Rioters threw stones at the windows, threatened to set fire to the Tour, and turned to assail three mills situated on the same bridge crossing. These mills belonged to the "entrepreneurs" of the Tour who also owned the grain that had been taken from the barge at La Roche-Guyon the previous day. Disturbances continued into the next day, as people raided merchants' supplies in Vernon. Even reinforcements totaling fifty men from the regiment of Penthièvre failed to restore calm.[45]

On 4 May, trouble reached several markets and villages in the Brie. The carters of the fermier Duclos at Messy drove two carts loaded with grain to the mill at Souilly. They entered Souilly at five o'clock in the morning, but before they could get to the mill, Louis Bonnefoy grabbed the first horse by the bridle and demanded grain. As one carter rose to hit Bonnefoy and drive him away, three women ran to assist Bonnefoy. They held the horses while Bonnefoy climbed up on each cart and threw down a sack of grain

43. Lenoir blamed the lack of preparedness on Turgot, who simply ordered watchfulness and alerting the watch (Darnton, "Lenoir," p. 615), but Turgot blamed Lenoir for not preventing the rioting (Schelle, *Oeuvres*, 4:428). The next day, Lenoir was dismissed as lieutenant of police, and Albert replaced him. Although the Paris debacle may have been the public reason for Lenoir's fall, most historians agree that Lenoir's opposition to Turgot's grain politics played a more powerful role in his dismissal.

44. That morning, many of the *gardes françaises* had attended the blessing of the regiment flags at the Cathedral of Notre Dame.

45. See the various accounts of these events in "Journal de ce qui s'est passé à l'occasion de la révolte qui a eu lieu dans la subdélégation de Vernon et dans celles qui en sont voisines (n.d.)," AD Seine-Maritime, C 107; "Information (9 mai)," AD Eure, 16 B 653bis.

from each. He offered 12 livres for each sack, but the carters refused to accept the money. He then announced to them: "You know me well, you only have to say to your master that I will bring him the money at the price of 12 livres like the others, or he can come get it himself." The forty-seven-year-old Bonnefoy was working as a day-laborer and woodcutter, but he was probably better known for his former status as baker at Souilly.[46]

Between 5 and 6 May, the number of riots occurring daily peaked, touching ten and fourteen markets and thirty and forty-two villages respectively. A particularly spectacular riot rattled through the town of Brie-Comte-Robert on the 5th. A poorly provisioned market catapulted a tense and panicking crowd into action. After quickly denuding the marketplace of its meager resources, the assembled people fell in behind the leadership of their "Princess," Madelaine Pochet, who then led them to the nearby granaries of large-scale cultivators on the town's edge. Maligning the farmers as *bougres de gueux* to their faces, and claiming that they "had been graced for entirely too long," Madelaine was visible to all as the "woman with the red scarf on her head."[47] The same day, in the market town of Conty, south of Amiens, the mayor reported that several women with knives had tried to split open sacks of grain for sale on the *halle*. Two or three men joined these women, and together they forced the mayor to assess the grain and distribute it in whatever quantities the people wanted.[48] On 6 May, locals invaded the *ferme* of the abbey of the Carmes Billettes at Ozouer-le-Vouglis. The monks distributed grain at 12 livres per setier to the 300–400 people who arrived to claim it.[49]

Although on Sunday, 7 May, riots disturbed only two markets (Braine and Soissons), trouble flamed in thirty-five villages. At the village of Signy-Signets, south of the Marne approximately five kilometers southwest of La Ferté-sous-Jouarre, the syndic, Etienne Alliot, delighted many fellow villagers but triggered official wrath when, at a public assembly, he ripped up a royal ordinance prohibiting interference in the grain trade and physically assaulted a laboureur from a neighboring community. He denounced the legitimacy of the ordinance and the ill will of the farmer, who had not only

46. "Information (15 mai)," AD Seine-Maritime, B 2387.

47. "Procès-verbal des déclarations contre Madelaine Pochet (18, 19, 21 mai)" and "Interrogatoire (9 mai, 11 juin)," AD Seine-et-Marne, B 3957(1); "Interrogatoire (1 juillet)," AN, Y 11441. See also the reports collected with her transfer to the Bastille in BA, Archives de la Bastille, MS 12,447.

48. "Procès-verbal (8 mai)," AD Somme, C 857.

49. "Interrogatoire de Ambroise Gérard (14 mai)," AN, Y 12997.

refused to accommodate local needs by selling his grain but also had the tactlessness to announce that "the poor could no longer complain, because the grass was growing and they could eat that."[50] A brigade of cavaliers stationed in Crépy-en-Valois encountered a "crowd of people" returning from a *taxation populaire* in the farm of a laboureur at Echampeu. The cavaliers attempted to convince the people to disband, but they stood their ground "with an unequaled obstinacy." The cavaliers found themselves forced to "put saber in hand" and "resist their outburst." The crowd finally dispersed, but not before one cavalier had broken his saber in two pieces during the struggle.[51]

Market disturbances resumed at the beginning of the week, extending to Dreux, Roye, Blérancourt, Buchy, Saint-Saëns, and Nemours on 8 May. At Nemours, south of Paris, "the popular riot was begun by several bands of women . . . [who] threw themselves on a large number of sacks of grain and pierced them with knives, while other women carried them away." During the tumult, one woman's husband joined in to assist with confiscating the sacks. She immediately pushed him away from the fray, saying, "Go away. This is women's business."[52] City authorities in Rouen managed to avoid a major upheaval on that day by a prudent, advance manipulation of bread prices[53] and by arresting several people.[54]

Rioting continued the next day at Beaumont-du-Gâtinais, Neufchâtel, Chauny, Dormans, and Château-Thierry, and at Coulommiers, Daréntal, and Bacqueville-en-Caux on 10 May. Threats to set fire to grain storage rooms leased to merchants who refused to bring grain to market provoked a panic among proprietors in Troyes on both 9 and 10 May. Proprietors demanded around-the-clock police surveillance, refused to lease space to other merchants for fear of provoking further popular hostility, and rotated night "watches" among themselves when police support appeared insuffi-cient.[55] Tensions were exacerbated by rumors that a wide-ranging "troop of

50. "Interrogatoire (31 mai)," AD Seine-et-Marne, B 2387.

51. "Procès-verbal (7 mai)," AD Oise, B non coté, maréchaussée de Clermont (1775).

52. "Lettre du procureur du roi à Nemours (8 mai)," BN, Collection Joly de Fleury, 1159, fols. 196–97; "Information: Déposition de Jean Héron (8 mai)," AD Seine-et-Marne, B 3957(1).

53. Authorities fixed bread prices in March, and then in April they exempted bakers from the monopoly (*droit de banalité*) for milling in the city mills. This allowed city officials to order that the fixed-price loaf be raised from 14 onces to 16, which may have stabilized conditions. I thank Judith Miller (personal communication, 24 June 1992) for her assistance with this problem.

54. By 8 May, officials in Rouen had managed to prepare for trouble. "Interrogatoires de Marie LeRoy et Marie LeRoux (20 mai)," AD Seine-Maritime, 202 BP 18*.

55. The subdelegate informed the intendant that Abbé d'Astrevigne, canon of the Eglise Papale

bandits, chased from the vicinity of Pont-Sainte-Maxence, [last] found in
the Gâtinais, might fall on [Troyes] from Sens."[56]

After 10 May, outright violence in the countryside apparently ended, but
trouble continued in some towns. Rioting erupted at the market of Auffay
in the Caux on 11 May and again, even more violently, on 13 May. North
of Laon, the town of Marle experienced disturbances on 12 May. In the
Champagne, a virtually empty market at Fismes on the 13th drove consumers to search houses (including the subdelegate's) suspected of hoarding
grain. On 15 May, rioters searched a farm at Argueil in Normandy. On the
18th, trouble flared in the market of Dieppe.

In the space of twenty-two days, the Flour War spread far beyond its point
of origin at Beaumont-sur-Oise. That small spark had ignited a formidable
blaze. The movement grew as word of trouble in one place traveled to
another. Inhabitants of Beaumont carried the news to Méru; at Gournay, a
gardener from Gisors related events of the previous day in her hometown; at
Magny, rioting ignited after news had arrived of disturbances in Pontoise;
and so on and on. Once lit, the conflagration spread rapidly, and in many
directions at once.[57]

Throughout this period, Turgot struggled to defuse potential trouble and
to contain and suppress the uprisings that did erupt. Concerned with scarcity
and rising prices at Reims, which had witnessed dislocations in March and
where Louis XVI's formal coronation would take place on 11 June, Turgot
moved to mobilize the *ateliers de charité* (charity workshops) to provide work
for the poor both in the city and along the route to Paris.[58] The April events

---

of Sainte-Urbaine, knew the identities of the potential arsonists but refused to reveal names on the
grounds of the seal of the confessional. See "Déclaration fait par la Demoiselle Fléchy (9–10 mai)"
and "Lettres du subdélégué Paillot à l'intendant (10 mai) (15 mai)," AD Aube, C 1908.

56. "Lettre du subdélégué à l'intendant (10 mai)," AD Aube, C 1908. These fears harked back
to the Hulan band of mid-century and forward to the Great Fear. This is the only reported rumor of
this sort to arise during the Flour War.

57. Rudé has clearly detailed this "contagion" for the Brie in "La Taxation populaire . . . région
parisienne," pp. 144–45, and more generally in *The Crowd*, p. 25.

58. A letter dated 27 April revealed that he had already granted 65,000 livres for the expansion
of the work shops and that he had just placed 40,000 livres more on account for the same purpose.
He also suggested replacing the roadwork conducted by *corvée* labor by a paid work force. Both
Turgot and the intendant clearly worried about the effects of high prices and unavailable grain on
the reception of the king during the *sacre*. See "Lettres (27 avril & 28 avril)," in AD Marne, C
414. Turgot had long worried about the cost of this coronation ceremony. In November 1774 he
had suggested that the king move the ceremony from Reims to Paris in order to save money (Herman
Weber, "Le Sacre de Louis XVI," in *Le Règne de Louis XVI et la guerre d'indépendance américaine*,
Actes du Colloque international de Sorèze, 1976 [Dourgne, 1977], pp. 11–22). In Troyes, authorities
began distributing rice to the poor and sick (AD Aube, C 1179). Turgot promised further assistance,

at Dijon that had preceded the Flour War catapulted him into action. The Conseil d'Etat began considering demands for the suspension, and perhaps elimination, of the various market fees and entry tolls (the *droits de marché et d'octrois*, which, as the property of a wide range of privileged interests, including the Crown, were not subject to the liberalization edicts) still collected on grain and flour on rivers, at the entrance to market towns, and in the markets themselves. In fact, they were suspended for the cities of Dijon, Saint-Jean-de-Losne, and Montbard on 22 April, and other suspensions followed, but too late for the Flour War.[59] Two days later another judgment ordered the payment of subsidies for all grain imported by sea into the kingdom, with additional incentives for grain transported directly from the ports to Paris or Lyon. The judgment also announced an increase in the number of *ateliers de charité* in order "to procure for the people the means to

especially to the 3,000 female cotton-spinners (*fileuses de coton*) employed in the city ("Lettre [29 avril]," AD Aube, C 1908). Rouen also received 20,000 livres for its charity work shop in April (AN, F11 1191–92). On Turgot's general plans for the charity work shops, which he hoped would ease the transition to liberalization, see Faure, *Disgrâce*, pp. 204, 229; Weulersse, *Turgot*, p. 207; Schelle, *Oeuvres*, 3:125–26; 4:46; Thomas M. Adams, *Bureaucrats and Beggars: French Policy in the Age of Enlightenment* (Oxford, 1990), pp. 132–33. On the many problems surrounding the charity work shops, see, e.g., Olwen Hufton, *The Poor in Eighteenth-Century France, 1750–1789* (Oxford, 1974), pp. 182–93; Cissie Fairchilds, *Poverty and Charity in Aix-en-Provence, 1640–1789* (Baltimore, 1976), pp. 147–53; Jean-Pierre Gutton, *La Société et les pauvres. L'Exemple de la généralité de Lyon (1534–1789)* (Paris, 1971); and Robert M. Schwartz, *Policing the Poor in Eighteenth-Century France* (Chapel Hill, N.C., 1988), pp. 172–78. There was nothing new in the idea of mobilizing the work shops during scarcity and high prices. See, e.g., M. Bricourt, M. Lachiver, and J. Queruel, "La Crise de subsistance des années 1740 dans le ressort du Parlement de Paris," *Annales de démographie historique*, 1974, p. 302.

59. Suspensions were ordered for Bar-le-Duc (14 mai), Château-Thierry (29 mai), and Lyons-la-Forêt (31 mai) in the Paris Basin. On 3 June a judgment reaffirmed these suspensions (with exceptions for Paris and Marseille) and extended them to include the seigneurial dues called *havage* that permitted some types of people (especially the executioners) to take grain, by hand or with a scoop from sacks of grain displayed on the markets. On 13 August an edict ordered that all seigneurs and proprietors of seigneurial dues on grains present their titles for examination. It appeared that general abolition was being readied, a policy Turgot actively endorsed. However, January 1776 witnessed a general reversal of policy on this front. Within the year, most collections were reestablished (but not the notorious *havage*). On these, see "Extrait des registres du Conseil d'Etat, 1774–1776," AN, F12, 6; "Arrêts du Conseil du Roi," AN, E 2512, 2514, 2515, 2516, 2517; "Lettre de M. le Duc de la Vrillière à M. de la Tour du Pin (22 avril)," AN, O*1 471, fol. 142; François Isambert et al., *Receuil général des anciennes lois françaises*, 29 vols. (Paris, 1822–33), vols. 23–24. I thank Al Hamscher for his helpful discussions with me on this subject. Precedent existed for such suspensions during subsistence crises. See, e.g., the general suspension of seigneurial dues on grain, flour, and vegetables issued by the central government from October 1740 to December 1741. In this case, however, the government intended only a temporary suspension (M. Bricourt et al., "Crise de subsistance," pp. 281–319).

afford the present *cherté* that the mediocrity of the last harvest had made inevitable."[60]

As rioting spread throughout the Paris Basin, the government took more emphatic action. Unwilling to trust entirely the insufficiently numerous and problematically loyal local police and authorities, on 4 May it ordered two armies to patrol the countryside and regional markets. For example, it took a detachment of light horsemen and two detachments from the regiment of Penthièvre to keep the peace in Etrépagny after the initial eruption on 2 May.[61] Troops guarded the capital. Although, 25,000 troops were deployed on the field. The next day, the king promised swift and severe repression of rioters and ordered the prévôtal courts to act as courts of first and last resort in all judgments.[62] On 9 May, he addressed a "call to the clergy" that outlined the official explanation of events. He ordered priests to present the state's case to their flocks just as they did other royal messages in less critical times. The official version steadfastly held to a conspiracy thesis and claimed that the disorder was caused not by "real dearth" or "excessive misery" but "by men from outside the parish" who intended to inflame the countryside and ultimately Paris itself. This call ordered the parish priests to recall parishioners to their duties, to chastise them for "having doubted the goodness of the King, his vigilance and his care," to "expose the sublime precepts of religion . . . that will assure the maintenance of order and justice." Other instructions directed parish priests to encourage their flocks to make restitution for their ill-gotten gains, to supervise and keep a record of its collection, and to denounce those who resisted.[63] And, on 11 May,

60. "Arrêt de Conseil de 24 avril"; also in Schelle, *Oeuvres*, 4:404–6. The judgment ordered the subsidies to begin 15 May and end 1 August (as the next harvest would begin). Unfortunately, even though many merchants initiated deals to begin importing immediately (Weulersse, *Turgot*, p. 193), the grain rarely appeared before June. See, e.g., "Lettre de 9 mai de Deslandes, directeur du manufacteur des glasses de St. Gobain à Hardy, premier secrétaire de l'intendance à Soissons," AD Aisne, C 68: "The grain that we are bringing from Holland is now en route, and we expect to receive it at the end of the month." Deslands also ordered grain from Russia; it arrived in June ("Lettre de 11 juin," AD Aisne, C 68). But according to the Ile-de-France intendant, Bertier de Sauvigny, the sum of 100,000 livres earmarked for work shops in the *généralité* of Paris "was less than that accorded the previous years" ("Lettre de Bertin à Turgot [25 mai]," AN, H2 2106). Seeking more money, Bertier claimed that "there has occurred neither movement nor murmurs in the parishes in which there are charity work shops." I have been unable to verify this assertion. On Bertier's attitudes toward charity, see Thomas M. Adams, *Bureaucrats*.

61. "Lettre de M. de Pommery à M. Crosne (10 mai)," AD Seine-Maritime, C 108, fol. 108.

62. "Déclaration du Roi portant attribution au Prévôts généraux des maréchaussées, de la conaissance et du jugement en dernier ressort . . . (5 mai)," AN, Y 18682. The Parlement of Paris protested this move as an infringement of its jurisdiction. See Bailey Stone, *The Parlement of Paris, 1774–1789* (Chapel Hill, N.C., 1981), p. 132.

63. "Lettre royale aux archévêques et évêques sur les émeutes avec une Instruction aux curés,"

Louis XVI promulgated an amnesty for all persons (except the "chiefs and instigators of sedition") who replaced, either in kind or in cash, the grain, flour, or bread taken during the riots.[64] Whether any of these measures, most of which were quite traditional responses to the crisis, helped end the Flour War is unclear. The subdelegate at Gournay-en-Bray argued that "the troops would not make the buyers more docile, they will be further inflamed."[65] Moreover, total calm had not returned. Throughout the summer, prices remained high while markets were unevenly supplied; disturbances flared sporadically and consumers "murmured" a great deal.[66] At the end of May, the subdelegate at Troyes wrote to ask the intendant to send troops to replace those that the celebration of Louis XVI's coronation would draw off to Reims. He was worried, he explained, about "containing a populace still very animated against the grain storage room from which is sold no grain."[67] On 3 June, troops had to be sent to Gonesse to ensure calm,[68] and throughout the month authorities in Crépy-en-Valois reported mounting tensions and occasional violence. The subdelegate reported:

> The fermentation is more lively than ever. . . . Everywhere work has stopped, no trade, no correspondence. The laboureur has sent away his threshers, no longer cultivates his lands, and shuts himself in with his servants to defend himself. The crowd of discontented people increases. The people accustomed to pillage know no other law and proclaim loudly that being hanged or dying of hunger is all the same.[69]

He reported trouble in the villages of Séry, Bonneuil-en-Valois, Chaversy, Vauciennes, and Trumilly, and menacing tensions at Villers-Cotterêts and Nanteuil-le-Haudouin.[70] Authorities reported similar disturbances in Nor-

---

in Schelle, Oeuvres, 6:437–41; see also the copy in AD Marne, C 419, and the cover letter for this circular to the bishops in AN, O·1 471, fol. 158. Turgot used the bishops as intermediaries (Faure, Disgrâce, pp. 276–78).

64. See copy of this promulgation in AD Oise, B 1584.

65. "Lettre (17 mai)," AD Seine-Maritime, C 109, n. 238.

66. Such murmuring could also be found outside the Paris Basin. François Lebrun notes that authorities in Angers reported that the people were "agitated" and that officials feared "sedition" ("Les Soulèvements populaires à Angers aux XVIIe et XVIIIe siècles," in Actes du 90e Congrès national des sociétés savantes, Nice, 1965 [Paris, 1966], p. 138, n. 82).

67. "Lettre (22 mai)," AD Aube, C 1908.

68. Weulersse, Turgot, p. 196.

69. "Lettre (9 juin)," AD Oise, C 318.

70. "Lettres à l'intendant (5 et 8 juin)," AD Oise, C 318.

mandy, and the subdelegate at Lyons-la-Forêt warned that high prices and insufficient provisions on the market were enraging and frightening consumers.[71] On 2 July, several bargemen provoked a riot at the port of Auxerre to prevent grain from departing for Paris.[72] And on 7 July, trouble again disrupted the market at Chauny.[73] Nevertheless, the presence of troops to supervise market days helped control disorders,[74] and throughout the summer the maréchaussée continued to search for and arrest people who failed to make restitution. In August, the maréchaussée of the Beauvaisis "disarmed with all the prudence possible approximately ten parishes" previously associated with the Flour War. Police confiscated thirty-seven muskets and thirty-three pistols.[75]

Thus ended the turmoil generated by the Flour War. In markets, rioters had descended on the displays of merchants and cultivators; they had ransacked storage rooms where sacks of flour and grain lay stored; and they had raided bakers' boutiques and flour merchants' homes. Along land and river routes they intercepted carts and barges transporting grain and flour for the provisioning of Paris and other regional centers. They raided the stocks of mills and religious communities. And, in the countryside, they invaded the granaries of laboureurs and fermiers as well as those of the occasional seigneur, to search for grain that had not come to market.

Protesters frequently demanded that local authorities supply grain at lower prices and engage regulations to enforce accessibility (what Kaplan has called a "pre-riot"), and only acted themselves after the police hesitated or refused to respond. For example, when the people led by Angelique Lefevre appeared before the lieutenant-general (*lieutenant-général civil et criminel*) at Pontoise "to summon him to reduce and fix the price of grain and to order the merchants to let them have it," he explained that he was not authorized to take such action. The protesters then withdrew, retorting, "We'll go take it ourselves. They [the authorities and merchants] are protecting each

71. "Lettre (14 juin)," AD Seine-Maritime, C 110; "Lettre à l'intendant (11 juin)," AD Seine-Maritime, C 109.

72. "Déposition d'Etienne Jobert (2 juillet)," "Interrogatoire de Joseph Charles Motherée (3 juillet)," and "Lettre (18 juillet)," AD Yonne, 1 B 591.

73. "Lettre de Deslands au premier secrétaire de l'intendance à Soissons (9 juillet)," AD Aisne, C 68.

74. Troops were not withdrawn from markets in the Parisian region until 22 November (Weulersse, *Turgot*, p. 198).

75. AD Oise, B 1585. I thank M. Samson for his assistance. There is no evidence of anyone, save Pierre Hamelin, wielding firearms at the time of the Flour War.

other."[76] Similar events occurred at Choisy-le-Roi, Vernon, Chaumont-en-Vexin, and, of course, Beaumont-sur-Oise.[77]

This movement thus took on the classic contours of the preindustrial food riot. Faced with short supplies and rising prices, rioters seized what grain and flour they found, distributed it among themselves, and engaged in the familiar rite of the *taxation populaire*. At Attichy, for example, rioters invaded two storage rooms and then "carried a part of it [the grain] to the *halle* to be measured" and distributed. When that quantity proved insufficient, they returned to the rooms to distribute the rest.[78] The inhabitants of Chaumes-en-Brie stopped several carts carrying grain from the market at Rozay-en-Brie. They unloaded eighteen sacks (out of fifty-six), stored them in the town chapel, and promised to sell them the following day at the local market.[79] Rioters at Méru and Choisy-le-Roi slashed sacks with knives and poured the contents onto the ground for others to scoop up into aprons, skirts, and pockets.[80] Occasionally grain was pillaged outright, but most people paid the fixed price established by the crowd or in some cases even left IOUs. The most common price, 12 livres per setier (Parisian measure), prevailed in the regions closest to Paris, while other frequently used prices included 15, 18, and 20 livres for grain.[81] Often rioters broke down doors

76. A free translation of "Allons en prendre ils se tiennent tous part la main." See "Lettre (29 avril)," BN, Collection Joly de Fleury, 1159, fols. 205–6; repeated in "Procès-verbal du pillage fait tant au marché que sur le port et chez différents fariniers de cette ville (29 avril)," AD Yvelines, 12 B 519.

77. For events at Choisy-le-Roi, see "Information (5 ami)," BN, Collection Joly de Fleury, 1159, fols. 23–24; for Vernon, see "Journal de ce qui s'est passé à l'occasion de la révolte qui a eu lieue dans la subdélégation de Vernon et dans celles qui en sont voisines (n.d.)," AD Seine-Maritime, C 107; for Chaumont-en-Vexin, "Lettre (6 mai)," AD Seine-Maritime, C 108; for Beaumont-sur-Oise, "Interrogatoire de Nicolas Bailly (11 juillet)," AN, Y 11441.

78. "Procès-verbal des émeutes arrivées pour la vente des grains d'Attichy (6 mai)," AD Oise, J (Châtellenie d'Attichy), non coté.

79. "Déclaration de Toussaint Jacquet (8 mai)," AD Seine-et-Marne, B 3957 (1).

80. "Information sur la sédition à Méru (29, 30 avril, 2, 3 mai)," AD Oise, B 1583; "Procès-verbal (4 mai)," BN, Collection Joly de Fleury, 1159, fols. 47–48. Similar behavior occurred during the *entraves* at Pontoise, Versailles, and the port of Beaumont-sur-Oise.

81. The price set depended on the size of the measure, the quality of the grain, the price paid at the previous market, and the authorities' or merchants' abilities to compromise with rioters. Sometimes prices varied during the course of the riot, as in Pontoise, where rioters started paying 15 livres at the marketplace and then paid only 12 livres for grain on the barges at the port ("Procès-verbal [29 avril]," AD Yvelines, 12 B 519). At Vernon, when rioters reduced the price they were prepared to pay for flour from 1 livres 6 sols to 1 livre, the authorities had to reimburse those who had paid the higher price ("Journal [n.d.]," AD Seine-Maritime, C 107). Occasionally, as in Dammartin, the merchants, confronted with threats of violence, set the price at 12 livres

and forced locks; more rarely, scuffles erupted between rioters and their targets or between rioters and the police.

Who Did It

Observations of authorities, witnesses, victims, and arrest records of rioters provide the traditional sources of information about participation in crowd action. If we supplement the information generated by these sources with others, such as tax records, character references from local notables, and other testimonies from police and official reports, we can further refine our picture of participation and its context.[82] From these we can not only sketch the general occupational or socioeconomic characteristics but also provide gender, age, and family life-cycle profiles of those who responded to the crisis of 1775 by rioting. The "average" rioter was a middle-aged, married, semiskilled wage-earning male or female with young children.[83]

The crowds during market disturbances frequently far exceeded the usual number of customers on ordinary market days. Although many authorities simply reported the presence of "a prodigious number of people" or "an infinite number of persons" (and most reports no doubt exaggerated considerably), some officials offered more precise descriptions of the dimensions of the problem. An authority at Crouy-sur-Ourcq explained that "more than five hundred people" came to the market on 9 May. Despite efforts to distribute small quantities to each individual, "they could only serve fifty

---

themselves ("Procès-verbal [4 mai]," AD Seine-et-Marne, B 2387). For more on price-fixing behavior, see Chapter 5.

82. Rudé pioneered our methods for analyzing participation, and the Flour War focused his earliest attention. It may therefore seem presumptuous to retrace his steps. I have no quarrel with his general observations about the preponderance of the *menu peuple* in such subsistence movements as the Flour War, but as social historians are all too aware, *menu peuple* is a highly amorphous term that simultaneously describes both much and too little. The additional sources (both quantitative and qualitative) I consulted make greater precision possible, but they must be used carefully. As noted below, one might want to present one image of oneself to the tax collector (that of being poorer than one really was) and an entirely different one to the judges who determined guilt in food riots (that of being more respectable than one really was, or more desperate). Supplications describing attenuating circumstances and character references generated to produce releases or reduced sentences also pose problems of accuracy. Despite these dangers, however, these sources can be helpful in generating information about relative occupational and economic condition, marital status, family composition (including larger kin networks), and specifics of family life.

83. Only in the region around Pontoise does this average middle-aged, married, child-ridden individual appear more frequently as a vine-grower than wage-earner.

people."[84] Estimates of the size of the crowd at Vernon on 3 May ranged from 2,000 to more than 6,000. At Marines, police officials reported that some "three to four thousand marauders" ransacked that market the same day as the events at Vernon.[85]

As for the countryside, the size of the bands of rioters (attroupements) varied enormously. Some observers reported groups as small as two or three individuals, while others counted hundreds. A laboureur at Cauffry kept a list of everyone who demanded grain during a two-day period. He counted 107 individuals.[86] Laboureurs and fermiers north of La Ferté-sous-Jouarre reported the incursion of a band of 200 people.[87]

Whatever the actual number of rioters, the police certainly arrested large numbers of people. The general recourse to the *taxation populaire* and the magnitude of the disturbances convinced many contemporaries, and especially Turgot, that the riots were directed by a conspiracy determined to discredit free trade in general and his ministry in particular.[88] As a result, the ensuing arrests were followed by intensive interrogations of rioters.[89]

84. "Lettre (10 mai)," BN, Collection Joly de Fleury, 1159, fol. 67.

85. For Vernon, compare "Information (9 mai), Déposition de Nicolas Jean François Ledoux," AD Eure, 16 B 653bis; "Lettre (16 juin)," AD Seine-Maritime, C 107. For Marines, see "Procès-verbal (3 mai)," AD Oise, B 1583bis.

86. "Déposition de Pierre Vachette (15 mai)," AD Oise, B non coté, maréchaussée de Clermont, 1775. I thank Guy-Robert Ikni for pointing out these unclassified documents.

87. "Information (17 mai)," AD Seine-et-Marne, B 2387.

88. The thesis of royal officials that there was a conspiracy behind popular movements was nothing new. The Flour War—a widespread and particularly threatening movement for the capital—provided a great opportunity to envision a plot to discredit the good intentions of the monarch and his minister. Many friends and foes of liberalization thought they saw evidence of a conspiracy, although they differed when they fingered the source. Métra blamed the recently undermined Abbé Terray; bookseller Hardy suspected the financiers of the recently ousted Jesuits and their supporters among the clergy (so did Voltaire, in his vintage anticlerical style); Dupont de Nemours, among others, indicted the Prince de Conti; and Miromesnil, a long-standing foe of liberalization while he sat in the Parlement of Rouen, accused no one specifically but argued that behind the rioting lay a "plan to harass the countryside, to intercept navigation, to prevent the transport of grain on the highways, in order to enflame the cities and above all Paris." Jules Flammermont, *Les Remonstrances du Parlement de Paris au XVIIIe siècle*, 3 vols. (Paris, 1888–98), 3:272–73. See the list in Soulavie, *Mémoires*, 2:299–300; Faure, *Disgrâce*, pp. 293–311; Rudé, "La Taxation populaire . . . région parisienne," p. 166; Schelle, *Oeuvres*, 4:51–55; Ljublinski, *Guerre des farines*, pp. 49–73.

89. That Turgot took the threat implied in the Flour War seriously was evidenced by the persistent search for conspirators that animates so many interrogations. The magistrates submitted rioter after rioter to an inquisition that, while it produced no results, indicated dedication to the search for conspirators. See, e.g., the interrogation of François Clairet, *ouvrier en laine*, accused of organizing (with other workers) the rioting at the Mouy market ("Interrogatoire [17 juillet]," AD Oise, B 1583bis; also cited in Rudé, "Picardie," pp. 307–8). Similar interrogations were conducted by the prévôtal courts at Melun and Meaux and by the *commissionnaires* of the châtelet of Paris.

Altogether police arrested 548 people for their roles in the disturbances outside Paris, Versailles, and Saint-Germain-en-Laye. In addition, they collected depositions from 447 "victims" and hundreds of witnesses.

The scale and ferocity of the government's response to the Flour War exceeded the traditional. In the past, the government had selectively danced its steps in the elaborate *pas-de-deux* between authority and popular protest, using strategic force to restore order. Ordinarily, arrests were counted in the dozens, prosecutions were few, and punishments, with specific and spectacular exceptions, were light and infrequent.[90] The Flour War, however, provoked a more massive response. The king decreed: "These acts of brigandage . . . must be suppressed, stopped, and punished." Authorities, he said, must inflict punishments according to the law, but "it is necessary that examples be made with celerity."[91] The forces of order hastened to carry out this mandate with vigor, particularly near Paris. Rioting erupted as far away as 150 kilometers from Paris, but the vast majority of arrests occurred within a 30- to 45-kilometer radius around the capital—northward to Noailles, westward to Marines, southward to Nemours, and eastward to Meaux. Within this smaller zone, the cavaliers of the maréchaussée of Beauvais, of Brie and Champagne, Melun and Nemours, and of the prévôté of the Ile-de-France made 92 percent of all arrests during the Flour War.[92]

90. Spectacularly violent punishments of the kind described by Michel Foucault were aimed at regicides, not at subsistence rioters (Michel Foucault, *Discipline and Punish: The Birth of the Prison*, trans. A. Sheridan [New York, 1977], esp. part 1). Occasionally, however, courts inflicted heavy penalties. For example, after an assault on a grain magazine in Rouen in 1752, five rioters (including two women) were hanged, and another was sentenced to life in the galleys (Lemarchand, "Troubles," p. 422). The 1774 riots in Tours resulted in twenty-one arrests. Terray, angered by the riots, demanded heavy repression and got it: three men were condemned to death, two men were sentenced to nine years in the galleys; one woman to branding, the stocks, and banishment; and one man to three years banishment (Brigitte Maillard, "Une Emeute de subsistance à Tours au XVIIIe siècle," *Annales de Bretagne et des Pays de Ouest* 92 [1985]: 31). More often, however, when judges dispensed severe sentences, the guilty party had fled the arm of official justice. For example, following a food riot at Arles in 1752, seven rioters were condemned to death and twelve to the galleys for life, but all sentences were rendered in absentia. Suzanne Pillorget-Rouanet, "Une Crise de colère des paysans d'Arles: Les Emeutes frumentaires des 2 et 3 janvier 1752," in *Actes du 92e Congrès national des Sociétés savantes, Strasbourg, 1967* (Paris, 1970), 1:393–91. The riots of the late 1760s prompted Laverdy to demand heavy sentences, but the courts ultimately returned "soft" ones (Kaplan, *Bread*, 1:219).

91. "Déclaration du Roi remettant les faits relatifs aux émeutes à la justice prévôtale (5 mai)," in Schelle, *Oeuvres*, 4:429–30.

92. The weight of repression varied enormously from region to region. Repression was most vigorous in the surplus-producing *pays de grande culture* itself or in the market towns that played a crucial role in provisioning Paris. Not only did huge differences exist in the size of territories covered by the jurisdictions noted below, but the regions close to Paris had always been more densely staffed with cavaliers than elsewhere. More discussion of the regional differences in attitudes toward the

Outside the zone of most intense repression, repercussions were much less severe and followed a more traditional pattern. Authorities ferreted out any leaders, isolated them from their followers when possible, and arrested them only as a last resort, occasionally making the arrest during the rioting itself. For example, the subdelegate at Braine applauded the way the town's maréchaussée, animated by a "spirit of detachment," arrested the leaders of the uprising and reestablished "calm and tranquillity" in the marketplace.[93] Of course, sometimes this response caused even more trouble. At Blérancourt, the cavaliers arrested the "most mutinous rioter," but were forced to release him when, "far from intimidating [the people] this act occasioned a worse disorder. The people armed themselves with rocks and sticks."[94] More frequently the police waited until after the tumult had died down, occasionally even weeks and as much as two months later. Indeed, the subdelegate at Dieppe suggested that the vulnerable police force at Bacqueville "take note of the names and domiciles of the leaders and the most bold and then go during the night to arrest them in their beds."[95] In fact, police at Mouy did exactly that. They rousted suspects from their beds and even engaged one in a chase through the neighborhood in the dead of night.[96] Some officials claimed that fear of popular reprisal for arrests kept them from arresting anyone at all. The *procureur du roi* at Chauny admitted, "While it is true that many people merited arrest, I thought the risk certain and the effect without remedy [if] these spirits, already in a surprising fermentation, were pushed to the final extremity."[97] The mayor of Conty claimed he was

---

rioting is in Chapters 4 and 6. The number of arrests per jurisdiction are as follows. The maréchaussée of Beauvais arrested 322 people; altogether the maréchaussée of Beauvais accounted for 59 percent of all arrests. Within this jurisdiction, moreover, the Pontoise market drew the most intensive repression of any place that experienced the Flour War: 28 percent (or 155 people) of all arrests. The maréchaussée of Brie et Champagne arrested 78. The maréchaussée of Melun et Nemours arrested 53; the prévôté of the Ile-de-France arrested 42; the châtelet of Paris arrested 22. The prévôté of the Hôtel du Roi arrested and tried many rioters for disturbances in Versailles (17 arrested, but not calculated into overall statistics) and carried on searches, but no arrests in Saint-Germain-en-Laye (which is outside the scope of this study). The prévôté of the Hôtel du Roi did arrest 2 other people, who were accused of rioting at a mill at Rennemoulin. The maréchaussée of Soissons arrested 7; the maréchaussée of Senlis arrested 3; the maréchaussée of Haute Normandie arrested 4; the maréchaussée of Clermont arrested 3; and the présidial and maréchaussée of Evreux arrested 11. The maréchaussée of Picardie arrested 1. The total number of people arrested was 548.

93. "Lettre (8 mai)," AD Aisne, C 13. Unfortunately there is no record of these arrests other than his statement.

94. "Lettre (8 mai)," AD Aisne, C 13.

95. "Lettre (15 mai)," AD Seine-Maritime, C 108, n. 276.

96. "Procès-verbal (22 mai)," AD Oise, B 1583ter. Searches for incriminating evidence also occurred at night. See "Procès-verbal (3 mai)," AD Oise, B 1583ter.

97. "Lettre (10 mai)," BN, Collection Joly de Fleury, 1159, fols. 40–41.

afraid to denounce any of the rioters "for fear of being exposed to their vengeance."[98]

Repression was most vigorous in the immediate Parisian hinterland, either in the surplus-producing *pays de grande culture* itself or in the market towns, which together with the grain-exporting regions played crucial roles in the provisioning of the capital. Moreover, the Parisian hinterland had always been better staffed with police than its neighboring provinces, and the addition of troops only furthered this imbalance.[99] By contrast, in regions farther from the capital more out of the direct line of the Paris provisioning system, and comparatively understaffed with police, repression was neither as swift nor as thorough. Indeed, some local officials from these regions used the opportunity provided by the Flour War to argue for a stronger police force. Both the subdelegate and the *procureur du roi* at Nanteuil-le-Haudouin argued in separate letters that it was "impossible to stop the rioting here, since we had only three cavaliers of the maréchaussée from Crépy-en-Valois."[100]

When police turned to the arrest and prosecution of suspects, they relied both on firsthand observation and on witness testimony to ascertain suspects. They sought riot leaders, of course, but they were also driven by other factors, such as the need to make a quick example, to dampen excitement, or to coerce restitutions. Among those arrested for rioting, very few denied their involvement, although they might attempt to reduce the punishment by underplaying their roles. The result was courtrooms full of people arrested for various types of behavior, from riot leadership to rank-and-file participation. Altogether the repression resulted in the arrest of hundreds, the conviction of scores, and sentences for several of the leaders ranging from death by hanging to life servitude in the galleys. Two men were condemned to the gallows, but the king later commuted their sentences: one to life in the galleys, the other to nine years banishment. The galley labor force swelled further: five men for life (plus two in absentia), three for nine years (one later received a pardon), four for five years (plus one in absentia and one later received a pardon), and three for three years. Four people received

98. "Procès-verbal (8 mai)," AD Somme, C 857.

99. See, e.g., the statistics provided by Iain Cameron for the distribution of the maréchaussée in 1790. This was after the reforms of 1776, when the force was better staffed than previously (Cameron, *Crime and Repression in the Auvergne and the Guyenne, 1720–1790* [Cambridge, 1981], appendix 1, p. 261).

100. "Lettre (6 mai)," AD Oise, C 318; "Lettre (6 mai)," BN, Collection Joly de Fleury, 1159, fols. 190–91.

sentences of three years in a royal prison (one was eventually pardoned); three drew six-month sentences, one three months, and one one month. A final person confronted three years of banishment. The courts issued many fines and probations as well as a great favorite—the *plus amplement informé*—that in this case released the suspect, but only provisionally lest more information became available.

Of course, the royal officials found no conspirators among those they arrested. Instead, as George Rudé has established generally, the great majority of rioters arrested belonged to the common people of the towns and villages in the zone in which the riots erupted, just as in previous subsistence riots. Close analysis reveals, more specifically, that certain elements of the common people were more likely to riot and face arrest than others. Table 1 identifies the occupational categories reported by rioters arrested.[101] The police arrested significant numbers of people from families of what Rudé called the *petit peuple*: rural and town day-laborers, rural and town artisans, tradespeople, and vine-growers.[102] That these groups should constitute a large portion of those arrested is neither surprising nor new: after all, these groups relied on the grain, flour, and bread they purchased for their families' subsistence.

Day-laborers—unskilled laborers (category 1), semiskilled laborers, and dependent skilled workers (cat. 2), such as journeymen in most trades who depended on wages to sustain them—constituted the largest cluster of rioters arrested: 30.3 percent of the total. Already victims of the disadvantageous movements in food prices and wages of the second half of the eighteenth century, these urban and rural groups were extremely sensitive to dramatic shifts in grain prices or accessibility, since they had to purchase what they ate.[103] In some towns, participation reflected the occupational structure of dominant local industries. Thus, in towns like Mouy, one of the largest woolen industrial centers in the Beauvaisis, the *ouvriers en laine* (wool

---

101. Using arrests as indications of participation in riots requires care. Confronted with far more rioters than even massive forces could detain, the limited forces of the maréchaussée had to make a selection even while carrying out a large-scale roundup. Their choices revealed their assumptions about who did and did not constitute a serious deterrent to the restoration of order. Nonetheless, these arrest records, when supplemented with other types of information—witness testimony, interrogation records—and placed in the larger context of social structures (from tax records, e.g.), can, as Rudé argued long ago, provide insight into the nature of participation and ultimately its significance.

102. For Rudé's description of Flour War participants, see "La Taxation populaire . . . région parisienne," pp. 174–75; idem, "Picardie," p. 325; idem, *Crowd*, pp. 205–9.

103. On movements in prices and wages, see Chapter 2.

Table 1. Occupations of Rioters Arrested

	Occupations[a]	No. of Rioters	Percent of Total
1.	Unskilled day-laborers	78	14.2
2.	Semiskilled & dependent skilled laborers	88	16.1
3.	Artisans/independent crafts (except milling, baking, etc.)	80	14.6
4.	Merchants/service (except grain/flour merchants, etc.)	30	5.5
5.	Innkeepers/publicans	9	1.6
6.	Vine-growers (rioted in Pontoise, 89 [16.3%]; rioted elsewhere, 55 [10.0%])	144	26.3
7.	Rural propertied groups (except vine-growers)	7	1.3
8.	Officials/notables	32	5.8
9.	Grain/flour traders/bakers/millers (including their workers)	17	3.1
10.	Others	8	1.5
11.	Unknown	55	10.0
	Total	548	100.0

Note: This table includes all rioters arrested outside Paris, Versailles, and Saint-Germain-en-Laye. See Appendix 1 for a specific breakdown of occupations for each category used.

[a] While male occupations can be documented in fairly straightforward ways, female and children's occupations pose problems because of their subordinate legal status and a legal system that focused on male heads of households whenever possible. I determined women's and children's occupations in two ways. I used their own designation of occupation wherever possible, and where that data was unavailable I relied on information about husband's and father's occupations.

workers) or *compagnons sergers* (journeymen serge-makers) predominated, or the *compagnons de la rivière* (river workers) at Saint-Leu-d'Esserent along the Oise River. In the villages of the *pays de grande culture*, agrarian day-laborers played similarly visible roles.

A close look at the occupations of the theoretically independent (i.e., those who ordinarily did not have to work for others) groups of artisans (cat. 3) and merchants (cat. 4), which together formed 20.1 percent of those arrested in the wake of the Flour War, reveals certain similarities between their conditions and those of the rural and town day-laborers. On the whole, those from these two categories who were arrested belonged to the lower occupational rungs of the common people. Moreover, we must doubt that economic independence was actually possible for many who had to supplement their craft with wage labor or for those whose trade was subject to the vagaries of the market for contract services. For example, one rioter declared his profession as a turner (*tourneur*) to the judges, but his tax roll recorded him as a day-laborer.[104] Jacques Rimbault was arrested for rioting in his village of Coubert and at the market of Brie-Comte-Robert. He reported his occupation as butcher (*boucher*) to the judges. The 1774 *taille* roll listed him as *petit boucher*, and he paid a tax of 8 livres 8 sols. The tax roll also indicated that the only other butcher in town, Thiabot, paid more than seven times as much in tax as Rimbault.[105] Ambroise Vivier testified he was a buckle merchant, and his *taille* roll substantiated this. Nevertheless, he paid a mere 2 livres in *taille* in 1774, a tax that situated him among the manouvriers, some of whom even paid more. Indeed, he earned less from his "industry" than many of his day-laborer neighbors.[106] Those who worked under contractual conditions included masons, quarrymen, and others involved in the construction business.[107] Although five blacksmiths, three horse merchants, a mercer, and one wig-maker were arrested, more numerous were the masons, sawyers, used clothes and shoe sellers, and even a traveling rat-poison seller. Moreover, this very vulnerability made them more dependent on collective survival nets (rooted in a range of social networks) and therefore inclined to communal solutions, such as rioting, to address their distress (see Chapter 5).

Innkeepers and publicans (cat. 5) played crucial roles in disturbances and were well placed to do so. Their shops were bastions of male sociability, and often they themselves were local celebrities. The wool workers at Mouy assembled in the Cabaret d'Egypte to plot "sedition" before the market opened on 29 April. The Pontoise publican, Peronard, let rioters store grain in his house, and his counterpart at Lizy-sur-Ourcq, Donna Jacquinot, incited women to attack a local merchant's storage room on 5 May and, two

104. Thus, the 1774 *taille* roll for Etienne Rénard, the professed *tourneur*, takes no substantive note of his artisanal status. Compare "Interrogatoire de 7 mai," AD Seine-et-Marne, B 3957(1); "Rôle de taille de Chevry, 1774," AN, Z1G 361a.

105. "Interrogatoire de 9 mai," AD Seine-et-Marne, B 3957(1); "Rôle de taille de Coubert, 1774," AN, Z1G 361a.

106. "Sentence (22 septembre)," AD Oise, B 1583; "Rôle de taille de Montsoult, 1774," AN, Z1G 360a.

107. I have been as generous as possible in attributing independent status to all those arrested who indicated artisanal and merchant occupations to their judges, yet tax records belie some of their assertions. Of course, in each source the individual pressed to present a very different image of himself or herself and thus must be treated carefully. Despite these opposing tendencies (to demonstrate either respectability or absolute destitution before the judges, and to claim penury before the tax collector), these sources can be usefully compared (after all, neither judge nor tax collector was stupid).

days later, urged the people assembled to ignore an ordinance of 7 May, which he styled as "nothing, [since] it has not been signed."[108] Indeed, innkeepers and publicans were often well informed about the nature of the grain trade, since merchants and producers relied on auberges and taverns for rest and for doing business.[109] Yet even among *cabaretiers*, degrees of independence varied tremendously. For example, Louis Thibault told inter-rogators that he was a taverner and vine-grower in his village of Chaton in the parish of Vendrest. Police authorities who arrested him and sought evidence against him declared him a day-laborer.[110] Many microproprietor vine-growers sold small quantities of their wine to neighbors as a way of supplementing their income. Many also worked "off-season" as day-laborers or protoindustrial workers, a source of income that could be more remuner-ative and more essential to family survival than their vineyard.

Vine-growers (cat. 6) represented the single largest category of rioters arrested—26.3 percent of the total. Although this proportion is skewed by the disproportionately large number of arrests that followed the disturbances at Pontoise, a town situated in the heart of the *pays de vignoble* and of central importance to the Parisian provisioning network, vine growers still occupied an important place among the arrested. As dependent as day-laborers on the grain, flour, or bread they purchased, vine-growers were equally vulnerable to fluctuations in the supply and price of grain. But their purchasing power depended on the vagaries of the wine market, the size of their holdings, and, for many, on rents. Thus, the vine-growers arrested represented a diverse economic spectrum in their communities.[111] Some, for example, lived the life of Jean Lavisse, who claimed when he was arrested for rioting in the village of Ully-Saint-Georges that he was a vine-grower, but whose tax roll revealed him to be "poor" in 1775 and subject to no tax at all.[112] Compare the relative standing of two men from Dieudonne in the Beauvaisis. Philibert Vaast declared himself a vine-grower to the magistrates, and his 1773 *taille* roll confirms that testimony. Yet he owned less vineyard,

108. On Mouy, see "Procès-verbal (22 mai)," AD Oise, B 1583ter; on Peronard, see "Interroga-toire (25 septembre)," AD Oise, B 1584; on Jacquinot, see "Interrogatoire (24 mai)," AD Seine-et-Marne, B 2387.

109. Meuvret, *Problèmes*, 3:107–8.

110. "Interrogatoire (14 mai)" and "Information (7 mai)," AD Seine-et-Marne, B 2387.

111. On the varied status of vine-growers, see Lachiver, *Vin*, pp. 434–41, and most recently, Beaur, *Le Marché foncier*, pp. 128, 178–79.

112. "Interrogatoire (n.d.)," AD Oise, B 1583. On the 1775 *taille* roll for his village of Cires-lès-Mello, he was listed as "pauvre" (AD Oise, C 524ter).

less property in general, and paid less than half the tax that François Vaast, who declared himself a day-laborer in the same village, did.[113] At the other extreme, sixty-two-year-old Guillaume Berenger ranked in the top 10 percent of taxpayers in his village of Cergy near Pontoise. He owned vines and arable land and leased even more land, but may not have produced enough grapes or grain for assured subsistence.[114] As one cavalier reported of events in a community of vine-growers, Cergy, "if we had to arrest everyone involved in the Flour War, we would have to arrest the entire community."[115]

Standing between hostile camps of rioters and merchants and producers, local authorities and notables (cat. 8) clearly occupied pivotal positions during subsistence crises. Driven by the responsibility to uphold royal policy, burdened by the expectations of their neighbors that they would also protect or advance the positions of their communities, and hopeful of shielding themselves from criticism while simultaneously protecting their private interests, they faced a confusing, conflicted, and tense situation at best. Moreover, as during earlier subsistence movements of the late 1760s and early 1770s, many local officials genuinely opposed liberalization on principle.

That some local authorities proved unequal to the test seems to have been inevitable, and during the Flour War thirty-two of them crossed this torturous line of duty and got caught, accounting for 5.8 percent of all arrests. Although we have no precise statistics about the numbers of officials among the overall population, their presence among the apprehended may approximate their general representation in the adult population in the eighteenth century. Certainly it constituted a symbolically significant level of activity, whatever the precise numbers and percentages involved.[116]

Given the symbolic importance of their behavior during civil unrest, local

---

113. "Interrogatoire de Philbert Vaast (1 mai)" and "Interrogatoire de François Vaast (n.d.)," AD Oise, B 1583bis. Compare these with the tax roll for repairs to the church at Dieudonne (1773), which reports 1773 *taille* tax and taxable property (AD Oise, C 472).

114. On Berenger, compare "Interrogatoire (20 septembre)," AD Oise, B 1584, and "Rôle de taille de Cergy, 1773," AD Yvelines, C 184, n. 85. Berenger owned 3 arpents of vines, 3 arpents of arable land, and rented 3⅓ arpents of land of unknown cultivation. Lachiver calculates that a vine-grower needed 2–3 arpents of vines to break even during an average year (*Vin*, p. 331). A grain cultivator needed at least 10 arpents of land. Compare ibid., p. 331, and Florence Gauthier, *La Voie paysanne dans la Révolution française. L'Exemple picard* (Paris, 1977), p. 32.

115. "Procès-verbal (5 septembre)," AD Oise, B 1583.

116. Kaplan appears to take this view, as he provides considerable evidence of the defection of local authorities from royal policy during the first period of liberalization (*Bread*, 1:220–28). His evidence is purely descriptive; he provides no statistics about arrests.

officials' behavior attracted scrutiny from all quarters. When, for example, they crossed over as individuals acting alone rather than as a body of officials acting together, they faced the certain angry denunciation of fellow authorities and the penetrating investigation of the state.[117] As officials charged with enforcing state policy, they ran a more serious risk of arrest than others (except only the most notorious leaders); as highly visible members of their communities, they had small chance of avoiding it. Accusations against individual local authorities and notables overwhelmingly resulted in arrest and prosecution. Those arrested came from a range of posts and levels of notability, such as Bailly, the temporary lieutenant general of police; Dubois, the mayor at Beaumont-sur-Oise; Boislabbé, the procureur du roi at Pontoise; seven parish priests; six village syndics (including the rowdy Alliot from Signy-Signets); a procureur fiscal; and several gamekeepers. All except the gamekeepers not only faced the local investigation reserved for the common rioter but also confronted more thorough interrogation in the Bastille.[118]

While millers, bakers, and grain and flour merchants (cat. 9) attracted much of the rage of the subsistence riot, some also knew how to take advantage of their situation during a crisis. Jean Mercier, a miller who leased the mill de Moineaux from the Prince de Conti at Mouy, sent his carters, mill guards, and milling assistants (chasseurs du moulin) to the market of Mouy on 29 April, where ordinarily they collected and transported grain destined for the mill after purchase. This time they helped themselves to sacks of grain abandoned or reduced in price by sellers frightened by the tumult.[119] The blatier, Brunet, sought a good opportunity for later profits when he joined rioters in the assault on a barge moored at Pontoise the same day.[120]

Among these categories of rioters, the rural propertied (cat. 7), appear underrepresented (only 1.3 percent of total arrested) among those arrested. Although they attracted the attention of authorities, victims, and witnesses, they rarely suffered arrest. For example, an official reported that "among the seditious" at Meaux "there were well-off people [des gens aisés], who already

---

117. Chapter 5 explores more fully the ways officials could slip over the line that separated full compliance with liberalization from resistance to it and emerge unscathed.

118. BA, Archives de la Bastille, MS 12,447.

119. "Procès-verbal (6 mai)," AD Oise, B 1583ter. On the mill, see Comte de Luçay, Angy-en-Beauvaisis. Son histoire, ses privilèges, sa prévôté royale (Senlis, 1876), p. 65.

120. "Procès-verbal (25 septembre)," AD Oise, B 1584.

had grain enough for subsistence and who arrived with horses and carts and audaciously demanded grain at the same price" as everyone else.[121] The subdelegate at Gisors observed: "In the number of rioters there were well-off and well-known people."[122] A fermier near Charmentray reported that, among the rioters who visited his farm, there were "well-off peasants, even those *petits laboureurs* called *harquotiers* [sic]."[123] Pierre Vachette, laboureur, fermier, and *receveur* at Cauffry in the Clermontois reported that the widow Jean Baptiste Bricogne came to his farm seeking grain, "and she even has enough grain in her granaries for her family's subsistence until the harvest."[124] The *taille* roll from her village indicated that she paid the highest tax in her community.[125] Others who testified before the police noted many other *petits fermiers*, *petits laboureurs*, and *haricotiers* among the rioters.[126] Despite their low representation among the arrested, this evidence underscores the important participation of the small- and medium-sized landed proprietor and landholder in the riots, a group occupying the middle ground between the day-laborers, artisans, and merchants, who rioted in much larger numbers, and the large-scale producers, who were their victims.[127]

A final group not shown in Table 1—the poor—deserves mention for its ambiguous place in the 1775 crisis. On the one hand, subsistence riots were indeed the domain of the poor, the near poor, and the potentially poor, or those who believed they were being denied what they were entitled to: the primary item of survival, bread. On the other hand, the poor as a quasilegal category (such as those who paid no tax, or who paid the tax of 6 deniers symbolic of poverty in the eighteenth century, or the homeless who were described as homeless, *sans feu ni lieu*) were virtually absent both from arrest

121. "Lettre (11 mai)," AD Seine-et-Marne, B 2387.

122. "Lettre (16 mai)," AD Seine-Maritime, C 109, n. 32.

123. "Plainte du Sr. Courtier, fermier des Incurables (5 mai)," BN, Collection Joly de Fleury, 1159, fols. 125–30.

124. "Procès-verbal (9 mai)," AD Oise, B non coté, bailliage de Clermont, maréchaussée, 1775.

125. "Rôle de taille de Mogneville, 1775," AD Oise, C 519.

126. See, e.g., "Mémoire de Jean Crapard, fermier à Pontault (5 mai)," BN, Collection Joly de Fleury, 1159, fols. 203–4; "Déposition de Jean Philippe Gillet, laboureur à Pierre-Levée (12 mai)" and "Déposition de Denis Eustache Billion, laboureur à Jouarre (12 mai)," AD Seine-et-Marne, B 2387; "Déclaration de Nicolas Borde fermier de la ferme seigneuriale de Mouchy-le-Châtel (3 mai)," AD Oise, B 1583.

127. For more on the explanation for their presence, see Chapters 1 and 6. Why police arrested so few in light of so much testimony of their participation is unclear. Officials undoubtedly believed they were less of a threat to public order than the historically more disorderly common people, yet their presence in Flour War crowds could also have appeared more threatening because it was less expected.

records and from witness and victim accounts of the disturbances. Although there are isolated images of obviously poor participants, such as that of seventy-year-old Madeleine Grandée, a day-laborer's widow scooping up two hatfuls of grain scattered on the ground after the assault on a barge on the river Oise near Beaumont-sur-Oise, there is virtually no evidence of their direct involvement in the rioting.[128] We need to account for this, because it seems to fly in the face of evidence of growing poverty in the eighteenth century.

One approach explains the absence of the poor among food rioters by noting their notorious passivity, their seeming willingness to accept their fate—their grinding misery—without protest. This "culture of poverty" was characterized by submissiveness, "a psychology of acceptiveness" that blocked the possibility of self-generated positive action.[129] Thus, the argument goes, the poor did not riot because they did not share in the culture that saw benefit in collective action. Persuasive though it might be, this approach fares ill against mounting evidence of activism among some of the Ancien Régime poor. Some activity constituted criminal behavior such as theft, but other forms of "everyday resistance" and collective action generated considerable political concern in the eighteenth century.[130] The "culture of poverty" approach is thus an unconvincing explanation for the absence of poor in food riots.

Indeed, the eighteenth century was obsessed with the problem of the poor: they were growing in number; some were legitimately poor, but most were shirkers; some should be helped, but most warranted repression.[131]

128. "Interrogatoire (18 mai)," AD Oise, B 1583ter.

129. Jeffry Kaplow, especially, has developed this point in his *Names of Kings: The Parisian Laboring Poor in the Eighteenth Century* (New York, 1972), pp. 153–70.

130. For the most systematic study of "everyday resistance" but in a region remote from France, see James Scott, *Weapons of the Weak: Everyday Forms of Peasant Resistance* (New Haven, 1985). Closer to the Flour War, see Thompson, "Patrician Society, Plebian Culture," *JSH* 7 (Summer 1974): 382–405; Eric Hobsbawm, *Primitive Rebels* (Manchester 1959), for England; Olwen Hufton, *The Poor of Eighteenth-Century France* (Oxford, 1974), and Arlette Farge, *Vie Fragile* (Paris, 1986), for France. See also the suggestive work of David Garrioch, *Neighborhood and Community in Paris, 1740–1790* (Cambridge, 1986).

131. As historians have long noted, despite real physical evidence of poverty (such as actual deprivation and starvation) that seems to transcend time and place, definitions of poverty also depend largely on perspective and are thus social constructs. On the problems of defining the poor and official attitudes toward the poor, see, e.g., Jean-Pierre Gutton, *La Société et les pauvres* (Paris, 1971); Harry C. Payne, "Pauvreté, Misère, and the Aims of Enlightened Economics," *Studies on Voltaire and the Eighteenth-Century* 154 (1976): 1581–92; Olwen Hufton, "Towards an Understanding of the Poor in Eighteenth-Century France," in *French Government and Society, 1500–1850: Essays in Memory of Alfred Cobban*, ed. J. F. Bosher (London, 1973), pp. 145–65; idem, *The Poor of Eighteenth-Century France*; Robert M. Schwartz, *Policing the Poor in Eighteenth-Century France* (Chapel

Everyone assumed that a dangerously thin line divided poverty and crime. The Physiocratically minded admitted that, bad harvests aside, prices would rise with liberalization and that this might pose a problem for the poor and those on the margins. So it comes as no surprise that the poor generated considerable concern in 1775. As we have already seen, Turgot planned a more extensive system of *ateliers de charité* for the long term and he had moved quickly to assist cities like Reims, Rouen, and Troyes as they worked through efforts to offer their poor aid in the form of work and food. Other towns also offered official sympathy, and sometimes support, as the crisis worsened in April and May. For example, the subdelegate at Villers-Cotterêts explained: "What excites the most general consternation is that the miserable (*malheureux*), that is, the poor who are ashamed to beg (*le pauvre honteux*), remain denuded of all resources."[132] During the Flour War, such towns as Marle, Gournay-en-Bray, and Argenteuil attempted to provide some kind of assistance for those they deemed the worthy poor.[133] This dose of charity and poor relief may be one reason that the poor were so rarely among rioters.[134] Moreover, the combination of charity and repression the state reserved for its poor may have served not only to neutralize them but also to fragment them so that they were unable to maintain the kinds of networks that fostered or made collective action possible. Consequently, the poor found themselves isolated from other communities by a variety of barriers: by the polarization between rich and poor, the high and the humble; by the stigma of moral denigration as poor and thus wicked or unworthy; by society's fear of them as vagabonds and criminals bred by

---

Hill, N.C., 1988); Adams, *Bureaucrats*. For a general description of ways of defining the poor, see Amartya Sen, *Poverty and Famines: An Essay on Entitlement and Deprivation* (Oxford, 1981), esp. chap. 2, "Concepts of Poverty."

132. "Lettre (4 mai)," AD Aisne, C 13.

133. On Marle, see "Lettre (6 mai)," BN, Collection Joly de Fleury, 1159, fol. 110; on Gournay-en-Bray, where the Duc de Montmorency made a grand gesture of seigneurial paternalism, see "Lettre (3 mai)," AD Seine-Maritime, C 109; on Argenteuil, "Lettre (4–5 mai)," BN, Collection Joly de Fleury, 1159, fols. 3–4.

134. The poor had traditionally commanded the concern of authorities confronting subsistence crises. Previous crises had mobilized massive efforts to alleviate the suffering of the poor. See, e.g., the attempts of authorities and church described by Bondois for 1662 and Boislisle for 1709: P.-M. Bondois, "La Misère sous Louis XIV: La Disette de 1662," *Revue d'histoire économique et sociale* 12 (1924): 53–118; A.-M. Boislisle, "Le Grand Hiver et la disette de 1709," *Revue des questions historiques* 73 (1903): 442–506, 74 (1903): 486–542. Bohstedt argues that in Devon the "country's relief program was specifically designed to aid [and] forestall potential rioters without stigmatizing them as paupers" (*Riots and Community Politics in England and Wales, 1790–1810* [Cambridge, 1983], p. 40). He notes that few people described as poor participated in food riots during the 1790–1810 period in Devon (ibid., p. 39).

poverty. Even more destructive of potential solidarity, the poor found themselves separated from each other by despair, competition for scarce resources, and police surveillance determined to break up bands or gangs, of potentially disorderly poor. This isolation precluded, as it was meant to, the solidarity among themselves and between them and others that might have molded the backbone of collective behavior.[135]

Another possible reason for the absence of the poor from riot reports lies in the role other active rioters played in providing for them themselves. The pattern of slashing sacks and scattering grain over the ground for others (like Madeleine Grandée) to scoop up made grain accessible to those who could not even afford grain at the "just price." This behavior thus made the role of the poor a mere secondary or accessory part and rarely worthy of repression.

Finally, authorities combined their precautions to provide for those they defined as the honest poor with a conscious decision to shield them from repression. Miromesnil, Garde de Sceaux, set the tone when he told the maréchaussée of Beauvais to differentiate between "those incapable of making restitution" and "those who rioted without being motivated by need."[136] The cavaliers responded by indicting only those they designated as "well-off" or "at ease" (aisé) in their reports. Admittedly, the cavaliers of the maréchaussée saw poverty in relative terms, and from their perspective— as a body recruited from the lower ranks of the common people themselves and paid very little—the poor were a very small segment of those who may have had actual claims to poverty, if need were the only test. Nevertheless, such clemency accorded even this narrow category of people helps to account for their virtual absence from the ranks of the arrested.

Middle-aged working men and women with family responsibilities that included young children formed the majority of rioters arrested. They thus occupied a stage in family life-cycle that made their vulnerable relationship to the food supply even more precarious. The average age of all men arrested was 38.4 years; for women it was 40.1.[137] Most were married.[138] And

---

135. For more on this, see Chapter 5.

136. "Lettre (10 juillet)," AD Oise, B 1584.

137. Ages are known for 83.3 percent of all men arrested and for 95.7 percent of all women arrested. Median ages are 38 for men and 41.5 for women. Compare these results with the figures of Rudé, who calculated that the average age of men arrested was 30 (Crowd in History, p. 209).

138. Marital status is known for 100 percent of the women, among whom 67.7 percent were married. Marital status is known for only 41 percent of the men, a difference that reflects the concern of police and judges to locate women specifically within their familial structures but also the tendency to view men as autonomous individuals (they simply did not ask men whether they

significant numbers were members of families that included dependent persons: the young, the sick or disabled, the elderly.[139]

Women provide the most classic cases. For example, thirty-eight-year-old, pregnant Marguerite Chapelain, wife of a journalier and mother of two, admitted that she had come to the market at Choisy-le-Roi with her eighteen-month-old child and had laid the baby on some grass while she scooped up grain scattered over the ground.[140] The police reported that the forty-eight-year-old wife of a shoemaker, Marguerite Cithère, arrested for rioting at the market of Pontoise, had "8 or 9 children."[141] The twenty-seven-year-old widow of a vine-grower near Pontoise, Marie Anne Laroche, supported "a sick child and an over-eighty-year-old father."[142]

Men also carried familial burdens, sometimes in ways remarkably similar to women. The forty-year-old journeyman serge-weaver at Mouy, Michel Biet, had "six young children."[143] Forty-year-old Jean Louis Lamy, a vine-grower at Vauréal near Pontoise, had been a widower for two years and had four children.[144] And the twenty-three-year-old day-laborer Jean Petitfrère explained that "his father was dead and he lived alone with his mother, his brother and sister were married, and had very little to get by on with his mother."[145] At the age of thirty, the carter Pierre Leguay supported a blind father as well as a large family at Noisy-sur-Oise.[146]

Thus, family obligations focused and directed the involvement of both women and men in the Flour War, a characteristic of riot participants that enables us to refine further our understanding of their relationship to the subsistence question. They rallied to defend their vulnerable family econo-

---

were married, as they always did women). Among the men whose marital status is known, 67.4 percent were married.

139. Judges never asked this question. Rioters sometimes provided such information as part of a defense. More frequently, attestations by parish priests or other village notables often underscore familial responsibilities. We must be wary of this evidence because defenders of the arrested no doubt hoped that evidence of such "extraneous" circumstances would work in favor of the accused. Nevertheless, such information is useful if it is corroborated by such other data as age and marital status.

140. "Procès-verbal (11 mai)," "Supplique (12 mai)," and "Interrogatoire (13 mai)," AN, Y 18682.

141. "Interrogatoire (n.d.)," AD Oise, B 1584.

142. "Interrogatoire (29 septembre)," AD Oise, B 1584.

143. "Attestation du curé et sindic (17 juillet)," AD Oise, B 1583bis.

144. "Attestation pour Jean Louis Lamy (n.d.)," AD Oise, B 1584.

145. "Interrogatoire (n.d.)," AD Oise, B non coté, bailliage de Clermont, maréchaussée, 1775.

146. See his character reference supplied by the parish priest, "Attestation (n.d.)," AD Oise, B 1584. Jean Mathurin Partois, age 38, *tisserand* at Auvers, claimed that both his wife and his mother were sick, thus leaving him without support ("Interrogatoire [25 septembre]," AD Oise, B 1584).

mies—vulnerable generally, in terms of economic and social access to grain and its products, and precarious specifically, in terms of family life-cycle. Not all men or women who rioted were middle-aged and responsible for dependent persons, nor did all middle-aged dependent-supporters riot, but such a condition, coupled with uncertain entitlement to grain during crises, obviously was an important precondition for rioting.

The Flour War also generated the same general gendered behavior found by historians of previous subsistence movements. Although women were most prominent in specific theaters of action (see Chapter 4), we have already seen that they were present wherever trouble occurred. Along the Oise, women raided barges transporting grain to Paris; they stopped carts carrying grain in the Brie; they ransacked mills where sacks of flour lay stored; they invaded granaries of cultivators in search of grain that had not come to market; and, most visibly, they took part in and often led marketplace riots. Women instigated riots, worked with other women in small groups sharing the grain or flour they seized, brought their children with them to help scoop up the grain that lay scattered on the ground after the sacks were torn open, and joined the bands that visited the country-side.[147] Yet, despite the repetitive nature of reports locating women at the head of or among Flour War rioters, authorities arrested only 93 women, compared with 455 men. This gender-specific pattern of arrests stems from a combination of traditional attitudes about both men and women and from actual gendered behavior during the Flour War, as we shall see.

Identifying leaders of crowd behavior poses certain problems. When confronted by interrogators, a few arrested rioters admitted leading riots, but most flatly denied all accusations. Therefore, identifying leaders requires using other sources. Rather than rely exclusively on the observation of the police (who had their own perception of what constituted riot leadership), I combined their testimony with evidence from other witnesses and rioters' interrogations, as well as with testimonies of the accused leaders them-selves.[148] I therefore define a leader as someone who, according to a convincing sample of available sources, instigated and/or assumed direction of a riot or a significant dimension of a riot.

A profile of those arrested as leaders (Table 2) reaffirms the pattern seen

147. Indeed, it was in specific reference to the riots associated with the Flour War that François Métra observed their central role. See his *Correspondance secrète*, 1:341.

148. This important problem merits further study. Defining leaders of crowd activity depends heavily on perception and is far from a clear-cut issue. See the discussion of arrests, above, for the type of behavior that drew repression during the Flour War.

Table 2. Occupations of Riot Leaders

	Occupations[a]	No. of Leaders	Percent of Total
1.	Unskilled day-laborers	10	11.6
2.	Semiskilled & dependent skilled laborers	29	33.7
3.	Artisans/independent crafts (except milling, baking, etc.)	14	16.3
4.	Merchants/service (except grain/flour merchants, etc.)	6	7.0
5.	Innkeepers/publicans	3	3.5
6.	Vine-growers	6	7.0
7.	Rural propertied groups (except vine-growers)	0	0.0
8.	Officials/notables	5	5.8
9.	Grain/flour traders/bakers/millers (including their workers)	3	3.5
10.	Others	1	1.2
11.	Unknown	9	10.5
	Total	86	100.1

Note: This table includes all rioters arrested outside Paris, Versailles, and Saint-Germain-en-Laye.

[a] I determined occupations for leaders the same way as for all rioters. See footnote to Table 1 for my procedure. Appendix 2 contains detailed information about occupations.

among rioters in general. Despite the occasional role of local authorities or notables, the overwhelming majority of identifiable leaders arrested or accused came from the same socioeconomic strata and experienced similar precariousness in their families as the rioters themselves. The only difference was that they belonged even more frequently to the lower rungs of society than the rioters in general, were a little bit younger (with average ages of 35.1 for women and 38.4 for men), and in a few cases could be considered veritable "marginals" within their communities.

Forty-five percent of the leaders indicted belonged to the laboring classes (cats. 1 and 2), with the largest number from the wage-earning semiskilled and skilled laborers. And even more clearly than among rioters arrested in general, many leaders from the artisanal and merchant/service categories (cats. 3 and 4) shared characteristics similar to their counterparts among the rank-and-file—their independence was at best uncertain. Charles Degaast, one of two rioters condemned to hang, furnishes an example. On 28 April he joined rioters at the market of Méru, where he cut open several sacks of grain and struck a laboureur on the head with the handle of his whip when the farmer tried to stop Degaast from further violence. He then led the pillage of a mill at Blainville. Forewarned, the miller's brother lowered the vanes, stopped milling, and locked the door. Degaast broke down the door, seized the mill watchman by the neck, and brandishing a knife, declared, "I have the bugger." He thought he had captured the miller, and threatened to slit his throat. Others, who realized the man held was not the miller, stopped him, "because he was the servant not the master." Degaast then led the other assembled rioters in opening and carrying away the flour stored in the mill. The thirty-eight-year-old Degaast styled himself an inlaid-ware worker (*tabletier*) in his first interrogation, but in subsequent interrogations claimed he also worked as a day-laborer and as stable boy on market days, to supplement the income on which he and his mother subsisted.[149] Jean Renault, accused of attempting to incite rioting at Bonneval, reported his occupation as weaver (*tisserand*) but claimed that "for the past two years he and his family had eaten only rye bread or *mouture*"—a sign he used to signify that the family was faring poorly.[150]

The case of Pierre Hamelin, an inhabitant of the parish of Nesles, further underscores the both precarious and ambiguous nature of some members of the artisanal world who emerged as leaders during the Flour War. On 4 May, he climbed up on a sack at the market of Beaumont-sur-Oise and threatened cultivators with further rioting. He told the police who arrested him and the judges who prosecuted him that he was a "publican, baker, and butcher" in his parish. The thirty-eight-year-old tycoon further testified to his entrepreneurial inclinations when he defended himself by explaining, "If M. et Mme. la Marquise de Nesles were against him, it was because he had had an oven built" against their will. Moreover, he explained, "If he did not enjoy a good reputation in his *pays*, it is because a lot of people owe him money and he demands repayment." With so many irons in the fire, one might expect to discover that Hamelin was among the more notable inhabitants of his community, and not just the more notorious. However, the *taille* roll of Nesles indicates that he ranked among the most disadvantaged taxpayers in his town of 163 households. Although three households paid more than 200 livres, Hamelin paid a mere 6 livres 4 sols in 1773.[151]

As with the rank-and-file, the 1775 subsistence crisis coincided with

149. "Interrogatoires (2,5,13 mai)," AD Oise, B 1583.
150. "Interrogatoire (11 juillet)," AN Y 11441.
151. "Rôle de taille, 1773, Nesles," AD Yvelines, C 224. Granted, Hamelin could have experienced a meteoric rise since 1773, but that seems unlikely. A survey of neighboring parishes revealed that he derived no obvious sources of taxable income in any of them either.

family difficulties for many leaders. The police arrested Paul Felix Rougeaux at the market of Arpajon on 5 May, after he had announced publicly to a grain merchant "that it was necessary to contribute to the relief of the poor" by selling his grain more cheaply. Rougeaux himself then began measuring and distributing the grain to the others assembled. This thirty-eight-year-old shoemaker from the nearby village of Cheptainville headed a family of six children and a sick wife.[152] The forty-year-old ragpicker (*chiffonier*) from Bougival, Remy Cirier, led inhabitants of Reuil to raid a baker's shop, where he then incited them to riot. During his imprisonment, local notables from Bougival wrote to explain that Cirier's family was "in misery, with four children [and] one crippled."[153] The twenty-nine-year-old tailor from Soisy-sous-Etoile was arrested after leading a band of rioters to a farm in the parish of Saint-Germain-lès-Corbeil on 7 May. A supplication from his wife and a character reference from local notables revealed that André "was burdened with two children and a wife who is blind and pregnant."[154]

A small but striking set of examples show some leaders as marginalized within their societies. For example, a forty-seven-year-old father of six children, Louis Bonnefoy, provides an image of downward mobility. He was arrested for leading the *entrave* in his village of Souilly and for threatening both a local fermier and a baker from Claye with violence. He proclaimed publicly that "all he had to do was give the word and the entire *pays* would follow him. . . . He alone was worth four *mutins*." The police report noted that "everyone fears him in the *pays*." Bonnefoy claimed he was a former baker but was now working "for someone else as a woodcutter and sometimes as a day-laborer."[155]

Pierre Cadet had obviously fallen on hard times. On 1 May, he incited people to riot in the marketplace and then again before the door of a farm defended by several cavaliers of the maréchaussée. He insulted the cavaliers and yelled to the people assembled, "Pick up stones and let's throw ourselves on these bastards. They are made of skin and bones like ourselves." A widower for some time, he worked as a day-laborer and thresher at Gonesse, where he supported an eleven-year-old son and lived with his sister-in-law.[156]

152. "Interrogatoire (11 mai)," and "Attestation (10 mai)," AD Seine-et-Marne, B 3957(2).

153. "Interrogatoire (12 mai)" an "Attestation (n.d.)," AN, Y 18682.

154. "Interrogatoire (11 mai)," "Supplique (14 mai)," and "Attestation (14 mai)," AD Seine-et-Marne, B 3957(2).

155. "Interrogatoire (16 mai)," AD Seine-et-Marne, B 2387.

156. "Procès-verbal (11 mai)" and "Interrogatoire (12 mai and 21 juin)," AN, Y 18682.

Others confronted unemployment in their families. Louis Denis was fifty-seven years old and an unemployed miller's assistant (*garçon meunier*) with a wife and a child when he was arrested for inciting the crowd at Vernon to greater violence. Although he was out of work, he was well positioned occupationally to know a lot about the trade. Forty-one-year-old Madelaine Louette's husband could find no work as a gamekeeper when she used her knife to slit open sacks of grain and threaten sellers at the market of Méru. Madelaine's actions were mirrored by thirty-eight-year-old Catherine Clerfeuille, whose work as a lace-maker probably did not compensate for the unemployed state of her husband, a former schoolteacher.[157] Twenty-five-year-old Nicolas Marchais "spread the word" of rioting in the region of Colombe as he passed through villages seeking work as a gardener's helper (*garçon jardinier*).[158]

Those who rioted during the Flour War thus resembled, in general, those who had rioted in previous and subsequent subsistence movements. Rioters, both male and female, did indeed come overwhelmingly from the ranks of the food-purchasing common people: wage-earners, artisans, and shopkeepers constituted the largest percentage, and vine-growers played a significant part as well. It is certainly not difficult to envision how vulnerable many were at the first hint of scarcity and rising prices, how frustrated they would be by what they might interpret as improper business practices, official negligence, and lack of control over food, and how furious they could become during the crisis. Over and over, voices exclaimed that "starving or being killed by the police was all the same to them."[159]

If we include in our analysis of participation information on age and location in the family life-cycle and supplement interrogation information with tax records to flesh out the occupational situation of rioters, we get an even more refined picture. Rioters in 1775 tended to belong to the lower

157. On Denis, see "Interrogatoires (23 mai and 4 août)," AD Eure, B 398; "Sentence (17 août)," AD Seine-Maritime, C 108. On Louette, see "Interrogatoire (24 juillet))," AD Oise, B 1583ter; on Clerfeuille, see "Interrogatoire (14 juillet)," AD Oise, B 1583ter.

158. "Procès-verbal (5 mai)" and "Interrogatoire (7 mai)," AN, Y 18682.

159. A statement employed at Beaumont-sur-Oise, repeated at Pontoise ("Procès-verbal [29 avril]," AD Yvelines, 12 B 519), at Brie-Comte-Robert ("Information [5 mai]," BN, Collection Joly de Fleury, 1159, fols. 23–24), and at Gonesse ("Information [16 mai]," AN, Y 18682). During an attack on a transport of grain from a parish near Ancenis in Brittany in 1694, rioters proclaimed: "Ils aimaient mieux être pendus que de mourir de faim" (Boislisle, *Correspondance*, 1:362, no. 1314). Iain Cameron notes the same phrase in Bergerac in 1773 (*Crime and Repression in the Auvergne and the Guyenne, 1720–1790* [Cambridge, 1981], pp. 63–69). It is interesting that John Bohstedt had observed that English food rioters often used the same language: "If they were to suffer, they might as well be hung as starved" (*Riots*, p. 36).

rungs of the common people; some had experienced downward occupational mobility, and many confronted some of the darkest stages in their family cycle. What is evident for the arrested in general is even more salient among the indicted leaders of riots. As we will see in the following chapter, even more precise patterns emerge when the characteristics of participation are compared with particular types of action.

Chapter 4

TYPOLOGY OF THE FLOUR WAR

The outbreak of the Flour War, like the outbreak of riots whenever and wherever they occur, not only exposed the distress among the people but also manifested a shared feeling of outrage powerful enough to bind individuals together into groups that shared, if only briefly, a common purpose. This apparent unity of purpose, however, invariably reflects not a single grievance but many, not one perception of injustice but an array of them, focused on points of action. By starting from these focal points and pursuing the various perceptions to their sources, the popular disturbance may open a way to see a hitherto obscured patterned texture in a society stressed by the pressure of change on tradition. Certainly late eighteenth-century France—with its growing population, changing patterns in the grain and flour trade and diversification of those who participated in them, its multiplying varieties of business practice, and its shifting royal policies—constituted such a society. The Flour War, once parsed into its common and particular patterns, offers a prime vantage point from which to view that society.

The observable form of disturbances during the Flour War—the *taxation populaire*—predominated throughout the Paris Basin, thus providing clear links of similarity between previous subsistence movements and that of 1775. Moreover, as they did in previous movements, the common people overwhelmingly made up the rank-and-file as well as the leadership of the rioters. Yet, beneath these general observations, and to some extent obscured by them, behavior and the composition of the "crowd" could and did vary, both over time and from place to place. In the Flour War as in other food riots, participation and behavior manifested characteristics specific to local patterns of economic and social development in general and to the local pattern of production or marketing of grain and its products in particular. This linkage of grain production and trade and the Flour War not only underlay the varieties of local actors and actions, it also exposed the overlapping but more general problem of uneven development and its consequences to France in the late eighteenth century.

Four general patterns of riot behavior emerge from a close examination of the Flour War.[1] These patterns surface clearly when the riots are plotted on a map of grain production and trade, and they closely correspond to a typology of specific geographic regions, each of which defined by whether it (1) depended on "imported" or locally produced grain for its needs; (2) contained markets that attracted surplus grain designed for "exportation" to such places as the capital; (3) was located along important trade routes; or (4) produced a grain surplus intended for "exportation" to Paris or other provincial cities.[2] Some regions performed combinations of these functions,

---

1. Maurice Agulhon emphasized the need to consider "geographical typology . . . in any study of the sociology of revolutions" (*The Republic in the Village: The People of the Var from the French Revolution to the Second Republic*, trans. J. Lloyd [Cambridge and Paris, 1982], p. xi). We need to extend this call to include the less spectacular but no less applicable cases of popular movements such as food rioting.

2. By analyzing not only the collective profile of rioters but also that of the Flour War's "victims," patterns become more visible. Ironically, despite all the studies dedicated to identifying the rioters during popular uprisings, there has been virtually no comparable study of the victims themselves. The lone voice of Guy Lemarchand has emphasized the importance of knowing more about the identities of targets of popular movements. See his "Les Troubles de subsistance dans la généralité de Rouen (seconde moitié du XVIIIe siècle)," *AHRF* 35 (Oct.–Dec. 1963): 401–27. The police collected from 449 victims depositions that detail their experiences and their losses, and local authorities' reports further chronicled their plights. Turgot promised to indemnify victims (basically via a local tax) for the losses incurred during the Flour War, thus encouraging them to come forward with their stories. These lists have many disadvantages, of course. They were not comprehensive and therefore cannot give definitive information on all who serviced a particular market. They omit the merchant who traded only occasionally at specific markets (unless the "riot day" was his "market day"), and they may include some traders who visited a particular market only rarely. Moreover, when news of rioting spread, some traders might have remained home rather than risk pillage or worse. This was the case during later stages of the Flour War. Nevertheless, these lists

but (as we shall see) rioters adjusted their tactics according to their knowledge of their regions' functions.[3]

Patterns of Behavior / Theaters of Action

TYPE 1

In the first, traditional form of market riot, rioters wielded the *taxation populaire* largely within the physical confines of the marketplace. Rioters seized grain displayed for sale by producers and merchants, distributed it among themselves at a "just price," and, after denuding the marketplace, returned home with their provisions. Such actions were often preceded by

---

provide a useful snapshot of the grain trade. Although the numbers of traders and their names may have changed some over the course of the year, it is doubtful that the basic contours of the trade changed in any significant way. And a close analysis of lists provides a much needed counterpart to similar analyses of arrest records.

I am not the first to generate a model for approaching the Flour War. Edgar Faure isolated three patterns: (1) conflicts in markets, (2) expeditions to more distant areas, (3) eccentric conflicts, distant from principal trouble spots (*La Disgrâce de Turgot* [Paris, 1961], pp. 283–92). Although this categorization is helpful in analyzing some forms of behavior (and parallels my own, in certain aspects), it does not take into consideration the context that produced that behavior. Vladimir Ljublinski argued that determining the place of action was not significant for understanding the Flour War (*La Guerre de farines. Contribution à l'histoire de la lutte des classes en France, à la veille de la Révolution* [Grenoble, 1979], p. 145). I disagree strongly. Knowledge of the theaters of action contributes significantly to our understanding of motives and behavior. Other historians have also generated food riot typologies. See, e.g., Charles Tilly, "Food Supply and Public Order in Modern Europe," in *The Formation of National States in Western Europe* (Princeton, 1975), p. 386; Andrew Charlesworth, ed., *An Atlas of Rural Protest in Britain, 1548–1900* (Philadelphia, 1983), esp. chap. 3.

3. Recent work has contributed greatly to our understanding of Ancien Régime markets and marketing in general and to the Paris provisioning system in particular. To the "standard" works on the subject—such as Abbot P. Usher, *The History of the Grain Trade in France, 1400–1710* (Cambridge, Mass., 1913); Charles Desmarest, *Le Commerce des grains dans la généralité de Rouen à la fin de l'Ancien Régime* (Paris, 1926); Camille Bloch, *Le Commerce des grains dans la généralité d'Orléans (1768) d'après la correspondance inédite de l'intendant Cypierre* (Orléans, 1898); George Afanassiev, *Le Commerce des céréales en France au XVIIIe siècle*, trans. P. Boyer (Paris, 1894), e.g.,—must now be added the important contributions of Steven L. Kaplan, *Provisioning Paris: Merchants and Millers in the Grain and Flour Trade During the Eighteenth Century* (Ithaca, N.Y., 1984); Jean Meuvret, *Le Problème des subsistances à l'époque Louis XIV*, vol. 3, *Le Commerce des grains et la conjoncture* (Paris, 1988); Dominique Margairaz, *Foires et marchés dans la France préindustrielle* (Paris, 1988). Kaplan and Margairaz (who relied in part on Kaplan's work), in particular, have offered a typology of markets that correlates well with my typology of riots, derived from examining riot behavior.

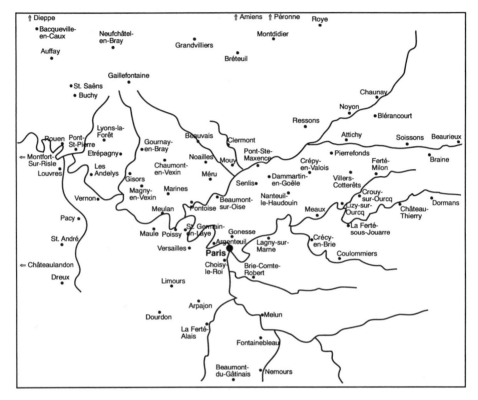

Map 2.   Locations of Market Riots During the Flour War (Types 1 and 2)

attempts to get local authorities to lower prices, increase supplies, or punish what the people declared as abuses, such as hoarding, price-gouging, or adulterating supplies. Occasionally, especially in larger towns, rioters might attack bakeries. Disturbances of this type erupted in many places during the Flour War (see Map 2), but its clearest manifestation occurred either in market towns that serviced local needs largely with local supplies, such as parts of the pays de Caux and the Beauvaisis, or in the grain-importing regions, where markets brought grain from surplus-producing regions and sold it locally, such as the pays de Bray and the Gâtinais. In these regions, local entrepôt or elementary[4] markets provisioned local consumers and those

4. On the different types of markets in the Paris Basin, see Chapter 2 and Margairaz, Foires, p. 177. Elementary markets served a smaller area than entrepôt markets. I have differentiated between grain markets and other types of markets that could exist in any town. While Auffay or Gournay-en-Bray might support an elementary or entrepôt grain market, they were far more integrated into national markets in other areas of the economy (see below).

from the neighboring area; this trade took place in the marketplace or *halle*, and rarely anywhere else.

In the largely self-sufficient regions, grain came from nearby producers of the hinterland and was destined specifically for local consumption. The marketplace retained its centrality as a trading nexus. Designed to reduce travel time both for producers and for consumers, to privilege locals and their needs, and to enforce a degree of competition among producers assembled with their grain, these markets rarely involved large quantities or broader trading interests. Yet when provisions became scarce and prices rose, and when the market was invaded by "strangers" (*étrangers*) representing metropolitan interests, solutions such as finding alternative sources of subsistence could be difficult precisely because the market was not geared toward linking with outside grain-marketing networks. Thus, tensions between producers and consumers, who no doubt knew well the state of their local market, could produce violent clashes. Indeed, Meuvret has shown that it did not take much of a change in harvest size, particularly in the types of regions defined in Chapter 2, for there to be a dramatic effect on the grain available for the market.[5] He has also emphasized that small variations in harvest size could produce equally dramatic changes in the number of consumers seeking grain.[6] Small-scale producers who occasionally supplied markets or who managed to make ends meet with family provisions might quickly turn into grain purchasers for subsistence or harvest-seed needs.

Just such a clash occurred at Auffay, a town of 1,000 inhabitants located in the eastern pays de Caux, which experienced violent upheavals on 11 and 13 May.[7] The pays de Caux was largely self-sufficient in grain, and although in some places cultivators occasionally produced a small surplus for export, local supplies provisioned Auffay.[8] These producers were not, however, marginal landholders, but rather laboureurs and fermiers of substantial holdings.[9] At the same time, the penetration of domestic cotton industry

---

5. *Problèmes*, 3:152.

6. Ibid., p. 153.

7. On Auffay, see esp. the work of Gay L. Gullickson, "The Sexual Division of Labor in Cottage Industry and Agriculture in the Pays de Caux, Auffay, 1750–1850," *FHS* 12 (Fall 1981): 177–99, and idem, *Spinners and Weavers of Auffay: Rural Industry and the Sexual Division of Labor in a French Village, 1750–1850* (Cambridge, 1986). On the period of the Flour War, see AD Seine-Maritime, "Etat des pertes causées à quelques laboureurs de la subdélégation de Dieppe (27 juin)," C 107; "Rôle de taille, Auffay, 1775," C 1730; "Rôle de vingtième, Auffay et les hameaux, 1770, 1773," C 537; "Lettres (13 mai et 15 mai) du subdélégué à l'intendant," C 108. Auffay was clearly integrated into the national (and international) market in textile production as a major protoindustrial center for cotton manufacturing.

8. According to lists of losses incurred during the riots, twelve of thirteen victims were local residents of Auffay or nearby parishes.

9. For example, Charles Julien, laboureur at Auffay, paid the highest tax for the *taille* in town

produced a significant population of microproprietors, who subsisted with their families only with the aid of the cottage industry.[10] This latter group was extremely sensitive to changes in grain prices. So the subsistence crisis pitted "the poor people from the canton" against the powerful cultivators in the marketplace.

On 11 May, protesters in the marketplace "demanded grain at whatever price it pleased them to offer and threatened violence to obtain it." Several scuffles erupted, as grain sold for half- and three-quarters price that day. On 13 May, the situation worsened. Producers had been "frightened by their experiences" on the 11th, and only a few brought grain to sell. Infuriated by the diminished supply, rioters ripped open sacks on display and paid less than half price for the grain. Some of them even assaulted a brigadier of the maréchaussée from Tôtes who attempted to intervene.

These laboureurs who provisioned the Auffay market found themselves in "very critical circumstances." On the one hand, "if they brought their grain to market, they risked being pillaged and mistreated." On the other hand, if they stayed home, "they ran the chance of pillage and perhaps having [their farms] set on fire" by rioters. Moreover, the local police force was too small to provide protection, despite assistance from Tôtes. Local authorities, largely overwhelmed by circumstances themselves (whatever their sympathies), ordered the cavaliers "to use moderation" in responding to the crisis and then counseled the producers "to give in to the circumstances [and sell] the grain at whatever price [the rioters] wanted to pay." After all, as the subdelegate from Dieppe reported in his memo to the intendant, "everything [that] happened here [was the work of] people from the canton, most of them well known." He concluded that it would not be difficult to "make several exemplary punishments." The local nature of the Auffay grain supply created a traditional form of trade focused on the marketplace. Thus, when the Flour War erupted in Auffay, it remained traditional in form and content.

---

in 1775. Jacques Boyard, also a laboureur at Auffay, placed a close third behind the "holders of the tithe and the miller. The collector of the 1773 *vingtième* estimated Boyard's combined revenue at 1,550 livres, which included proprietorship of two houses, a grange, enclosures, and equal amounts of owned and leased arable land. In the nearby Sevis, victim Michel Terrien lived with his widowed mother on a large ferme totaling 1,600 livres in revenue and owned 8 cows and 104 sheep. In 1775 he paid five times more tax for the *taille* than any other villager and also served as syndic. Some of these producers who provisioned Auffay may have engaged in a more extensive grain trade (as they probably did in stock-raising), but if they did there is no evidence about its magnitude or direction.

10. According to Gullickson, more than 39 percent of the population of Auffay worked either as spinners or weavers in 1796, and a good many of these also worked as rural day-laborers, especially during the peak agricultural periods (*Spinners and Weavers*).

In the grain-importing regions, suppliers—usually small-scale merchants, or *blatiers*—might travel long distances, scouring the countryside and more distant markets for their supplies, but they normally traded in small quantities.[11] They linked markets by buying up small quantities in one market and selling them in another, and they connected cultivators to markets by collecting small amounts produced by others and carrying them to market for sale. In many ways, the vicissitudes of the trade made these petty traders as vulnerable as the consumers.[12] Meuvret has argued that the socioeconomic position of the *blatier* "was closer to that of the manouvrier than that of the laboureur. . . . The returns that a *blatier* made from the sale of sacks from one market to another was probably not higher than the customary wage of a simple day-laborer."[13] Subsistence crises in such areas reflected great desperation felt by both sides, and rioting there sometimes took a particularly frantic turn.

Consider the example of Gournay-en-Bray, a town of just over 2,000 in the heart of the pays de Bray, some twenty-two leagues from the capital along the main route from Dieppe to Paris. It experienced a food riot of this "classic" type on 2 May and again on 9 May. Gournay lay in a region characterized by a largely pastoral but diversified agriculture, where the soil discouraged wheat-growing, and the town relied heavily on grain imported from the Vexin and Picardy.[14] The majority of traders who serviced Gournay were *blatiers*, and by pursuing their businesses aggressively they could take

11. On *blatier* trade and traders in the Paris provisioning system, see Kaplan *Provisioning*, pp. 214–20. As Kaplan says, the "socioeconomic function of the *blatier* was to buy up what others did not want or were unwilling to travel to obtain or were unaware of" (p. 215). See also Usher, *Grain Trade*, pp. 13–19, 46–47; Meuvret, *Problèmes*, 3:101–5.

12. As Kaplan points out, "information was the *blatier*'s keenest need" (p. 215), and without accurate information about prices and demand they stood to lose much. Unlike Antonio in the *Merchant of Venice*, few, with their small quantities, could say that their "ventures are not in one bottom trusted, / Nor to one place" (1.1.42–43)—a situation exacerbated by their dreadful reputations as corrupt speculators (recall that it was a *blatier* who, as the first target of the Flour War, ended up in the fountain at Beaumont-sur-Oise)—found themselves extremely vulnerable in times of stress.

13. *Problèmes*, 3:104.

14. "Etat de la subdélégation de Gournay (1787)," AD Seine-Maritime, C 185; "Etat des pertes des laboureurs et marchands de bleds aux marchés de Gournay, les 2 et 9 mai 1775," AD Seine-Maritime, C 107. Gournay was tightly connected to the larger market in dairy (especially butter) and cattle products, providing a lively trade with Paris (and was distinctly not an elementary market in this area), a sign of ongoing specialization that furthered its dependence on imported grain for its subsistence. On this aspect, see Pierre Goujard, *L'Abolition de la féodalité dans le Pays de Bray (1789–1793)* (Paris, 1979), pp. 18–20. See also Jules Sion, *Les Paysans de la Normandie orientale. Pays de Caux, Bray, Vexin normand, vallée de la Seine* (Paris, 1909), pp. 103–9, 244–50.

advantage of the local and dependent character of the Gournay market.[15] They and other traders engaged in what many thought were less than "moral" marketing practices. A miller from Dampierre-en-Bray, operating as a merchant at Gournay when he brought there to sell grain he had purchased at the market of Gaillefontaine on 28 April,[16] elicited the suspicion of the subdelegate who wrote: "Millers buy grain at higher prices than others do, and thus are not exempt from suspicion of the interest they have in making grain prices rise."

And prices certainly did rise at Gournay throughout the year. The subdelegate reported that the price of a boisseau of wheat had risen from 4 livres 10 sols in October 1774 (immediately after the harvest), to 6 livres 2 sols at the last market in April.[17] On 2 May "the *halle* was adequately provisioned," but prices had fallen very little (to 5 livres 10 sols). Reports of the previous day's *taxation populaire* at Gisors excited already angered "little pockets" to demand a similar reduction to 4 livres 10 sols.[18]

Frightened by the mounting tension in the marketplace, merchants hesitated to open their sacks. Although the market normally opened at noon, grain-traders stalled for two more hours. As soon as it opened, tempers flared and rioting erupted. Scared, the merchants ran "to demand the protection of the Duc de Montmorency and to ask him to fix the price at which they should sell their grain." In a magnanimous paternalist gesture that great seigneurs thought themselves born to make,[19] Montmorency ordered that the merchants "sell to the poor at a cheaper price, but to the better-off people at the price it was worth, and he would indemnify the merchants for their losses in sales to the poor." He distributed some of his

15. The subdelegate at Gournay submitted a list of declarations of losses incurred during the riots of 2 and 9 May, thereby providing information about the nature of the Gournay market. This "Etat des pertes des laboureurs et marchands aux marchés de Gournay les 2 et 9 mai" lists fifteen *blatiers*, three *blatiers/laboureurs*, two *boulangers*, one *meunier*, one *fermier des dîmes* de Gerberoy, and one *curé* (AD Seine-Maritime, C 107). None of these sold local grain. For example, Charles Gaudet, *blatier* and laboureur at Villers-sur-Auchy, a village close to Gournay, had purchased his grain at the market of Grandvilliers, more than six leagues away. Similarly, the *meunier* Boutellier from Dampierre had bought his grain at the even more distant market of Gaillefontaine on 28 April. A sign of the expected return, but also the vulnerability, of such operations is provided by the baker Pelletier from Morvilliers, who declared he had incurred a heavy loss on the four sacks of "good wheat" (*bon bled*) he had brought to Gournay on 9 May. The "Etat" reported that "he had bought [the grain] for 36 livres a sack and had counted on selling it for 39 livres but only received 24."

16. On millers in their multiple roles as grain merchants and flour merchants, see Kaplan, *Provisioning*, pp. 264–80.

17. "Lettre (4 juin)," AD Seine-Maritime, C 107.

18. "Lettre (3 mai)," AD Seine-Maritime, C 109.

19. For more on aspects of paternalism, see Chapter 5 below.

own grain to the poor and parceled out a 120 livre indemnity to vendors who cooperated by selling at a loss to the poor.[20]

Calm returned, but only briefly. When supplies ran out, many people discovered they could not buy at any price. Riots erupted again as frustrated consumers accosted merchants with sticks and stopped local bakers from provisioning their boutiques. The violence continued until well past dark. When "the traders left [Gournay] very late that evening and very unhappy, they threatened not to return for the next market [9 May]."[21] Nevertheless, many did return—the *blatiers*, whose survival depended on every possible transaction. Again, supplies ran drastically short and tensions still ran high. A fresh eruption again rattled the marketplace.[22]

Merchants, rioters, police, and seigneur thus played out their traditional roles on the Gournay marketplace. Clashes embroiled small-scale merchants and "little pocket" consumers, both of whom lived close to the margin of subsistence and for whom changes in the supply and price of grain could soon mean hunger. Gournay's grain market functioned to facilitate consumer access to the means of subsistence; the merchants supplied these means. But merchants could not produce supplies out of nowhere, and merchants' motives were not consumer-oriented. When other areas with as strong if not stronger purchasing power competed with the town for supplies, merchants turned elsewhere. Gournay's food riots thus marked the breakdown of the traditional market system, a system that, as Dominique Margairaz emphasizes, functioned largely as a service to consumers.[23]

Markets in neither Auffay nor Gournay collected grain for more distant consumers so the trade retained its traditional and local character. The free-trade judgment did little to alter the character of the grain trade in these elementary markets and others like them: producers and merchants both continued to bring grain to the local market, when they brought it. What

20. Despite the indemnity distributed by Montmorency, compensation was generally inadequate. Only one victim emerged entirely recompensed: a baker from Loueuse. While some victims could absorb the loss, at least for a while, others, like the *blatier* François de Saint-Aubin, also from Loueuse ("a very poor man burdened with four children"), probably could not ("Etat des pertes . . ." AD Seine-Maritime, C 107). Moreover, victims had to wait a long time until the indemnity promised by Turgot arrived. Reports listing final amounts for indemnification were not sent to Turgot until the end of January 1776. See "Etat des grains et farines pillés et donnés à vil prix dans le commencement de mai 1775 (20 janvier 1776)," AD Seine-Maritime, C 107.

21. "Lettre (3 mai)," AD Seine-Maritime, C 109.

22. Unfortunately, the documents do not permit a close examination of this eruption. The 2 May disturbance is detailed carefully in official reports, but the 9 May upheaval is mentioned only briefly.

23. Margairaz, *Foires*, pp. 199, 211.

Table 3.   Types of Flour War Riots

Type	No. of Riots	Percent of Total
Type 1	45	14.2
Type 2	37	11.7
Type 3	12	3.8
Type 4	203	64.0
Other	14	4.4
Unknown	6	1.9
Total	317	100.0

Note: This table includes all riots (including those of Paris, Versailles, and Saint-Germain-en-Laye). See Table 4 for a specific breakdown of rioting for each category used.

emerges in such regions, therefore, is a portrait of the *taxation populaire* in its most traditional form. Riots of this sort also erupted in places like Beaumont-du-Gâtinais, Chaumont-en-Vexin, and in various markets of the Beauvaisis such as Mouy. The subdelegate at Chaumont explained specifically "that there are no storagerooms in Chaumont, no commerce in grain, and the small number of laboureurs who live here have only small occupations."[24]

True elementary and entrepôt markets were, however, relatively rare in the Paris Basin, compared with other parts of France analyzed by Dominique Margaraiz.[25] The pull of the capital's needs for subsistence grew stronger all the time, and even these local markets experienced broader ties via other commodities with more distant markets, rendering them susceptible to supralocal forces. Nevertheless, more than half of all market rioting during the Flour War represented "type 1" behavior,[26] suggesting that these types of markets were far from disappearing from even the increasingly integrated Paris Basin. Although several of the markets that experienced this type of behavior performed feeder or collector-market services (Beaumont-sur-Oise, Gonesse, Soissons, and Rouen, for example), the limited riot behavior they experienced reflected more effective police powers or negotiation skills by authorities. With the exception of Beaumont-sur-Oise, the scene of the first

24. "Lettre (6 mai)," AD Seine-Maritime, C 108, n. 327.
25. See maps 17–18 in *Foires*, pp. 268–71.
26. Type 1 incidents represented 54.9 percent of all market rioting and 14.2 percent of all rioting of any type. See Table 3 for more information.

eruption of the Flour War, police in all the other more extensive markets mustered preventative measures that kept disturbances from spreading beyond marketplaces. For example, cavaliers of the maréchaussée reacted swiftly to arrest agitators in the markets of Rouen. In so doing, they managed to squelch more widespread unrest. The experience of more limited riot behavior in feeder and collector markets was relatively rare, however. The majority of type 1 riots occurred in the smaller markets serving largely local needs that continued to function in the Paris Basin. These subsistence crises, such as that preceding the Flour War, generated tensions sufficient to produce severe marketplace food rioting.

TYPE 2

In the Paris Basin, riots of a second type were more pervasive—riots in which extensive disturbances rocked towns that provided market services broader than the local provisioning needs described above. Although this second type usually began as a traditional market riot, rioters soon expanded their activities to attack grain and flour held in public and private storage rooms, mills, granaries of local cultivators, town-based religious communities, bakeries, and occasionally even the seigneur's residence. They thus widened the uses of the *taxation populaire* in response to the kind of grain trade they confronted.

During the Flour War, this type of riot erupted predominantly either in market towns in the grain-exporting regions of the *pays de grande culture* (the breadbasket of the Paris Basin) or in those that provisioned Paris or other regional centers by land or by water (see Map 2). As major distribution centers (collector, relay, or feeder markets) for the grain trade, these wholesale markets often far exceeded entrepôt and elementary markets both in the total quantity handled and in the value of individual transactions. Moreover, these markets operated through a complex structure that offered multiple targets to protesters, a structure facilitated but not innovated by liberalization.

Although merchants and cultivators still transacted some of their business (often negotiating deals via *echantillons*, samples) in the traditional marketplace and serviced local consumers, much more frequently they handled the big transactions with merchants from Paris or other regional centers outside the physical confines of the public *halle*. They stored large quantities of grain and flour in, and negotiated sales directly from, private storage rooms scattered throughout the market towns. Local residents—publicans, inn-keepers, artisans, bourgeois, and occasionally seigneurs and monasteries and convents—developed a modestly profitable sideline leasing space in which producers and merchants stored grain prior to sale. Furthermore, towns sometimes provided public storage space, and church institutions occasionally participated in public provisioning schemes by storing grain. Ecclesiastical institutions (monasteries, cathedral chapters, etc.) were widely known as repositories of often considerable quantities of grain: they stored for their own needs, collected it as revenue from seigneurial dues and tithes, and sometimes amassed it to participate in other provisioning schemes. They generally made charitable donations to the poor, and some participated in the "community" granary system devised for Paris.[27] Three examples from the Flour War demonstrate the nature of rioter behavior in this type of environment.

Magny-en-Vexin, a small town in the heart of the fertile Vexin on the route between Paris and Rouen, served as "the entrepôt for grains from the Vexin normand destined for consumption in Paris, Versailles, and Saint-Germain."[28] Both the Vexin français and the Vexin normand constituted an essential region of the surplus-grain-producing Paris provisioning zone, characterized by an almost exclusive concentration on grain production. Dupâquier's studies show that forty-eight parishes in the élection of Magny produced an excess of grain ranging from one-third to one-half. They also sold oats, veal, and wool.[29] Magny functioned as the major collection and shipping center for the surplus produce of the Vexin. Cultivators and merchants there, as in similar entrepôt market towns elsewhere, had developed the use of private storage rooms, either owned or more frequently

27. On charity, see Colin Jones, *Charity and Bienfaisance: The Treatment of the Poor in the Montpellier Region, 1740–1815* (Cambridge, 1982), as well as other sources cited in Chapter 1. On the community granary system, see Steven Kaplan, "Lean Years, Fat Years: The 'Community' Granary System and the Search for Abundance in Eighteenth-Century Paris," *FHS* 10 (Fall 1977): 211–15. It is not clear how much of this system remained functional by 1775, for Lenoir claimed that "the former regulations according to which the *corps et chapitres* possessing lands in the environs of Paris had been required to store in their granaries enough grain and flour for several years' consumption were no longer observed. M. de Turgot could no longer count on this resource; it had been entirely destroyed by him." In "Le Lieutenant de police J.-P. Lenoir, la guerre des farines et l'approvisionnement de Paris à la veille de la Révolution," ed. R. Darnton, *RHMC* 15 (1969): 616.

28. In 1787, Magny's population totaled 360 households (*feux*): "Tableaux des élections de la Généralité de Rouen, subdélégation de Magny, la ville de Magny," AD Seine-Maritime, C 185; see also "Questionnaire (mai 1775)," C 109. In 1791 the population was 1886, counting six satellite villages (Jacques Dupâquier, *Ainsi commença la Révolution . . . Chaumont-en-Vexin et Magny-en-Vexin* [Pontoise, 1989], p. 38).

29. *Ainsi . . . Chaumont*, pp. 50–54.

leased, for their grain. Thus, cultivators leased rooms where they deposited grain intended for the wholesale market; merchants (and principally the merchants involved in the ever-growing Paris flour trade of the eighteenth century)[30] then visited the rooms, paid the cultivator for the desired quantity, and paid the proprietor of the magazine an additional sum to hold the grain until they removed it.[31] These flour merchants, or *fariniers*, then transported their purchases overland to Pontoise, where they had the grain milled into flour,[32] and then sent it by land or river to the Paris markets.[33]

The wholesale trade at Magny thus involved a triangle of grain handlers: producers, storage-room owners, and merchants. Such trade never passed through the traditional marketplace that served only a small local retail trade. When supplies ran short or prices rose in the marketplace itself, local consumers, aware of the magnitude of this aspect of the trade, suspected (usually correctly) these dealers of hoarding and speculation, or favoring "outside" buyers rather than local consumers. Before liberalization, authorities relied on their policing powers to inspect and requisition the contents of these private storage rooms during shortages.[34] Liberalization withdrew these powers. During the Flour War, rioters in these towns took this action themselves. As a result, dealers often suffered tremendous losses, a situation that was exacerbated by the complexities of managing the wholesale trade. Declarations of losses from the Flour War provide clear evidence of the functioning of business relationships in the grain trade in a feeder market. The storage rooms formed the front line in the battle for grain. The proprietors of these storage rooms, who suffered damage to their property, threats of personal violence at the hands of rioting consumers, and occasionally losses themselves, in fact had more in common with their attackers than with the clients they served, for the storage-room owners, like the

30. See Kaplan, *Provisioning*, pp. 345–54.

31. As one victim of the Flour War described the system in a letter to Turgot designed to engender understanding and support, "the laboureurs of the Vexin have granaries [in Magny] as much for their commodity as for that of the flour merchants. These latter pay 1 sol per setier of grain to the proprietor of the storage room when they don't pick up the grain the day they buy it" ("Lettre de Jean-Charles Brunel [n.d.]," AD Seine-Maritime, C 107).

32. Kaplan describes how Pontoise emerged as a major center for the flour market in the eighteenth century (*Provisioning*, pp. 306–9).

33. Similar markets existed throughout the Paris Basin. For example, the town of Roye, not far from the Oise in Picardy, also performed a similar function. An "Etat des marchés . . . dans la généralité d'Amiens" reported that merchants "come here [Roye] to buy grain in order to transport it to the market at Pont-Sainte-Maxence, which serves the provisioning of Paris" (AD Somme, C 90).

34. See, e.g., Paris, "La Crise de 1709."

rioters, came from the common people of Magny. Among the eleven owners of storage rooms invaded during the Flour War were four innkeepers and publicans, one widow of a harness-maker, one apprentice shoemaker, one miller's aide, one widowed cheese-monger, one draper, and one grain merchant.[35]

On 1 May, "the people, excited by the revolt at Pontoise" quickly stripped the sparsely provisioned marketplace and then moved to batter down the doors to the private storage rooms, demanding that the grain stored there be distributed.[36] Rioting continued to rock the town until "around 11 o'clock in the night, . . . but the next morning several troops of peasants arrived to begin again." The police finally forced the crowd to dissipate, so they "went straight to the market at La Roche-Guyon, threatening to return in the evening if they didn't find grain there." Officials at Magny quickly armed the *garde bourgeoise* to confront the possible returnees.

35. "Etats . . . de mai 1775 and 20 janvier 1776," AD Seine-Maritime, C 107; "Rôles de la taille, Magny, 1775," AD Yvelines, C 347, nos. 33, 34. The Flour War also disequilibrated business relations between sellers and buyers. The case of Jean-Charles Brunel, laboureur at Hacqueville, demonstrates some of the problems ("Lettre à Turgot," AD Seine-Maritime, C 107). He explained that "being in the habit of selling the greatest part of the grain from his harvest at the market of Magny for the provisioning of Paris," he like other laboureurs leased a magazine in town. On 22 April he sold 12 setiers of grain at 33 livres to François Boissy, a flour merchant from Pontoise; on 29 April he sold Boissy another 12 setiers at 33 livres 10 sols. Boissy paid Brunel, but during the week removed only 7 setiers from the magazine, thus leaving 17 setiers that Brunel "no longer regarded as his responsibility, but the flour merchant's." On 1 May those 17 setiers formed part of the massive loss incurred during the rioting. Boissy declared Brunel responsible for the loss and brought his case before the lieutenant general of police for adjudication. As the subdelegate (who also filled the position of lieutenant general of police) pointed out to the intendant, this method of doing business "raised a delicate and difficult-to-resolve question: does the cost of the loss fall on the laboureur who sold the grain that never left [the magazine] or on the flour merchant who bought it [but expected] to pick it up during the course of the following week?" ("Lettre de 2 mai," AD Seine-Maritime, C 109). Six weeks after the riots, the lieutenant general/subdelegate finally decided in favor of the merchants: the laboureur owed the merchant either the grain lost during the rioting or his money back. Thus, Brunel owed Boissy 17 setiers or 402 livres. The cultivator, and many others like him for whom the decision also applied, incurred a serious loss from this sale as well, he explained, as "a more modest loss for grain he delivered willingly during the crisis to various *pauvres honteux.*" Brunel complained bitterly, yet he was no mere small-time laboureur but a big-time fermier in his village. Although he owed only a very modest holding of just over 10 arpents of "mediocre land" and rented just over one arpent of land from the heirs of another resident, he had shared since 1774 a nine-year lease with Nicolas Defontenay of "three fermes with buildings of different usages, three banal wine presses, a dove-cot, 24 arpents of enclosure, and 331 arpents of arable" for a rent of 9,550 livres ("Rôle de vingtième, Hacqueville, 1781" AD Eure, C 229, n. 65).

36. On events at Magny, see "Lettres (1 mai et 2 mai)," AD Seine-Maritime, C 109; "Etat du bled pillé ou vendu à vil prix au marché de Magny (mai 1775)" and "Etat général des bleds qui ont été vendu à un bas prix au marché de Magny (20 janvier 1776)," AD Seine-Maritime, C 107.

Widespread rioting also erupted on 5 May at Nanteuil-le-Haudouin, a town similar to Magny in size and function and located between the Valois and Multien.[37] As the subdelegate at Crépy-en-Valois observed, Nanteuil was "one of the storage rooms for Paris, and if grain is lacking here, [Paris] feels the consequences."[38] Indeed, as we have seen, the Valois and the Multien, in particular, supported vast holdings dedicated almost exclusively to cereal production, and cultivators from this region provisioned both the wholesale trade and the retail trade transacted in the marketplace.

Thus situated, Nanteuil served as a major distribution center for the provisioning of Paris, and this wholesale trade constituted by far the most important part of its grain-trading business. The relative predominance of the wholesale trade over retail can be assessed by comparing losses on 5 May. Under the *nouvelle halle du marché*, losses totaled 108 setiers of grain, a quantity admittedly smaller than usual because producers, aware of the turbulence in the region, hesitated to expose their grain and themselves to potential violence. Nevertheless, one grain dealer alone, Sieur Félix, a Paris baker, held more grain, 150 setiers, in a storage room located above the former *halle*, than the sum total of losses at the marketplace. Sieur Contour, a Saint-Denis baker, held 80 setiers, and Sieur Desaubry, a miller also from Saint-Denis, stored yet another 100 setiers in rooms nearby.[39]

The merchants, bakers, and cultivators who traded at Nanteuil employed a system, like that at Magny, of storing grain in rooms leased from local residents. But in addition to the Magny-type storage space, the stables and granges of the château belonging to the Prince de Condé, the seigneur, served a similar purpose. One cultivator leased a room above the stables, and another leased a space above the council chamber, and auditory of the château.[40]

Rioters at Nanteuil also ventured beyond market and magazine to search and requisition stocks held by local cultivators in their farms. The people knew where to look: the fermier Sieur Frémin, who incurred heavy losses

37. "Le dénombrement des habitants de cette ville [Crépy-en-Valois] et des plus fortes paroisses du département (1773)," AD Oise, C 767. This document reported 1,164 inhabitants at Nanteuil.

38. "Compte-rendu des incidents qui se sont produits la veille au marché de Nanteuil (6 mai)," AD Oise, C 318.

39. "Extrait des minutes du greffe du Bailliage et Comté de Nanteuil en Nanteuil-le-Haudouin (5 mai)," AD Oise, B non coté, procès-verbaux, maréchaussée de Clermont, 1775; copy in BN, Collection Joly de Fleury, 1159, fols. 192–95. These "country-buying" bakers and millers formed part of the very active Paris provisioning system. See Kaplan, *Provisioning*, pp. 470–94.

40. Sieur Robinet, a laboureur from Droizelles, leased the first room; Sieur Frémin, a fermier from Nanteuil, leased the one above the council chamber.

during a raid on his stock of grain stored above the Condé stables, experienced incursions into the two fermes he exploited on the edges of town. At first he resisted, and for his refusal to open his doors to the people outside he saw his locks ripped out and his doors battered down. From one ferme, called La Couture, rioters removed 270 setiers, and from the other they removed 300 setiers.[41] Although Frémin was by far the biggest loser from the 5 May explosion, four other local laboureurs confronted similar attacks.

No longer constrained by former regulations to provision regularly the local marketplace, and fearful of the consequences of appearing there during the crisis, these cultivators had attempted to protect their property by staying home with it. The people of Nanteuil were enraged by the meager display in the *halle* and went looking for supplies withheld from the public place. The magnitude of grain production in the region made large-scale cultivators obvious targets.

The day after the riots at Nanteuil, a similar upheaval ravaged Meaux, an important focal point for grain traveling by land from the Brie or by barge along the Marne. This much larger town served a multiple function for the grain trade as a feeder market.[42] Located in the heart of the grain-exporting Brie, it attracted cereal from both sides of the river to its market; critically situated along a major river route to Paris, it served as a point of embarkation and through-passage for grain and flour heading west to the capital. Itsposition on the banks of the Marne favored the construction of water-powered mills that not only ground grain for local consumption but also served Parisian bakers, who converted grain they purchased at Meaux and its environs into flour for ready transport to their bakeries.[43] Finally, by serving as an important administrative and ecclesiastical center for the Brie, as well as having a sizable population, Meaux generated a consumer need that encouraged the proliferation of bakeries to provide ready-made bread.[44]

The specific events of the Flour War in Meaux followed the same pattern

41. "Extrait des minutes (5 mai)" (note 39 above).

42. In 1771 there were 1,283 *feux* counted at Meaux: "Tableaux contenant l'état et la situation des paroisses de l'Election de Meaux pendant l'année 1770 (1771)," AD Seine-et-Marne 34 C 7. The significance of Meaux for the Paris grain trade is discussed by Kaplan, *Provisioning*, pp. 126, 140, 173, 304. He notes the advanced development of merchant trading and miller and baker trading with the capital. Margairaz also notes the importance of Meaux as a feeder market (*marché-relais*) for Paris (*Foires*, p. 180).

43. Using the 1768 "Cassini" maps, Kaplan counted eight watermills and two windmills at Meaux and also noted the presence of a boat mill on the Marne (*Provisioning*, p. 304). The 1770 "Tableaux . . . de Meaux" (see note 42 above) lists four mills on the Pont de l'Echelle, five mills on the Pont du Marché, and one boat mill, but does not mention the windmills.

44. The 1770 "Tableaux . . . de Meaux" (note 42 above) lists fifteen bakers.

as those in Magny and Nanteuil.[45] Even before the market officially opened, rioters assailed the first arrivals on the *halle* and stopped carts en route with grain for sale. Fearing trouble, some cultivators had, as at Nanteuil, decided to stay home that day. It did not take long, therefore, for rioters to denude the marketplace. They then turned to attack the public "reserve" where merchants and cultivators stored grain designated for future sale or eventual removal.[46] They also invaded private storage rooms and searched "homes that had the reputation for storing grain."

Rioters at Meaux further expanded the uses of the *taxation populaire* to include other activities. They battered down the door to the Hotel Seigneurial of the Cathedral of Meaux and made off with 180 setiers of grain. Abbé Mathieu Servant, a canon and priest at the chapter, reported attacks on his private supply of grain and the pillage of 6 setiers he had sent by cart to the *halle*. Rioters also invaded bakeries and assaulted several mills in town.

Behavior such as that described for Magny-en-Vexin, Nanteuil-le-Haudouin, and Meaux found echoes throughout the part of the region engulfed by the Flour War where the Paris provisioning system had engendered feeder markets of different sizes and dimensions. After denuding markets, rioters invaded public and private storage rooms at Pontoise, Crépy-en-Valois, Vernon, Lyons-la-Forêt, and Lagny-sur-Marne while they threatened those at Troyes; they requisitioned supplies from ecclesiastical institutions in such towns as Lagny-sur-Marne, Crépy-en-Valois, Montdidier, and Senlis; they assailed mills at Poissy, Brie-Comte-Robert, and Lagny-sur-Marne.[47] All were logical targets for rioters searching for grain outside the marketplace. Altogether, I counted thirty-seven such type 2 eruptions, which constituted just under half of all market disturbances.[48]

45. On events at Meaux, see AD Seine-et-Marne, "Lettre au Prévôt Général de la maréchaussée de la Généralité de Paris (11 mai)," B 2387; "Information (8, 9, 10, 13, 17 mai)," B 2247; "Information (17 mai, 1 juin)," B 2387.

46. This "reserve" had functioned traditionally as the repository for grain whose movement was restricted by previous paternalist regulation ("Lettre [6 mai]," AD Seine-et-Marne, B 2247). Two out of the four victims who lost grain during the assault on the reserve were Parisian merchants and bakers. The merchant-miller Jean Philippe Obron claimed that just over one-third of the grain at his mill on the Pont du Marché belonged to Parisian bakers "for whom he had made purchases." Jean Baptiste François, also a merchant-miller on the Pont de l'Echelle, declared that the 100 setiers rioters took from his mill "had been destined for Paris." "Information de 8, 9, 10 mai," AD Seine-et-Marne, B 2247.

47. Among type 2 disturbances, I have counted only those that contained market disturbances as well as other types of rioting. I counted the relatively few isolated attacks on mills or ecclesiastical institutions among type 4 incidents.

48. Type 2 incidents represented 45.1 percent of all market riots and 11.7 percent of all Flour War disturbances. See Table 3.

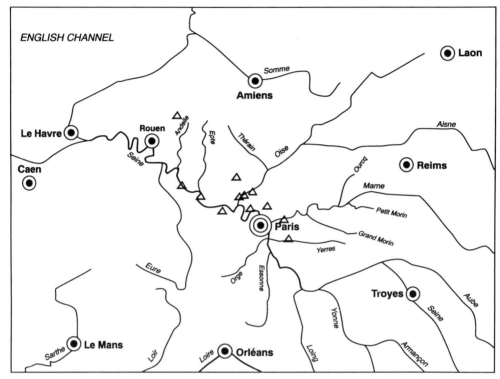

Map 3.   Locations of "Entraves" (△) During the Flour War (Type 3)

TYPE 3

During the Flour War, in addition to enacting the *taxation populaire* by targeting markets and their related services, rioters continued to resort to another traditional form of food riot behavior—the *entrave*, a type of behavior with a long history that involved intercepting barges and carts that transported grain or flour along river or land routes (see Map 3).[49] The *entrave* had a clear goal: to restrict the movement (*enlèvement* or *exportation*) of grain or flour, either to prevent it from leaving its place of origin or to

49. Both Louise Tilly and Olwen Hufton distinguish between the market riot and the *entrave*. See L. Tilly, "The Food Riot as a Form of Political Conflict in France," *JIH* 2 (1971): 23; Hufton, "Social Conflict and the Grain Supply in Eighteenth-Century France," *JIH* 14 (Fall 1983): 327. Indeed, Louise Tilly is responsible for applying the term *entrave* itself to the behavior. Contemporaries sometimes spoke of "entraves à la circulation des subsistances."

commandeer it en route to provision a hungry community. Because a number of important markets of the second type described above (the feeder or collector markets) were usually located along significant trade routes (which gave them their provisioning significance), riots that erupted in their markets often expanded to include riots of the *entrave* type when grain or flour was discovered in transport.

Such was the fate of the barges moored at the port of Pontoise on 29 April. Rioters turned from the marketplace to ravage one barge anchored in the middle of the river and another moored at the port. The one in the river belonged to Guillaume Touzel, merchant and bargeman at Pontoise, but he did not own the 363 setiers of wheat it carried. The Maison de Scipion, which formed part of the Hôpital Général of Paris, had purchased the grain "on account" in Pont-Sainte-Maxence on 26 April. Rioters dragged the barge to the bank, fixed the price of grain at 12 livres per setier (although most neglected to measure it and some paid nothing at all), and stripped its contents. They left "two very damp setiers . . . and 294 empty sacks marked 'Scipion,' many of which were slashed and torn." Nicolas Jessard, a merchant and bargeman from Pont-l'Eveque near Noyon, owned the barge moored at the port. He carried grain for several Pontoise merchants, which he had unloaded and distributed the day before the rioting erupted, and 168 setiers sold to a merchant at Saint-Germain-en-Laye by a merchant from Noyon. The Saint-Germain merchant had paid 31 livres 10 sols per setier for the grain; the rioters paid only 12 livres.[50]

Other *entraves* erupted in villages or along rivers along the major routes. On 28 April, rioters "pillaged" a barge at Stors, a small village on the river Oise seven leagues from Paris.[51] The grain on the barge belonged to Jean Martin, merchant-miller, flour dealer and fermier, who leased both his mill at Stors and his land at Presles from the Prince de Conti.[52] Martin had purchased his grain at Soissons (on the Aisne) and at Pont-Sainte-Maxence (farther up on the Oise). He had stopped the barge at Stors on the morning of 28 April "to convert it into flour at his mill and then transport the flour for the provisioning of Paris."[53]

50. "Procès-verbal qui constate le pillage du bateau de bled appartenant au Sieur Guillaume Touzel, 1 mai," AD Yvelines, 12 B 519; "Procès-verbal qui constate le pillage du bateau de bled appartenant au Sieur Nicolas Jessard, 1 mai," AD Yvelines, 12 B 519.

51. The population numbered under 80 in 1776 (Jacques Dupâquier et al., *Paroisses et communes de France. Dictionnaire administrative et démographique, Région Parisienne* (Paris, 1974), p. 526.

52. "Rôle de la taille, Presles, 1774," AN, Z1G 360A.

53. On these events, see "Procès-verbal (n.d.)," AD Oise, B 1584.

Unhappily for Martin, the location of his mill meant that he docked at a place grain-poor even in normal times. In 1768, an état had explained: "There are no tenures in this parish, it is composed only of day-laborers and woodcutters, and its badland is under the forest of Ile-Adam. There is nothing grown in this parish."[54] Seven years later, in the midst of a subsistence crisis, the local residents hastened to seize the windfall docked in their midst. Before Martin could unload his barge, the people began arriving to strip it of its contents. Although the rioters were not actually responsible for stopping the barge, they quickly took advantage of the situation, ensuring that this food, at least, would not pass hungry rural mouths to fill the growing maw of the metropolis.

Villagers similarly assailed two carts carrying flour destined for Paris passing through the village of Epinay-sur-Seine on 2 May.[55] One cart and its contents belonged to Jean-Baptiste Danneville, miller and flour merchant at Chars near Marines. The flour in the second cart belonged to Sieur Plessier, a flour merchant at Pontoise.[56] When they arrived in the village, according to the cart drivers (voituriers), children began running after the carts and yelling, "They must be stopped. It is flour." The men also observed that neither men nor women were working—everyone "was standing at their doors as if it were a Sunday." When they stopped to tend to the horses, the wheelwright and joiner, followed by a "prodigious number of people," ran up to them, took hold of the bridle of the first horse, and said, "We need flour, we have waited long enough." Both drivers put up a determined struggle to protect their cargoes, and one, who had traveled this route often enough to know and to have done business with several of the inhabitants, tried to talk them out of taking the flour. Another said to the wheelwright, "How can you stop me who exists to help you earn a living?" The wheelwright responded, "Just the same, we need flour." The people began unloading the carts and prepared to pay for what they took, when cavaliers of the maréchaussée arrived. After an exchange of insults and blows, the cavaliers withdrew, unable to prevent the inhabitants of Epinay from distributing the flour.[57] But their efforts achieved nothing.

Other entraves included several barges on the Oise near Beaumont-sur-

54. AD Oise, J 2589.

55. "Information (22 mai)," AN, Y 18682.

56. Danneville had leased his mill since at least 1773 ("Rôle de la taille, Chars, 1773," AD Yvelines, C 186). I could find nothing else about Plessier.

57. "Information (22 mai)" and "Interrogatoires de Pierre Pérard et Jean François Guyard (15

Oise on 29 April, a barge stopped at La Roche-Guyon on the Seine on 2 May, another barge passing by Tosny on the Seine on 3 May, a cart carrying grain near Ully-Saint-Georges in the Beauvaisis on 29 April, and a cart near Calais on 4 May. I counted twelve such stoppages: seven river vessels (four on the Oise, two on the Seine, and one on the Marne) and five land transports. These represent a mere 3.8 percent of all riots (see Table 3).[58] Yet, given the pervasiveness of rioting during the Flour War and the context of a highly developed Paris provisioning network, this number seems small, especially for the early days of the movement before transporters might have refused to venture forth for fear of not reaching their destination undisturbed. Later, Turgot ordered troops to accompany and protect grain and flour en route to Paris.

The most likely explanation for the relative paucity of *entraves* during the Flour War is to see the events in the feeder and collector market towns, particularly the attacks on storage rooms and mills, as "preemptive" *entraves*. Rioters knew well the intended destination of grain and flour stored in these places, and raids thus functioned as a way of diverting stores from Paris or other urban "collector" markets for local use. Such moves were designed to halt the very departure of grain and flour marked for transport. Thus, stopped at the local market during the Flour War, little grain exited town to confront the classic *entrave* later in passage.

TYPE 4

The fourth and final—and perhaps most dramatic—type of disturbance erupted in the countryside of the *pays de grande culture* (see Map 4).[59] Directed principally against stocks held in the farms of large-scale cultiva-

---

mai)," AN, Y 18682. On another occasion, cart-drivers actually overcame the efforts of rioters to take their cargo ("Procès-verbal des événements à Moisselles, 2 mai," AD Oise, B 1583). Employees did not always defend wholeheartedly the property of their employers. The *contre-maître* of a barge, stopped at Petit Andely on the Seine for assistance in getting its tow-horses to the other bank, offered to let the inhabitants who helped his barge have the grain saying, "You can take it. I don't count on taking it far" ("Lettre de 31 mai," AD Seine-Maritime, C 108).

58. Six other *entraves* related directly to events taking place in markets, and I have counted these among type 2 behaviors.

59. This type erupted in all parts of the *pays de grande culture* discussed in Chapter 2, except Picardy.

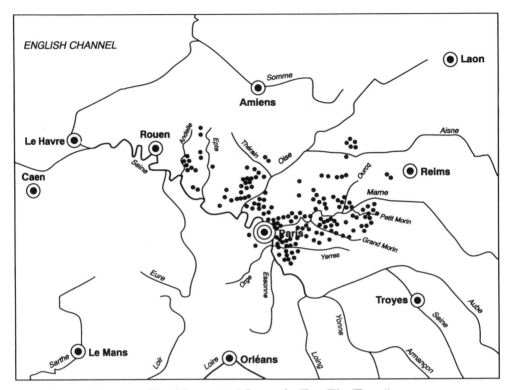

Map 4. Locations of Rural Rioting (●) During the Flour War (Type 4)

tors, it sometimes included forays against stores in rural mills and religious communities, and more rarely against those in seigneurial residences. Some of these rural disturbances were obviously related to the second type of feeder market riot described above, such as that in Nanteuil-le-Haudouin, where riots born in towns moved to the countryside and appeared as natural extensions of activities of the town to its producing hinterland. At Brie-Comte-Robert on 5 May, rioters descended on the marketplace first, assailed the storage rooms of merchants and cultivators next, and finally visited "all the laboureurs in the city and the *faubourgs*, from whom they took all threshed grain."[60] But the overwhelming majority of such disturbances erupted independent of activities in specific market towns. During the Flour War, they constituted a massive movement in the countryside.

For those who produced and still retained surplus grain, the troubles

60. "Lettre (5 mai)," BN, Collection Joly de Fleury, 1159, fols. 21–22.

associated with this movement began on 29 April, two days after the initial eruption at Beaumont-sur-Oise, in the villages of Berne, Morancy, Bruyères, and Boran. They continued daily until the last known incident at Boismetot on 11 May. The number of episodes accelerated, reaching a maximum between 5 and 7 May, when rioters struck as many as thirty-five farms daily. Altogether, I counted 150 such rural disturbances.[61]

These disturbances took a similar form everywhere. Bands of rioters "from the *pays* and *environs*" presented themselves at the doors of the farms, demanded grain at a reduced price, searched granaries, and immediately distributed among themselves what grain they found. These country confrontations were local affairs; rioters and their targets frequently knew each other by name and could almost always identify each other by community. On 7 May, for example, "approximately thirty people" visited the farm of the widow Notaire, *fermière* at Champdeuil, to demand grain. When she told them she had none, they responded that "she had better find them some, and then they climbed into her granary where she distributed 19 setiers and one minot of grain." She recognized thirteen people from her own village and six from two nearby parishes.[62]

Occasionally rioters pillaged grain outright, but many others left IOUs, and the overwhelming majority paid for it at the popularly adjusted price. The amount of violence mounted by the rioters was proportional to the nature of resistance victims turned against rioters. Although most cultivators simply let the rioters "work their will, without account and without measuring," a few attempted to retain some control over their fates. Then the rioters often broke down doors and forced locks; more rarely, scuffles erupted between victims and rioters. A few successfully hid their stores from watchful assailants, and a handful even managed to mount an effective defense. Cultivators frequently attempted to make the most of a dangerous situation by privileging known locals over unknown "strangers" in the distribution of their grain. Others delivered grain as charity to those who appeared at their farms. Sometimes rioters demanded money, drank the farm's wine, or helped themselves to other possessions.[63]

Although laboureurs and fermiers constituted by far the largest category

61. Although rioters who participated in these incursions may have had knowledge of marketplace disturbances, I specifically included in this count only activities for which there was no direct connection between market and rural rioting.

62. She even named them ("Procès-verbal [7 mai]," AD Seine-et-Marne, B 3956[1]). For more on the local nature of these events, see Chapter 5.

63. For more on this, see Chapter 5.

of victims during the rioting in the countryside, they were not the only targets. Rioters also descended on a few rural religious communities, rural mills, and resident seigneurs.[64] The 30 April attack on the Benedictine monastery at Saint-Leu-d'Esserent on the Oise is the best-documented case of an attack on a rural religious community during the Flour War.[65] The monks accused four riverworkers, "all of whom were simple day-laborers at St.-Leu possessing no land," of leading the assault. These leaders, armed with sticks, incited the inhabitants of the nearby hamlet of Boissy to join them. Three hundred rioters invaded the monastery and demanded grain at 12 livres per setier and bread at 1½ sous per livre. They further demanded a kind of forced charity when they told the monks to give grain "even to those who had no money." When the Prior attempted to bargain for a higher price, "since grain was worth 38–40 livres at the market," several rioters responded by sounding the tocsin "to excite the rest of the inhabitants to make common cause with them." The monks finally agreed to have the village bakers, provisioned with grain from the monastery, bake all the bread necessary at 2 sous per livre. The rioters agreed and retired, and the monks "fait battre la caisse" and posted their announcement.[66] Altogether, rioters attacked five rural ecclesiastical institutions.

On 29 April, several hundred rioters descended on two mills at Mours on the river Oise, one leased by Jacques Lierval and the other by Jacques Dorival.[67] Despite the efforts of Lierval and his wife to intimidate their assailants by arming themselves with a large hook and a knife, rioters responded to an exhortation from an unknown member of the crowd to "be bold," broke down the door to the mill, and took four sacks of flour, each one weighing more than 300 livres. When Dorival confronted them in turn,

64. Differentiation between attacks on these rural targets and those located in the towns may seem artificial because rioters turned against both for many similar reasons. Yet this behavior is different from the behavior in town actions, which required less premeditation. When rioters turned against these rural targets, they did so by making a conscious decision to act and often constituted the only violent act they committed. In the towns, the momentum derived from the initial uprising in the marketplace carried rioters to other places where grain was stored.

65. "Procès-verbal (n.d.)," AD Oise, B 1583bis; "Extrait des minutes du greffe du Bailliage Provincial de Senlis (1 mai)," BN, Collection Joly de Fleury, 1159, fols. 249–50. On the monastery itself, see Albert Fossard, Le Prieurie de Saint-Leu-d'Esserent (Paris, 1934).

66. Tensions remained high, however, and the monks worried about a resurgence of violence for some time after the initial eruption. For twelve days they posted guards outside the monastery and kept the price of bread at 2 sols until 20 June (and the price of grain between 18 and 24 livres per setier). They calculated that the monastery incurred a loss of more than 3,000 livres.

67. "Procès-verbal de la sédition et des déclarations faites à Mours (29 avril)," AD Oise, B 1583bis. On Dorival and Lierval, see "Rôle de la taille, Mours, 1774," AN, Z1G 360a.

he explained that "the grain wasn't his and the flour was for the provisioning of Paris." The people retorted that "they didn't give a damn about the provisioning of Paris and they were going to lift the roof off his house and dash it to ruins." Dorival submitted and turned over twelve sacks of flour.[68] I counted twelve attacks of mills during the Flour War.[69]

On 6 May, rioters attacked the one of only three seigneurs to experience direct rural incursions during the Flour War.[70] Sixty-year-old Nicolas Deshuissards, seigneur of Saint-Martin-lès-Voulangis, was compelled to distribute "7–8 muids" of grain to people from neighboring parishes, most of whom he recognized by name.[71] Rioters also raided the residence and granaries of the seigneur of Roncherolles-en-Bray on 8 May.[72]

These type 4 rural confrontations constituted the overwhelming majority of disturbances of the Flour War, thus comprising an important facet of popular behavior.[73]

As the population of France (and especially that of Paris) grew during the eighteenth century, as the wholesale grain and flour trade expanded, as the network of participants diversified, as the forms of business practices multiplied, and as liberalization facilitated processes well under way before the attempted implementation of the policy, consumers watched attentively and suspiciously. When dearth loomed, when prices rose, when the people moved to assert control over this "item of the first necessity," they knew well where to look. They widened the range of uses of the *taxation populaire* to respond to the multiple dimensions of the grain trade. If behavior during subsistence movements appears more sophisticated by the end of the century than at the beginning, it was in part because grain production and trade had become more sophisticated, more multidimensional. The Flour War thus stands as testimony to the development of the producing and marketing systems.

68. Again, this evidence might support a broader definition of what constituted an *entrave*-type pattern of behavior.

69. Rioters assailed far fewer mills than any survey of possible targets would suggest as likely. For such a survey, see Kaplan, *Provisioning*, pp. 250, 276, 304–15.

70. Attacks on seigneurs themselves were rare, which is not surprising because in the Paris Basin—especially in the *pays de grande culture*, where most of these country actions took place—most seigneurs chose to live elsewhere. Their estate managers and *fermiers* controlled the grain their lands produced and collected the dues associated with their privileged status. For more on this, see Chapter 6.

71. "Information (16 mai)," AD Seine-et-Marne, B 2387.

72. "Lettre (30 mai)," AD Seine-Maritime, C 107.

73. Type 4 rioting comprised 64 percent of all rioting, while types 1 and 2 combined, market riots, tallied 25.9 percent. See Table 3.

When the subsistence crisis struck the Paris Basin in 1775, it generated a massive movement in the countryside as well as in the elementary, feeder, and urban collector markets in the region. Those who rioted drew on a combination of accurate information about grain production and marketing, on traditions of paternalist practice that included price-fixing, searches and requisitions, and distributions, and on their own heritage of previous *taxations populaires*. The Flour War, in this respect, was consistent with earlier patterns of behavior, and at the same time, by virtue of its scale and scope as well as patterns of participation, constituted a further stage of sophistication and development in this form of popular movement. Tables 3 and 4 provide an overview and chronology of Flour War incidents by type of action.

Patterns of Participation

To these four types of behavior and theaters of action also correspond particular gender and class patterns of participation. Market rioting may have been "women's work," but the independent incursions into the farms of cultivators fell to men. Moreover, men were more inclined than women to venture beyond neighborhood and village to wage either the town or the countryside battles of the Flour War. And the rank-and-file of the country confrontations came more frequently from the wage-laboring occupations than did those who challenged merchants, producers, bakers, and authorities in the market towns.

Historians (not to mention contemporary observers) have frequently noted the important presence of women in subsistence riots. The Flour War, of course, was no exception, and Chapter 3 has already provided some examples. Indeed, the very first episode of the Flour War, at the market of Beaumont-sur-Oise on 27 April, revealed the role of women. Not only did many witnesses indict "the women of the waterfront" as probable co-instigators, but all who testified about what they saw at the start of the market claimed that "women threw themselves upon a [female] grain merchant, insulting her, swearing that she wanted to sell her grain too dearly, punching her and knocking her to the ground." Angelique Lefevre played a crucial role during the "pre-riot" at Pontoise; the red-scarved "Princess" Madelaine Pochet led the riots at Brie-Comte-Robert; and Marie

Table 4. Chronology of Flour War Incidents by Type of Action

Date	Type 1[a]	Type 2[b]	Type 3[c]	Type 4[d]	Other[e]	Unknown[f]
27 April Thursday	Beaumont-sur-Oise					
28 April Friday	Méru		Stors		Pont-Sainte-Maxence	
29 April Saturday	Mouy	Pontoise	Beaumont-sur-Oise Royaumont	Berne Boran Bruyères Morancy Mours (m) Presles (m)	Beauvais	
30 April Sunday				Saint-Martin-lès-Nonnettes (r) Saint-Leu-d'Esserent (r) Presles (m)	Pontoise	
1 May Monday		Magny-en-Vexin Gisors Saint-Germain-en-Laye Noailles Meulan Gonesse	Triel-sur-Seine Framicourt	Belloy Cauvigny Cavillon Maffliers Moisselles Montsoult Mouchy-le-Châtel Novillers-lès-Cailloux Tillard	Pont-Sainte-Maxence Nanterre	
2 May Tuesday	Gournay-en-Bray	Etrépagny Versailles Poissy Argenteuil Senlis	La Roche-Guyon Franconville Epinay-sur-Seine	Ully-Saint-Georges Asnières Baillet Belloy-en-France Bouffémont Cauvigny Champlâtreux Fontenay-en-Parisis Franconville		

Table 4. (Continued)

Date	Type 1[a]	Type 2[b]	Type 3[c]	Type 4[d]	Other[e]	Unknown[f]
3 May Wednesday	Bréteuil Marines	Crépy-en-Valois Paris Vernon		Grand Gournay Méru Maffliers Moisselles Montsoult Mouchy-le-Châtel Ully-Saint-Georges Aulnoy-les-Bondy Avernes Cauffry Genainville (m) Louvres Rennemoulin (m) Rougemont Saint-Marcel Savigny Sevran Thiverny Us Vétheuil (m) Vienne-en-Arthies (m) Vigny Villepinte	Boulogne Rueil	
4 May Thursday	Limours Pacy Gonesse	Vernon Villers-Cotterêts Lyons-la-Forêt Dammartin-en-Göele Choisy-le-Roi	Souilly	Chelles Fresne-sur-Marne Monté-en-Göele Annet-sur-Marne Crépy-en-Valois Breuil-le-Vert Cauffry Bouillant	Gressy (m)	

5 May
Friday

Arpajon
Fontainebleau
Gaillefontaine
Chaumont-en-Vexin
Saint-André
Crécy-en-Brie

Brie-Comte-Robert
Lagny-sur-Marne
Lizy-sur-Ourcq
Nanteuil-le-Haudouin
Ferté-Milon

Les Andelys

Bièvres
Bobigny
Drancy
Groslay
Rosny
Bondy
Gagny
Villepinte
Crosne
Aulnay-lès-Bondy
Sevran
Le Blanc-Mesnil
Compiègne
Coyolles
Pissaleux
La Noue
Lognes
Guermantes
Gisy
Combault
Cossigny
Brégy
Ferrières
Couilly
Charmentray
Bertichère
Villerest
Mesnil-Verclives
Touffreville
Gaillardbois
Dorais
Brémule
Charleval
Grainville

Pierrefonds
Pont-Sainte-Maxence
Arnoult

Table 4. (Continued)

Date	Type 1[a]	Type 2[b]	Type 3[c]	Type 4[d]	Other[e]	Unknown[f]
				Mussegros		
				Croutoy		
				Férolles		
				Créteil		
				Sucy-en-Brie		
				La Queue-en-Brie		
				Chennevières		
				Roissy-en-Brie		
				Montévrain		
				Artilly		
				Pontault		
				Chanteloup		
				Jossigny		
				Haute Maison		
				Combault		
				Coyolles (s)		
6 May	Jouarre	Meaux	Chaumes-en-Brie	Favières	Linas (m)	
Saturday	La Ferté-Alais	Nemours		Signy-Signets	Charenton (m)	
	Louviers	Lizy-sur-Ourcq		Saint-Martin-lès-Voulangis (s)	Crépy-en-Valois	
	Clermont	Noyon		Réez-Fosse-Martin		
	Maule	Montdidier		Chauconin		
	Ressons	Attichy		Marcilly		
		Melun		Boutigny		
		Dourdon		Presles		
				Poincy		
				Saint-Fiacre		
				Trilport		
				Cossigny		
				Vaucourtois		
				Forfry		
				Bailly		

7 May Sunday	Soissons		
		Villemareuil	
		La Celle-sur-Morin	
		Ertépilly	
		Barcy	
		Coutevroult	
		Lissy	
		Yerres	
		Boutigny	
		Nanteuil-lès-Meaux	
		Soignolles	
		Chevry	
		Gretz	
		Armainvilliers	
		Ozouer-le-Voulgis (r)	
		Alfort	
		Villeneuve-Saint-Georges	
		Limeil	
		Valenton	
		Cordon	
		Grisy	
		Montévrain	
		Dommier	
		Saint-Pierre-Aigle	
		Crécy-la-Chapelle (m)	
		Torcy	
		Sancy	
		La Chapelle	Jaignes (m)
		Signy-Signets	Braine
		Pierre-Levée	
		Jouarre	
		Saint-Germain-lès-Corbeil	
		Maupertuis	
		Plessy-Placy	
		Congis (m)	

Table 4. (Continued)

Date	Type 1[a]	Type 2[b]	Type 3[c]	Type 4[d]	Other[e]	Unknown[f]
				Chauconin		
				Puisieux		
				Crisenoy		
				Haute Maison		
				Barcy		
				La Celle-sur-Morin		
				Errépilly		
				Varreddes		
				Penchard		
				Champdeuil		
				Giremoutiers		
				Maisoncelles-en-Brie		
				Vendrest		
				Villemareuil		
				Coutevroult		
				Champigny		
				Limeil		
				Cossigny		
				Crépoil		
				Tancrou		
				Echampeu		
				May-en-Multien		
				Braine		
				Dammartin-en-Brie		
				Malmaison		
				La Chapelle		
				Soignolles-en-Brie		
				Périgny		
8 May Monday	Buchy	La Ferté-sous-Jouarre	near Rouvray	Jouarre		
	Les Andelys			Saint-Germain-les-Corbeil		
	Roye			Grand Champ		

9 May Tuesday	Blérancourt Dreux Rouen Beaumont-du-Gâtinais Neufchâtel-en-Bray Saint-Saëns Gournay-en-Bray Dormans	Chaunay Crouy-sur-Ourcq		Rouvray Roncherolles-en-Bray (s) Saint-Rémy (r)
10 May Wednesday	Coulommiers Bacqueville-en-Caux Darnétal			Sablonnières Saint-Léger
11 May Thursday	Auffay-en-Caux			
12 May Friday	Gaillefontaine		Beaurieux	
13 May Saturday	Auffay-en-Caux	Fismes	Melun	Saint-Gilles
15 May	Dieppe			
18 May Wednesday				Argueuil
Date Unknown	Montfort-sur-Risle Pont-Saint-Pierre Chateaulandon Grandvilliers Péronne		Mantes Fére-en-Tardenois	Saussay Chézy Heubécourt Brumets Tilly Surcy Haricourt Boismetôt

Note: This table records all the incidents (including Paris, Versailles, and Saint-Germain-en-Laye) associated with the Flour War.

[a] In type 1 incidents, rioters wielded the *taxation populaire* largely within the physical confines of the marketplace. Although most of the markets that appear in this category were elementary or entrepôt markets, a few, such as Beaumont-sur-Oise, Gonesse, Rouen, and Soissons, functioned as broader feeder or collector markets. In these cases, rioters limited their actions despite other opportunities. This limited behavior usually (with the exception of Beaumont-sur-Oise, where the first rioting erupted) reflected either effective repressive power or successful negotiations by authorities.

b In type 2 incidents, rioters expanded their activities from the marketplace to claim grain and flour held in public and private storage areas, mills, granaries of local cultivators, town-based religious communities, bakeries, etc. The markets that appear in this category were feeder or collector markets.

c In type 3 incidents, rioters resorted to the *entrave*: the interception of barges and carts transporting grain along river or land routes. This category includes only those *entraves* that occurred outside of market disturbances (such as type 2 incidents).

d In type 4 incidents, rioters directed their attacks against stores in farms of large-scale cultivators, rural mills (designated by a letter "m" after the place name), religious communities (designated by a letter "r" after the place name), and against seigneurial residences (designated by a letter "s" after the place name). I have not included rioting that was directly related to type 2 disturbances. Many places listed here experienced more than one incident, such as forays against more than one farm in the same village. For example, rioters invaded the farms of seven different fermiers and laboureurs at Berne on 29 April. I have listed main village names rather than hamlet or farmstead names.

e This category "Other" includes incidents of potential but not actual rioting in markets (such as Beauvais and Pont-Sainte-Maxence) or elsewhere (such as the mill at Gressy); unrest that persisted after initial riots (such as Melun, Crépy-en-Valois, or Pontoise) but that did not produce new eruptions; and rioting that swept storage areas but nowhere else (Braine). It also includes rioting in towns within the ten-league *cercle interdit* around Paris from which significant markets were prohibited and where rioting took the form of trouble at bakeries (Nanterre, Rueil, and Boulogne) or flour merchants (Argenteuil).

f The category "Unknown" includes references to incidents that do not give sufficient information to determine the type of action involved.

Table 5.   Gender and Type of Action

Type of Action	Men (%)	Women (%)
Types 1 and 2	53.6	79.6
Type 3	3.7	7.5
Type 4	27.9	9.7
Other actions[a]	11.9	2.2
Unknown	2.9	1.1

Note: Each column is calculated as a percentage of either all men or all women who rioted and were arrested. The total number of men is 455 and the total number of women is 93.

[a] "Other actions" includes (1) arrests of local authorities and notables for nonfeasance and misfeasance but not actually for rioting; (2) arrests of people for not making restitution but providing no indication of where rioting occurred; and (3) arrests for rioting at a bakery at Nanterre.

Margarite Lefevre and Catherine Clerfeuille led women with knives to rip open the sacks of grain displayed on the market of Méru. Rioting erupted at the markets of Gaillefontaine and Bacqueville-en-Caux when women became violent after bartering for lower prices broke down. Women also played prominent roles at such towns as Beaumont-du-Gâtinais, Gisors, Choisy-le-Roi, Conty, Lagny-sur-Marne, and Nemours. One is tempted to conclude with historian Olwen Hufton that this evidence further substantiates her argument that the grain riot was a "female terrain," except that female participation was rarely completely exclusive and it varied according to the type of riot described above.

Market town riots (of either the first or second type) constituted a female action par excellence, and rioting there was visibly "women's business." *Entraves* (type 3) tended to involve more balanced proportions of men and women. The rural manifestations of the Flour War (type 4), however, were overwhelmingly male in composition. These patterns emerge clearly both from an analysis of arrests as an indicator of proportional representation (see Table 5) and from an examination of witness testimonies.

Almost 80 percent of all women arrested had participated in market and market-related riots; fourteen of the fifteen women arrested for leading rioting had acted in market town disturbances. Almost 54 percent of all men arrested had engaged in similar behavior. With few exceptions, such as the textile manufacturing town of Mouy, where male wool and serge workers dominated most aspects of the rioting and appeared exceptionally well organized, women emerged as crucial figures in market rioting and, as we have already seen, observers were quick to signal their roles.[74] Relatively similar proportions of men and women were arrested for participation in *entraves*: 3.7 percent men and 7.5 percent women, figures largely substantiated by witness testimony.

The gender composition of the crowd is reversed for rural confrontations (type 4). Although women sometimes participated in these disturbances and even, very rarely, led the rioting,[75] men constituted and led these actions with greater frequency and visibility than women. Almost 28 percent of all men arrested rioted, a number that contrasts significantly with the 10 percent female participation. More striking is that only one of the twenty-four leaders arrested for leading rural *attroupements* was female. The galvanic effects of rioting men coursing through the countryside ring clearly in witness accounts. When asked to identify those who rioted, victims and witnesses invariably named men. Nicolas Deshuissards, seigneur at Saint-Martin-lès-Voulangis, recognized thirteen people from among the hundreds he claimed raided his château on 6 May. All were men. Louis Rougeolle, fermier at Mousselen, identified six men and one woman from among the crowd that appeared at his farm on 3 May. Remy Martin, laboureur at Le Bois-de-Brie near Villemareuil, listed twenty-two men and only five women. The widow Taveau at Cossigny named only men from the crowd who came to her farm on 5 May. This violent group not only took grain "at a low price," but also "forced the door to the laundry room, where they took and emptied the sacks, . . . entered the kitchen and took bread, wine and cheese and, not content with that, when they were full, . . . threw [the food] on the floor and crushed it under their feet."[76]

---

74. Although authorities arrested far more men than women during the Flour War (see Chapter 3), this is more a reflection of differences in the perceived threat that men vs. women posed than in actual numbers involved. This is the only way to interpret the contradiction between arrest figures and testimony (a situation that does not exist for rural confrontations discussed below). For this reason, I rely on proportion figures for gendered behavior rather than directly comparing female vs. male figures.

75. The examples are few indeed and included the band of 20–30 (some said 40–50) women who visited Sieur Roger, fermier at Alfort on 6 May and Jacques Day, fermier at Créteil on 5 May ("Procès-verbal de 6 mai" and "Information de 13 mai" AN, Y 18682). These women may have been associated with the band of women who accused the miller on the bridge at Charenton of hiding his grain at Roger's farm ("Information de 13 mai," AN, Y 18682). Louis Gilbon, fermier at La Tour, parish of Saint Germain-lès-Corbeil, claimed that on 7 May "approximately 20 women led by 2 men" appeared at his farm ("Procès-verbal de 7 mai" and "Information de 15 mai," AD Seine-et-Marne, B 3957[2]).

76. On Deshuissards, see "Information (16 mai)," AD Seine-et-Marne, B 2387; on Rougeolle,

Therefore, differently gendered theaters of action existed, and only some kinds of subsistence riots were female terrain; others belonged to the men. Women tended to operate most prominently within the marketplace or in related spaces; men tended to form the rural battalions of the Flour War. Of course, no marketplace was occupied exclusively by female rioters, and neither was the countryside invaded exclusively by male rioters, but each type of action carried gendered characteristics and gendered meanings as well (see Chapters 5 and 6).

Men and women differed in another aspect of rioting too. Men were more inclined than women to venture beyond their village or neighborhood of residence to ply the tools of the *taxation populaire* in either market or countryside; women's actions remained linked more to the context of village or neighborhood than men's actions.[77] Over 50 percent of all men who were arrested during the Flour War rioted outside their own locale; only slightly over one-third rioted where they lived.[78] More than 60 percent of all women who were arrested did so where they lived, and just over one-third went elsewhere.[79] Although rioters from the Beauvaisis and other regions with more mixed agriculture and less integrated markets tended to rove less than those from mono-cultural surplus-grain-producing regions with large-scale collector and feeder markets, this gendered pattern of behavior remains generally applicable. At the market of Pontoise, for example, more than 70 percent of female rioters were locals, while only 46 percent of male rioters came from local neighborhoods. Only at the site of the first riot of the Flour War, Beaumont-sur-Oise, did local men and women appear in equal percentages: just over 80 percent were locals.[80] Altogether, police arrested

see "Déposition (8 mai)," AN, Y 18682; on Martin, see "Information (12 mai)," AD Seine-et-Marne, B 2387; on Taveau, see "Déposition (13 mai)," AD Seine-et-Marne, B 3957. Charles Vachette, fermier and laboureur at Cauffry, kept an exact list of all those who came to his farm on 2 and 3 May. Out of 107 rioters, he counted almost twice as many men as women ("Information de 15 mai," AD Oise, B non coté, maréchaussée de Clermont, 1775; see also list published in Ikni et al., *Rochefoucauld-Liancourt*, pp. 379–82.

77. This observation is substantiated by David Garrioch, *Neighborhood and Community in Paris, 1740–1790* (Cambridge, 1986), and Temma Kaplan, "Female Consciousness and Collective Action: The Barcelona Case, 1910–1918," *Signs* (1982): 545–66. This evidence is no doubt partially skewed by assumptions governing arrests, but as will be discussed in later chapters, even if authorities saw "foreign" men as most dangerous and arrested them in greater numbers, the arrest of "local" women makes little sense.

78. Some 53.6 percent of all men went elsewhere; 36.9 percent stayed home and rioted; information is unknown for 9.5 percent (such as those arrested for failure to make restitution without any record of where grain to be restituted was to be acquired).

79. Some 61.3 percent of the women rioted at home; 37.6 percent rioted elsewhere. This information is unknown for only 1.1 percent of the women.

80. For Pontoise, 53.6 percent of the men arrested came from outside, while 46.4 percent came

slightly more "outsiders" than "insiders" for their behavior during the Flour War.[81]

Men were also more likely to make multiple incursions into different farms or involve themselves in more than one type of situation. Louis Thibaut, a publican and vine-grower from the parish of Vendrest, traveled to two different farms at Lizy-sur-Ourcq on 5 May and then to two mills (one at Lizy and one at Jaignes) and another farm (at la Trousse) on 7 May. His activities involved two days of traveling totaling sixteen miles and two different types of behavior. On 1 May, François Laurent traveled a circuit of more than ten miles when he went from his home at Dieudonne to the farms at Cavillon, Fercourt, Châteaurouge, Fayel, and Cauvigny.[82] Although Madelaine Pochet, the red-scarved Princess of Brie-Comte-Robert, may have totaled three farms as well as the earlier market, she stayed within the confines of the town of Brie.[83] Only Veronique Prévôt voyaged as readily, but still not as far, as many men. On 29 April she traveled to the mills at Mours, to the mill at Presles, and to two barges in her home town of Beaumont-sur-Oise. The circuit totaled just over four miles.[84]

As in most food riots, there was very little violence in the Flour War. Only 2 percent of all rioters arrested used violence against another person. Among these, the women arrested were as violent as the men, although a higher percentage of women arrested were more violent than men. Five women engaged in some form of physical assault against people (5.4 percent of all women arrested); six men behaved similarly (1.6 percent of all men arrested). Françoise Martin was accused of being the most violent and seditious person at the market of Beaumont-en-Gâtinais on 9 May. She announced publicly that "the sacks [of grain] must be split open," and she hit a merchant and grabbed him by the hair.[85] Madeleine Louette, Catherine

---

from Pontoise or very close neighboring parishes (such as Saint-Ouen-l'Aumone); 28.2 percent of all women arrested came from outside, while 71.8 percent were locals. At Beaumont-sur-Oise, 83 percent of all men and women arrested were locals. Only at the market of Brie-Comte-Robert is this gendered pattern reversed (100 percent of all women arrested came from outside), but the sample is so small that it tells us little. Moreover, a record number of male outsiders (77.3 percent) were arrested too.

81. Some 50.9 percent were outsiders; 41.1 percent were insiders; the information is unknown for 8.1 percent.

82. "Interrogatoire (n.d.)," AD Oise, B 1583bis.

83. On Thibault, see "Interrogatoire (14 mai)," AD Seine-et-Marne, B 2387. On Pochet, see Chapter 3.

84. "Interrogatoire (25 mai)," AD Oise, B 1583ter.

85. "Interrogatoire (16 mai)," AD Seine-et-Marne, B 3957(1). After this interrogation she was sent to the Bastille ("Interrogatoire [1 juillet]," AN, Y 11441).

Clerfeuille, and Marguerite Beauvais engaged in various forms of violence during the rioting at Méru on 28 April. Catherine and Madeleine roughed up some laboureurs. Marguerite did the same thing, but also brandished a knife.[86] Marie Louise Archer punched a cavalier of the maréchaussée during the rioting at Pontoise on 29 April.[87] All the women arrested for physical violence had done so in the marketplace, and three of them had acted together in the same place. Two out of the six men turned violent in the marketplace, and both acted together. Pierre Pavis and Jean-Claude Bertrand helped to carry the *blatier* to the fountain at Beaumont-sur-Oise and dunked him.[88] André LeGrand discovered the doors to the town of Pontoise closed the day after the rioting there and tried to enter by throwing stones at the guards.[89] Etienne Alliot and Pierre Lamotte brawled with laboureurs during a type 4 disturbance: Alliot attacked a laboureur in Signy-Signet, and Lamotte attacked one in May-en-Multien.[90] Charles Degaast began his exploits at the market of Méru, but not until he got to the mill at Blainville did he turn violent and attack one of the miller's helpers.[91] Although these examples are too few to permit great generalization, they do seem to exhibit some of the basic patterns in gendered behavior associated with different types of rioting: women in type 1 and 2 disturbances, men in type 4 riots.[92]

The Flour War also comprised different occupational theaters of action (see Table 6).[93] Although both the marketplace (types 1 and 2) and rural (type 4) actions attracted participants from the full spectrum of occupations discussed in Chapter 3, the rural manifestations drew more heavily from the wage-labor force. Almost three times as many unskilled day-laborers (journaliers and manouvriers) participated in the independent raids on the farms

86. "Interrogatoires (24 juillet)," AD Oise, B 1583ter. For more on the situation on Méru, see Chapter 5.
87. "Interrogatoire (29 avril)," AD Oise, B 1583bis.
88. "Sentence (22 novembre)," AD Oise, B 1583.
89. "Interrogatoire (n.d.)," AD Oise, B 1583bis.
90. On Alliot, "Interrogatoire (31 mai)," AD Seine-et-Marne, B 2387; on Lamotte, "Interrogatoire (1 november 1775)," AD Oise, B non coté, maréchaussée de Clermont, 1775."
91. "Interrogatoires (2, 5, 13 mai)," AD Oise, B 1583.
92. Furthermore, they suggest another difference between French and British food riots. John Bohstedt argues that "women's riots were significantly less violent than men's" ("Gender, Household, and Community Politics: Women in English Riots, 1790–1810," *Past and Present* 120 (Aug. 1988: 104). My numbers are too small to do more than suggest that further research is necessary.
93. Although it would be partially accurate to dismiss occupational variations in different types of rioting as a reflection of the variations in the socioeconomic environment of each geographical type, this does not explain all the variations present. As seen above, rural "outsiders" were frequently arrested for actions in marketplaces, thus mingling "ecotypes" and making such generalizations more difficult. More analysis will follow here and in later chapters. See also Appendix 3.

Table 6. Rioter Occupations and Type of Action

Occupations	Types 1 & 2	Type 4
1. Unskilled day-laborers	8.8%	25.7%
2. Semiskilled & dependent skilled day-laborers	19.2	18.4
3. Artisans/independent crafts (except milling, baking, etc.)	13.8	14.0
4. Merchants/service (except grain/flour merchants, etc.)	5.0	4.4
5. Innkeepers/publicans	1.6	2.2
6. Vine-growers (Pontoise, 28; elsewhere, 8.8)	36.8	18.4
7. Rural propertied groups (except vine-growers)	0.9	0.7
8. Officials/notables	3.5	5.9
9. Grain/flour traders/bakers/millers (including their workers)	4.4	1.5
10. Others	1.6	1.5
11. Unknown	4.4	7.4
Total	100.0	100.1

Note: The figures in this table are derived by calculating the percentage of all rioters arrested for participating in each type of action. Type 3, the *entrave*, did not produce a statistically useful sample for comparison here. It is discussed separately in the text.

of laboureurs and fermiers or on the occasional rural mill or monastery, than in the marketplace riots. Twice as many vine-growers sought grain in the marketplace, and at Pontoise especially, than in the farms of the countryside. Yet outside Pontoise, vine-growers visited more farms than markets.

Witness testimony confirms these statistical observations in every case except that of the non-vine-growing propertied groups. Officials and victims reported the presence of the small- and medium-sized laboureur or fermier in all types of rioting (see Chapter 3), but they were especially visible in the countryside, joining fellow villagers to search the granaries of large producers and to distribute and carry off the grain found there. They appeared with horses and carts and, perhaps most significant, were known to everyone.

Riots associated with *entrave* behavior drew from a more diverse cross section of society, involving day-laborers, artisans, and shopkeepers, rich and poor, propertied and propertyless, in mixed proportions. The leaders of the *entrave*, a blacksmith and a cobbler, on two carts passing through Epinay-sur-Seine, came from the artisanal elite of that village's society. Those who ransacked the barge at Stors came from the poorer sections of a rural environment, where "nothing is grown." An attack on a barge raided in the village of Tosny near La Roche-Guyon provides the most staggering example of elite participation in the Flour War. The subdelegate reported that a certain Pierre Deshaye took eleven sacks of flour during the *entrave*. Styled the "coq des pillards," he was reported to have 40,000 livres in property in his village of Freneuse. For all that, the police never arrested him, and we are left to wonder about the power of rumor (or the power of 40,000 livres in property). Despite these difficulties, however, the *entrave* appears to have mobilized more diverse interests around its goal—the interdiction and immediate dispersal of grain or flour departing from or passing through a community—than any other form of behavior.

Closely examined, the Flour War thus reveals an economic society that was more complex and diverse than the superficial similarity of events suggests. Within the complexity, however, discernible patterns of geography and behavior emerge. These reflect the nature of grain production, trade, and consumption in specific regions interacting with such factors as class and gender. Together these factors cemented disparate individuals into cohesive communities that mounted collective actions of self-defense during the Flour War.

Chapter 5

THE ROLE OF COMMUNITY
IN THE FLOUR WAR

Flour War rioters operated in what contemporaries called *attroupements*, bands or groups. Not just individuals who happened to be on the same mission in the same place at the same time, they were people engaged in a collective action in which the bonding agent came from some prior sense of solidarity or "community." Many historians have emphasized a relationship between "community" and collective action such as food riots. In general, they describe this community as both organizational and normative, engaging social networks and shared values.

Subsistence crises mobilized social networks, stimulated the moral economy, and provoked action. As a general statement, however, this description lacks precision in a dynamic world such as late eighteenth-century France, where changing market relations, socioeconomic structures, and administrative organization and royal policy restructured social networks and provoked defection from the community in its social and cultural senses. Defectors—most frequently commercially oriented surplus-grain producers, grain and flour merchants, and physiocratically minded officials—embraced the free market as opposed to the regulated one, private property as opposed to contingent property, individuality as opposed to mutuality. As defection from paternalist practice on the subsistence issues accelerated, the common people refined its own position. Thus, new forms of community or collective solidarity develop that include class but are not limited to class alone. When, during subsistence crises, the people found that defectors refused to fulfill their collective responsibilities, the people resorted to the *taxation populaire*.

General statements about the relationship between community and collective action demand refinement in the light of growing, detailed knowledge of such disturbances. Indeed, some historians have questioned the very existence of shared values embodied in the moral economy; others have emphasized the presence of power struggles within the mobilized crowd; and still others have questioned our current understanding of the consequences of food riots.[1] The Flour War demonstrates the necessity to accommodate historical explanation to both broad-gauge and particular (sometimes individual) concerns, for both were present, interacting sometimes in concert, sometimes in conflict. This chapter will address both the nature of cohesive forces in the community(ies) galvanized by the Flour War and the tensions that emerged within these communities during the crisis, including those that resulted in the defection of some members. The 1775 subsistence crisis also generated community efforts to recall these real or perceived defectors back to their collective obligations and their membership in the community.

---

1. Robert Woods, "Individuals in the Rioting Crowd: A New Approach," *JIH* 14 (1983): 1–24; Suzanne Desan, "Crowds, Community, and Ritual in the Work of E. P. Thompson and Natalie Davis," in *The New Cultural History*, ed. Lynn Hunt (Berkeley and Los Angeles, 1989), pp. 47–71; Tim Harris, *London Crowds in the Reign of Charles II: Propaganda and Politics from the Restoration Until the Exclusion Crisis* (Cambridge, 1987); Samuel L. Popkin, *The Rational Peasant: The Political Economy of Rural Society in Vietnam* (Berkeley and Los Angeles, 1979).

Moreover, the subsistence crisis that produced the Flour War mobilized communities of various constructions. This mobilization sometimes provoked a cacophony of voices claiming to represent their communities, and this resultant discourse often signified attempts to realign the community. Riots in 1775 were the product of still-functioning but incomplete communal networks that were simultaneously social and normative. Where traditional communal bonds held on the subsistence question, disturbances were modest or nonexistent; where these bonds had frayed while others had endured or new ones knitted together, disturbances could be more severe. Different types of communities thus produced different types of responses. In preindustrial France, therefore, the character of food riots reflected the particular nature of the historically constructed community that existed in particular places, and the way in which these conditions shaped individual responses to crises.

The Nature of Community

As historical constructions, communities vary with the specific formation of the society in which they are embedded. They nevertheless exhibit common sets of characteristics, among which two of the most important are social bonds and behavioral norms.[2] Historians and anthropologists have detected social bonds in many forms: kinship, occupation, class, gender, patronage, neighborhood (village), ethnicity, religion, and friendship, among others. Communal bonds and solidarities can also help to structure the relationships involved in property, production, and exchange. The more multiplex the bonds, the more dense the relationships, and the stronger the community.

The second characteristic of community—behavioral norms—reflects the

2. As any survey of the literature shows, "community" turns out to be a frustratingly elusive and debatable concept, especially when studies have sought universally applicable definitions. The recent analyses of community most useful for this study are J. C. Calhoun, "Community: Toward a Variable Conceptualization for Comparative Research," *Social History* 5 (Jan. 1980): 105–11; John Bohstedt, *Riots and Community Politics in England and Wales, 1790–1810* (Cambridge, Mass., 1983), pp. 4, 21–23, 26, 51–52, 84, 207–23; David Garrioch, *Neighborhood and Community in Paris, 1740–1790* (Cambridge, 1986), pp. 2–6, 253–56; William Reddy, "The Textile Trade and the Language of the Crowd in Rouen, 1752–1871," *Past and Present* 74 (Feb. 1977): 82–83; David Sabean, *Power in the Blood: Popular Culture and Village Discourse in Early Modern Germany* (Cambridge, 1984), pp. 3, 28–30. Also helpful is Jean-Pierre Gutton, *La Sociabilité villageoise dans l'ancienne France* (Paris, 1979).

underlying social process whereby individual perceptions of events are "mediated by values embedded in concrete practices" into recognized, patterned responses.[3] This "consensus on the sense of the world"[4] anchors in two sorts of traditions: "that which is taken for granted" and the "imaginative reconstruction of the past in the service of current interests."[5]

That a community shared behavioral norms does not, however, imply that sweet reason dominates human folly to produce an atmosphere of "mutual agreement, friendship, or equality,"[6] but rather that its members engage in "the same argument, the same discourse" that hammers out "alternative strategies, misunderstandings, conflicting goals and values."[7] Community members thus share not only a "sense of belonging" but also a willingness to shape their actions "on the basis of communal relations."[8]

A community thus consists of "networks of individuals, bound together more closely than they are linked to outsiders."[9] It manifests its cohesion by embracing certain behavioral norms, certain interpretations of behavior, that resonate with the social environment and are enforced through social pressure or community sanctions. Of course, there is never an exact match between the actual social organization and specific cultural assumptions.[10] Nevertheless, the extent to which members of the community conform to

3. James Scott, *Weapons of the Weak: Everyday Forms of Peasant Resistance* (New Haven, 1985), p. 305. Scott emphasizes the importance of a "normative environment" to community cohesion. His work deals specifically with Malaysian peasant society but has a general applicability as well.

4. Pierre Bourdieu, *Outline of a Theory of Practice*, trans. R. Nice. (Cambridge, 1977; French ed., 1972), p. 167. Bourdieu refers to this as *"doxa."*

5. Scott, *Weapons*, p. 345. Scott describes the latter sort of tradition as a "recognizable but partisan facsimile of earlier values and practices drawn up to legitimize essential class interests." This process of revision illustrates the principle that tradition is never fixed but in fact is constantly being adapted to changing circumstances (Gerald Sider, *Culture and Class in Anthropology and History: A Newfoundland Illustration* [Cambridge, 1986] , pp. 185–86). See also William Roseberry's insistence on this in *Anthropologies and Histories: Essays in Culture, History, and Political Economy* (New Brunswick, N.J., 1989), p. 57.

6. Scott, *Weapons* (New Haven, 1985), p. 305.

7. Sabean, *Power*, p. 29.

8. Ibid., p. 30; Calhoun, "Community," p. 110.

9. Garrioch, *Neighborhood*, p. 12.

10. As Robert Wuthnow stated with reference to the relationship between such movements as the Enlightenment and social structure, "articulation always implies disarticulation . . . a search for features of ideology that resemble features of the social milieu must also include an account of the ways in which an ideology becomes at least partially free of contextual determination" (*Communities of Discourse: Ideology and Social Structure in the Reformation, the Enlightenment, and European Socialism* [Cambridge, 1989], p. 12). This is also true of what we have called the "moral economy." Historians who attempt to discount the normative elements in the moral economy by denying it any objective historical presence appear to assume that there must be a one-to-one relationship between the subjective and objective frames of reference.

and can hold others to the behavioral norms, and thus fulfill their collective responsibilities, is an indication of the strength of the community.

Therefore, neither the mere presence of these ties nor even the frequency of contact is enough to denote a community, and members of one community can, at the same time, have ties in other communities. Communities are rarely, if ever, closed entities without outside contacts, and most certainly this could not characterize eighteenth-century French communities of any kind.[11] Similarly, the mere presence of a normative environment is insufficient to distinguish a community unless members can be seen to behave in accordance with it. But these ties and norms, at least in some form, are preconditions for community. Members of a community should be able to predict correctly what fellow members will do, as well as interpret correctly what such behavior signifies. From such communal bonds and norms come the possibility and context for collective action.

Historians have repeatedly emphasized the relationship between community and collective action. For example, William Reddy has argued that there must be "a community base that made coherent action possible, a sense of membership that stands in a prior relationship to the motives of individuals. . . . It is necessary that participants have shared expectations of each other."[12] John Bohstedt observed: "Threats that provoked riots did not create crowds from simple 'pools' of individuals—they mobilized networks of people and relationships that already existed—networks of kinship and camaraderie, in work, play, marketing, worship, or neighborhood, as well as institutional networks."[13] The more dense the communal bonds, the more readily members can be mobilized for collective action. How these communities are organized depends on the historical-social context; once constituted, they then contribute to constructing social relations and culture. Communities are constantly subject to change as the context in which they are embedded changes, and as the actors within them act.

THE KING AND THE PEOPLE

In Ancien Régime France, the relationship between the king and the people transcended local ties and could form an important element in the building

---

11. See the debate around the concept of the closed peasant community generated by the work of Eric Wolf, "The Vicissitudes of the Closed Corporate Peasant Community," *American Ethnologist* 12 (May 1986): 325–29.

12. "Language," pp. 82–83.

13. *Riots*, p. 23.

of food riots. In times before the Flour War, rioters had sometimes invoked the king's name to legitimize claims for lower prices and more accessible subsistence and fixed the price of grain at 12 livres per setier and the price of bread at 2 sols per livre, "by order of the King." In October 1789 the marchers to Versailles set out in a confrontational mood to collect and escort to Paris the King, the Queen, and the Dauphin (their son and heir to the throne), whom they styled the "boulanger, la boulangère, et le petit mitron" (the baker, the baker's wife, and the baker's little helper). The people thus proclaimed directly the relationship between the monarchy and bread. The image of a king as ultimate patron, associated with subsistence issues and responsible for them, emerges vividly from this scene.

Steven Kaplan has argued, "[The] king was considered the baker of last resort. According to the unwritten compact between king and people, in return for their submission, the king promised to assure them their subsistence."[14] By 1789, however, the king had, according to Kaplan, "desacralized bread" by his commitment to liberalization, or at least his penchant for vacillation, and had thereby "violated a consensual taboo." As a result, kingship itself was desacralized—opening the way for popular revolution against the monarchy.[15] Michel Vovelle suggests a more subtle but compatible vision of popular perception of the king at the time of the writing of the *cahiers de doléances*, one that differentiates between rural and urban understanding. In the countryside, the people emphasized their own subordination coupled with an image of the paternal role of the king. When rural people addressed the king, they "supplicated, begged, and solicited" royal attention and assistance. They believed that, as their "father," he would provide. They articulated a request for and a hope of help, but not the demand for it associated with fulfilling a "contract." In the cities, however, people cast themselves as the "collective partner" of the king. They "reclaimed" and "required" royal action and compliance. They embraced a notion of compact or contract similar to that described by Kaplan.[16] In June 1776 Abbé Véri observed that the "middle order of society" (*étage mitoyen [de la société]*) regards "the sovereign merely as the agent of the nation" and that they no

14. *The Famine Plot Persuasion in Eighteenth-Century France* (Philadelphia, 1982), pp. 66–67.

15. Jeffrey Merrick also analyzes a parallel process of the desacralization of the monarchy, but from a different perspective (*The Desacralization of the Monarchy in the Eighteenth Century* [Baton Rouge, La., 1990]).

16. "La Représentation populaire de la monarchie," in *The French Revolution and the Creation of Modern Political Culture*, vol. 1, *The Political Culture of the Old Regime* (Oxford, 1987), pp. 79–81.

longer manifested "the veneration for royalty that our ancestors had for its divine origin."[17] Vovelle states that in 1775 "everywhere there was reference to the direct will of the King or to a supposed order by the King to justify the *taxation populaire*. . . . They appealed without intermediary to the King."[18] And without result, as well, for in 1775 the king never intervened in the pricing of grain.

In fact, however, in 1775 few rioters, rural or urban, lowly or elite, Parisian or provincial, explicitly invoked either image of the king while wrangling with merchants, producers, or officials. Rioters in many places, even before the events of 2 May at Versailles, fixed the price of grain at 12 livres per Parisian setier and that of bread at 2 sols, or the local equivalent.[19] At Dourdan, a basket-maker declared before magistrates and people assembled after mass that "the price of 12 livres per setier was just."[20] But only in the Brie did they claim to represent the will of the king when they did so, and there only in the rural confrontations. Most simply set the price by threat of force. They frequently said "they would have grain at 12 livres per setier or they would use force." Moreover, during the Flour War, rioters at Versailles could have—as the rumor said they did—stormed the château to present their demands to the king himself, but they did not. In fact, events in Versailles took the same course as in countless other towns in the Paris Basin that spring.

Rioters in some villages in the Brie did claim that the price of 12 livres came from royal orders. At Fresne-sur-Marne on 4 May rioters demanded that laboureur Jacques Gibert accept 12 livres for a grand setier because this price "était de la part du Roi."[21] Rioters visiting the laboureurs at Chelles the same day claimed that 12 livres per grand setier was "the order of the King" and "la taxe du Roy."[22] On 6 May, rioters told the laboureur at Saint-Martin-lès-Voulangis that they wanted grain "à raison de 12 livres qui était

---

17. *Journal de l'abbé de Véri*, ed. Baron de Witte, 2 vols. (Paris, 1928–30), 2:8. Merrick incorrectly cites the date as June 1775 (*Desacralization*, p. 129).

18. "Répresentation," p. 83.

19. On what happened at Versailles, see Chapter 3. The monks at Saint-Leu-l'Esserent agreed to 2 sols on 30 April. In Rouen, Gournay-en-Bray, and many other places, rioters declared they wanted prices fixed at 12 livres or its local equivalent because "that was the price it had been sold at in other markets." See, e.g., "Interrogatoire, Marie LeRoux (20 mai)," AD Seine-Maritime, 202 BP 18*.

20. "Procès-verbal (7 mai)," AD Yvelines, 4 B 1352.

21. "Information, Jacques Gilbert (17 mai)," AD Seine-et-Marne, B 2387.

22. "Information, Louis Nicolas Bourgeois & Jean Vincent Lamotte (17 mai)," AD Seine-et-Marne, B 2387.

la taxe du Roy."[23] On 7 May, a "crowd of people" beat on Denis Eustache Billion's farm door, "demanding on behalf of the king that the door be opened or they would open it by force." They also announced "that they needed grain on behalf of the king at the price of 12 livres per grand setier."[24] Similar events occurred at Pierre-Levée and Favières, where rioters cast themselves as loyally obedient to and executors of the king's will, before which everyone had to submit.

When Thomas Blaison, a *procureur fiscal* at Villemomble, worried that "it was not possible that the price of bread could have fallen so suddenly from 33 livres to 12," he was reassured that "that was true, bread had been *taxé* at 2 sols for bread, and that cavaliers of the maréchaussée at Bondy said that they were distributing grain at Gonesse for 12 francs and that they had orders for that." He then "imagined that the king had, out of munificence, made a gift to the people by having grain distributed at a low price and indemnifying the farmers."[25] So convinced, he joined with other rioters that day to visit farms and fix the price of grain. Even in the Brie, however, such direct statements were uncommon.

Some magistrates worried about the seditious character of rioters' attributions of price-fixing to the king. Several specifically asked the rioters they interrogated whether they had heard people say "they had orders from the king to have grain distributed at 12 livres [or 9 in a few instances] per setier." Like the search for conspiracy, however, they never identified a source.[26]

Closer to Versailles, some people were well informed about the events of 2 May. On 3 May, rioter Remy Cirer admitted saying to a baker in Rueil he wanted a bread that weighed 12 livres for 24 sols. When the baker told him he could not give it to him for that price, Cirer retorted: "That makes no difference to me. I saw it given at Versailles for 2 sols per livre and I won't pay any more than that."[27] One hundred people appeared before a farm in the parish of Bièvres on 4 May and announced that they wanted grain "paying on the basis of 2 sols per livre because it was only worth that much at Versailles."[28]

Laying claim to royal will may therefore have helped reinforce and

23. "Information, Pierre Frabit (n.d.)," AD Seine-et-Marne, B 2387.
24. "Information (12 mai)," AD Seine-et-Marne, B 2387.
25. "Interrogatoire (23 mai)," AN, Y 11441.
26. See, e.g., the interrogations of Pierre Julliard and Jacques Huguenin (24 mai), AN, Y 13555.
27. "Interrogatoire (12 mai)," AN, Y 18682.
28. "Information, Jean Baptiste Philippe (14 juillet)," AN, Y 18682.

legitimize some rioters' claims, and orders emanating from Versailles may sometimes have carried punch. For some, it had perhaps become part of the script of subsistence riots, as had the demand for grain at 12 livres per setier. Most rioters, however, leaned much more heavily on the levers of local politics. We have already seen how frequently rioters pressured local authorities, indicating that they expected more from the officials in place than from the king far away. Indeed, the king was not the only noble source of legitimation. In Villepinte on 4 May, rioters appeared before laboureur Nicolas Prévost and declared: "We need grain for money. You should have orders to give it to us. It is on behalf of Monseigneur le Duc d'Orléans."[29] Similarly, some rioters in and near Méru claimed they operated under orders from the Prince de Conti.[30] In both cases, rioters appealed to the authority of local seigneurs rather than to the seigneur in Versailles.[31]

A few rioters appear to have believed the king was irrelevant to subsistence matters. When 600–700 people raided a farm in the village of Montsoult and were told it was wrong to pillage, they retorted that they "did not recognize the king, they only recognized God and bread."[32] Fifty-year-old Louis Philippe Dubois denounced the continuing high price of grain on the market of Melun on 13 May, saying publicly, "Here is a fucked up piece of work. If in fifteen days bread isn't at 2 sols per livre in Paris, the King is fucked; there are four thousand men who will set fire to the four corners of Paris."[33] On Sunday, 7 May, after the reading of the king's declaration that ordered swift and severe repression of rioters and gave the prévôtal courts jurisdiction, Donna Jacquinot in Lizy-sur-Ourcq and Etienne Alliot in Signy-Signets responded by tearing it up and declaring it fraudulent because it was not signed.[34] In his journal entry for 7 June 1775, Abbé Véri, a Turgot supporter, worried that Louis XVI "would be upset by the intrigues at court and even more by the smouldering populace whose sparks increase every-

29. "Déclaration de Nicolas Prévost (7 mai)," AN, Y 18682.

30. See "Interrogatoires, Gaspard Guieffe (24 mai) & Charles Degaast (2, 5, 15 mai)," AD Oise, B 1583ter.

31. There may have been more here than an appeal to a local seigneur. The Conti and Orléans were chronically insubordinate members of the royal family. Perhaps appeals to them carried subversive messages. Unfortunately, the evidence indicates that, although rioters knew they invoked the name of a very powerful lord, they meant no more than to call on local clout. Moreover, in the case of Conti at least, exalted status offered no protection from attack. Rioters raided one of the Conti fermes near Méru.

32. See "Interrogatoire, Jean Richardier (10 juillet)," AD Oise, B 1583bis.

33. "Interrogatoire (15 mai)," AD Seine-et-Marne, B 3957(2); "Interrogatoire (1 juillet)," AN, Y 11441.

34. See "Information (17 mai)," AD Seine-et-Marne, B 2387, for these separate incidents.

day." He predicted that "a slow and hidden fire would ultimately escape through some opening."[35]

Yet such direct defiance of royal authority as that of Dubois and Jacquinot was as rare an event as invoking that authority explicitly in support of the *taxation populaire*. In 1775 the common people in general seem to have regarded the king as apart from if not above the fray. According to Condorcet, "a month after the Flour War, the king crossed, to go to Reims [for the coronation ceremony], a part of the theater of sedition, and found there only a people who blessed his government."[36] Indeed, among all the interrogations and testimonies stemming from the Flour War, no direct evidence suggests that the common people attributed their woes to changing royal policy. They recognized abuses, as they saw it—such as selling too high, not privileging local consumers, hoarding grain, and so on—and demanded action to rectify them, but they did not openly attack the policy behind this behavior.

Far more seditious than popular behavior, perhaps, was the attitude of other local notables, such as parish priests (*curés*) who potentially could exercise considerable influence within their communities.[37] While serving as the most important representative of the church at the local level and as mediator between his flock and the next world, the parish priest performed an array of official and unofficial secular tasks within his community. He administered charity and poor relief; he kept the parish register; he appointed and oversaw the schoolteacher, and often taught himself. His unofficial tasks included mediating local disputes, offering advice on all topics, making loans, recommending parishioners for jobs, and interceding in court cases. Moreover, the eighteenth century witnessed increased state reliance on the parish priest for worldly purposes. The government enjoined him to transmit its messages to his flock, to gather information on local affairs, to watch over public behavior and report transgressions, in addition

35. *Journal*, 1:298.

36. *Vie de Turgot*, p. 111, cited in Schelle, *Oeuvres*, 4:55, n. 1. Even Abbé Véri admitted that the coronation drew "popular acclamations," although he also claimed that "most of the people of Paris and the provinces could hardly stand the cost of the *sacre*" (*Journal*, 1:304).

37. On the parish priest in Ancien Régime France, see, e.g., Bernard Plongeron, *La Vie quotidienne du clergé français au XVIIIe siècle* (Paris, 1974); Timothy Tackett, *Priest and Parish in Eighteenth-Century France: A Social and Political Study of the Curés in the Diocese of Dauphiné, 1750–1791* (Princeton, 1977); Tackett, "L'Histoire sociale du clergé diocésain pendant le XVIIIe siècle," *RHMC* 26 (1979): 198–234; Tackett and Claude Langlois, "Ecclesiastical Structures and Clerical Geography on the Eve of the French Revolution," *FHS* 11 (Spring 1980): 352–70; Gutton, *La Sociabilité villageoise*, pp. 183–254.

to preaching obedience and submission to the state, as well as to the church and God. The *curés* had thus become "men of the king" as they were "men of the bishop."[38]

The parish priests occupied a unique place among local notables. The church not only provided the symbol around which the community united in joy, festival, and mourning, but also seethed with potential tensions that focused largely on the priest himself. Inhabitants had little say in the selection of their priest, and most *curés* were recruited from well outside the *pays* of their flock. Moreover, as keepers of the confessional, they remained well informed—perhaps too well informed for some—about what went on in the communities. The position required a delicate balancing act between the dictates of the state, the demands of the office, and the pressure exerted by one or more factions within the parish. The Flour War tested priests' abilities to sustain the balance.[39]

Parish priests responded to the crisis of 1775 with a wide range of strategies. A few performed their duties with exemplary zeal, and three received pensions for their attention to their duty. Most walked a line that kept them out of danger from both parishioners and the state. However, seven stepped over the line and found themselves arrested and sent to the Bastille. Although the clergy never lived up to Voltaire's cynical expectations,[40] in all seven cases, the priests were arrested for giving improper advice to their parishioners.[41] Two of these were accused of seditious behavior with regard to the king or his ministers during their sermons. According to witnesses, the parish priest at Gournay-sur-Marne, Pierre-Claude Dourdan, announced in his sermon "that perhaps it [the crisis] was not the fault of the king, but that of his ministers [and that] he had around him ministers who turned his head and spoiled him, and supported the high price of grain."[42] François Edouard Tirel de la Martinière, priest at Auger-Saint-Vincent, reinterpreted the king's circular to the clergy. He claimed

---

38. Plongeron, *Vie quotidienne*, p. 132.

39. On the tasks the state expected the clergy to perform, see Chapter 3.

40. Voltaire saw clerical machinations behind everything he did not like, and the Flour War was no exception. In a purely fictitious story about the events, he wrote: "As we approached Pontoise, we were surprised to see ten to fifteen thousand peasants who were running and howling like madmen who cried, 'The grain, the markets, the markets, the grain.' I heard a small priest who with a stentorian voice was saying [to the peasants], 'Let us sack everything, my friends. God wills it.' " "Diatribe à l'auteur des Ephémérides (10 mai)," cited in V. S. Ljublinski, *La Guerre des farines* (Paris, 1979), p. 58.

41. On the seven arrested, see their interrogations in AN, Y 11441, and BA, Archives de la Bastille, MS 12,447.

42. "Interrogatoire (23 juin)," AN, Y 11441.

that "it was not the king's intention" to require restitution from people who
had received grain as a free gift from the cultivators. This, of course, left
much open for interpretation. Moreover, he told his parishioners it was
unreasonable for them to pay full price for grain, much of which was "of
very poor quality and full of dust and bad seeds."[43] Such behavior drew
heavy penalties, as those who ended up in the Bastille learned. Parish priests
stood at the nexus of their communities, and their sermons and advice
gained a wide audience. By simply changing the inflection in their voices
while reading a royal edict, or by commenting on current conditions, they
could foment discontent and focus anger. For instance, the curé at La
Queue-en-Brie denounced the police as "flour merchants" and as "dogs
[anyone] could make bark."[44]

No doubt this sort of public critique of royal policy—a critique that was
by no means new, since unhappy subjects had long adopted a "the king is
good, but his ministers are evil" position—or of agents of royal authority
contributed to a general sense that government was not being conducted in
the people's welfare. However, most notables steered a path well clear of a
direct confrontation with royal will.

More frequent were indirect and guarded criticisms of policy. For example,
in their correspondence some local officials openly denounced the effects of
liberalization and its relationship to popular distress. They and their predecessors had had the brutal experience of vacillating policy for more than ten
years, and as Steven Kaplan has shown for the first experience of the 1760s,
local authorities handled the episodes poorly. Repetition of the experiences
of this first episode only brought more bitterness. The subdelegate at Lyons-
la-Forêt wrote critically of the surplus-producing cultivators and millers in
his region for shamelessly pursuing their interests just as liberalization
permitted. He blamed diminished supplies and higher prices in his market
on "the bad will of the laboureurs who do not punctually furnish the market,
even though grain isn't lacking in the area." He chastised them for a "too
opinionated and prideful" attitude and concluded that their scornful behavior stemmed "no doubt from all their riches." Furthermore, he requested a
return to regulations that would "prohibit millers and their valets from
entering the grain market before the people had been served."[45]

At Gournay-en-Bray, the subdelegate was even more suspicious of the
effects of free trade. After describing rising prices since the harvest of 1774,

43. "Interrogatoire (19 juin)," AN, Y 11441.
44. "Information (13 mai & 19 juin)," AN, Y 18682.
45. "Lettre (11 juin)," AD Seine-Maritime, C 109, n. 151.

he asked, "Was it not possible that this continuous progression . . . is caused by the unlimited protection the government accords to the cultivator, thus authorizing his cupidity?" and observed, "When we tell the people that the revolt of 2 May has prevented the laboureurs from bringing their grain to market since that time, and therein lies the cause of the increasing price of that commodity, they tell us that if this *émotion* hadn't come, grain would now cost 8 livres per boisseau [that is, twice as much]."[46] The situation in the Normand village of Monancourt underscored this point. No riots erupted in this market town, but prices rose nonetheless. The market of 18 May saw a tremendous increase in the number of sacks displayed for sale (from 45 to 150 sacks), but the price rose 20 sols per sack. Prices continued to rise in June.[47] Many more officials wrote no letters, but, as we have seen, they did make common cause or at least compromises with the rioters.

The Bases of Community

While the repeated use of the "king's price" by the Flour War rioters may reflect some traditional assumption of royal empathy for the plight of hungry subjects, the relationship between king and people only rarely provided that explicit "community base that [makes] coherent action possible." The time to recall the national defector, the baker-king, to his family of subjects lay in the future.[48] Most often, rioters turned to local solutions for their local problems. They demanded reactivation of local regulations and the intervention of local patronage and charity networks. They relied on their local communities and recalled local defectors to them.

We must therefore turn to a closer examination of local communities and the nature of communal bonds mobilized during the Flour War. I have identified three main types of communities.[49] The first type of community

46. "Lettre (4 juin)," AD Seine-Maritime, C 107.
47. "Lettre (18 mai, 8 juin)," AD Seine-Maritime, C 110.
48. The Flour War served to further politicize the subsistence question and, by extension, royal policy among the more educated members of France: the philosophes, the members of Parlement, etc. This needs further study.
49. For its analysis of Flour War participation and social bonds, this section relies on interrogation records, witness and victim testimony, and police reports, supplemented by other information, such as tax records, but such sources have shortcomings. First, even supplementing with other forms of testimony, we can find information about only a small percentage of those who rioted. Second, although we can isolate various types of social bonds and even determine the density of ties, we have no way of knowing how powerful these bonds were or the relative weight of each bond. Third,

linked common people and elites along patronage relations and largely shared the relations and assumptions of paternalism and its regulationist practices. The second type was generated by the common people, who in their status as grain consumers relied on preexisting social bonds that they could mobilize against grain-holders who rejected paternalism. The third type united the defectors from patronage relations who embraced some form of the physiocratic vision of the free market in grain. The second and third types were products of both the ongoing breakup of patronage relations and the defection from the paternalist normative environment of grain proprietors and those that associated with them.

Food riots were less likely to erupt in the first type of community, and when they did they tended to be mild. But this type of community had experienced considerable stress and fragmentation—economic, social, and administrative (see Chapter 2). Consequently, only a few communities of this sort remained strong enough in the Paris Basin to activate their particular forms of crisis resolution successfully. More common were communities of the second and third types, communities that ultimately clashed with one another during the Flour War. These communities were rooted in preexisting social bonds that could be mobilized during a subsistence crisis. Relations based on neighborhood (or village), occupation/workplace, kinship, and gender could be invoked by the common people for a *taxation populaire*. Kinship, occupation/workplace, and political networks as well formed the basis of the social bonds that linked this third community of grain producers, merchants, bakers, and many local officials in 1775. For both these communities, the experiences of food riots, such as the Flour War, served further to shape and reshape their contours, both social and normative.

PATRONAGE AND COMMUNITY IN 1775

Patronage in a variety of manifestations functioned as a social relation that could be mobilized during subsistence crises in Ancien Régime society and formed part of a "normative environment" in which discourse could take

---

there might be other forms of bonds that do not appear in these sources. Nevertheless, the evidence we do have provides us with some information about the kinds of bonds mobilized during food riots. This information—compared with that generated for the next section, which analyzes ties that create ruptures among groups that might otherwise be linked together—helps us determine the characteristics of participation and the role of community in food riots like the Flour War.

place on subsistence issues. Ancien Régime patronage networks included relations and expectations traditionally embedded in the seigneurial order; those linking local notables and common people; those involving the king and his subjects; and those involving employer and employee in ways that transcended wages.[50] These vertical relationships embodied asymmetrical social relations, relations of domination and dependency. They manifested relations of power, ultimately reducible to the exercise of force by the dominant over the dominated. Yet while inequality might, in the final analysis, be maintainable only by force, it cannot exist long with coercion as its only mainstay. Godelier has suggested that "the strongest and most effective [way of] guaranteeing the long-term maintenance of . . . power is not violence . . . but consent in all the forms in which the dominated acquiesce in their own domination." For such consent to exist, "the exercise of power must appear as a service rendered by the dominant to the dominated that creates a debt of the latter to the former which can only be discharged by the gift in return of their goods, their labor, their services or even their lives."[51] Thus, various practices associated with patronage—gifts, charity, job opportunities, and so on—functioned as what Pierre Bourdieu has called "euphemized" power.[52]

Furthermore, as Thompson and others have argued, the relation between elites and the common people, between rulers and ruled, between employers and employee, "always runs in both directions and the same relationship, when turned around and viewed in reverse, may present an alternative heuristic."[53] While the patron might view the act of providing grain at a reduced price as charity, the common people might view it as a right. This approach helps us to explain, on the one hand, the readiness of the people in 1775 to believe the rumor that the king (in honor of the coronation) or the Duc d'Orléans or the Prince de Conti had ordered the sale of grain at a reduced price and, on the other hand, the "boldness" with which they pursued what they saw as their rights to benefit from such largess. As one

50. Patrons and clients could be linked by other social bonds, such as kinship and neighborhood, yet patronage differs from these in the necessary inequality that is embedded in this relation.

51. Maurice Godelier, *The Mental and the Material: Thought, Economy, and Society* (London, 1986), pp. 13–14 (French ed., 1984).

52. *Outline*, pp. 191–192. See also Scott, *Weapons*, pp. 306–7.

53. Thompson, "Folklore, Anthropology, and Social History," *Indian Historical Review* (Jan. 1978), reprinted as a Studies in Labor History pamphlet (Sussex, 1979), p. 13. See also, idem, "Eighteenth-Century English Society: Class Struggle Without Class," *Social History* (May 1978): 133–66, esp. 150, where he calls this relationship for eighteenth-century England the "patronage-deference equilibrium"; Scott, *Weapons*, p. 309.

official at Nanteuil-le-Haudouin observed, "all the inhabitants from here and the environs . . . regard these 'thefts' as things they have a right to take."[54]

As long as both parties, despite their disagreements over the meaning of the transaction, continued to interpret that transaction as part of the expected, legitimate behavior of social relations, the community could function relatively smoothly. Both accepted the principle of the "social use of property" such as grain. Neither overtly questioned the basis of the patronage system. But this does not mean that property owners always accepted the claims of others to their property, or that property owners and claimants always developed the same sense of timing about when claims could be appropriately made. Nor does this mean that the dominated accepted their status uncritically or passively. As Olwen Hufton has shown, the dominated could muster virtually incessant acts of harassment, or what James Scott has called "everyday forms of resistance," against their dominators, a pattern that formed part of general community interaction or discourse.[55] Within this patronage relation, both elites and common people thus attempted to manipulate the patronage system to their own advantage.[56] Every time common people or elites manipulated the system for a particular reason in a particular context, they shaped and reshaped it, sometimes in small, invisible ways, sometimes in significant and visible ways, for patronage relations and the norms of paternalism were not immutable or univocal.

The Flour War provides numerous examples of such reciprocal manipulation of the patronage system in late eighteenth-century France. First, the seigneurial system continued to provide opportunities for classical patronage and paternalist intervention during a subsistence crisis. As previously described, the 2 May market at Gournay-en-Bray provided an opportunity for the seigneur, the Duc de Montmorency, to intervene in a quintessentially paternalist style. Moreover, by demanding his protection, merchants transferred responsibility for the situation to him rather than assuming it themselves or blaming the invisible hand of market forces. Montmorency engaged in both mediation and charity, determining who should benefit

54. "Compte rendu des incidents qui se sont produits la veille au marché de Nanteuil (6 mai)," AD Oise, C 318.

55. Hufton, "Attitudes Toward Authority in Eighteenth-Century Languedoc," *Social History* (Oct. 1978): 281–302. The phrase "everyday forms of resistance" forms the subtitle of Scott's book, *Weapons*.

56. Scott, *Weapons*, p. 309.

from the sales at reduced prices, as well as indemnifying merchants and providing grain to the needy (as he defined them) from his own stocks.[57] Although he failed to avoid rioting later in the day, he had performed his role as seigneurial patron, at least for a while. Merchants and poor had, at least for a while as well, manipulated the patronage system to their advantage. The seigneur at Coyolles deplored events of 5 May when people from the town of Villiers-Cotterêts raided his farm for grain. He explained in classic paternalist fashion, "I have in my village several families and elderly to support. There is only myself and the parish priest to aid them and this miserable populace has taken the means to do so."[58]

Second, although absentee seigneurialism and the overall weakening of seigneurial control in absolutist France had diminished opportunities for the exercise of classical paternalism, the late Ancien Régime provided plenty of examples of a latter-day version of it. Fermiers and laboureurs, as elites within their villages and the resident successors to seigneurs, sometimes donned their predecessors' cloaks of paternalism.[59] Thus, for example, the laboureur Cosme Charlemagne at Petit Groslay explained his role, declaring he was "moved with surprise and compassion when he saw the crowd . . . and to find among it several people burdened with families in need." He determined to distribute some of his grain as charity.[60] Louis Salmon distributed "as charity" grain, a pitcher of cider, and bread to eight men and one woman who visited his farm at Cauvigny on 1 May. "They drank and ate, and then withdrew thanking him."[61] On 8 and 9 May, at Lizy-sur-Ourcq, the fermier of the seigneurie, the fermier of the tithe, and a local grain merchant "voluntarily distributed grain to the poor of the parish." The grain came from "a depot for that purpose" they had established.[62] Pierre Martin, a laboureur at Sablonnières, refused to name the people who had come to him to ask for grain (and got it for 12 livres) because "they were all people from the *pays* . . . and neither impertinent nor threatening."[63] When the maréchaussée arrived to collect depositions from the

---

57. See Chapters 3 and 4.

58. "Lettre de Sr. Desfosses (5 mai)," BN, Collection Joly de Fleury, 1159, fols. 272–73. Seigneurial patronage proved to be a difficult system to make work in much of the Paris Basin in 1775 (see below).

59. For more on this, see Chapters 2, 4, and 6.

60. "Déclaration (6 mai)," AN, Y 18682.

61. "Procès-verbal (2 mai)," AD Oise, B 1583.

62. "Déposition de Jacques Robert, Information (17 mai)," AD Seine-et Marne, B 2387. I was unable to find out any more about this store of grain.

63. "Déposition, Information (16 mai)," AD Seine-et-Marne, B 2387.

laboureurs and fermiers at Lévignen, Betz, and Acy-en-Multien, "they responded that they had no complaint to bring against anyone, that they had voluntarily delivered grain to the inhabitants of their parishes."[64]

Sometimes the common people knew well how to manipulate paternalist relations to their advantage. On Wednesday, 10 May, "strangers" threatened to denude the farm belonging to a laboureur at Le Jariel near Sablonnières. Many of the locals asked the parish priest for permission to sound the tocsin "in order to assemble themselves to go prevent the 'marnois' from taking the grain." When the priest observed that it was illegal to form bands (de s'attrouper), they responded "that they only intended to serve Sieur Dele-tain," adding, "if the strangers tried to force the farmer" to give up his grain "they would demand preference." In fact, Deletain decided to turn grain over to his neighbors and divulged no names to the authorities.[65] As one of the men arrested for his part in several incursions into the farms of local cultivators explained, "Sieur Deletain gave him [grain] without paying because he knows him well." Inhabitants of La Celle-sur-Morin turned to the defense of a local laboureur when people from outside the pays broke into his courtyard and threatened to take all the grain away. They sounded the tocsin, assembled the inhabitants, and chased the strangers away. He then distributed grain to his protectors.[66]

Such behavior served the interests of property owners as well. The local nature of these events ensured that victims would recognize their assailants and could resolve more readily any trouble that occurred. As Pierre Afforti, laboureur at Villepinte, explained, incursions of people from "outside" the village posed serious difficulties. He testified that he "knew no one" who came to his farm to demand grain; all the parishes were "foreign" to him. He had received no restitution.[67] Indeed, there was a direct correlation between the success in enforcing restitution (when victims demanded it, and some did not) after the Flour War and the local nature of revolt.

Moreover, a legacy of good local relations not only enabled effective crisis resolution in 1775, it could also save local elites from devastation. These sorts of relations between propertied and local common people appear

64. "Procès-verbal (16 mai)," AD Oise, B non coté, maréchaussée de Clermont, jugements prévôtaux, 1775.

65. "Information (14 mai)" and "Interrogatoire de Claude Etienne Janvier (14 mai)," AD Seine-et-Marne, B 2387.

66. "Dépositions de Jean Dominique Aureau and François Raoult (17 mai)," AD Seine-et-Marne, B 2387.

67. "Information (16 mai)," AN, Y 18682.

clearly in the case of Jean Crapard, fermier at the farm of Pontillault in the parish of Champigny-sur-Marne. Crapard reported that on 5 May inhabitants from Champigny and Villiers-sur-Marne visited his farm to demand grain at 12 livres per setier. When his wife begged them to leave enough for their subsistence and explained that "they had had such a bad harvest for the past two years that they had had to sell it all," the band's first response was, "They knew that, but needed grain anyway." When, however, the inhabitants from Villiers (who were, as Crapard explained, from "outside" the *pays*) started cursing and threatening Madame Crapard, those from Champigny rallied to her defense. They retorted, "It's not here that you should say this. We have always been well paid here, and these are good people." Those from Villiers emptied their sacks, and so too did those from Champigny, who admitted, "There is barely enough grain here for you."[68] The inhabitant of Ully-Saint-Georges rallied to arrest three men from another village who had threatened a local laboureur who had no grain for them. As soon as the men declared to the cultivator, "You might not have grain this morning, but you had better have some by this evening or we will set a fire," local inhabitants arrested them and summoned the maréchaussée.[69]

Yet Geneviève Boucher, sixty-three-year-old widow of a laboureur at Barcy, probably expressed the most common pragmatic motive behind such paternalist behavior. She explained that "because she was afraid of pillage, she had distributed [grain] to her servants and to other inhabitants of the village for 12 livres."[70] Such local patronage also fostered better local relations and in the long run reinforced the authority of the local propertied elite within their villages.

Nevertheless, such relations also served those who depended on the propertied for their survival. The behavior had its pragmatic side. Not only did the potential rioters want affordable, accessible grain or bread, but the majority of them still had to live side by side with and often work for the fermiers and laboureurs after the crisis was over. Sieur Bertaux, laboureur at Charleval, had grain enough for the locals and distributed it without

68. "Lettre (9 mai)" entitled "Mémoire d'un fermier," BN, Collection Joly de Fleury, 1159, fols. 203–4.

69. "Procès-verbal (2 mai)," AD Oise, B 1583bis.

70. "Déposition (10 mai)," AD Seine-et-Marne, B 2247. Similarly, Sieur Parreux, fermier at Coubert, sent his servants around to the entire parish to announce he would sell grain to them at 12 livres rather than deliver it to others ("Interrogatoire Jacques Rimbault [9 mai]," AD Seine-et-Marne, B 3958[1]).

demanding restitution. He explained that "since he had distributed grain to people from the environs, all known to him, he did not want compensation."[71]

Third, the marketplace also served as a nexus for paternalist relations that mitigated against the more violent clashes generated in much of the Paris Basin during the Flour War. The marketplaces of eighteenth-century France varied tremendously in levels of integration into the national market, and all continued to involve face-to-face relations where "the relationship between the two parties concerned exists before and after the exchange" and the amount of mutual information necessary to make marketing decisions depended in part on these relations.[72] Of course, even in the least nationally or regionally integrated markets, or even in the least anonymous markets, there had always existed risks and tensions between buyers and sellers. Nevertheless, resolutions to tensions might be found more readily when face-to-face relations persisted. For example, a potentially violent riot was averted at the Normandy market of Saint-André on 5 May when "the gentlemen who brought [grain to market] fixed the price themselves in order to help the unfortunate indigents."[73] On 12 May, the inhabitants of the city of Marle, "who had grain, voluntarily brought [it to market] to provide for the poor."[74] Poverty and indigence were themselves social constructions that paternalists defined when they selectively distributed their charity. Yet residents such as these local elites responded to the plea to shoulder their collective responsibility as local notables and provide a collective good to members of their community. Rather than calling for some form of violent resolution, such as the maréchaussée or army or arming themselves, they resolved the crisis peacefully and through negotiation.

Moreover, subsistence crises provided opportunities (albeit highly stressful ones) for local authorities and notables to assume paternalist roles: by price-fixing, requisitions, and, above all, compromise.[75] These traditional strate-

71. "Etat (9 juin)," AD Seine-Maritime, C 107.

72. Bourdieu, Outline, p. 186.

73. "Lettre (5 mai)," AD, Seine-Maritime, C 208, n. 194.

74. "Lettre (16 mai)," BN, Collection Joly de Fleury, 1159, fol. 110.

75. On earlier periods, see André Paris, "La Crise de 1709 dans le Bailliage de Montfort-l'Amaury, le marché des grains vu à travers le contrôl de l'administration royale," in Actes du 101ère Congrès national des sociétés savantes, Lille, 1976 (Paris, 1977); Steven Kaplan, Bread, Politics, and Political Economy in the Reign of Louis XV, 2 vols. (The Hague, 1976). On the Flour War, see Cynthia Bouton, "National Policy and Response to the Guerre des Farines," in Proceedings of the Fifth George Rudé Seminar, ed. Peter McPhee (Wellington, N.Z., 1987), pp. 282–97. On Normandy, see Judith Miller, "The Pragmatic Economy: Liberal Reforms and the Grain Trade in Upper Normandy, 1750–1789" (Ph.D. diss., Duke University, 1987).

gies had been developed as a means not only to mitigate the worst effects of dearth, but also to strengthen the authority of the state by both serving the interests of the "little pockets," as the common people were often called, and broadening opportunities for intervention on many fronts. The liberalization edicts of 1774, like those of 1763–64, created a role crisis for many officials: traditional crisis management strategies were specifically prohibited by the dictates of free trade—a circumstance that placed officials at risk not only with the common people but also with Turgot's regime, which was prepared to prosecute deviants. While nonintervention may have been a wise strategy for local officials seeking royal favor, it often was a disaster at the local level. With angry consumers at the doors of the town hall, stampeding the marketplace, or invading private and public granaries, local officials who followed royal policy without the firepower to enforce it risked not only loss of control in their communities in the short run, but also a breakdown of long-run local relations.

Most managed to steer a course between the strict observance of nonintervention dictated by liberalization and the open and now illegal intervention of the traditional variety. At Roye, in an effort to avert violence on 8 May, officials "opened the reserves and [brought] the grain to the market and fixed it at a moderate but reasonable price."[76] On 2 May, when rioters threatened to break down the doors of flour merchants' granaries at Argenteuil, officials "avoided a worse disaster" by "engaging the public, with the consent of the merchants, to pay between 40 and 45 sols per bushel [of flour]" although the people had first insisted on only 30 sols and the merchants on at least 46 sols.[77] The *procureur du roi* wrote from Gaillefontaine that he had received "nothing but thanks" from suppliers and consumers on 5 May, when officials had served as intermediaries in the marketplace to negotiate prices.[78] At Bacqueville-en-Caux on 10 May, a woman demanded the sale of a sack of grain at 15 livres while the *laboureuse* insisted on 31 livres. As a crowd gathered, the cavaliers of the maréchaussée intervened to advise the seller to accept the price offered "to avoid a great *rumeur*." She agreed. Her actions triggered a similar response among the other sellers who were scared by the threat of disorder. Although the cavalier did not actually fix the price of grain for sale, his intercession clearly influenced the course of the market.[79] Similar arrangements lessened ten-

76. "Lettre (8 mai)," BN, Collection Joly de Fleury, 1159, fols. 227–28.
77. "Lettres (4, 5 mai)," BN, Collection Joly de Fleury, 1159, fols. 3–6.
78. "Lettre (6 mai)," AD Seine-Maritime, C 110.
79. "Lettre (13 mai)," AD Seine-Maritime, C 108, n. 275.

sions and reinforced the paternalist roles of local officials at Clermont on 6 May, Blérancourt on 8 May, Auffay on 13 May, and Choisy-le-Roi on 4 May.[80]

These examples illustrate several of the characteristics of community as outlined at the beginning of this section. First, despite great differences of power and property, those belonging to a particular collectivity (classically the village, but also in market towns) saw themselves as bound together more closely than to outsiders. Second, those who saw themselves as belonging to this collectivity actually modified their behavior on the basis of these relations. Third, common people and elites (locals and cultivators, common people and bourgeois, consumers and officials) all shared the same normative environment. Indeed, what is most striking is the assumption on the part of local inhabitants (including the propertied) that the property they defended from outside threats was still, in crucial ways and at a particular moment, community property. This kind of relationship did not, of course, reflect some kind of idealized harmony within the community. Its members might still agree that such property as grain carried social obligations, but it recognized as well that it belonged to private owners and that inequities existed in the right to command access to that property, and to the other resources property owners controlled.[81] Hence, tension was always a product of these relations. The past was no more orderly, stable, or friendly than the present or the future.

Such relatively peaceful resolutions to the 1775 subsistence crisis, which depended on the successful workings of the patronage system—even if in its transformed, late eighteenth-century form—occurred infrequently. More commonly we find, instead, striking examples of failure to manipulate patronage relations. The Duc de Montmorency may have succeeded for a time in mediating between consumers and merchants in Gournay, but his counterpart at La Roche-Guyon failed totally. No one listened to the

80. On Clermont, "Lettre (6 mai)," AD Oise, C 295; on Blérancourt, "Lettre (8 mai)," AD Aisne, C 13; on Auffay, "Lettre (15 mai)," Seine-Maritime, C 108; on Choisy-le-Roi, BN, Collection Joly de Fleury, 1159, fols. 47–48. Not long after the Flour War had subsided in Normandy, trouble continued to simmer in the market town of Pavilly. The market of 14 June experienced considerable tension as consumers tried to set a low price for grain on display. The commander of the militia unit stationed in the town attempted to dissipate the "mutiny" by subsidizing the people's bids by using coins from his own pockets, thus pacifying sellers and raising the people's bids to the market price. See "Lettres (14 & 18 juin)," AD Seine-Maritime, C 110.

81. The common people could be just as avidly committed to their property as any large-scale landowner or merchant. There could also be severe disagreements over which conditions were necessary to legitimate communal claims to property. But *at some time* and *in certain contexts*, such agreement was still possible.

attempts of the Duchesse d'Enville, seigneur of the town, to calm rioters. In fact, "she was insulted and forced to leave."[82] When villagers presented themselves to fermier François Guichard at Grand Champ on 8 May to demand grain, he responded with hard-core resistance rather than paternalism. He defended his farm all day with the assistance of "his children, guards, and servants armed with guns and pistols."[83] Pierre Gaffet, laboureur at Brinches, successfully hid his stores from locals and outsiders alike.[84] The subdelegate at Vernon, Doré, resorted to armed defense and wounded several rioters when he determined to defend the local grain depot, the Tour de Vernonnette, from attack.[85] The dimensions of this problem are examined more thoroughly later, but these examples demonstrate the failure of these actors to operate within the same paradigm, the same "normative environment." Without a common point of departure, neither party could achieve resolution.

Where patronage relationships held most strongly, where the normative environment and social bonds that sustained it coincided most closely, food riots were less likely to erupt. In fact, 1775 provides a useful insight into the vexing question that has plagued historians of social protest: what was happening in the communities that *did not* riot? Because in 1775 police sought depositions from everyone they thought was even a potential victim (cultivators, merchants, millers, etc.), regardless of overt evidence of disturbance, they sometimes received testimony from people who, under other circumstances, would not have come forward to report trouble, because they did not see what had happened as significant.[86]

What distinguished the perception of trouble from the perception that nothing extraordinary had happened resided in the shared acceptance of the same normative environment and the willingness of elites and common people to negotiate within it. Paternalist patronage thus simultaneously served threatened consumers and sustained the authority of elites. When such strategies failed to resolve the crisis adequately, as when similar

82. Luckily for her, just as rioters were on the verge of attacking her château, a barge loaded with 1,400 sacks of flour appeared on the Seine to distract them ("Lettre [3 mai]," AD Seine-Maritime, C 107).

83. "Déposition, Information (17 mai)," AD Seine-et-Marne, B 2387.

84. "Information (16 mai)," AD Seine-et-Marne, B 2387.

85. "Journal de ce qui s'est passé à l'occasion de la révolte qui a eu lieu dans la subdélégation de Vernon et dans celles qui en sont voisines," AD Seine-Maritime, C 107; "Information (9 mai)," AD Eure, 16 B 653bis.

86. This behavior reminds us that in 1775 not all potential defectors from the community had defected.

responses to a crisis failed to produce the expected result, or when one of the sides repudiated the previously shared assumptions, trouble occurred. Then patrons and people squared off against each other, each sustained by assumptions forged in a different context. As the embodiment of social bonds and shared norms, the community fragmented. Yet it was no aggregate of disconnected individuals.[87] It was the product of other, coexisting social bonds that also linked people together and formed other types of communities. What we see, therefore, is not the disappearance of community but the reshaping of solidarities in changing historical circumstances. These forces shaped new communities, which turned against each other over the subsistence issue.

This process of restructuring the community had long been under way by 1775. Just as patronage relations themselves had undergone transformations as seigneurs departed from the land and left behind tenant farmers, estate managers, and rich peasants to fill the patronage gap as they saw fit, so too had other relations changed. Chapter 2 outlined some of the most salient of these for the Paris Basin. We now turn to the other types of communities that connected rioters, and then to communities of defectors that included the propertied, officials, and other notables, as well as their dependents.

COMMUNITIES OF RIOTERS IN 1775

Neighborhood or village ties, a bond that may or may not have included local patrons, were one of the most common types of bond linking food rioters in 1775.[88] Under normal conditions, people from the same village often traveled in groups to market towns, to buy and sell as well as to manage administrative affairs and find entertainment. Times of crisis proved no exception. For example, inhabitants from the village of Cergy gravitated "in great number" to Pontoise, where they amassed grain from the port, storage rooms, and marketplace. They played such a notable role that the lieutenant of the maréchaussée reported he "could name all the inhabitants of the parish without risk" of inculpating an innocent person. As it was, authorities arrested twenty-two people from Cergy. The village in 1776 had

87. Nor do I mean to suggest that these communities break with each other completely. In fact, significant ties persist among these communities.

88. Historians have often noted this connection. Unfortunately, evidence will not permit an analysis of town neighborhood ties, because there is no way to know exactly where people lived in some of these towns.

205 households. Thus, the police arrested a member from more than 10 percent of the households.[89]

Local authorities in market towns could rarely name individual rioters, but they had no difficulty identifying them by their village because they tended to arrive together and riot together. Arrest and interrogation records reveal similar patterns, despite the maréchaussée's inclination to make selective rather than blanket arrests. Only 15 percent of those arrested overall found themselves in jail without some fellow villager in a similar predicament. Of the 164 people arrested for rioting in Pontoise, 78 (or 48 percent) came from outside of Pontoise. Of these, only four stood as the sole detainee from their village, and one of these reported to the magistrates that she had traveled to the market town with three others from her village.[90] At Brie-Comte-Robert, where 77 percent of those arrested came from outside the market town and many fewer rioters (22) were arrested altogether, three were the lone representatives from their villages arrested. One of these, however, also testified that she had traveled to the market with a fellow villager.[91] Although most arrested villagers willingly provided a list of their fellow travelers in order to demonstrate that they had simply "done as the others," thus legitimizing their actions by grounding them in communal solidarity, some adamantly refused to turn in their accomplices. When judges asked Guillaume Moreau to name those from Cergy who had joined him in pillaging the barge at the port, he should have been able to list dozens, but he responded that "there were many from Cergy, but he couldn't name any of them."[92] When the judges insisted on pursuing the search for accomplices with a fellow resident of Cergy, Jean Lechaudé, the recalcitrant vine-grower stonewalled them: "he saw no one . . . he knew no one . . . he met no one and he was alone."[93]

89. Only one husband-wife set was arrested from Cergy. All the other arrests represented separate households. Only 182 were households headed by men. See "Procès-verbal (5 septembre 1775)," AD Oise, B 1583. Demographic information derived from J. Dupâquier et al., *Paroisses et communes de France. Dictionnaire d'histoire administrative et démographique: Région parisienne* (Paris, 1974), p. 468.

90. "Interrogatoire de Marie Anne Rousselet, veuve Cochon (17 juillet)," AD Oise, B 1583bis. Rousselet was a forty-one-year-old widow of a vine-grower in Herblay. Police continued to collect information about riot participation well into the following fall. Reports always clustered rioters by residence. For a classic example of this, see, for Pontoise, "Procès-verbal (5 septembre)," AD Oise, B 1583.

91. "Interrogatoire de Madelaine Pochet (9 mai)," AD Seine-et-Marne, B 3957(1).

92. "Interrogatoire (9 juillet)," AD Oise, B 1583bis.

93. These were answers to the questions: "Who were the persons from Cergy? . . . He must have recognized people from Cergy who were carrying grain from Pontoise to Cergy [after the riot]."

Villagers also mobilized local networks when they set out to search for and requisition grain from cultivators. Laboureurs and fermiers reported repeatedly that villages turned out groups of rioters. Remy Martin, a laboureur from Villemareuil in Brie, testified that on Sunday, 7 May, "about sixty people from Montceaux and two from Trilport" came to his farm at three o'clock in the morning to demand grain.[94] A large group of villagers from the parish of Sablonnières spent Wednesday morning, 10 May, searching the farms of cultivators in Saint-Léger and Grand Marché near Rebais. One cultivator numbered the group at 50, another estimated 100, another "a foule," another "une troupe," and a last simply claimed that "the inhabitants from Sablonnières came to demand grain."[95] Eight inhabitants of the village of Dieudonne in the Thelle spent Saturday, 29 April, at the market of Mouy, and Monday, 1 May, traveling to the farms of several cultivators.[96]

Of course, the *entrave*—the interception of barges and carts transporting grain or flour along river or land routes—was the prime example of potential village/neighborhood solidarity on subsistence issues. On 6 May grain merchant Toussaint Jacquet led a train of wagons carrying his grain from Guignes to the town of Rozay-en-Brie. As the train passed through Chaumes-en-Brie, the inhabitants rallied to sound the tocsin, halted the carts, commandeered nineteen sacks, and sequestered eighteen of them in the chapel. The people claimed they would sell it the next day at the market at Chaumes, for 12 livres per setier.[97] As already noted, the *entrave* could rally more diverse social participation because it directly pitted "outside" interests, such as those of nonresident merchants, and abstract needs, such as of consumers elsewhere, against the deeply felt local and thus more concrete needs of the community.

Social bonds catalyzed by geographic proximity often intertwined with those forged in the workplace or in general occupational solidarity. Certain types of occupations produced significant numbers of rioters in particular regions (see Chapters 3 and 4). Thus, Monsieur de Pommery advised intendant Crosne to "visit the houses of the woodcutters and day-laborers of

---

. . . There were more than 100 people who 'stole' grain from the barge and he must have met some people from Cergy on his way home." See "Interrogatoire (9 juillet)," AD Oise B, 1583bis.

94. "Information (12 mai)," AD Seine-et-Marne, B 2387.

95. Altogether, six cultivators reported visitations from Sablonnières. See "Information (17 mai)," AD Seine-et-Marne, B 2387.

96. They went to farms at Fayel, Cauvigny, Fercourt, and Châteaurouge. See "Interrogatoires (n.d.)," AD Oise, B 1583bis.

97. "Déclaration (8 mai)," AD Seine-et-Marne, B 3957(1).

the parishes of the forest and vineyards [in and around Vernon and La Roche-Guyon], and he would discover proof of crime."[98] Police arrested five river workers for their roles in "plotting" with eighty others in a barge on 29 April to force the Benedictine monastery of Saint-Leu-d'Esserent to give bread. The next day, they armed themselves with clubs, forced the inhabitants of Boissy to join them, rang the monastery's bell to summon more people, demanded grain at the characteristic 12 livres per setier, and terrorized the monks.[99] Six men from Ronquerolles raided the mill at Blainville on 1 May, all day-laborers.[100] Seven of the eight rioters from Dieudonne were day-laborers. Of the twenty-three arrested for rioting at the market of Mouy on 29 April, ten worked in woolen textile manufacture as *ouvriers en laine* or *compagnons sergers*, and five worked for a local miller who had attempted to profit from the unusually low prices.[101] The *tabletiers* of Méru played an active role (alongside women) in rioting in that market.[102] We have already seen how the *portefaix* and the "women from the waterfront" (classically the laundresses) were involved in the first eruption of the Flour War at Beaumont-sur-Oise. Rouenais officials held three spinners responsible for fomenting sedition at the marketplace on 8 May. All these occupations were notorious in the Ancien Régime for their ability to generate solidarity among their practitioners.[103]

Vine-growers also were a densely bonded group. Deeply attached to the vines planted by generations past, and inserted in work-cycles and life-cycles that related directly to viticulture, vine-growers had developed strong solidarities that often transcended differences of wealth and were distinct from the ties generated from farming arable land.[104] Of the twenty-two

98. "Lettre (10 mai)," AD Seine-Maritime, C 108, n. 108.

99. "Procès-verbal (11 juillet)," AD Oise, B 1583bis. There were two *compagnons de la rivière*, one *canayeur*, one *charpentier de bateau* and *compagnon de la rivière*, and one *pêcheur* and *compagnon de la rivière*. On this episode, see Chapter 4.

100. AD Oise, B 1583bis and 1583ter. A seventh was arrested; no evidence remains of his occupation.

101. Many more textile workers were accused. See "Procès-verbal (23 mai)," AD Oise, B 1583ter.

102. Ten out of 22 people arrested were *tabletiers*. Moreover, when one claimed that he was accused falsely, he marshaled the signed testimony of four other *tabletiers* to swear that he had not left his doorway during the riots in the marketplace. See "Certificat (24 septembre)," AD Oise, B 1584.

103. The Rouenais spinners already had a long history of disruptive behavior. In 1752 their demonstration against changes in their trade helped trigger a grain riot. See Guy Lemarchand, "Troubles de subsistance dans la généralité de Rouen aux XVIIIe siècle," AHRF 35 (Oct.-Dec. 1963), p. 408.

104. On this, see, for the Paris Basin in particular, Marcel Lachiver, *Vin, vigne, et vignerons en la région parisienne du XVIIe au XIXe siècles* (Paris, 1982), pp. 431-32, 500. Lachiver suggests that the

rioters arrested from the parish of Cergy, all but two were vine-growers.[105] All arrested from the village of Eragny who rioted at Pontoise were vine-growers, with the exception of one cooper, whose world was equally bound by the vine. All who went to Brie-Comte-Robert from Saint-Méry were vine-growers.

Occupational networks sometimes extended to the shop or workplace. For example, at age thirty-six Benoit Trabe already employed many workers as sawyer (*scieur-de-long*) in Pontoise. Trabe had hired and housed at least the five journeymen who were arrested with him when they lifted grain off a cart, raided a barge at the port, and took a sack of grain from a flour merchant.[106] A mason from Chelles and all his workers presented themselves before a local laboureur to demand the distribution of grain at a reduced price.[107] A carter from Chevry let his fourteen-year-old day-laborer take a horse to the local fermier to get grain.[108] Jean LeRoy, a saltpeter-maker, hid the grain he had taken from a flour merchant in Pontoise at his employer's house.[109] Officials reported that Sieur Etienne, who owned some forest near Lyons-la-Forêt, was observed "at the head of his workers." Etienne "spoke first and for all the others."[110] This evidence suggests that despite mounting evidence of a growing gap between employers (patrons) and workers in the Ancien Régime, some forms of solidarities remained, perhaps most saliently outside the big cities.[111]

Kinship connected clusters of rioters in a variety of ways. Among closest relatives, the most common bonds linked brothers or sisters, but rioters also engaged parent-child relations and husband-wife pairings. For example,

vine-growers formed ties of solidarity that were more intense than among peasants who worked arable land.

105. Cergy's 1773 *taille* roll reveals that 68 percent of the resident inhabitants were vine-growers, 17 percent held other occupations, and 15 percent had unknown occupations ("Role de taille, Cergy, 1773," AD Yvelines, C 184, n. 85). Of the two who were not vine-growers, one was a day-laborer and one was a carrier.

106. "Interrogative Benoit Trabe (1 & 26 mai)," AD Oise, B 1583ter; "Interrogatoires" of workers Simon Levault, Jean Nisard, Jean Maitre, and François Cresson (n.d.), AD Oise B 1583bis.

107. "Déposition de Louis Bourgeois, Information (17 mai)," AD Seine-et-Marne, B 2387.

108. "Interrogatoire de Julien Himbert (7 mai)," AD Seine-et-Marne B 3957(1).

109. "Interrogatoire (24 juillet)," AD Oise B, 1583ter.

110. "Lettre (12 juin)," AD Seine-Maritime, C 109; "Lettre (6 juillet)," C 107. Also cited in Lemarchand, "Troubles," p. 404.

111. See Robert Darnton, *The Great Cat Massacre* (New York, 1984); George Rudé, *The Crowd in the French Revolution* (Oxford, 1959); Arlette Farge, *La Vie fragile: Violence, pouvoirs, et solidarités à Paris au XVIIIe siècle* (Paris, 1986); Steven Kaplan, *Work in France: Representations, Meaning, Organization, and Practice* (Ithaca, N.Y., 1986); Michael Sonenscher, *Work and Wages: Natural Law, Politics, and the Eighteenth-Century Trades* (Cambridge, 1989), among many others.

brothers Nicolas François (age twenty-two) and Pierre Delaloy (age twenty-nine) of Théméricourt visited together a farm in the village of Us to demand grain on 3 May; brothers Pierre (age thirty-eight) and Bernard Serrain (age forty-two) from Dieudonne joined fellow villagers during their 1 May incursions into several farms.[112] Sisters Marie and Rose Leroy (both age twenty-eight) lived together with Marie and her husband in Franquevillette and "incited sedition" together at the market of Rouen on 8 May.[113] A father Antoine (age fifty-eight) and his son Jean Louis Delaplace (age nineteen) rioted on a barge at Pontoise together; authorities had to arrest the Allongé father and son because they refused to restitute the grain from their incursions into the farms in the region of Signet in the Brie.[114] Although police arrested fathers and daughters, they had not been rioting together. A mother Suzanne Mandart (age forty-four) and her daughter Catherine (age sixteen) scooped up grain from the ground during the riots at Méru.[115] Cavaliers arrested both Geneviève Gremvin and her husband Jean Marin when they traveled together from their village of Groslay, where they were vine-growers, to coerce a farmer in Moisselles to give them grain.[116] The miller on the bridge of Poissy reported that an entire family comprised of wife, husband, and "three or four children" had threatened him on 2 May.[117]

But such kinship bonds were not common among rioters arrested. Only 3 percent of all rioters arrested found themselves imprisoned with other members of their immediate family who shared the same household, and even fewer of those interrogated reported that other household members had accompanied them.[118] This suggests that families rarely mobilized more than one member of the household for this kind of activity. This strategy made it

112. On the Delaloy brothers and the Serrain brothers, see "Interrogatoires (n.d.)," AD Oise, B 1583bis. Pierre Delaloy was married; Nicolas François Delaloy was single. The Serrain brothers were the oldest pairing. The youngest pairing involved the Rousseau brothers (ages 17 and 18) of Beaumont-sur-Oise (AD Oise, B 1584).

113. "Interrogatories (20 mai)," AD Seine-Maritime, 202 BP 18*.

114. On the Delaplace pairing, "Interrogatories (1 mai)," AD Oise, B 1583ter; on the Allongé family, "Procès-verbal (11 août)," AD Seine-et-Marne, B 2387. Unfortunately, there is no age or other information on this father-son pairing.

115. "Interrogatoire, Suzanne Mandart, femme Saligny (24 juillet)," AD Oise, B 1583bis; "Interrogatoire, Catherine Saligny (23 septembre)," B 1584.

116. "Interrogatoire (4 mai)," AD Oise, B 1583bis.

117. "Information (17 juin)," AN, Y 18682.

118. Arrest records indicate the following occurrences: six brother pairings; two sister pairings; four father-son pairings; two mother-daughter pairings (not counting infants and very small children, who played no active role in the Flour War); and three husband-wife pairings. Witness and police testimony reveal very few additional cases.

possible to preserve family viability if a rioting member was arrested; family testimony indicated repeatedly that imprisonment of even one adult household member could bring serious hardship. Indeed, one of the father-son pairings involved two separate households, not a son living under a father's roof.[119]

Rioters may have mobilized, instead, more distant kinship ties that did not threaten household stability. Although eighteenth-century rural society was more mobile than its reputation has allowed,[120] villages still demonstrated certain specific kinship patterns. Another 7 percent of rioters arrested not only participated in the Flour War together but also shared the same surnames or in-law status, as well as the same village of residence.[121] For example, Nicolas Walle raided a mill at Gué-à-Tresmes and a farm at Beauval with his brother-in-law Claude Denis.[122] Marie Leroy joined her sister-in-law Marie Leroux in inciting a riot at Rouen.[123] However, kinship in these forms did not function as a powerful bond linking rioters in 1775. The need to defend the family economy during subsistence crises certainly mobilized women and men to invoke the *taxation populaire*, but when they headed for market, bakery, or farm they usually sent one member from a household and rarely mobilized along kinship lines. Neighborhood, occupation, and gender were stronger bonds.

As we have already seen, gender also functioned as a social bond. Not only did certain spaces carry gendered characteristics, but women and men created gendered networks. Veronique Prévost explained to the judges that

119. Nicolas Fontaine, *père* (age 55) maintained a household separate from Nicolas Fontaine, *fils* (age 25) ("Interrogatoires [28 septembre] AD Oise, B 1584). The rareness of such interhousehold arrests suggests that this is more than simply the product of random arrests. The only other explanation lies in a police force unwilling to arrest more than one from each household. This appears an unlikely explanation for arrests that took place at the time of the rioting, but a more likely possibility when arrests occurred after the rioting had died down. Then, police may have targeted only heads of households. See Chapter 6 for men who claimed they had not rioted but their spouses and children had.

120. Micheline Baulant, "Groupes mobiles dans une société sédentaire: La Société autour de Meaux aux XVIIe et XVIIIe siècles," in *Les Marginaux et les exclus dans l'histoire,* ed. Bernard Vincent (Paris, 1979), pp. 78–121.

121. More distant kinship ties are particularly difficult to trace through records such as these; they run the risk of establishing relations that did not exist and overlooking more important ones entirely. Even though only a more sophisticated demographic analysis could ascertain kinship ties with greater certainty, this type of evidence is useful if used cautiously. Lachiver suggests that endogamy among vine-growers was so common that entire villages could share close kinship relations (*Vin,* pp. 428–29).

122. "Interrogatoires (31 mai)," AD Seine-et-Marne, B 2387.

123. Both had married a brother from the Goupy family. "Interrogatoires (20 mai)," AD Seine-Maritime, 202 BP 18*.

she had belonged to a group of ten to twelve women who had gone to ask for bread from the two millers/flour merchants at Mours on 29 April.[124] Men accused of plotting the riot at Mouy admitted to meeting in a tavern, the Cabaret d'Egypt, the morning the market opened.[125] One interesting manifestation of the separateness of these networks is that neither the men nor the women referred to the other network when confronted by the judges. Even in the two cases mentioned above, when fathers and daughters were both arrested for riot activity, they had not acted together. Only husband and wife sets linked the sexes, and these occurred infrequently.

The women and men who rioted at Méru formed two interlaced but largely separate networks. On the one hand, many men belonged to an occupational network of inlayers (*tabletiers*), a network in which women, as wives and daughters, sometimes played a part. On the other hand, women had constructed their own networks. We can see aspects of these bonds in the relations reported by female rioters arrested. At the center of this network stood thirty-eight-year-old Catherine Clerfeuille, *femme* (the wife of) Claude Leternelle. A lace-maker, she reported that her husband had formerly worked as a schoolteacher but listed no current occupation for him. Catherine claimed that she had heard of the previous day's "pillage at Beaumont" from "the *femme* Emery, an old clothes seller at Chambly, who told *la mère* Gentil who lives with her [Catherine's] son-in-law, Basquin, a cobbler in Méru." Catherine told all this to Madelaine Louette, *femme* François Fourier, gamekeeper at Berville, who then ate lunch with Marie Suzanne Daudry, *femme* Pierre Legros, horsetrader and publican at Méru. Both later joined Clerfeuille and others in the tumultuous marketplace. Marie Marguerite Beauvais, *femme* Pierre Lemaire, a journeyman blacksmith at Méru, and Marie Anne Lefebvre, a fellow lace-maker and *femme* Jean Mabille, cattle trader and day-laborer, attended the market with Catherine, helped her get the grain she took from the market, and shared it with her. At the same time, Suzanne Mandart, a seedswoman married to a *tabletier*, and her sixteen-year-old daughter followed the example provided by Marie Lefebvre, who was the only woman Mandart recognized in the marketplace. Police arrested all of these women for rioting. Clerfeuille and Beauvais were accused of specific violence: of roughing up laboureurs and tearing sacks of grain open with knives.[126] Different types of identifiable ties linked various combinations of these women, and the nature of some bonds remains

124. "Interrogatoire (18 mai)," AD Oise, B 1583ter.
125. See, e.g., "Interrogatoire Marc Agé," AD Oise, B 1583bis.
126. "Interrogatoires (24 juin, 18, 24 juillet)," AD Oise, B 1583bis, 1583ter.

unclear. What is clear, however, is that some women in Méru and elsewhere formed networks, both informal and formal, that they could mobilize to form the core for organizing a violent riot in the marketplace.

Many if not most of the women arrested worked for wages: protoindustry, day-laboring, marketing garden products, and so on. However, even housework involved them in frequent and various interactions outside the home. Marie Catherine Derlot was a thirty-eight-year-old wife of a journalier in the village of Noisy-le-Roi near Versailles.[127] She described what she did to the judges: "she took care of her household and her children and was a wetnurse, currently weaning the son of Sieur LeBlanc, *officer du Roi*." She was also four months pregnant. On Monday, 1 May, she left Noisy at 7:00 in the morning for Neauf [Neauphle-le-Château] to get haricot seeds for planting, accompanied by the son of a neighbor who sought eggs. They got there at 10:30, negotiated their businesses, left at 1:00 and returned to Noisy between 5:00 and 6:00 that evening, so she could not have participated in the rioting at Saint Germain-en-Laye on 1 May. The next day, she was at home until 2:00 in the afternoon, when she discovered she was out of flour and headed for Versailles, "not knowing there was a revolt there." When she arrived there, at 3:30, the worst was over and soldiers were organizing the distribution of bushels of flour at the market price. She bought some flour and returned home. She got into trouble on 3 May. In the afternoon, "she heard that flour was selling at Rennemoulin for 20 sols per boisseau," 10 sols below the price she had paid at Versailles, but three other women were waiting to buy. Police were on guard, and the miller, Sieur Robine, went ahead and sold her 8 boisseau for 20 sols (later she claimed the flour was of bad quality). Only after she returned home was she arrested. Now she stood before the court; her activities had looked quite suspicious to the police. Marie Catherine Derlot's work of caring for her household drove her outside the home into multiple and diverse activities and social exchanges. She never explained how she heard about the sale at Rennemoulin, but her various encounters during the day provided her with plenty of information networks, both formal and informal: neighborhood, marketing, and perhaps news from other people on the road.

Eight men arrested for rioting at Versailles formed relationships that were no less complex than those forged by women but that were still quite distinct.[128] The masonry shop of Sieur André on the rue de Belair stood at

---

127. See her "Interrogatoire (10 mai)," AD Yvelines, 1 B 219.

128. On what follows, see the "Interrogatoires" of François Portoux, Jacques Bontot, Mathurin Thevenet, Jacques Aubin, Pierre Gentil, Jean Sisterne, Jacques Chabot, and Mathurin Dardant (4 and 5 May), AD Yvelines, 1 B 219.

the center of this network. Five men worked there as journeymen and day-laborers. Two came from the same town in Basse Marche: one, twenty-two-year-old François Portoux, had moved to Versailles when he was eleven and worked as a day-laborer; the second, twenty-year-old Jacques Bontot, had arrived a year earlier to join his father, who also worked for André and was "known and protected by the Duc de Villeroy and Sieur LeBrun, an architect in Versailles." They also shared the same lodging. Two other journeymen came from Limoges: twenty-one-year-old Pierre Gentil and forty-year-old Mathurin Thevenet. These three journeymen masons and one day-laborer shared work space and time with another journeyman, twenty-year-old Jacques Aubin. Gentil and Thevenet lived at the same address with an unemployed journeyman mason also from Limoges, twenty-one-year-old Mathurin Dardant, and with a forty-four-year-old digger (*terrassier*) from the Auvergne, Jacques Chabot. Chabot worked with another Auvergnat *terrassier*, Jean Sisterne. Only Portoux and Thevenet were married, and they to women from their own *pays* whom they visited in the Basse Marche only during the winter.[129]

On 2 May the masons who had come to work for Sieur André at 5:00 A.M. took their lunch at 9:00. While eating lunch, they heard a great commotion coming from the market. Sieur André heard it too and, like the other shop owners in the area, closed everything up, forcing those who had come to work later to leave. As the masons went to see what all the excitement was, they ran into Dardant looking for work. Jean Sisterne had worked all morning at the Parc. Right around lunchtime he broke his mallet and had to return to town to get another one. He had lunch with Chabot, his friend, fellow Auvergnat, and workmate, who had not felt well for several days and had not gone to work. After lunch, as they passed by the market, they ran into Gentil and Thevenet, with whom Chabot lived. Gentil and Thevenet had already joined the masons, and the entire band entered the Poids le Roy and carried off six sacks of flour. It took them two trips. They took the sacks to the Chabot-Gentil-Thevenet lodging and agreed to sell two and split the proceeds. This they did, except for Aubin, who said he "preferred flour to money, because he could cook" and took three sacks and left. Then the rest of the band went to a cabaret, used the money to buy a round of drinks, divided up the rest, and went their separate ways, some like Sisterne to pay a debt he owed a comrade. Sieur André's shop remained

129. It is interesting that the judges in Versailles were among the very few that asked men about their marital status.

closed the rest of the day. As workers returned to work in the next few days, the police arrested them, ultimately grabbing the whole network of eight men.[130] These men were linked by overlapping ties involving occupation/ workplace, lodging, and geographic origins.

Men and women sometimes worked together in rioting during the Flour War, but (as we have seen) although they engaged in similar behavior in the same place, they often formed separate clusters of rioters.[131] Occasionally our sources enable us to discern these separate groups, which no doubt explains apparent discrepancies in witness testimony at Beaumont-sur-Oise over whether the "women from the waterfront" or the market sack-carriers had started the uprising. Both groups of witnesses were correct: the women and the men had activated their own separate networks and took similar action in the same place at the same time. Events at Méru suggest the same thing.[132]

These types of bonds—geographic, occupational, kinship, and gender— intersected in various ways to form dense relations, or communities, among rioters in 1775. The men who "plotted" the *taxation populaire* at the market of Mouy on Saturday, 29 April, shared not only links forged in neighborhood (several of the most active came from the hamlet of Moineau in the parish of Angy, just outside Mouy), gender, and sociability (the tavern), but also links through occupation. Witnesses claimed repeatedly that most were "workers" (*ouvriers*) in the "manufacture of Mouy." The three women arrested for "inciting riot" at the market of Rouen shared kinship, geographic, and occupational ties. All three worked as spinners in the cotton industry. The "women from the waterfront," whom witnesses accused of fomenting sedition at Beaumont-sur-Oise, combined gender and workplace bonds; the sack-carriers whom witnesses indicted similarly shared occupational, workplace, and gender bonds. The rioters of Méru shared a diverse cluster of ties: occupation (such as lace-making for the women and inlay work for the men), kinship, gender, and sociability (or friendship). Although not all people who rioted in the Flour War related in such multiple ways with others, these sorts of ties helped to create organizational nodes for stirring protest during the subsistence crisis.

130. The police at Versailles arrested only sixteen people in all.

131. Dominique Godineau speaks of " 'parallel' worlds, which both sexes respected" ("Masculine and Feminine Political Practice During the French Revolution, 1793–Year III," in *Women and Politics in the Age of Democratic Revolution*, ed. H. B. Applewhite and D. G. Levy [Ann Arbor, Mich., 1990], p. 73).

132. See a similar situation at Vannes in 1765 described in T.J.A. LeGoff, *Vannes and Its Region* (Oxford, 1981), pp. 103–5.

Moreover, some of these social bonds could transcend ties to other communities and thus give us an idea of their strengths. For example, the overwhelming majority of village syndics arrested for openly siding with fellow villagers or for rioting themselves during the Flour War came from the same social ranks as the rioters themselves. Etienne Alliot, the syndic of Signy-Signets, was a day-laborer.[133] Louis Hudde from Baillet held several occupations—a carter of paving stones, a fruit-seller, and a shepherd—but none very remunerative.[134] Louis Suplice Metat of Montsoult worked as a basket-maker and paid 3 livres for the *taille* in 1774. By contrast, his victim Delacour paid 1,706 livres in *taille*.[135] When the lieutenant of the maréchaussé galloped into the village of Moisson, the home of large numbers of rioters who attacked the barge at Tosny, with his patrol of cavaliers, he discovered that the "parish was peopled only by women, and there was no man except the syndic." The villagers had been warned of his arrival and fled. And as the syndic guided him around "to the houses where there were people to arrest," he saw the syndic "making signs . . . to the women to warn their husbands to escape if they had not done so already."[136] The parish of Moisson was composed overwhelmingly of vine-growers, most of whom were very poor. In 1775 Magny's subdelegate wrote that "at least half of the inhabitants of Moisson go to beg near Paris during the winter."[137] In these cases, bonds of inferior social status bound village syndics more tightly to those with similar class status than to fellow officials and overcame whatever sense of duty they felt toward their official positions as administrative intermediaries.

People who belonged to these networks clearly shared expectations about one another's behavior. Thus, Suzanne Mandart emulated the actions of Marie Lefevre, a role model, in the marketplace of Méru. When arrested rioters protested before the magistrates that "they were simply doing as everyone else," they signaled that they had acted within a community, not as isolated deviants. The poor who were noticeably absent from the Flour

133. "Interrogatoire (31 mai)," AD Seine-et-Marne, B 2387.

134. "Interrogatoire (24 septembre)," AD Oise B 1583; "Attestation (20 septembre)," B 1584; "Rôle de taille, Baillet, 1774," AN Z1g 360A. Huddle held some property in nearby parishes of Bouffémont and Chauvry, but none of his properties or revenues amounted to much ("Rôle de taille, Bouffémont, 1774" and "Rôle de taille, Chauvry, 1774," AN Z1g 360A).

135. "Procès-verbal (15 novembre)," AD Oise, B 1583. Grand Gournay formed part of the parish of Montsoult ("Rôle de taille, Montsoult, 1774," AN Z1g 360A).

136. "Lettres (24, 26 juin)," AD Seine-Maritime, C 108, pièces 310, 312.

137. "Lettre," AD Seine-Maritime, C 995, also cited by Jacques Dupâquier, *Ainsi . . . Chaumont*, p. 72.

War's food riots may have been unable to draw on some of these communal ties. Although some villages took care of their own, many poor were marginalized through efforts of charity and social control (hôpitaux-généraux, dépôts de mendicité, ateliers de charité, and even prison). Sometimes driven to individual acts of begging or theft, they were repressed quickly when they were found joining together as begging bands. Thus, the poorest people of the Paris Basin were too atomized to access collective networks that could lead to collective protest.

Indeed, experiences such as food riots like the Flour War manifested the continued vitality of community among the common people; moreover, as E. P. Thompson and others have suggested, food riots were also practices by which communities were expressed, consolidated, and transformed under changing historical circumstances. In the longer-term perspective of previous and subsequent food riots and their historical contexts, the Flour War indicates that the *taxation populaire* itself—a product of collective action grounded in community—was undergoing transformations. As we shall see, changes took place unevenly, differently, or more visibly in some places than in others. Despite these variations, these changes manifested community responses to shifting circumstances that in turn imposed the necessity and created opportunities for reshaping both social bonds and the normative environment, thus stimulating and sustaining the process of change.

COMMUNITIES OF DEFECTORS IN 1775

What differentiated the communities described in the first section of this chapter from those described in the second and this third one is that, in the former, patronage relations functioned relatively effectively because, although changing the interpretation of the extent and nature of that responsibility sometimes generated disputes and tensions, general agreement persisted over the legitimacy of that relationship. In the latter two types, these relationships had broken down on subsistence issues. This breakdown was a product of shifts in social structure that polarized the village or town and reordered social bonds. Ultimately there occurred a defection of many grain proprietors from the normative environment that accepted the social use of grain and its products and that food producers and merchants carried collective responsibilities.

When grain-holders thus rejected as illegitimate the assumption that grain was a collective good and redefined food distribution at lower than market price as theft (pillage) rather than part of the paternalistic practice of charity, while grain consumers clung to their traditional views of sustenance as a right, the community confronted a crisis. Such defections from the previous communal normative environment distinguished the communities that rioted in the Paris Basin in 1775 from those that did not or those that experienced mild disturbances. Riots erupted when the parties could no longer agree on the terms of debate. This situation was exacerbated by the shifting sands of royal policy that vacillated between embracing its traditional paternalist position, on the one hand, and the physiocratic vision of free trade on the other, thus injecting a further solvent of uncertainty into a crisis of expectations.

Armed resistance to local demands for grain distributions, a "bunker mentality" that drove some producers to bury their grain or hunker down behind closed courtyard doors, and the refusal to take even the usual 12 livres per setier that rioters offered as payment, reflect abandonment of the traditional postures on the subsistence issue. For example, Nicolas Tronchon, laboureur at Marcilly, declared he had refused payment from the people who came to his farm on 6 May because "he preferred taking no money at all to taking only 12 livres."[138] Those who refused to sell at 12 livres repudiated the principle of the just price. In effect, they declared it illegal for authorities to set a price other than the market price, and pillage for rioters to do so. They repudiated the social use of grain that was not calculated in market terms.

Producers and merchants, millers and bakers, local authorities and other local notables, had themselves developed multiple community relations. Identifying the community that linked "defectors" proves more difficult to document than finding it among rioters. They did not congregate in bands the way the common people did during subsistence crises. Indeed, the very fact that they often stood alone in farm or mill or shop made them more attractive targets. Roger Dion has observed for the Paris Basin that isolated blocks of land separated from the village and village lands on which a group of buildings, including the farmhouse, sat was a fairly common feature, particularly in the *pays de grande culture*. This living arrangement for proprietors and their fermiers could sever some types of ties with the village itself, further isolating them from the village community.[139] Although some accepted the collective obligations and assumptions that shaped the pater-

138. "Information (10 mai)," AD Seine-et-Marne, B 2247.
139. Roger Dion, *Essai sur la formation du paysage rural français* (Tours, 1934). See also Jean Meuvret, *Problèmes*, 2:88.

nalist approach to the food issue, many others had forged (and continued to forge) communities of their own, communities that, like all others, comprised both social bonds and norms, which could in turn modify behavior among members, including the substitution of capitalist ideals for traditional ones. While such people never completely severed ties with their local communities, and never completely eschewed the local, paternalist normative environment, they simultaneously continued to forge stronger ties with the larger communities of others more like themselves, ties that dictated new forms of behavior. They did this through kinship ties, through channels of political power, and through networks facilitated by commercial and property relations.[140] In this process begun long before 1775, we can see elements at work at the time of the Flour War.

In the countryside of the Paris Basin, substantial laboureurs and fermiers constituted an extremely small percentage of the population.[141] Despite their numerical weakness and spatial isolation, however, they were not socially isolated. Historians have discovered strong kinship networks that stretched beyond the farm.[142] Indeed, kinship linked much of the landed elite of rural France, and a small number of families often controlled the economy of a large region. Endogamy characterized their marriage alliances. Fermiers tended to form marriages more often with other fermiers than with laboureurs.[143] Children of fermiers and laboureurs tended to follow in their fathers' footsteps, either taking up the family land or establishing themselves on lands nearby.[144] Predictably, therefore, 1775 revealed these relations in the region engulfed by the Flour War, as when rioters attacked the farms of the two most propertied inhabitants of the parish of Belloy: Claude Meignan, fermier of the seigneurie, and his brother-in-law, Jean Baptiste Sainte-Boeuve, receveur of the fief of Puy d'Aulnoy.[145]

140. On aspects of this process, see, e.g., the works of Kaplan, *Provisioning*, pp. 321–38 (on millers); Marc Venard, "Une Classe rurale puissant au XVIIe siècle: Les Laboureurs au sud de Paris," *AESC* (1955) 10: 517–25; Jean-Marc Moriceau, "Mariages et foyers paysans aux XVIe et XVIIe siècles: L'Exemple des campagnes du sud de Paris," *RHMC* 28 (July 1981): 481–502; idem, "Un Système de protection sociale efficace: Exemple des vieux fermiers de l'Ile-de-France (XVIIe–début XIX siècles)," in *Annales de démographie historique*, 1985, pp. 127–44; Jean-Pierre Jessenne, *Pouvoir au village et Révolution: Artois, 1760–1848* (Lille, 1987), pp. 205–22; Jean Jacquart, *La Crise rurale en Ile-de-France, 1550–1670* (Paris, 1974), pp. 541–95, 731–40.

141. See Chapter 2.

142. See note 140 above. Jean-Marc Moriceau and Gilles Postel-Vinay, *Ferme, Entreprise, Famille* (Paris, 1992), pp. 73–128.

143. For the late eighteenth century, see Jessenne, *Pouvoir*, pp. 206–9.

144. Ibid., pp. 214–21.

145. "Lettre (3 mai)," AD Oise, B 1583ter; "Rôle de taille, Belloy, 1774," AD Z1g 360B; and personal correspondence with Jean-Marc Moriceau. By 1775, Sainte-Boeuve himself had died, and

Events also demonstrated more diverse kinship networks. Cultivators made alliances with people other than cultivators. For example, the fermier at Sucy-en-Brie called on his brother-in-law, an innkeeper at Créteil, to help handle the crowds that arrived on 6 May to demand grain. The innkeeper was particularly useful for his ability to identify faces in the crowd.[146]

Testimonies of some of those present when rioters invaded farms in 1775 provided a picture of surplus grain producers' larger networks. For example, a fermier at Genouilly in the parish of Crisenoy distributed grain with the help of the seigneurial receveur, who was also the procureur fiscal et concierge of the Château of Crisenoy;[147] the fermier of the seigneurie at Crosne was assisted by the seigneurie's receveur;[148] and the fermier of Chenay, parish of Gagny, found a helper in his neighbor, the procureur fiscal of the bailliage of Neuilly-sur-Marne.[149] In all three cases, visitors clearly linked the proprietor with the seigneurial or administrative order of the Ancien Régime.[150]

Even on the farm itself, surplus-grain-producing cultivators and their families were never alone at the time of the Flour War. As employers of domestic as well as farm labor, the courtyards, barns, fields, and houses held not only the laboureur's or fermier's kin, but also other people. These people stood ambiguously between rioters and their victims in 1775. Though themselves a part of the common people, they were immediately dependent on the grain proprietor for their livelihood, sometimes even fed directly from the farm's stocks (as were certain day-laborers, harvesters, etc.) and housed on the premises. Consequently these individuals often found themselves defending farm and grain against those with whom they held other strong ties. The strength of the defense often depended on their cooperation. François Guichard managed to stave off the assault on his farm by local

---

his widow headed the household. Rioters did not assail the properties of the two other large-scale cultivators in the village: Claude Gavignot and Etienne Cousin. Although their respective tax payment (590 livres and 747 livres, respectively) paled in comparison to Meignan's (1,912 livres) and Sainte-Boeuve's (1,281 livres), it still qualified them as significant landholders in the village. As far as I can tell, they were not related, as were the other two. Of course, this evidence testified more to rioter perception than to functional ties linking local elites.

146. "Information (13 mai)," AN, Y 18682.

147. "Procès-verbal (7 mai)," AD Seine-et-Marne B 3957(1).

148. "Information (14 mai)," AN, Y 18692.

149. "Déclaration (7 mai)" and "Information (17 mai)," AN, Y 18682.

150. We cannot discount the market relationship that often governed estate management by the eighteenth century. See Robert Forster, The Nobility of Toulouse in the Eighteenth Century (Baltimore, 1960); Jonathan Dewald, Pont-St.-Pierre: Lordship, Community, and Capitalism in Early Modern France (Berkeley and Los Angeles, 1987).

villagers with the assistance of his guards and servants, as well as his
children.[151] In such cases, the individual farm functioned as a surviving,
albeit partial, paternalist microcosm, though the proprietor may have embraced the emerging market-driven world outside.

Surplus-producers formed ties in towns as well as countryside. The
marketplace served not only as the focal point of interactions between
consumers and grain proprietors, but also as a center of networks joining
merchants, producers, millers, bakers, and so on. Steven Kaplan elucidated
the nature of networks engendered by the grain trade:

> Labyrinthine kinship ties united millers, bakers, grain and flour
> merchants, and laboureurs (and stretched in some cases to embrace
> brokers or market officers). . . . Further extended by friendships,
> these family linkages significantly lowered transaction costs by
> transmitting trustworthy information, reducing uncertainty, intro-
> ducing parties who could count on each other, building exchange
> rules on mutual identity and confidence, and focusing on long-term
> relations, . . . defended the group against external threats, punished
> renegades in its midst, [and] formed an arena of sociability.[152]

In essence, grain proprietors were actively creating their own solidarities.
Small wonder that frustrated rioters who had demanded in vain that
authorities at Pontoise take paternalist measures in 1775 denounced officials
and merchants alike, saying, "Ils se tiennent tous par la main." These
solidarities differed in the range of social relations from that of the common
people. Among the common people, the community that could be effectively mobilized was largely local and, at most, regional; among grain
proprietors, the solidarity was not only local and regional, but national as
well. The common people shared strongest community ties with other
relatively powerless people like themselves; grain proprietors forged ties
among other powerful groups.

These grain proprietors also shared a different normative environment.
Although quick to demand state protection when it suited them, and

---

151. This relationship demonstrates that community fragmentation was always incomplete (see
below). Economic and social dependency tied laborers to employers, and these vertical links help
to explain some aspects of the struggles between the community of rioters and those among them
whose ties to the group of defectors kept them alienated from those who rioted.

152. *Provisioning*, pp. 602–3. He also notes that these ties were brittle. For more on this, see
below.

equally quick to seek patronage when it served them, they denied the people's version of paternalism and had largely abandoned the even modified version that traditional elites had accepted. Instead, they demanded absolute control over their property and the right to dispose of it as they saw fit, although few could have articulated this in theoretical terms.

Over time, food riots served to shape not only popular community and consciousness, but also community and consciousness among surplus-grain-producing cultivators, grain and flour merchants, millers, bakers, and so on. The common people drew on past practice and the "mobilizing myth" of the just price to address present crises. Their targets responded by drawing not only on past experiences but also on perceptions and responses modified by such changing conditions as growing market opportunities, reconstructed social networks, and altered political sanctions that combined to undermine previous relations and assumptions. Food riots themselves operated as formative agents in the shaping of this grain-holders' culture that mixed paternalist and free-market assumptions and behaviors in a concoction reworked by each experience.[153]

Recalling Defectors to the Community

Actual rioting signaled that paternalist relations had failed to provide a generally acceptable resolution to the subsistence crisis and that the communities that had formed around patronage ties and the culture of the moral economy were breaking down. However, the persistence of the *taxation populaire* and other ritual elements in subsistsence crises also demonstrates that neither party had entirely severed ties with the other. Royal authority and grain proprietors never declared themselves opposed to paternalism or denied their concern for the needs of the common people, although they increasingly disputed the means to achieve the common good.[154] This left them subject to manipulation by the people, who invoked the moral

153. Dale Williams sees these experiences as central to the shaping of middle-class consciousness in England ("Morals, Markets, and the English Crowd in 1766," *Past and Present* 104 [August 1984]: 72). Although this is undoubtedly a component of the French experience—and Kaplan's analysis of French grain merchants tends to suggest something like this was under way—the deeper links with the seigneurial system produced a different mix in France.

154. See the discussion about the morality of the classical economists in A. W. Coats, "Contrary Moralities: Plebs, Paternalists, and Political Economists," *Past and Present* 54 (Feb. 1972): 130–33.

economy response to subsistence crises. The common people attempted to recall potential defectors to the paternalist/patronage community.

The ritualistic practices of the common people reflect an overwhelmingly optimistic attachment to the principles of cause and effect. The repetition of similar patterns of behavior and discourse from one subsistence crisis to another and from place to place indicated that actors were attempting to reproduce a paternalist response. Nowhere is this more obvious than in the early stages of a subsistence crisis. When the people assembled to present themselves and their demands for cheaper, more accessible grain to local authorities, to merchants, or to producers, they hoped to trigger a particular paternalist response. They were sending reminders to those who controlled grain and its products that the time had come to shoulder their collective responsibilities.

Thus, what Steven Kaplan has called the "pre-riot" and John Bohstedt called the "protocol of riot" was the attempt of the common people to call potential defectors back to the community.[155] In some cases the strategy worked, but in many others it failed miserably. The Flour War presents examples of both outcomes. Some cultivators, like Cosme Charlemagne, or merchants, like the "gentlemen" at the Saint-André market, responded quickly to local demands for paternalist charity. Responding to popular appeals to common interests, marketplace authorities sometimes ignored royal injunctions, interfered with the grain trade, and negotiated compromises between protesting consumers and merchants. Officials at Louviers allowed sales of grain only in half-bushel quantities, while those at Dourdon fixed bread prices and ordered bakers to bake enough bread "continuously and daily for the needs of inhabitants of the city and environs until they exhausted their supplies."[156] Local officials at Argenteuil and Roye furnished similar examples.[157]

In other cases, cultivators, merchants, and authorities missed, ignored, or even openly rebuffed the people's calls for paternalist consideration. A laboureur from the parish of Signy-Signets, Charles Touprix, enraged fellow villagers when he declared at a public meeting that "the poor" could eat "grass."[158] Doré, subdelegate at Vernon, gained the approval of his intendant for mounting an armed defense of the stored grain destined for both the

---

155. Kaplan, *Bread*, 1:194–95; Bohstedt, *Riots*, pp. 5, 193.

156. On Louviers, see "Lettre (9 mai)," AD Seine-Maritime, C 109, pièce 35. On Dourdon, see "Procès-verbal (6 mai)," AD Yvelines, 4 B 1352.

157. See earlier in this chapter.

158. See Chapter 3.

local and Parisian markets—he ordered the clerk to close the doors and refuse sales—but he was alienated from town notables for the same behavior.[159]

Both Touprix and Doré incurred public wrath when they refused the call to respect the requests of the needy. The village syndic physically assaulted Touprix while fellow villagers cheered. Doré's actions not only escalated the violence, which resulted in injury to several people, but made him the object of local hostility. He wrote, "I was almost alone against 6,000 rioters, I succeeded, and this glorious success produced an effect contrary to my hopes. . . . It has attracted the scorn of the entire city. . . . Everyone flees from me since this event and is convinced that my resistance was due only to my interest in the Tour, and that I am a despicable man who gets fat like all grain merchants."[160]

Because even in the liberalization era neither the king nor the grain proprietor, producer, or merchant, was prepared to forgo publicly his paternalist image and the social authority it imparted, subsistence crises created ambiguous circumstances. The increasingly attractive prospect of following the logic of the market demanded behavior that was inimical to paternalism. Yet the fact that notables usually left at least one foot in the paternalist community encouraged the common people to hope that they could be convinced to step back with the other. Hence, the repeated rituals embedded in the *taxation populaire* aimed to transmit the call to return to the community. When producers, merchants, and authorities failed to heed the call, when they demonstrated that they had defected definitively, the community that remained turned to violence to force compliance. As British historian Roger Wells has observed, "the crowd, with its actual power in numbers, and its inherent threat of violence, was the people's institution."[161] Thus, the ambiguity created by growing market opportunities, by the mobilization of increasing numbers of entrepreneurs willing to embrace them, and ultimately by royal decree, on the one hand, and the dynamic and adaptable traditions of patronage, on the other, engendered the poten-

159. "Journal de ce qui s'est passé à l'occasion de la révolte qui a eu lieu dans la subdélégation de Vernon," AD Seine-Maritime, C 107; "Information (9 mai)," AD Eure, 16 B 653bis. See Chapter 3 and discussion earlier in the present chapter. Doré had earlier been involved in attempting to calm a tumultuous marketplace. He had forced the display and sale of grain stored in a local warehouse that belonged to Rouenais merchant Planter. Moreover, he had required its sale in small quantities for more widespread distribution. But it was the defense of the Tour that polarized opinion at Vernon. See "Lettres (10, 12, 13 mai)," AD Seine-Maritime, C 110; "Lettre (7 mai)," C 108.

160. "Lettre (16 juin)," AD Seine-Maritime, C 107.

161. *Wretched Faces: Famine in Wartime England, 1793–1801* (New York, 1988), p. 74.

tial for disorder and the formation of opposing fronts during subsistence crises.

Struggles Within Communities in 1775

I have been arguing that people who joined or opposed subsistence move-ments shared a similar normative environment and that when they mobi-lized they drew on many of the same aspects of community. But some historians have recently noted the general failure to acknowledge the presence of individual interests and power struggles within the ranks of the crowd.[162]

When food rioters clashed with bakers, farmers, merchants, and millers in 1775, and when the people invoked the traditional *taxation populaire* as a strategy to convey their distress, contemporary observers assumed that rioters shared similar motives. Subsequent historians often contested the reasons observers gave, but joined with them in assuming a largely unanimous motivation. This position has now come under attack by such historians as Suzanne Desan, who has suggested that "the 'moral economy' might have different meanings or levels of significance for various members of the community," and by Robert Woods, who challenges that "a crowd's motives might vary as widely as the number of its participants."[163] Despite generally similar patterns, the Flour War provides broad evidence of different types of crowd behavior (see Chapter 4). The longer-term significance of these differences is examined in Chapter 6. This section looks at the sources and meanings of diversity within Flour War crowds themselves, a diversity that sometimes caused dissension but that more often reveals the diversity of motivation underlying a common unity. It focuses first on the problem of motivation and then on the types of social interactions that could emerge within crowds themselves.

Not all who rioted in 1775 had the same priority list. Some were driven by actual need, some freeloaded, some planned in advance, some simply "found themselves swept up by the crowd," some may have been coerced. Some were driven by personal motives, some expressed grievances that transcended the immediate subsistence issue, some joined to advance their relative positions within their communities.

162. See note 1 for this chapter.
163. Desan, "Crowds," p. 59; Woods, "Individuals," p. 2.

Rioters frequently explained their behavior in terms of immediate or imminent need. For example, sixty-three-year-old day-laborer Sébastien Titout, arrested for rioting at the farms of laboureurs and fermiers at Château Morin and Grand Marché, claimed "it was need that had made him act that way."[164] Louis Lecan, a day-laborer with four children, testified that when "he saw that all the grain in the area was disappearing, he feared that there wouldn't be enough for his family's subsistence."[165] No doubt Titout and Lecan, as well as many others, calculated that this explanation might move judges to clemency, but need constituted a clear issue among many of those who rioted (see Chapter 3). Moreover, among those whose families depended largely on wages for survival, need motivated more directly than an image of halcyon days of paternalism. The pronouncement at Beaumont-sur-Oise that "starving or being killed by the police amounted to the same thing to them" was echoed at the markets of Brie-Comte-Robert, Pontoise, and Gonesse.[166] Yet there was nothing incompatible between the "mobilizing myth" of the moral economy and need itself.

The crowds of the Flour War also contained a certain number of parasites who sought to profit from riot-induced cheap grain without legitimate reason (according to the logic of the moral economy). On 6 May a miller in Mouy accompanied his assistants to the market, where they made off with thirty sacks of grain during the rioting.[167] Interrogated rioters sometimes denounced those among them whose claim to benefit from the *taxation populaire* appeared to be illegitimate. For example, Antoine Leguay, a vine-grower in Vauréal, testified that the son-in-law of the village syndic, "a man well-off," had also taken grain during the disturbances at Pontoise.[168] Simon Nicolas Delarivière, a vine-grower at Saint-Leu-lès-Taverny, accused Caron, a cooper, who is "very well-off," of making his wife go get grain from the barge at Stors.[169] Freeloading, like need, was a matter of perception; indeed, the presence among rioters of people who appeared unlikely to need paternalist help—such as cultivators, bakers, grain merchants, millers, and notables—may have indicated their general support for the cultural assumptions underlying the *taxation populaire*, rather than a desire to ride on the back of the community.[170] Of course, complaints against freeloaders might

---

164. "Interrogatoire (14 mai)," AD Seine-et-Marne, B 2387.
165. "Interrogatoire (15 mai)," AD Seine-et-Marne, B 2387.
166. "Interrogatoire (5 mai)," BN, Collection Joly de Fleury, 1159, fols. 23–24; "Procès-verbal . . . Pontoise (29 avril)," AD Yvelines, 12 B 519; "Information (16 mai)," AN, Y 18682.
167. "Procès-verbal (6 mai)," AD Oise, B 1583ter.
168. "Interrogatoire d'Antoine Leguay (21 septembre)," AD Oise, B 1584.
169. "Interrogatoire (17 juillet)," AD Oise, B 1583bis.
170. According to Judith Miller, bakers might find themselves in financial distress during crises

also be interpreted as evidence of a coherent vision of the moral economy. By differentiating between those who did and those who did not have legitimate claims to grain and its products, rioters articulated a social right to property.

Cases of individuals who protested their arrests by arguing they had simply been swept along by the excitement, or in a few cases coerced, appear more frequently. Riot leaders Madelaine Pochet and Pierre Cadet both explained that they had been caught up in the crowd without understanding the implications. Cadet tried to excuse himself further by recourse to the not uncommon explanation that he had been drunk at the time of the riots. Pochet testified that the "crowd made her do it." Such explanations aside, both knew how to animate the rioting—to mobilize the community for collective action—once they had become involved.[171] The *procureur fiscal* of Villemomble claimed villagers had coerced him to join them in their requisitions at local farms. Then he admitted he had taken grain, "like all the others."[172] Villagers at Boissy claimed that the Oise river workers forced them to assail the Benedictine monastery at Saint-Leu-d'Esserent.[173]

The Flour War also offers examples of rioters motivated by narrow personal vendettas against grain proprietors or officials. One case involved the parish priest at Gournay-sur-Marne who turned against the local fermier during the Flour War. The maréchaussée arrested the priest, Pierre Claude Dourdan, when they learned that on 6 May, when two men from Vincennes visited "one of his granges" to demand grain, he sent them instead to the farm of Dufresne. During the testimonies, the source of the dispute between Dourdan and Dufresne emerged. Dufresne's wife explained that they "hated him because of a court case between him and her husband" over 12 livres. The couple argued that Dourdan had misappropriated the money from the wife's sister just before she had died. Dourdan claimed that the sister donated it for ornaments for the church. Dourdan had lost the court decision and had

---

such as food riots. When grain prices went up (and during liberalization they could rise dramatically because there were no formal constraints), municipal officials might attempt to address the issue by controlling bread prices. Thus, bakers, like the consumers, were hit hardest during the crisis itself. Moreover, officials might suspend milling fees, thus hurting millers. See Miller, "Politics and Urban Provisioning Crises: Bakers, Police, and Parlements in France, 1750–1793," *JMH* 64 (June 1992): 227–62.

171. See above, Chapter 3.

172. "Interrogatoire de Thomas Blaison (6 mai)," AN, Y 11441 and AB, Archives de la Bastille, MS 12,447.

173. See fuller discussion of river worker involvement earlier in this chapter.

to give the money back. His church lost its ornaments, and he acquired a motive for revenge.[174]

Food riots could thus provide opportunities to express other, broader grievances. Agricultural day-laborers turned against the surplus-grain producers who controlled their destinies in multiple ways. When day-laborer LaMotte threatened a laboureur at May-en-Multien with "You won't be the master today, because it's our turn," he expressed a general hostility against the power such village elites wielded.[175] Madelaine Pochet, a day-laborer herself, denounced fermiers, declaring, "They had been gluttons (*gras*) for entirely too long,"[176] while Veronique Prévost complained that "the rich were so evil that the poor person was truly unfortunate."[177] Some rioters thus protested their relative powerlessness and poverty and found the food riot a useful outlet for the expression of such frustrations.

In addition to expressing the frustrations of the poor and the dominated, the crowd could also serve as a locus for a variety of social and political interactions that transcended the immediate subsistence issue. The food riot could become, as Desan has suggested, a site for consolidating or transforming local roles.[178] Food riots generated opportunities to speak as the voice of authority for the community—to express collective demands—and to confirm or renounce attachments to the community. These dimensions appeared most obviously in the interactions of notables and common people, in gender relations, and in other social relations at the local level.

As we have already seen, subsistence crises placed local notables in ambiguous circumstances, a situation exacerbated by the on-again off-again nature of liberalization policy. Food riots not only embroiled local officials in potential struggles with each other and the royal government, but also revealed the tenuous nature of their relations with the local community. Thus, some notables clearly calculated the relative advantage offered by siding with the crowd or grain proprietors and the Crown, calculations based on their assessments of local relations. The vine-grower and village syndic of Cergy, Denis Charles Caffin, who had joined fellow parishioners in an

174. "Interrogatoire (23 juin)," AN, Y 1141, and AB, MS 12,447.

175. "Procès-verbal (16 mai)," AD Oise, B non coté, jugements prévôtaux, 1775.

176. "Interrogatoire (9 mai)," AD Seine-et-Marne, B 3957(1).

177. "Interrogatoire (25 mai)," AD Oise, B 1583ter. When rioter Pierre LeBlond presented himself to a local notable's widow to demand grain, she explained that she had none because she cultivated no arable. He terrified her with the declaration that "if she had no grain, she had property" ("Information [1 juin]," AD Seine-et-Marne, B 2387).

178. "Crowds," p. 59.

assault on the market and port of Pontoise, emerged with a fine for his actions—and what may have constituted local hero status. In 1789 he appeared as one of two deputies elected to take the village cahier to the secondary bailliage meeting at Senlis.[179] In contrast, the subdelegate at Vernon, Doré, had obviously miscalculated the nature of his relations with the community.

Food riots not only manifested gendered characteristics but also served to align gender relations within communities. Women's particular relationship to the provisioning process and the family economy empowered them in certain contexts.[180] When the woman at Nemours pushed her husband from the sacks of grain on display at the market and announced, "This is women's business," she not only may have saved him from the more severe retribution the state reserved for rioting men, but also delineated female space and reappropriated her place in the community as well as in her family. She assumed the right, the authority, to speak for the community on subsistence issues, to define and activate the normative environment by which its members lived, and to order public behavior.[181] Mothers—women with children, pregnant women—spoke for future generations as well as their own and carried particular authority within this sphere.[182]

A final and related arena in which the food riots could function as the vehicle for consolidating or transforming local roles was the opportunities they provided for advancing the position of some individuals over others, equalizing conditions, or achieving notoriety. The case of Pierre Hamelin, the armed and entrepreneurial provocateur of Nesles (a self-proclaimed butcher, baker, innkeeper, and moneylender who dared to challenge seig-neurial authority), demonstrated how local infamy could manifest itself on different fronts.[183] The Flour War also presents several examples of failed

179. Ernest Mallet, ed., *Les Elections du bailliage secondaire de Pontoise en 1789* (Pontoise, 1919), p. 245.

180. On the discussion of female power and informal power networks, see, e.g., Susan Carol Rogers, "Female Forms of Power and the Myth of Male Dominance: A Model of Female/Male Interaction in Peasant Society," *American Ethnologist* 2 (Nov. 1975): 727–56; idem, "Women's Place: A Critical Review of Anthropological Theory," *Comparative Studies in Society and History* 20 (Jan. 1978): 123–62; Ernestine Friedl, "The Position of Women: Appearance and Reality," *Anthropological Quarterly* 40 (July 1967): 97–108; Diane Rothbard Margolis, "Considering Women's Experience: A Reformulation of Power Theory," *Theory and Society* 18 (1989): 387–416; Desan, "Crowds," pp. 58–59. See other citations in Chapters 1 and 6.

181. For more on this, see Chapter 6. Compare this with Bohstedt, "Gender," p. 100.

182. Compare events during the Flour War with those in Bergerac in 1773 as described by Iain Cameron, *Crime and Repression in the Auvergne and the Guyenne, 1720–1790* (Cambridge, 1981), pp. 63–64.

183. See Chapter 3.

attempts by individuals to empower themselves by manipulating the crowd. Louis Bonnefoy, the forty-seven-year-old father of six children and former baker now working as a woodcutter and day-laborer, led an *entrave* in his village of Souilly, threatened a local *fermier* and baker with violence, and declared that "the entire *pays* would follow him." Bonnefoy apparently thought more of his influence than observers did, because testimony revealed that "everyone fears him in the *pays*." Instilling fear constituted a kind of power, but not necessarily one that carried much honor,[184] and riot leadership did not in this case translate into local leadership.

Once arrests began, new opportunities to manipulate social relations emerged. Interrogations certainly provided evidence of solidarity when arrested rioters refused to implicate others, but they could also open avenues for retribution when rioters denounced others for clearly partisan reasons. The rioter Leguay, who had denounced the "well-off" son-in-law of the syndic of Vauréal (discussed above) for rioting in Pontoise, was himself "burdened with four young children and had much difficulty getting by in his condition."[185] Nicolas Rousseaux, a vine-grower in the Faubourg Saint-Ouen-l'Aumone outside Pontoise, whom officials believed to be "very well off," incriminated three others from his neighborhood "who had taken a lot and who are well-off and in a situation to pay an honest restitution."[186] A carter, Jacques Biebille, complained to the judges that fellow rioter Pierre LeBlonde had threatened that he would denounce Biebille if the police arrested him. Biebille explained that LeBlonde "was after him because of a debt, and LeBlonde had owed him the money for the past two years." If Biebille ended up in jail, LeBlonde could extricate himself from the debt.[187]

The Flour War thus validates the argument that in order to understand why people participated in food riots, we need to go beyond assuming that because the crowds themselves embraced similar modes of behavior and values, those who joined them did so for similar reasons. Rioters rioted for a variety of individual reasons, but they also shared different concerns, depending on whether they lived in country or town, depended on wages or held property, were male or female, etc. Subsistence crises mobilized different communities of people, as well as drawing on individual needs and goals to create the context for collective action. When these individuals and groups joined the crowd, the individual motives, the class interests, the

184. See Chapter 3.
185. See note 168 above and "Attestation du curé de Vauréal," AD Oise B 1584.
186. "Interrogatoire (26 septembre)," AD Oise, B 1584.
187. "Interrogatoire (12 juin)," AD Seine-et-Marne, B 2387.

gendered perspectives, while influencing certain aspects of behavior, tended simultaneously to be blended in the context of local conditions and subsumed in the broader concerns of the moral economy. And, this broader dimension of culture helped reinforce the larger communities to which the common people belonged. It also proved adaptable to changed conditions.

Chapter 6

FOOD RIOTS AND CHANGE

Although the Flour War resembled many previous subsistence movements, it also reflected transformations wrought by differences of time and place. This chapter focuses on three important developments in the context of the changing economic, social, and political conditions described in previous chapters. These developments are (1) a riot participation characterized by increasing numbers of French men and women who came from a narrower section of the common people, including those of the wage-laboring ranks and/or those whose condition was generally deteriorating; (2) a level of male participation that suggests that they, especially and increasingly, felt the effects of their relatively low or declining status and responded to it, in part, as women had before them (even if authority didn't interpret their behavior that way); and (3) a rural dimension to the riots that had expanded considerably in scope and size from previous movements.

While previous subsistence movements contained all these elements—men and women rioters from the lowest ranks of the laboring population, male rioters and spheres of action, and incursions into the countryside in search of grain or flour—the Flour War represented a significant evolution in all three areas. For explanations, we must look to the transformations in French economic, social, and demographic development during the eighteenth century and, particularly after mid-century, to the alternating set of policies designed by the Crown, as well as to the changing entitlements to food that attended these transformations.

The literature on subsistence movements is large and growing. The Bibliography contains a special section enumerating the printed primary and secondary sources consulted for this study. The information derived from these sources provides the data for my analysis of the evolution of food riots in Ancien Régime France. Using printed materials, especially secondary sources, carries particular problems because the method relies on the selective interests of other historians. For example, as John Markoff observed in his work on rural revolt during the Revolutionary period, French historians have worked disproportionately on rural zones around large cities, focused on areas where other dramatic events occurred, and "underrepresented smaller, less dramatic, and less openly confrontational events."[1] Indeed, as Markoff admits, "the hope of a representative sample is usually as hopeless as the dream of a complete enumeration."[2] Despite these limitations, this approach can provide some useful information about certain dimensions of change. From the work on such extensively researched topics as Early Modern French subsistence movements, it is possible to study variations or tendencies in target selection, types of behavior, and crowd composition. Thus, from the sources enumerated in the Bibliography (which

1. See esp. John Markoff, "Constructing a Conflict-Event File from Heterogeneous Sources" (forthcoming). See also his "Social Geography of Rural Revolt at the Beginning of the French Revolution," *American Sociological Review* 50 (Dec. 1985): 761–81; "Contexts and Forms of Rural Revolt: France 1789," *Journal of Conflict Resolution* 30 (June 1986): 253–89; and "When and How Did the Countryside Revolt? A Statistical Study of Revolutionary France, 1788–1793" (Paper presented to the Western Society for French History, Reno, 1991). I thank Markoff for his help on these questions and others.

2. "Constructing a Conflict-Event File."

is a product of an extensive literature search for printed materials), I documented 540 subsistence riots (not counting the 317 Flour War incidents, which would bring the total to 857) in the seventeenth and eighteenth centuries to 1789.[3] The first documented food riots erupted in Amiens in 1614.[4] More widespread rioting erupted in 1630 in Angers, Caen, Orléans, Pertuis, Reillane, and Amiens.[5] Thereafter, riots erupted sporadically in 1631, the 1640s, and 1660s. The 1690s produced a massive wave of rioting, as did the period 1708–10. Other clusters of riots before 1775 included those in 1725, 1728–31, 1739–40, 1747–48, 1752, 1764–68, 1770, and 1773–74. Altogether, I have documented 376 riots before 1775. After 1775 there were outbreaks of riots in 1778–79, 1784, and of course 1788–89. I found 164 outbreaks after 1775, with the overwhelming majority from the period 1788–89 (84.1 percent). Thus, the chronological boundary for my study is the period from 1614 to 1789.

A Wide But Narrowing Social Base

Over the course of the eighteenth century, French subsistence movements drew their "crowds" from an increasingly narrow section of the population.

3. This information compares favorably with that beginning to emerge from the team of researchers headed by Jean Nicolas and Guy Lemarchand in France. See Nicolas, "Les Emotions dans l'ordinateur: Premiers résultats d'une enquête collective" (Paper presented at the conference on Troubles populaires en France aux XVIIe–XVIIIe siècles, University of Paris–VII, 1986); Lemarchand, "Troubles populaires au XVIIIe siècle et conscience de classe: Une Préface à la Révolution française," AHRF 279 (Jan.–Mar. 1990): 32–48. Nicolas and Lemarchand have counted 182 subsistence movements between 1690 and 1720, and 652 between 1760 and 1789; I found 112 disturbances between 1690 and 1720, and 668 between 1760 and 1789. They are interested in all forms of popular revolt and, so far at least, have concentrated their efforts on forms other than subsistence riots. Moreover, their typology of subsistence movements is not particularly useful to the concerns here, because they differentiate very little on the basis of different forms of behavior. On this see Annexe A, "Typologie et Grille de Dépouillement," in Mouvements populaires et conscience sociale, XVIe–XIX siècles (Paris, 1985), pp. 761–63.

4. Pierre Deyon, Amiens, capitale provinciale: Étude sur la société urbaine au 17e siècle (Paris, 1967), pp. 436–37. There may have been earlier food riots, such as those now being documented for England. Indeed, evidence suggests that English food riots date back to at least the Late Medieval period. British medievalist Buchanan Sharp has discovered an entrave in the fourteenth century (Communication to the "Moral Economy Twenty-One Years on Conference," Birmingham, U.K., March 1992).

5. François Lebrun, "Les Soulèvements populaires à Angers aux XVIIe et XVIIIe siècles," in Actes du 90e Congrès national des sociétés savantes, Nice, 1965 (Paris, 1966), p. 126; Michel Caillard, "Recherches sur les soulèvements populaires en Basse Normandie (1620–1640) et spécialement sur la Révolte des Nu-Pieds," in A Travers la Normandie des XVIIe et XVIIIe siècles (Caen, 1963), pp. 37–38; René Pillorget, "Essai d'une typology des mouvements insurrectionnels ruraux survenus en Provence de 1596 à 1715," in Actes du 92e Congrès national des sociétés savantes, Strasbourg, 1967 (Paris, 1970), p. 379; and Deyon, Amiens, p. 437.

Although property owners and vine-growers in particular also rioted in large numbers during the Flour War, their participation was topographically localized and the majority of male and female rioters arrested came from the lower strata of the common people. Urban and rural wage-laborers and marginal craft and trade workers, and full- or part-time workers in protoindustrial production, constituted the largest percentage of rioters arrested. Even for the "propertied" participants in the Flour War, the last half of the eighteenth century represented a time of uncertain and sometimes deteriorating circumstances, and those who rioted came most frequently from among those made most vulnerable by the conjuncture.

Previous subsistence movements had drawn from a broader, more diverse section of the French population.[6] In Reims in 1709, for example, observers testified that bourgeois were seen assailing houses known for storing grain.[7] Although the 1709 Rouen riot was largely the work of women (mostly spinners), whose ranks were later swelled by other textile workers, observers reported that "several bourgeois joined in."[8] In Valenciennes, "bourgeois and soldiers from the garrison" took five sacks of grain from a transport.[9] And the same year in Marans, after a "sedition" that erupted in April and required troops to quell, "the principal inhabitants declared their solidarity by public act, with all the pillage that might come in the future."[10] In La Ferté-sous-Jouarre, a crowd that included "a number of solid citizens" stopped a barge carrying wheat on the Marne.[11] In 1747 "bourgeois and inhabitants allied to prevent grain from being exported from Autun and Dijon."[12] When police emphasized the role the "inhabitants" played in

6. I have been able to find information about the socioeconomic status for only 13.3 percent of all riots before 1775. This depressingly small number is the product of several problems with sources. Police and witness reports, particularly from the earlier periods, were either largely unconcerned with reporting social status or extremely imprecise. Sometimes they pointed out that "the people" rioted, sometimes it was "the inhabitants," and occasionally "the poor people" or the *canaille*. Moreover, police arrested and punished very few people for their roles in riots. Because of this frustrating imprecision, therefore, historians have been inclined to grasp at every detail available and report it.

7. A.-M. de Boislisle, "Le Grand Hiver et la disette de 1709," *Revue des questions historiques* 73 (1903): 442–506; 74 (1903): 486–542.

8. A.-M. de Boislisle, *Correspondance des contrôleurs généraux des finances avec les intendants des provinces*, 3:179–80, no. 475.

9. Ibid., p. 93, no. 282.

10. Ibid., p. 117, no. 346; also quoted in Louise Tilly, "The Food Riot as a Form of Political Conflict in France," *JIH* 2 (1971): 51.

11. Jacques Saint-Germain, *La Vie quotidienne en France à la fin du Grand Siècle* (Paris, 1965), p. 216; L. Tilly, "Food," p. 48.

12. Léon Blin, "La Face administrative d'une crise frumentaire en Bourgogne, 1747–1749," *Annales de Bourgogne* 189 (Jan.–Mar. 1976): 10.

entraves, in particular, their language suggests that rioters were drawn from a community that included elites as well as common people.

Historians have also noted the heavy participation of independent artisans and shopkeepers in the riots of the earlier part of the century as well as in many *entraves.* In 1643 a violent riot erupted in Vannes in Brittany, led by artisans who, panicked by the outflow of grain from the town, sacked houses belonging to the grain merchants on the port.[13] Artisans were also found in riots in Toulouse in 1694, in Paris in 1709, in Albi in 1747, in Vannes in 1765, and in Carcassonne in 1773. Peasants also formed a significant category of early rioters. "Peasant crowds" rioted in Libourne in 1708 and were shut out from the town of Sainte-Foy in 1709 when they tried to enter to get food.[14] Peasants halted carts carrying grain through the Forez in 1709 and stopped grain shipments in Mâcon.[15] They prevented the departure of grain from the diocese de Castres and the Vivarais in Languedoc in 1748.[16] Peasants were also reported in riots along the Saône River and Mâcon in 1709, in Arles in 1752, and in Marmonde in 1773. The term "peasant" is ambiguous at best, often used to describe a wide range of occupations from microproprietor to laboureur, and even someone who worked the land but did not own it. But everywhere it distinguished rural (not urban) dwellers, whose primary link was to the soil, not to manufacturing or trading, and who laid some claim to land as opposed to completely landless, day-laboring status.

Moreover, authorities seeking to repress disorder and witnesses asked to name names rarely signaled the presence of unskilled day-laborers during these earlier movements. They did, however, note the participation of workers in urban manufacture in towns where it had become an important employer of labor. The 1709 riot in Rouen, as we have seen, allied bourgeois and textile workers. It was the cotton workers of Rouen who controlled the town for three days in 1752 while they ransacked the granaries of ecclesiastical institutions and the warehouses along the quay.[17] In Troyes in 1740,

13. T.J.A. LeGoff, *Vannes and Its Region: A Study of Town and Country in Eighteenth-Century France* (Oxford, 1981), p. 103.

14. Julius Ruff, *Crime, Justice, and Public Order in Old Regime France: The Sénéchaussées of Libourne and Bazas, 1696–1789* (London, 1984), pp. 148–49. I thank Ruff for his help in answering my questions about rioting in this region.

15. On Forez, see Henri Hours, "Emeutes et émotions populaires dans les campagnes du Lyonnais au 18e siècle," *Cahiers d'histoire* 9 (1964): 138–39; on Macon, Pierre de Saint-Jacob, *Les Paysans de la Bourgogne du Nord au dernier siècle de l'Ancien Régime* (Paris, 1960), p. 190.

16. H. Bourderon, "La Lutte contre la vie cher dans la généralité de Languedoc au XVIIIe siècle," *Annales du Midi* 25–28 (1954): 161.

17. R. B. Rose, "Eighteenth-Century Price Riots, the French Revolution, and the Jacobin

some 600–700 workers demanding bread protested before the home of the Bailli, invaded houses suspected of having grain, and threatened to set them on fire.[18] The presence of significant numbers of unskilled or semiskilled laborers in riots testifies to the development of local and regional manufacturing, a development that in the seventeenth century was still quite rare and localized.

By the time of the Flour War, the social base from which rioters came had narrowed further. Arrest records and witness testimony underscore the important presence of unskilled rural laborers and the crucial participation of textile workers in such towns as Mouy. As we have seen, many of the artisans arrested came from the more vulnerable crafts, and many of the more independent artisans who faced arrest did so not for taking bread, grain, or flour but for egging on those who did. There were no reports of bourgeois participation as either rioters or rooters in the market disturbances of the Flour War. Furthermore, among the propertied rioters, those arrested or inculpated came from the struggling middle or lower ranks of the peasantry. For example, Pierre Vachette, laboureur and fermier at Cauffry, testified that the widow of Jean Baptiste Bricogne came to his farm seeking grain, although, he asserted, she "has enough grain . . . until the harvest." The widow Bricogne may have paid the highest tax in her village of Mogneville, but Vachette paid more than five times as much in his nearby parish of Cauffry.[19]

There are several ways to explain this development. We could conclude that the nature of participation during the Flour War simply reflected the socioeconomic composition of the regions in which it erupted, just as participation reflected that of previous movements in different places with different economic structures. Of course, this was true. We therefore find vine-growers in the *pays de vigneron*, woodcutters near forested regions, agricultural laborers in the *pays de grande culture*, and so on. Yet this only predicts the likelihood of finding certain categories of people in certain areas. We need to understand better why certain types of people were

Maximum," *International Review of Social History* 4 (1959): 432–45; William Reddy, "The Textile Trade and the Language of the Crowd at Rouen, 1752–1871," *Past and Present* 74 (Feb. 1977): 62–89.

18. Jean Ricommard, *La Lieutenance général de police à Troyes au XVIII siècle* (Paris, 1934), p. 240.

19. "Procès-verbal (9 mai)," AD Oise, B non coté, maréchaussée de Clermont, 1775. The widow Bricogne paid 90 livres and Pierre Vachette paid 464 livres ("Rôle de taille de Mogneville, 1775," AD Oise, C 557; "Rôle de taille de Cauffry, 1775," C 519).

mobilized and comprehend the implications of a changing pattern of participation.

Therefore, another approach focuses on the process by which economic prosperity, an increased division of labor, and a more intense competition for scarce resources had developed by 1775 as compared with, say, 1709. Capitalism—commercial, agricultural, and industrial (or protoindustrial)—had made significant progress over the course of the century. Indeed, the very fact that few people starved in 1775, despite the growth of the population, testifies to the advance of both agricultural productivity and commerce.[20] The narrowed social base of riot participation serves as further testimony to this. On the one hand, the advanced stage of proletarianization in the Paris Basin both in the surplus-grain-producing regions, among agricultural workers, and in the grain-importing regions, among protoindustrial workers and small property owners threatened with further fragmentation of their properties, created an ever-larger population of consumers who were extremely sensitive to even small variations in food prices and supplies. Thus, when the 1775 crisis developed, those most vulnerable constituted a fairly homogeneous but very numerous slice of the society of the Paris Basin.[21]

We might thus expect to find that the social composition of the "crowd" varied not only from place to place but also over time, as economic development transformed social structure and entitlements to food. This is in fact what happened. From the late seventeenth century onward, subsistence riots drew larger numbers from an ever narrower social base: cotton workers in Rouen in 1752, the textile workers at Pont-Saint-Ours near Nevers in 1768, spinners and weavers in Reims in 1770, and ever-larger

20. But people did occasionally starve during crises; see the report on the death of a woman at Saint-Lô in August 1784 during a dearth. After her public collapse and quick death, a search where she lived revealed "neither grain, nor bread, nor flour. . . . Cabbage cooked in water, without salt or butter, constituted her entire nourishment for days" (in Maurice Lantier, "La Crise de subsistance en 1784 à Saint-Lô," *Annales de Normandie* 25 [Mar. 1975]: 31).

21. Compare these findings with those related by Dale Williams for the food riots of 1766 in England: "Morals, Markets, and the English Crowd in 1766," *Past and Present* 104 (Aug. 1984): 58–59. Williams argues that the people who were most integrated into industrial capitalism already—textile workers, protoindustrial laborers, and so on—were most likely to riot. John Bohstedt suggests that in Devon the townspeople most independent from the traditions of landed paternalism and deference rioted (*Riots and Community Politics in England and in Wales, 1790–1810* [Cambridge, Mass., 1983], pp. 37–38). Most authors also conclude that rural wage-laborers rarely participated in food riots (ibid., p. 44; E. P. Thompson, "The Moral Economy of the English Crowd in the Eighteenth Century," *Past and Present* 50 [1971]: 119). For France, Lemarchand observes that rural day-laborers were less well represented than their proportional representation in the population in general ("Troubles," p. 405).

numbers of agricultural workers in Normandy throughout the eighteenth century.[22]

On the other hand, the prosperity of growing numbers of landowners and urban merchants and manufacturers in these same regions shielded them from some of the dangers presented by high prices. Of course, no one dependent on buying food for consumption needs could be protected from absolute dearth, but those with sufficient resources had access to the available subsistence at much higher prices than those denied the wherewithal to buy when prices rose even slightly. The increased polarization of urban and rural society further separated interests as consumption needs predominated less among the growing number of prosperous urban commoners.

The third approach to understanding what had happened by 1775 is related to the second in that it suggests that, although price rises in 1775 were significant enough to create a crisis for workers or small producers with dependent families and the expenses associated with sustaining them, they were not as threatening as rises during previous crises to those with greater resources.[23] Elites, and the upper levels of the common people, such as the independent artisans, were probably not threatened by the crisis of 1775 as they had been in 1709 or even 1752, for example. The sight of suffering or the threat of a more extensive crisis may have offended the sense of justice they shared with the laborers but did not trigger active participation in the movement itself, except possibly as rooters.

Moreover, this helps to put the great movements that erupted in 1788–89 and throughout the Revolution in perspective. The Revolutionary subsistence crises, as well as other economic factors, such as unemployment, were more severe[24] and therefore more threatening to a broader spectrum of

22. On Rouen, see Lemarchand, "Troubles," pp. 401, 404, 408; Reddy, "Textile Trade," pp. 62–66. On Pont-Saint-Ours, see Leguai, "Moulins," p. 49; on spinners and weavers in Reims, see Rose, "Eighteenth-Century Price Riots," pp. 433–34; on agricultural workers in Normandy, see Lemarchand, "Troubles," p. 405.

23. On prices, compare those in Micheline Baulant, "Le Prix des grains à Paris de 1431 à 1788," AESC 23 (May–June 1968): 520–40. Baulant (p. 540) shows that yearly grain-price averages were considerably higher during the crisis years of 1708–9 (41.04 livres), 1741 (37.00), 1768 (32.80), 1769 (32.40), and 1771 (33.45) than in 1775 (29.50). See similar evidence in Ernest Labrousse, Esquisse du mouvement des prix et des revenues en France au XVIIIe siècle, 2 vols. (1933; reprint, Paris, 1984), 1:104, 106–13, 183; and L. Tilly, "Food Riot," pp. 37–45. More detailed information can be found in J. Dupâquier et al., Mercuriales du pays de France et du Vexin français (1640–1792) (Paris, 1968), who record the market-by-market prices that yearly averages cannot show.

24. Ernest Labrousse, La Crise de l'économie française à la fin de l'Ancien Régime et au début de la Révolution (Paris, 1944).

people.[25] Although there is no direct correlation between price rises and rioting, and the Revolutionary period further injected a more formal political content into many subsistence movements, thus making generalizations about relationships between prices and participation tentative, the connection between threats posed to existence by rising prices and the class basis for participation might be more direct than previously supposed.

Finally, subsistence movements directly threatened claims of absolute proprietorship. As we have seen, rioters and their supporters asserted a contingent public character to grain and its products; the Physiocrats and their supporters demanded instead absolute ownership and control. Over the course of the century, as the paternalist model of provisioning lost ground, property owners may have found the implications of subsistence riots increasingly discomfiting. As Colin Lucas has observed, "property owners become more uncomprehending and more quickly frightened of the crowd."[26]

Subsistence riots may have thus furthered the polarization of elite and popular cultures. Assaults on the property of producers, merchants, millers, and bakers, as well as forays into the homes of notables suspected of hoarding grain or storing it for others, the on-again, off-again support of their interests generated by the Crown, and the ambiguous and sometimes overtly hostile posture of local authorities, may have driven a wedge deep between common people and the bourgeoisie (in its Ancien Régime meanings), as well as between this bourgeoisie and the state. Viewed over the course of the eighteenth century, the gradual disappearance of significant property owners from among the supporters of subsistence movements might reflect the growth of middle-class consciousness around the idea of property.[27] A striking example of this phenomenon occurred at Troyes in 1775. Rumors

25. A few of the smaller local disturbances manifested unique characteristics. For example, the outbreak of violence at Saint-Lô, which involved an *entrave*-type riot as well as marketplace eruptions and some physical violence, was the work of almost 1,000 children (Lantier, "Saint-Lô," pp. 13–31). Although children sometimes participated in riots, and especially in *entraves*, this stands as the most salient example of such activity.

26. "The Crowd and Politics in France," *JMH* 60 (Sept. 1988): 430.

27. Compare this with the observations of Dale E. Williams, "Morals, Markets," pp. 71–72. The process of defining absolute private property rights was long and took place on many fronts. See, e.g., Sarah Hanely, "Family and State in Early Modern France: The Marriage Pact," in *Connecting Spheres: Women in the Western World, 1500–Present*, ed. M. Boxer and J. Quataert (Oxford, 1987), pp. 53–63. William Sewell provides one of the best discussions of the problem of property in the Ancien Régime and Revolutionary periods, but he underestimates how much this process was already under way in the Ancien Régime itself (*Work and Revolution in France: The Language of Labor from the Old Regime to 1848* [Cambridge, 1980]).

that rioters planned to set fire to homes storing grain and flour for merchants in the town panicked proprietors and their neighbors. They demanded around-the-clock police surveillance and rotated night watches among themselves.[28] The sister of a grain merchant reported hearing rioters plot arson just below her window while she guarded her brother's granary on the night of 9 May. "It is time to strike our blow," said one voice. Another responded, "What will we do? We don't have a light." Then they noticed the light in her room and withdrew. The next day, her sister-in-law overheard two men say, "It is not the granary that must be set on fire, it is the house on the corner, so that [the fire] will spread to it."[29]

These fears were not groundless. We have already seen how rioters in 1740 turned violent and threatened arson. Widespread rioting in 1767 had also resulted in violent searches of homes belonging to grain merchants. Rioters damaged property and seized grain. In 1770 a grain merchant was roughed up by "the populace."[30] By 1775, conditions had worsened in the city. In March, municipal officers and the subdelegate wrote to the intendant to report that a rise in the price of thread and cotton had caused a suspension of commerce. So there was "a very great misery among the people," and "especially the spinners who number 2,000 to 3,000 people." Officials reported that the countryside was actually drawing grain from the market rather than supplying it.[31] The subsistence crisis, particularly the repeated nature of it—for Troyes had experienced significant disturbances in 1709 as well as in 1740, 1767, and 1770—had generated widespread tension that pitted textile workers, especially spinners, against merchants and property owners associated with them.[32] The 1767 riots resulted in the arrest of more than 100 people and the sentencing of three women to a public whipping and life in prison as "seditieuses pour les grains," an unusually harsh sentence for women.[33] This scenario is quite different from the one that took place in the midst of a subsistence crisis in Amiens in 1693. The intendant explained that he had not only made distributions of 3,000 loaves of bread to the poor (a not uncommon strategy, even in later periods), but he also required the "rich to lodge the poor and nourish them" (an uncommon strategy even in 1693).[34]

28. "Lettre du subdélégué (10 mai)," AD Aube, C 1908.

29. "Déclaration faite par la Demoiselle Fléchy (9–10 mai)," AD Aube, C 1908.

30. Ricommard, Lieutenance, pp. 241–43; Kaplan, Bread, 1:190–91.

31. "Lettre du subdélégué (22 mars)" and "Lettre des officiers municipaux, échevins, procureur sindic, maire de Troyes (14 mars)," AD Aube, C 1909.

32. On the 1709 riots, see L. Tilly, "Food Riots," p. 53; on 1740, see Ricommard, Lieutenance, p. 240.

33. Ricommard, Lieutenance, p. 242.

34. Boislisle, Correspondance, 1:315, no. 1174.

The narrower social spectrum from which Flour War rioters came is therefore best explained with reference to the complex of economic, social, and even cultural transformations at work over time in the particular regions in which it struck, and in the severity of the crisis itself. This evidence also raises questions about the role community played in constructing collective action in food riots.

Many British historians have noted that English food rioters came more frequently from the ranks of those who had experienced greater "independence" from the paternalist world of Early Modern "patrician society." As E. P. Thompson has argued, "economic rationalization nibbled . . . through the bonds of paternalism," and it was from among "people whom the gentry saw as . . . withdrawn from their social control" that "food rioters were likely to come."[35] Although French society had not experienced the same degree of social differentiation and economic rationalization as the English, the Paris Basin was one of the most developed regions in the country.

This evidence for social dislocation conflicts with arguments for strong communal ties in the making of collective action (Chapter 5). Seen through the prism of developmental time, however, the paradox disappears. Communal solidarities certainly played an active role in some forms of subsistence rioting, such as the traditional forms (especially the type 1 [marketplace] riots and the type 3 [entrave-type] riots discussed in Chapter 4). The very erosion of such solidarities in more developed regions contributed to the emergence of other forms of behavior, such as rural/country riots in the farms of large-scale cultivators (type 4 riots). Riots of this latter type drew largely from the ranks of unskilled and semiskilled male laborers, groups less likely (compared with the artisanal groups) to have retained strong traditional collective ties. This class of rioter needed to forge its own collective identity and in doing so began to alter patterns of behavior in such domains as food riots.

Feminized Men

Before the Flour War, subsistence riots were, within certain spheres of action, predominantly female terrain. In 1775, however, men swelled the

---

35. E. P. Thompson, "Patrician Society, Plebeian Culture," *JSH* 7 (Summer 1974): 382–405. See a similar argument in Williams, "Markets, Morals." John Bohstedt (*Riots*) also observes changing forms of behavior in English food riots, changes that related to the extent of integration into the market economy; see especially his discussion of behavior in Manchester.

ranks of protesters, particularly in the countryside actions. That so many men played such a prominent role in what was traditionally "female business," as the woman explained to her husband at Nemours, lies in a long-term and short-term deteriorating male status[36] among the lower ranks of the common people that subjected them to concerns similar to those of their wives, sisters, mothers, and daughters. Thus, men's precarious material, social, and political conditions drove them, on the one hand, to embrace traditional female responses to a subsistence crisis and, on the other hand, to confront massive repression from authorities who saw them as politically more dangerous than women.

Women played crucial and visible roles in Early Modern French subsistence movements.[37] Women instigated riots in the market of Lyons in 1699;[38] a woman was arrested in the wake of a "great eruption" (*grosse émotion*) at the market of Nevers in 1698.[39] In 1709, women led and joined bands of rioters that initiated *entraves* or disrupted marketplaces as far removed as Paris, Aix-en-Provence, Tarascon, and Vaison in the Vaucluse.[40] In Rouen, women "who were accustomed to assemble before a certain house that gave alms" started a disturbance that included rock-throwing at the intendant's house. The rioting continued for two days before men got involved.[41] Women continued in prominent roles at Laval in 1725, Montluçon in 1736, Dreux in 1739, Langres in 1740, Toulouse and Albi in 1747, Arles and Rouen in 1752, Abbeville in 1765, Amiens, Tonnère, and Marseille in 1766, Troyes and La Ferté-Gaucher in 1767, Dijon in 1770, Aix-en-Provence and Toulouse in 1773, and many other places, including the riots of 1775, as we have already seen.[42] Altogether, women participated

36. I use the term "status" in this context as a measurement used by the men themselves as an internal yardstick. Of course, this yardstick differed significantly from that which authorities imposed when they saw men rioting. This was also true of women.

37. The literature on female participation in subsistence riots is growing (see Chapter 1 and specific references below). The gender of rioters is known for almost one-quarter of all riots before 1775.

38. Boislisle, *Correspondance*, 1:522–23, no. 1854.

39. Louis Gueneau, *L'Organisation du travail à Nevers aux XVIIe et XVIIIe siècles (1660–1790)* (Paris, 1919), p. 393; also cited in André Leguai, "Les 'Emotions' et séditions populaires dans la généralité de Moulins aux XVIIe et XVIIIe siècles," *Revue d'histoire économique et sociale* 43 (1965): 55.

40. On Paris, see Boislisle, *Correspondance*, 3:123, no. 361; Jacques Saint-Germain, *La Vie*, pp. 186–87. On Aix and Tarascon, see Pillorget, "Essai," p. 380. On Vaison, see Serge Marzaux, "La Révolte des femmes en 1709 à Vaison: Crime, Punition, Pardon," in *Actes du 107e Congrès national des sociétés savantes, Brest, 1982* (Paris, 1984), pp. 305–11.

41. Boislisle, *Correspondance*, 3:179–80, no. 475.

42. On Laval, see Em.-L. Chambois, "Emeute populaire à Laval relativement à la cherté des grains, 1725–1726," *Province du Maine* 10 (1902): 226–34; on Montluçon, see Edouard Janin,

in 95.5 percent of all riots in which the gender of the participants is known. Women led 93.5 percent of all riots for which the gender of the leader is known.

Nevertheless, even in the past, there were exceptions to female predominance. In 1647, for example, reports noted the presence of "more than 150 armed men, making seditious cries, [who] forced the guardian of the entrance to the city [of Nevers] to give them the keys, entered the city and demanded bread."[43] Men were certainly present among the woodcutters and charcoal burners who attacked merchants in the generality of Moulins in 1709[44] and among the cotton workers of Rouen in 1752 (although the instigators there were the female spinners).[45] Men predominated among the 2,000 peasants armed with sticks who gathered in front of the town hall of Bergerac in 1773.[46] Men also participated in movements in which women led or predominated, such as in Toulouse in 1694. There, women led and predominated, but men also got involved.[47] What the Flour War reveals, therefore, is not the emergence of male participation for the first time, but

Histoire de Montluçon d'après les documents inédits (1904; reprint, Marseille, 1975), p. 104; on Dreux and Langres, see M. Bricourt et al., "La Crise de subsistance des années 1740 dans le ressort du Parlement de Paris," in Annales de démographie historique, 1974, pp. 296–97, 318. On Toulouse in 1747, see Bourderon, "Lutte," pp. 160–61; Marcel Marion, "Une Famine à Guyenne (1747–48)," Revue historique 46 (1891): 255; Robert Schneider, Public Life in Toulouse, 1463–1789: From Municipal Republic to Cosmopolitan City (Ithaca, N.Y., 1989), p. 315 (I thank Schneider for answering my questions on rioting in Toulouse). On Albi, see Bourderon, "Lutte," p. 160; on Arles, Suzanne Pillorget-Rouanet, "Une Crise de colère des paysans d'Arles: Les Émeutes frumentaires des 2 et 3 janvier, 1752," in Actes du 92e Congrès national des sociétés savantes, Strasbourg, 1967 (Paris, 1970), pp. 383–81. On Rouen, see Charles Desmarest, Le Commerce des grains dans la généralité de Rouen à la fin de l'Ancien Régime (Paris, 1926), pp. 85–87; Lemarchand, "Troubles," p. 401. On Abbeville, Amiens, and Tonnerre, see Kaplan, Bread, 1:190; on Marseille, René Pillorget, "Les Mouvements insurrectionnels de Provence, 1715–1788," in Mouvements populaires et conscience sociale, ed. J. Nicolas (Paris, 1985), p. 354. On Troyes, see Kaplan, Bread, 1:190; Ricommard, Lieutenance, pp. 241–43. On La Ferté-Gaucher, see Kaplan, Bread, 1:190. On Dijon, see Charles Tilly, The Contentious French: Four Centuries of Popular Struggle (Cambridge, Mass., 1986), p. 21; Léon Blin, "Face," pp. 5–42; Kaplan, Bread, 1:190. On Aix, see Pillorget, "Mouvements," p. 354. On Toulouse, see Bourderon, "Recherches sur les mouvements populaires dans la généralité de Langue-doc au XVIIIe siècle," in Actes du 78e Congrès national des sociétés savantes, Toulouse, 1953 (Paris, 1954), p. 116; Schneider, Toulouse, p. 317; C. Tilly, Contentious, p. 188; Nicole Castan, Les Criminels de Languedoc (Toulouse, 1980), p. 314; Kaplan, Bread, 2:565.

43. Leguai, "Moulins," pp. 48–49.

44. Ibid., p. 48.

45. Lemarchand, "Troubles," pp. 401, 404, 408. See also Reddy, "Textile Trade," pp. 62–66, who also notes the significant female presences in these crowds.

46. Yet even here, women had played crucial roles until this point. Iain A. Cameron, Crime and Repression in the Auvergne and the Guyenne, 1720–1790 (London, 1981), pp. 64–65.

47. Schneider, Toulouse, p. 314; Boislisle, Correspondance, 1:363, no. 1319.

rather the proliferation of male involvement and the expansion of male roles in market riots, *entraves*, and, even more prominent, in the rural confrontations.

Men certainly risked greater punishment than women for their roles in subsistence rioting. During the Flour War, as during previous subsistence movements, women emerged less severely penalized than their male counterparts. The police, and then the judges, conducted the arrest and punishment of women rioters with more leniency. After the last sentence was rendered, it was clear that women evaded the repression that similar behavior brought on male malcontents.

Men received much stiffer sentences than women.[48] Two men, Charles Degaast and Louis Bonnefoy, faced death by hanging until the king commuted their sentences to life in the galleys for Degaast and nine years banishment for Bonnefoy.[49] The galley force—a male punishment par excellence—swelled further as a result of these riots: five men for life (plus two in absentia), three for nine years (one later received a pardon), and three for three years. One man received a three-year prison sentence, another was given three years of banishment.

Only three women who manifested commensurate violence received the harshest sentence given to a woman—three years in prison—and one was eventually pardoned.[50] As we saw in Chapter 4, women's violence rivaled what men did, but the sentences were not comparable. The courts condemned three other women to six months in prison, one to three months, and one to one month. Certainly no man could provide the excuse that allowed Marie Louise Jardin to get only a reprimand after inciting the crowd to riot at Beaumont-sur-Oise, punching a grain merchant, and paying for grain at the rate she helped to set for the *taxation populaire*: she was "pregnant and ready to give birth."[51] The Duc de Mouchy observed during

48. For the seventy male leaders arrested I found sentences for forty-eight, and for the sixteen female leaders I found sentences of fourteen. Furthermore, the maréchaussée and other authorities identified ten other people (nine men and one woman) as leaders but were unable to arrest them. Five of these were sentenced in absentia.

49. For Degaast, see "Judgement rendu en la Chambre criminelle (27 juillet)," and the accompanying "Lettre de grâce," AD Oise, B 1583; for Bonnefoy, see the sentence dated 10 July and 21 July in AD Seine-et-Marne, B 2387.

50. One of these women (Marie Anne Vautier, femme Pierre Legrand) was accused of inciting riot at Meaux and of leading a band of women through the streets and received multiple sentences. A sentence dated 10 July condemned her to three years in prison (AD Seine-et-Marne, B 2387). Another sentence dated 19 August condemned her to life in prison (AD Seine-et-Marne, B 1147). Finally, in September 1776, the king awarded her a pardon and she was released (B 2387 and 2247).

51. "Lettre de Miromésnil (10 juillet)," AD Oise B 1584; "Jugement (27 juillet)," B 1583.

the arrest and prosecution of rioters following the disturbances that, although he had advised the arrest of suspected rioters, he "had not meant the women, among whom one is pregnant."[52] A similar situation occurred in 1699 in the wake of arrests after an *entrave* at Saint-Pierre-le-Moutier in Burgundy. The intendant wrote: "As to the unfortunate women who have babies at the breast, I had them released."[53] Women knew how to take advantage of the sympathy evoked by the sight of maternal distress. An observer of the mounting prices in Paris in 1709 wrote of "the cries of women in the marketplace who said it was better to butcher their children than watch them starve to death."[54]

Yet the logic that explains female participation in subsistence riots makes the male presence problematic. Men had always participated, but the arguments that explained female roles in such forms of popular movements made men seem out of place. Indeed, as we have seen, they ran a much greater chance of arrest than women (the police arrested five men for every woman in 1775) and faced much stiffer penalties. One might expect men to leave the task of the food riot to women, as the Nemours episode suggests was sometimes the case. In fact, many men did attempt to take advantage of elite assumptions about female roles. Some, like the cooper Caron, "had his wife go pillage the grain at the barge of Stors."[55] When brought before the judges, many men protested their arrest and blamed their wives for the riots. Adrien Cauchois argued that his wife had "encouraged" him to go to the market of Mouy for fear there would not be any grain later.[56] Some men blamed their children, particularly their daughters.[57] John Bohstedt helps us to understand better what happened when he warns us not to accept the notion that only women did the marketing, but this only begins to explain what happened.

The explanation for male participation in subsistence riots lies in the condition of male economic, social (including familial), and political status during the Ancien Régime. Ideally, males would be independent in status, an assumption that transcended social status in Ancien Régime France and was shared by the common people.[58] Men achieved this via land, a craft, or

52. "Lettre (n.d.)," AD Yvelines, 1 B 219.
53. Boislisle, *Correspondance*, 1:527, no. 1873.
54. Ibid., 3:212, no. 549.
55. "Interrogatoire de Simon Nicolas Delarivière (n.d.)," AD Oise, B 1583bis.
56. "Interrogatoire (4 mai)," AD Oise, B 1583ter. On other men who blamed their wives, see, e.g., the interrogations of Nicolas Belargent, age 56, *maçon* at Auvers; Antoine Brard, age 50, *vigneron* at Eragny; and Toussaint Hebert, age 41, *coquetier* at Belloy (AD Oise, B 1584).
57. See interrogations of Claude Decrois, age 59, *tabletier* at Méru, and François Gilquin, age 51, *couvreur* at Saint-Leu-lès-Taverny (AD Oise, B 1583).
58. See P. M. Jones, *The Peasantry in the French Revolution* (Cambridge, 1988), p. 8; Colin

a shop, coupled with a head-of-household function. By these specifications, however, most males who rioted fell short of the ideal, in 1709 as well as 1775. Theirs was a life of precarious and declining socioeconomic position, disequilibrium in a familial structure, and political alienation, a situation remarkably similar to those of their mothers, wives, sisters, and daughters. The men who rioted had, in crucial ways, been feminized, if by feminization we mean that men were becoming more like women of their own class, so that their behavior resembled women's and for similar reasons.[59] Men therefore assumed a quintessentially female role when they appeared in marketplace, granary, or farm to demand grain at a "just price."

Men who rioted, like the women who did, were victims of their failure to command access to grain, flour, or bread for themselves and their families. In the second half of the eighteenth century, the disadvantageous movements in wages, rents, population, and subsistence prices accentuated and accelerated their vulnerability. They therefore reacted swiftly but, more important, in large numbers, rallying to defend their precariously balanced family economies against the grain-producers, the grain and flour merchants, and the millers who threatened their survival. These rioting men found themselves in a situation of low and even declining status, a condition that rising prices in 1775 only exacerbated. A thirty-two-year-old vine-grower from Saint-Méry, a village northeast of Melun, thus explained his already deteriorating situation to the judges. He claimed he supported two children and a wife himself but that his third child was forced to live as a charity case in Andrézel. On 8 May, he discovered that his family lacked bread or grain,

---

Jones, *Charity and "Bienfaisance"* (Cambridge, 1982), p. 95; Alan Forrest, *The French Revolution and the Poor* (New York, 1981), p. 3. See also the description of laborers in protoindustry provided by William Reddy, "Textile Trade," pp. 69–70. Associations between male honor and autonomy appear to have played an even more pervasive role in southern France, as described by Yves Castan, *Honnêteté et relations sociales en Languedoc* (Paris, 1974), esp. chap. 3, pp. 162–207; Nicole Castan, *Les Criminels de Languedoc. Les Exigences d'ordre et les voies du ressentiment dans une société prérévolutionnaire (1750–1790)* (Toulouse, 1980), pp. 159–92.

59. Historians have used the term "feminization" to explain a variety of phenomena. I am applying a rather narrow definition here. In the second half of the eighteenth century, the conditions of existence for some men of the lower rungs of the common people were deteriorating. There are, of course, many different images of dependent, lowly status in the Ancien Régime—the poor, debtors, servants, and even children. However, many of these images share with what I call "feminization" similar attributes, similar descriptions, attached to these groups by such outside groups as elite men as: references to disorderliness, irrationality, unpredictability, lack of autonomy, and inferiority. My evidence from 1775 and other historical contexts suggests that authorities and other elites viewed these men differently, relegating them to a position that resembled that of women of the same class. Men never became women, of course, neither in their own eyes nor wholly in those of authorities.

so he and his brother-in-law went with three others from the village to the market at Brie-Comte-Robert, where they believed they were more likely to find grain than in the closer but smaller markets, such as Chaumes-en-Brie. No sooner had they arrived after this long journey than they were arrested as potentially seditious characters.[60]

Deterioration in the conditions of existence, evidenced by landlessness, deskilling, destabilized households, the breakdown of the sexual division of labor, and even joblessness implied feminization. Increasingly dependent on forces beyond their control, their status reduced to that of great vulnerability not unlike women's economically dependent status within the family economy of Early Modern society, many men found themselves in the women's domain of subsistence rioting.

We are even presented with some striking examples of what we might call "male mothers"—men who performed within their families the role of mother at the time of the Flour War. We can draw from cases noted in previous chapters: the widower Lamy, with four children; Froment, with two children and a pregnant and blind wife; Rougeaux and Partois, with children and sick wives; the widower Pierre Cadet, with an eleven-year-old son. The forty-one-year-old vine-grower from Sucy-en-Brie, Philippe Louis Fouré, is another case. On 6 May, Fouré climbed on his horse and headed for Brie-Comte-Robert with three neighbors. He explained he was "burdened with family, having no bread at home, and hearing that grain had sold at 12 livres per setier" the day before, it had seemed like a good idea. Unhappily for him, he was arrested promptly on arrival while his companions escaped. An "attestation" written on his behalf by several local notables elaborated on the desperation of his condition by explaining that "for the past two months, his wife has been sick in bed and is ready to give birth, he is burdened with six daughters and one son aged four years and his oldest girl is fifteen."[61] These men not only experienced the tensions associated with their roles as heads of precarious households in times of rising prices, but confronted the necessity of acting as surrogate mothers and shouldering the functions of wives.[62]

60. "Interrogatoire (9 mai)," AD Seine-et-Marne, B 3457(1).

61. "Interrogatoire (7 mai)" and "Attestation (6 mai)," AD Seine-et-Marne, B 3957(1).

62. The severity of the domestic crisis engendered by male single parenthood is further substantiated by the number and tone of the supplications men wrote (or had written for them) in the wake of the Flour War after the arrest of their wives. Over and over again, they stress the inability to keep the household going (children fed, work done, etc.) while the wife was gone. More men sent pleas like this than did women whose husbands were arrested. Indeed, widowers remarried more often than widowed women, which suggests that women managed to survive better in a single-adult household than did men. See, for an earlier period, James B. Collins, "The

Changing economic conditions wrought by agricultural capitalism, the demand for agrarian wage labor, and protoindustrialization contributed to the breakdown or realignment of the sexual division of labor in many families. Women had always worked and performed diverse tasks. Indeed, they may have constituted the largest domestic wage-labor force as spinners, lace-makers, and so on. Increasingly, men took jobs similar to those held by women, and women held some jobs similar to those held by men. Women worked as agrarian day-laborers (as the case of Madelaine Pochet indicates) and as weavers, and they sometimes held jobs while their husbands were unemployed.[63] This does not necessarily indicate an improvement in female roles (although it does not exclude that), because, for example, they were often paid less than men for similar work, but such developments might threaten men who saw their own positions jeopardized by female competition or by the necessity to do "women's work."[64] Certainly, converging roles might indicate that less and less distinguished men from women in such spheres.

Moreover, these men were excluded from political participation in even the broadest context. In most places of the Paris Basin, the meetings of the traditional *assemblée des habitants* of local communities had become, by 1775, increasingly restricted to the direct rule of or indirect control by local notables at the expense of other residents, and increasingly limited in scope and responsibilities by the centralizing state.[65] Furthermore, proletarianization, protoindustrialization, and the disadvantageous conjuncture at work in

Economic Role of Women in Seventeenth-Century France," FHS (Fall 1989): 440–41. Gay Gullickson argues a similar point in *Spinners and Weavers of Auffay: Rural Industry and the Sexual Division of Labor in a French Village, 1750–1850* (Cambridge, 1986), p. 174.

63. On the breakdown of the sexual division of labor under protoindustrial conditions, see Gullickson, *Spinners and Weavers*, pp. 162–66.

64. Other questions arise. Did domestic violence rise? Did "antisocial" male behavior rise? See, e.g., the work of John Gilles, "Peasant, Plebeian, and Proletarian Marriage in Britain, 1600–1900," in *Proletarianization and Family History*, ed. David Levine (Orlando, 1984), pp. 87–128. See also the interesting work by Alan Williams on family grievances: "Patterns of Conflict and Grievance in Eighteenth-Century Parisian Families" (Paper presented to the Western Society for French History, Reno, 1991). Obviously, it is difficult to answer such questions with the sources available.

65. On this, see Albert Soboul, "The French Community in the Eighteenth Century," *Past and Present* 10 (1956): 78–95. Compare the strength of the rural community in the Paris Basin with that described for Burgundy by Pierre de Saint-Jacob, "Etudes sur l'ancienne communauté rurale en Bourgogne," *Annales de Bourgogne* 13 (1941): 169–202; 15 (1943): 173–84; 18 (1946): 237–50; 25 (1953): 225–40; idem, *Les Paysans de la Bourgogne du nord au dernier siècle de l'Ancien Régime* (Dijon, 1960); Jean Jacquart, "L'Administration locale en Ile-de-France des origines à la Révolution: Jalons pour une recherche," *Paris et Ile-de-France* 38 (1987): 4–5; Hilton Root, *Peasants and King in Burgundy: Agrarian Foundations of French Absolutism* (Berkeley and Los Angeles, 1987). On the actions of the centralizing state in the village community, see Chapter 2 above.

the second half of the eighteenth century served to shake loose bonds that may have linked male heads of peasant or artisanal households to their wider community and contained their behavior within conventional limits.[66] With the seigneurial system of paternalism a pale reflection of its former self, loss of the land that had formerly linked peasants to their communities, and the dissolution of personal ties by wage-labor, few traditional bonds remained to constrain protest movements. Thus, rioters such as Pierre Cadet who, with his eleven-year-old son, lived with his sister-in-law, could no longer claim head-of-household status, a role essential for any political identity in the Ancien Régime.

The active participation of village syndics in the Flour War can serve as an example of the changes under way within the village communities of the Paris Basin. The position was usually nonremunerative, except for certain tax benefits in some places, and it was potentially controversial when royal dictates clashed with local interests or when the village community fractured into open conflict.

Although there surely existed syndics who joined rioters for personal reasons that did not include obvious economic, social, or broader political motives, information on syndics' socioeconomic positions provides a crucial guide to understanding behavior in 1775. Among the few syndics who repudiated their duties to uphold royal will and Physiocratic-inspired policies in 1775 and who rioted alongside fellow villagers were Louis Hudde, a paving-stone carter and sometime shepherd from Baillet-en-France; Etienne Alliot, day-laborer from Signy-Signets; Denis Charles Caffin, vine-grower from Cergy; Louis-Suplice Metat, basket-maker from Montsoult; Charles Jarlet, vine-grower from Saint-Leu-lès-Taverny; and Denis Duplessis, cooper from Taverny. Price rises and dearth threatened to unbalance what was already for most of these syndics a precariously structured family economy, a disaster that holding such a post would do little to deflect.

Class linked these syndics with fellow rioters against the urban merchant, but especially against the surplus-producing fermier and laboureur. The case of Etienne Alliot, the day-laborer serving as syndic at Signy-Signets, underscores the tensions embedded in village life in the surplus-producing pays de grande culture.[67] For his insubordination, Alliot was sentenced to five

---

66. As shown in Chapter 5, this did not mean that Early Modern French society was ever uniformly deferential or quiescent. Insults, mockery, and violence clearly characterized popular behavior. On this, see, e.g., Olwen Hufton, "Attitudes Toward Authority in Eighteenth-Century Languedoc," Social History 3 (Oct. 1978): 281–302; idem, The Poor of Eighteenth-Century France, 1750–1789 (Oxford, 1974), pp. 219–305.

67. On his role, see Chapter 3.

years in the galleys, but he spent only two months in a prison, and then the sentence was commuted to a fine, dispossession from office, and a prohibition against reelection. His actions may have made Alliot feel better and be a hero to the local common people, but they demonstrated ultimately that even holding village office (something few day-laborers did at the end of the eighteenth century, even before the reforms of 1787) empowered few male workers.[68]

By 1775 the vagaries of late eighteenth-century economic change, the complex transformation of the region around Paris under the impact of the growth of the Paris market for grain, and the continuing polarization of rural society turned ever-larger numbers of rural families to wage labor in its many forms or various other "expedients" and threatened many others with similar destabilization. Protoindustrialization sustained many families and shielded them from destitution and dispossession in the countryside, but it also left them dependent on national and international business cycles and required renegotiation of roles within families.[69] Thus, the grain crisis of 1775 mobilized men whose conditions, interests, and perceptions were less and less different from those of women. In effect, the increasingly difficult economic situation of the late eighteenth century feminized numbers of men.

Local authorities referred sometimes sympathetically, sometimes condescendingly, to the vulnerability and powerlessness of men in this position. They often spoke nervously of their unruly, uncontrollable, and unpredictable predilections—adjectives that found more fully developed echoes in reference to the early nineteenth-century working class—in the same way they had traditionally viewed women. Yet men were not women, and as we have seen, however economically and socially "feminized" and politically alienated these men were, authorities held them accountable to different, male standards of behavior.[70] Witnesses and police viewed men as more threatening and were prepared to denounce and arrest them.

---

68. I do wonder whether such behavior contributed to the creation of village "heroes." The vine-grower and syndic from Cergy, Denis Charles Caffin, who had joined fellow vine-growers in an assault on Pontoise, its market, and port, emerged with a fine for his actions. In 1789 his name appears as one of two deputies elected to take the villlage cahier to the secondary bailliage meeting at Senlis.

69. Reddy's description of the situation of textile workers in Rouen in 1752 makes this case forcefully ("Textile Trade," pp. 62–66).

70. Local authorities frequently expressed sympathetic concern for the common people, whose condition appeared to be deteriorating. Yet they also recognized the danger to the political and social order inherent in such developments and were particularly distressed about certain categories

During the Flour War, men, in particular, swelled the ranks of those who rioted in the countryside (Chapter 4). And in these countryside confronta-tions, the Flour War marks a change in scale and a further sophistication of purpose from previous subsistence movements.

The Flour War in the Countryside

The producing countryside had always attracted the attention of consumers and magistrates alike. The subsistence regulatory system that had governed the grain trade since the Middle Ages was grounded in assumptions about the productivity of the French countryside and about the behavior of the producers themselves.[71] In general, most thought the average French harvest sufficed to feed the population, but certain experiences had taught that producers and merchants were not reliable trustees of the people's right to this "primary necessity," so they had to be watched.

Since production started with the farmers, so too did regulation. At any time, but particularly during periods of dearth or the fear of it, officials could require producers (among others) to declare what quantities of grain or flour they held in storage. If these statements were not forthcoming, or appeared inaccurate, authorities had the right to search private property (to make *perquisitions*), seize unreported stocks, and compel sales. Moreover, while grain producers could sell their produce and were supposed to do so themselves without reliance on intermediaries, they could not engage in any further commerce; millers could sell grain (which they often received as payment for milling) but could not buy any for trading purposes. We now know that these regulations were never applied with complete consistency or complete equality. During good years, authorities relaxed their vigilance,

---

of men who were notorious for unruly behavior, such as the woodcutters and river workers, as well as the *ouvrier* or journalier, among others. See, e.g., Hufton, *The Poor*, pp. 254–78; Schwartz, *Policing the Poor in Eighteenth-Century France* (Chapel Hill, N.C., 1988), pp. 229, 244–46; Richard Cobb, *Police and the People: French Popular Protest, 1789–1820* (Oxford, 1970), pp. 26–37. For more general attitudes about the common people, see Harry Payne, *The Philosophes and the People* (New Haven, 1976); Gérard Fritz, *L'Idée de peuple en France du XVIIe au XIXe siècle* (Strasbourg, 1988). See also Louis Chevalier, *Classes labourieuses et classes dangereuses* (Paris, 1978); Joan Scott, "A Statistical Representation of Work," in her *Gender and the Politics of History* (New York, 1988), pp. 118–19.

71. The most comprehensive recent descriptions of the paternalist system of regulation is in Kaplan, *Bread*, 1:52–96.

because market forces (as unevenly developed as they were) appeared to provide sufficient supplies at reasonable prices. As long as producers and merchants avoided obvious acts of speculation, hoarding, and collusion, they could expect to operate quite freely. During bleak years, all could expect an intensification of regulation enforcement. But even in the bleakest years, officials tended to spare the nobility and other officers from searches for grain and regulation evaders.[72]

During subsistence crises, desperate consumers often pressured officials to make searches and determined to look for themselves if the requested action was not forthcoming.[73] Initially, this latter procedure involved forays of town-dwellers into the countryside. In the spring of 1693, the intendant reported from Amiens that the poor were spreading out to nearby villages to demand grain from the rich laboureurs and *receveurs* of the seigneuries.[74] In 1709, inhabitants of Beauvais attacked and burned the farm belonging to the Marquis des Marets, the Grand Falconer of France, while Parisians circulated in bands throughout the countryside stopping convoys of grain; in 1710, the inhabitants of La Chapelle-Hugon (generality of Moulins) gathered arms, hid in the woods, and from this vantage point threw themselves on *blatiers* as they passed; in 1738, a report told of bands of poor roving the Dunois near Châteaudun taking bread from farmers, searching their granaries, and taking what threshed grain they found; and in 1767, women from Montlhéry marched against laboureurs. In 1773, in the town of Créon, near Bordeaux, inhabitants forced the maréchaussée to organize a search for wheat and flour in the district.[75] Indeed, historian René Pillorget

72. On relaxing enforcement of regulations, see Kaplan, ibid., p. 78; George Afanassiev, *Le Commerce des céréales en France au XVIIIe siècle,* trans. P. Boyer (Paris, 1894), p. 18; Pierre Deyon, *Amiens: Capitale provinciale* (Paris, 1967), p. 141. On the inequities in enforcement, see André Paris, "La Crise de 1709 dans le Bailliage de Montfort-L'Amaury. Le Marché des grains vu à travers le contrôle de l'administration royale," in *Actes du 101e Congrès national des sociétés savantes, Lille, 1976,* pp. 209–10.

73. See above, Chapters 3 and 5.

74. Deyon, *Amiens,* p. 468.

75. On the 1709 events, see Boislisle, "Grand Hiver," p. 509; on the 1710 events, see Leguai, "Moulins," p. 48; on 1738, see M. Bricourt et al., "Crise de subsistance," p. 292; on the 1767 events, see Kaplan, *Bread,* 1:190. On Créon, see Julius Ruff, *Crime, Justice, and Public Order in Old Regime France: The Sénéchaussées of Libourne and Bazas* (London, 1984), p. 151. Boislisle also refers to the pillage of two châteaus as well as several religious communities in Burgundy in 1709 but gives no indication of who was involved ("Grand Hiver," p. 507). This form of town invasion of the countryside appears far more frequently in British subsistence riots than in France. See descriptions in Thompson, "Moral Economy," pp. 111–12; Andrew Charlesworth, ed., *An Atlas of Rural Protest in Britain, 1548–1900* (London, 1983), p. 63. Yet Charlesworth reads the French case incorrectly. True, more rural inhabitants participated in the French movements than in the British counterparts,

reports that in Provence what he called "hunger riots" came in two basic types during the period to 1715: either *entraves* or market riots.[76] Not until the 1770s is there any indication that subsistence crises were generating significant, rural disturbances conducted by those who lived in rural areas.[77] For example, in 1773, a band of "peasants" roved the region around Libourne in search of grain. In the Paris Basin, Kaplan reports that in 1770 "throughout the Brie 'considerable seditions' erupted in which 'the people forced the laboureurs to sell them grain at a price they set themselves.' "[78] Before 1775, of the riots whose "type" I have been able to determine (69.4 percent of all riots), only 4.2 percent were this type 4 riot.[79]

In contrast, in 1775, rural riots such as those of 1770 erupted throughout the *pays de grande culture*—in the Brie, of course, but also in the Valois, Beauvaisis, Vexin, and Soissonnais. Although some incidents involved incursions of town-dwellers into the countryside (as in 1767), most encounters pitted villager against villager. In particular, most of these confrontations pitted local agrarian wage-laboring and small- and medium-sized property-holding men against surplus-grain producers.

Rural rioters in 1775 were responding to pervasive and accelerating changes at work within their society. First, the increasingly polarized social structure of the *pays de grande culture* created at one extreme a narrow elite of rich and powerful fermiers and laboureurs who controlled both food production and the labor market as well as local political power, and at the other extreme a mass of wage laborers who depended on these large-scale cultivators (both laboureurs and fermiers) for jobs and food (see Chapter 2). Between the two extremes there persisted a shrinking number of smaller landholders who were losing to the large-scale laboureurs and fermiers the uneven struggle to control the profits from even small parcels of grain-producing lands. Over time, this battle for control of resources (especially

---

but except for rare incidents, such as the Libourne episode, French food riots were not composed largely of peasants, as Charlesworth suggests.

76. *Les Mouvements insurrectionnels de Provence entre 1596 et 1715* (Paris, 1975), p. 995.

77. I do not want to push too far the distinction between urban- and rural-dwellers in this preindustrial society where occupations overlapped and interchange was pervasive. However, there is a difference between the pull of the market town (which generated considerable rural attraction) or the actions of market-town dwellers (who might head for the countryside) and the independent action of rural-dwellers in their own setting.

78. Kaplan, *Bread*, 1:198. The Brie makes an interesting point of departure for this newer style of rioting, because in some parts of the region large-scale cultivators lived apart from the village proper in more isolated farmsteads, making them easier targets.

79. The most common form of riot was the *entrave*. More than half (53.6 percent) of all riots whose type is known were type 3 riots, 20.3 percent were type 1, and 10.7 percent were type 2.

food or the means to obtain food: food-producing land or the wages to buy
food) intensified, as evidenced by increasingly numerous outbreaks of rural
strikes, the complaints of violence and threats unleashed on the fermier or
laboureur by worker and lesser peasant alike, and various other forms of
"everyday resistance."[80] These tensions were rural in origin, and the Flour
War—this time a direct assault on the food held in the rural elite's
granaries—represents one form among myriad others in the uneven struggle.
Thus, it comes as no surprise to learn that among the victims whose
holdings can be detailed in the surviving tax records, all were by far the
largest landholders in their communities.[81] They farmed—usually as fermiers—the largest holdings and paid the most taxes.

The overwhelming majority of the victims—with the exception of certain
residents of the Vexin, where the average holding was smaller[82]—exploited
at least 200 arpents, and many held considerably more. For example,
Antoine Thuin, a fermier at Lissy in the Brie, held "from M. Payot in Paris
a ferme of 293 arpents of arable, 7 arpents of pastureland, and a grange"
and paid more than 400 livres for the taille, the highest in his community in
1774.[83] Charles Fillerin, a fermier at Maffliers, held a corps de ferme from the
Baron d'Heiss of 305 arpents of arable land and 40 arpents of pastureland
and paid a taille of 1,120 livres in 1774.[84] Not one victim was a significant
proprietor in his own right, although a few held a small number of arpents
of arable or vine "en propre."

The overwhelming majority also leased holdings belonging to more than
one proprietor. François Marc, laboureur and fermier at Touffreville in the

80. The term is James Scott's, Weapons of the Weak: Everyday Forms of Peasant Resistance (New
Haven, 1985). On strikes, see note 114 below; on threats, see the 1775 letter from the fermiers
from Chelles, cited in Chapter 2, note 81. See also Gilles Vinay-Postel, La Rente foncière dans le
capitalisme agricole. L'Exemple du soissonnais (Paris, 1974), p. 62; and Bricourt et al., "Crise de
subsistance," p. 297.

81. As noted previously, Turgot promised to indemnify victims for the losses incurred during
the Flour War, thus encouraging them to come forward with their stories. These depositions cover
the entire range of experiences of the victims. Some 186 reported incursions into their farms. Of
these, I have been able to find supplementary information—tax records (rolls for the taille, vingtième,
reparations to church properties, etc.)—for 34 percent. Because methods of tax assessment varied
considerably, I have used these records in a local and relative context, not in a comparative way.
Thus, these records can help us assess the condition of the victim relative to other members of the
same community.

82. Jacques Dupâquier, "La Situation de l'agriculture dans le Vexin français (fin du XVIIIe et
début du XIXe siècle) d'après les enquêtes agricoles," in Actes du 89e Congrès national des sociétés
savantes, Lyon, 1964 (Paris, 1965), pp. 321–45.

83. "Rôle de la taille, Lissy, 1774," AN, Z1G 361a.

84. "Rôle de la taille, Maffliers, 1774," AN, Z1G 360a.

Vexin Normand, is the most striking example. He held land belonging to fourteen different proprietors, including the seigneur of Touffreville and the parish priest of the nearby village of Hennézis.[85] André Baldé, fermier at Maffliers in the Valois, held land belonging to twelve different proprietors in his own village, as well as other land in the nearby parish of Montsoult.[86] One of Baldé's neighbors, Pierre Sainte-Boeuve, fermier at Chauvry, held land from five different proprietors, including the *corps de ferme* of the seigneurie belonging to Madame Lamassais comprised of 565 arpents of arable and pastureland. He also held land in Montsoult and Béthemont.[87]

Second, a significant portion of the laboureurs and fermiers singled out by the rioters were also intimately connected to the privileged orders of the Ancien Régime, either by leasing land belonging to them (which often carried certain benefits and exemptions) or by leasing the rights to collect seigneurial dues or the tithe. Examples include Pierre Vachette, fermier at Cauffry and *receveur* of the seigneurie of the Marquisat de Liancourt; Toussaint Bureau, fermier of seigneurial lands and the tithe at Bondy; Jacques Pierre Héricourt, fermier at Gagny who leased from the Prieur of Gournay "the land and seigneurie du Chenay" that included the seigneurial dues, the tithe, a plaster works, and a wine press; Adrien Hourdan and Pierre Delaissement, fermiers at Mussegros who shared the lease on two fermes and the seigneurial dues belonging to the President d'Anneuil; Antoine Bequin, fermier and laboureur at Heubécourt, where he leased from Sieur de Becdelièvre, seigneur, the ferme of Grumésnil, the ferme of Heubécourt, a wine-press, a dove-cote, a windmill, and the seigneurial dues; and Pierre Afforty, bourgeois de Paris, *archer-garde de la connétablie de la maréchaussée de France*, fermier, and *receveur* of the seigneurie, as well as *procureur fiscal* at Villepinte, where he exploited a *corps de ferme* belonging to the Abbaye of Saint-Denis totaling five charrues.[88] Attacks on seigneurs themselves were rare, a fact that is not surprising, given that most in the

85. "Rôle de la vingtième, Touffreville, 1772," AD Eure, C 92.

86. "Rôle de la taille, Maffliers, 1774," where he paid a tax of 1,045 livres 2 sols, and "Rôle de la taille, Montsoult, 1774," where he paid 43 livres 15 sols (AN, Z1G 360a).

87. "Rôle de la taille, Chauvry, 1774," "Rôle de la taille, Montsoult, 1774," and "Rôle de la taille, Béthemont, 1774," AN, Z1G 360a.

88. On Vachette, see "Rôle de la taille, Cauffry, 1775," AD Oise, C 519; on Bureau, "Rôle de la taille, Bondy, 1773," AN, Z1G 355c; on Héricourt, "Rôle de la taille, Gagny, 1773," AN, Z1G 355c; on Hourdan and Delaisement, "Rôle du vingtième, Mussegros, 1772," AD Eure, C 89; on Bequin (whose lease began in 1773), "Rôle du vingtième, Heubécourt, 1781," AD Eure, C 89; on Afforty, "Rôle de la taille, Villepinte, 1775," AN, Z1G 366b; Jean-Marc Moriceau and Gilles Postel-Vinay, *Ferme, Entreprise, Famille* (Paris, 1992), pp. 125, 363.

pays de grande culture chose to live elsewhere. Their estate managers and fermiers controlled the grain their lands produced and collected the dues associated with their privileged state, and often exercised the power previously belonging to the resident seigneur.

Laboureurs and fermiers also often concentrated and manipulated other forms of political power within their communities.[89] Yet far from shielding them from assault during subsistence riots, this further evidence of control may have intensified local hostilities and polarized positions. Some village syndics, for example, openly sided with their surplus-producing colleagues; others found themselves targeted for attack. Syndics in the villages of Berne and Moisselles turned over stocks of their grain to groups of rioters.[90]

Thus, the rural manifestation of the Flour War reflects the mounting tensions latent in the *pays de grande culture* in the late eighteenth century. Rioters targeted not only those individuals most likely to control grain, but also those who represented the various dimensions of their everyday distress and subordination. Rioters selected the laboureurs and fermiers who demonstrated either singly or simultaneously several characteristics: they held the largest exploitation, farmed the largest number of holdings, and/or were linked with the seigneurial system.

In the first two of these cases, rioters lashed out against the agricultural elite, not only as proprietors of surplus grain but also as holders of power, economic, social, and political (as well as cultural) within their communities. These fermiers and laboureurs were at the nexus of change in the second half of the eighteenth century. Shifting patterns of landholding accelerated their ascension as a narrow and resident elite. They amassed more and more land through concentration and reunions, often competing directly with the smaller peasantry. They therefore controlled increasingly the land and job markets within their villages. As we have already seen, the victims frequently recognized among the rioters two groups most affected by this power structure: the medium-sized landholders and the unskilled and semiskilled agricultural wage-laborers. In this sense we can agree with the assessment of Emmanuel Le Roy Ladurie when he concluded that the "1775 Flour War was waged by the lower classes against the land- and grain-potentates," whom he described as "big capitalist farmers."[91]

---

89. See Jessenne, *Pouvoir*, on the emergence of a "fermocracy" in areas of large-scale grain production, esp. part 2, pp. 147–244.

90. On Berne, "Procès-verbal (30 avril)," AD Oise, B 1584; on Moisselles, "Procès-verbal (2 mai)," AD Oise, B 1583; and "Rôle de la taille, Moisselles, 1774," AN, Z1G 360B.

91. "Rural Revolts and Protest Movements in France from 1675 to 1788," *Studies in Eighteenth-Century Culture* 5 (1976): 442.

Social and economic polarization in the surplus-grain-producing country-side created the conditions for suffering amid apparent and certainly relative plenty. For those who failed to produce any or enough grain to sustain themselves and their families, these large-scale producers appeared to control an abundance. Finding themselves without sufficient resources to purchase the grain rural laborers knew existed in farm granaries (often because they had themselves helped to store it there after the harvest or to thresh it to ready it for market), they had recourse to one of two courses of action. Either they could demand that farmers supply them via loans or charitable donations, thus conjuring up traditional relations of paternalism and patronage, or they could simply take it, by force if necessary. On occasion, the first policy succeeded; more frequently, they resorted to the latter.[92]

In many cases, however, these targets in the countryside represented more than the intrusion of capitalist business practices in agriculture. They were also clearly linked to eighteenth-century seigneurialism. Although as we have seen, direct attacks against the seigneurs were few—as were attacks on rural ecclesiastical communities (like the monastery of Saint-Leu-d'Esserent, which also held seigneurial powers)[93]—attacks on their immediate representatives in the villages, their fermiers and their receveurs, were numerous. They were the intermediaries between absentee seigneurs and the villagers. They administered seigneurial lands, collected the dues and the tithe, exploited the monopolies, enjoyed the exemptions such association brought, and often dominated the political life of the village.

Yet this function as representatives of seigneurialism was incompletely fulfilled (see Chapter 5). Disappearing (or realigning) were the traditional expectations of mutuality, such as charity and patronage, for example. True, examples such as a Cosme Charlemagne who distributed food to the poor of his parish during the Flour War in a style that emulated the Duc de Montmorency at Gournay-en-Bray showed that such traditions had not totally been lost in transit, but depersonalization was already under way.

These fermiers were more than "theoretical agents of the seigneur";[94] they

92. For example, the laboureur at Petit Groslay, Cosme Charlemagne, declared he was "moved with surprise and compassion when he saw the crowd and to find among it several people burdened with families and in need." He decided to distribute some of his grain as charity ("Déclaration de 6 mai," AN, Y 18682). See also Chapter 5.

93. The monastery shared juridical jurisdiction over the village. Albert Fossard, *Le Prieuré de Saint-Leu-d'Esserent* (Paris, 1934).

94. Le Roy Ladurie, "Rural Revolts," p. 442.

really were seigneurial representatives, not of the medieval type but of the
late eighteenth-century type. George Rudé observed that "in the Flour War
one does not see the hatred of the people erupt against the landed proprietor
as owner of feudal dues,"[95] but that one does see clearly that the people
turned against those who, at the local level, represented, by exploiting, the
seigneurial order, both secular and religious.

Third, the liberalization edicts further served to concentrate the resent-
ment of both rural and urban inhabitants of the *pays de grande culture* on the
large-scale fermiers and laboureurs during the second half of the eighteenth
century. Liberalization openly encouraged producers to become merchants
and further granted them the right to sell their produce directly from their
granaries rather than bring it to market. Thus, the potential for becoming
what paternalists referred to as "hoarders" or "speculators" increased dramatically and legitimately. In the Flour War we often find characters wearing
the multiple hats cultivators could and did wear openly from the 1760s. For
example, Charles Fessard was a walking manifestation of vertical and
horizontal integration in the grain trade. He declared himself a flour
merchant to authorities in Magny-en-Vexin, where on the eve of the rioting
that erupted on 1 May he had purchased grain stored in four different
magazines from five different laboureurs. Fessard also experienced an assault
on his farm in the village of Us on 3 May. There he towered above his
neighbors as laboureur and *garde étalon*. He held a farm called Bazincourt
that consisted of, among other properties, 250 arpents of arable land and
two mills. He leased over 160 more arpents from eight other proprietors,
and his commerce in flour was assessed at 10,000 livres for the *taille* in
1773.[96] He therefore presented multiple targets for rioters.[97]

95. "Taxation . . . région parisienne," p. 178.

96. "Etat du bled pillé ou vendu à vil prix au marché de Magny . . . (n.d.)," AD Seine-
Maritime, C 107; "Rôle de la taille, Us, 1773," AD Yvelines, C 240. Fessard had been doing
business in Magny for the Paris market since at least 1771, when he registered with the bailliage
court at Pontoise to declare that he ground the grain purchased at Magny into flour for Paris at his
two mills at Us. See "Registre . . . des laboureurs . . . dans le ressort du Bailliage de Pontoise (29
août 1770–28 janvier 1771)," AD Yvelines, 12 B 720. As Kaplan explains, the Terray regulations,
far from prohibiting cultivator involvement in the grain trade, probably legitimized it via required
registration (*Bread*, 2:538–39, 560–61).

97. Other examples include Antoinette Gaffet, widow of Jean Blot, fermier at Bélou in Boutigny
near Meaux, who lost 4 setiers of grain at the market of Meaux on 6 May and 36–40 setiers from
her farm on the same day ("Information de 12 mai," AD Seine-et-Marne, B 2387); and Sieur
Bertaux, fermier for the Prince de Conti at Bertichère, who suffered a loss at the 1 May market of
Gisors and an even greater loss from his farm on 5 May ("Etat des pertes . . . dans la subdélégation
de Gisors [7 juin]," AD Seine-Maritime, C 107, and "Lettre de 6 mai," C 108).

Furthermore, liberalization prohibited, at least in theory, former direct methods of addressing diminished supplies during a subsistence crisis: official searches and requisitions in the producing countryside. Authorities were instructed over and over again not to interfere in the free play of the grain trade, but as previous subsistence riots had shown, the people were prepared to act themselves when authorities refused to or hesitated. From the 1760s, the people confronted ever more authorities who hesitated to act, even though many persisted in sympathizing with the popular plight.[98]

On the one hand, therefore, liberalization legitimized and facilitated among producers behavior that already had a long history—long-term grain storage in and direct sales from farm granaries as well as active participation in the grain and flour trade. On the other hand, authorities were specifically prevented from taking previous paternalist steps to force grain to market and into the hands of local consumers. Indeed, the *procureur du roi* at Point-sur-Seine expressed the conundrum clearly in March 1775 when he observed that "the laboureurs" who were now "free to sell from their granaries hold [grain] there in piles . . . and the merchants go there to make their purchases." He complained that the markets were entirely devoid of grain and that, because the police could no longer "force the laboureurs and merchants to open their granaries and furnish the markets," prices had risen markedly.[99] Authorities and consumers alike had faced similar difficulties in the first experience with liberalization.[100]

Of course, most authorities in 1775, as in the earlier period, resorted to compromises that may have made the producers appear even more like evil speculators and hoarders than previously. Rather than adhere strictly to the new liberalization policy or repudiate it openly, officials resorted to a legally ambiguous combination of entreaty and bribery to encourage provisioning. The fermiers of the lands of M. Pommery in the Vexin normand complained bitterly that they had received "letters of invitation from both the subdele-

98. Kaplan on authorities' responses: *Bread*, 1:194–214, 220–29.

99. "Lettre (19 mars)," BN, Collection Joly de Fleury, 1159, fol. 222. See also a similar argument presented by the subdelegate at Lyons-la-Forêt, who blamed diminished supplies and higher prices in his market on the "bad will of the laboureurs who do not punctually furnish the market, even though grain isn't lacking in the area." He denounced them as "too prideful" ("Lettre de 11 juin," AD Seine-Maritime, C 109). The subdelegate at Gournay-en-Bray was as suspicious. After describing rising prices since the harvest of 1774, he asked: "Was it not possible that this continuous progression . . . is caused by the unlimited protection the government accords to the cultivator, thus authorizing his cupidity?" (AD Seine-Maritime, C 107). See Chapter 5 for more on this reaction of local authorities.

100. See Kaplan's discussion of the first episode in *Bread*.

gate of Gisors and the subdelegate at Gournay" to furnish their markets. They wanted to point out "that in the state of distress that [the rioters] have put them, they cannot [bring grain] as they would like, and even less to two different markets simultaneously."[101] The subdelegate at Chaumont-en-Vexin wrote that "in conformity with the dispositions of his majesty's edict, I interfered in no way in police affairs. I simply urged the laboureurs to give in to the circumstances."[102] In effect, local authorities placed the burden of responsibility for the subsistence crisis on the laboureurs and fermiers.

The Flour War represented not only the last great subsistence movement before the eruption of the Revolution, but also the last subsistence movement to occur in a context of a free grain trade until 1787–88, and then not again until after Thermidor.[103] The smaller subsistence crises of 1777 and 1784–85, and the greater ones of 1788–89 and 1792–93 occurred during times when officials were again empowered to interfere in the provisioning process. In 1789 many Paris Basin cahiers de doléances reflected this persistent belief that provisioning should not be left to the vagaries of free trade and self-interest and exhorted the Estates General to empower the local subsistence police. As we shall see below, many cahiers targeted the large-scale laboureurs and fermiers as the most likely to cheat the people of their right to subsistence.

Thus, the behavior of local authorities, coupled with the growing social polarization of the surplus-grain producing countryside, fostered increased tensions focused on the producers. Not only did Abbé Terray suspect cultivators of hoarding and speculating in the early 1770s,[104] but so did the people themselves. From the 1760s to the 1770s and after, the targets who wore the blackest of black hats in the subsistence issue—in the smaller

101. "Lettre (10 mai)," AD Seine-Maritime, C 108.
102. "Lettre (6 mai)," AD Seine-Maritime, C 108. For other examples, see "Lettre du subdélégué à Clermont (5 mai)," AD Oise, C 295; "Lettre des officiers du bailliage de Roye (10 mai)," BN, Collection Joly de Fleury, 1159, fols. 229–30; "Lettre du procureur fiscal de police à Blérancourt (8 mai)," AD Aisne, C 13.
103. The vacillations of government policies on the grain trade are well known. With the fall of Turgot in 1776 came the fall of liberalization. Loménie de Brienne had reintroduced it in June 1787; Necker dismantled it partially in September 1788 and more thoroughly in November 1788 and April 1789 when he forbade exports, then ordered all sales to take place in the marketplace, and finally empowered officials to intervene if necessary in the provisioning process to prohibit hoarding, speculation, and fraud. The convention moved furthest toward a regulated grain trade with the declaration of maximum prices in May 1793 and the creation of Revolutionary armies whose tasks included policing grain trade. The Thermidorians abolished the maximum and declared free trade, but also ordered bread rationing.
104. Kaplan, Bread, 2:570–76.

market towns and countryside—were increasingly fermiers and laboureurs rather than merchants, bakers, or millers who had been the evildoers of previous ages. For example, a certain Chocquet, at Fougerolles in the Beauvaisis, reported that after the rioting had subsided at the Mouy market and he ventured out to search for grain lost during the disturbances, a woman at the town mill told him "he was lucky he was a grain merchant and not a laboureur, because the miller's aide had just told her that had he been a laboureur he wouldn't have let him [Chocquet] have the grain and would have thrown him in the water instead." Chocquet wisely decided not to reveal his actual identity as both grain merchant and laboureur.[105] Of course, the black hat question depended on vantage point. In the big cities, the producer who did not directly market his grain because of intermediaries or the growth of the flour trade, was no doubt a relatively remote figure. The merchant or baker focused greater concern. But all of France was not Paris.

When the Flour War erupted in the Paris Basin, therefore, the large-scale cultivators of the *pays de grande culture* felt the brunt of intensified popular hostility, both urban and rural. By 1775, the larger context of the experience of uneven development and social polarization in the region meant that the agrarian movement embodied in the Flour War (and experienced less extensively before) often encompassed more than hostility toward these large-scale cultivators as hoarders of grain. As the *coqs de village*, they were masters in their villages in more ways than many of their neighbors could tolerate. And it was as this social, economic, and political elite that they inspired many of their less powerful neighbors to risk identification (without even superficial attempts to disguise themselves) and arrest to attack them during the Flour War. For example, on 7 May, the day-laborer Lemotte appeared before the laboureur Cariat at May-en-Multien with a band of people from the region, accosting him in his own kitchen and announcing, "You'll not be master today, because it's our turn."[106] Similarly, a rioter cornered the fermier of the seigneurial farm at Suisne on 6 May to declare that the fermier "was no longer the master of his own house (*chez lui*)."[107] On 4 May, Pierre Hamelin mounted several sacks piled up at the market of

105. "Déposition (3 mai)," AD Oise, B 1583. See also "Interrogatoire de Pierre Hamelin (25 juillet)" and "Interrogatoire de Jean Baptiste Portier (6 mai)," AD Oise, B 1583ter.

106. "Procès-verbal, déposition du Sr. Cariat," AD Oise, B non coté, maréchaussée de Clermont, 1775.

107. "Plainte de Germaine LaRoche, laboureur-fermier de la ferme seigneuriale de Suisne (7 mai)," BN, Collection Joly de Fleury, 1159, fols. 60–61.

Beaumont-sur-Oise and declared: "Messieurs laboureurs, you will no longer be the masters of your grain as you would like. You have trampled on the poor, and they will trample on you in turn." When the cavaliers arrested and searched him, they discovered a charged pistol in his pocket.[108] Rioters who searched the granaries of Cauffry laboureur Pierre Vachette declared, "You have grain in your granary and we want it, and if there is some in the barn we will winnow it as quickly as threshers can thresh it, and if we fast you will have to fast too."[109]

Rioters drew on long traditions of insubordination to annoy and frighten their targets. When rioters marched through homes, sat down uninvited at dining-room tables with their victims, drank their wine or cider, and ate their bread, their actions symbolized a reversal of power relations that day-to-day life prohibited. On 2 May, a band of rioters broke into the room where Etienne Delacour, a laboureur and fermier at Maffliers, kept the dirty laundry. They gathered it up and paraded it around in the streets, publicly humiliating his family.[110] Etienne's father, Louis Delacour, laboureur at Grand Gournay in the neighboring parish of Montsoult, experienced another version of an attack by hostile villagers. On 1 May, rioters "broke down the doors to his sheepfold [and took] 9 sheep" and drove them into the countryside.[111] Laboureurs and fermiers in certain parts of the *pays de grande culture* were often owners of large flocks of sheep and as such frequently found themselves engaged in long-running disputes over rights to common grazing lands. Unfortunately, the documents give no indication whether in this case there was any relationship between Delacour's freed sheep and debates over common grazing rights (*vaine pâture*) at Montsoult.[112]

Trouble continued in many of the same farms of the pays de France and the Valois even after the Flour War had subsided. In 1776, the fermiers in the villages of Baillet-en-France, Maffliers, Montsoult, Chauvry, and Moisselles confronted a wave of strikes among harvesters who demanded higher wages. The migrant workers—those principally from Picardy—told authorities that they were willing to work but that "the people from the parishes of the region threatened them" and even "mistreated them" to keep them from

108. "Procès-verbal (4 mai)," AD Oise, B 1583. Hamelin was later accused having accosted another laboureur earlier in the day. He was accused of warning, "It has been a long time that you have trampled the world under foot. Take care that you don't get trampled on in turn" ("Interrogatoire [25 juillet]," AD Oise, B 1583ter).

109. "Information (15 mai)," AD Oise, B non coté, Clermont.

110. "Déclaration (7 mai)," AD Oise, B 1583ter.

111. Ibid., B 1583bis.

112. On this, see, e.g., Meuvret, *Problème*, 2:21–22.

accepting the cultivators' terms.[113] Indeed, the cultivators targeted in 1776 were the laboureurs and fermiers who had experienced rioting in 1775: Delacour in Maffliers, Sainte-Boeuve at Chauvry, and the Benoists (father and son) from Baillet.[114]

The persistence of such hostility in many of the same places finds further articulation in the *cahiers de doléances* compiled some thirteen years after the Flour War had subsided.[115] The cahier from the small village of Baillet, where in 1775 two fermiers suffered incursions from rioting neighbors serves as an example:

> Art. 5: It is hoped that the seigneurs, for the well being and advantage of their vassals, would be willing to divide their lands into several lots and give everyone a portion. In this way, the seigneurs would have the consolation of seeing all their vassals survive. At least each fermier should enjoy no more than one ferme, rather than now when there are many who occupy two, others three, others four. And each should stick to cultivation without undertaking other commerce, rather than now when there are many who are still not content and engage in other commerce and employ only half of the laborers that four fermiers would employ. . . . He [the fermier] holds all the laborers under his domination, pays the workers what he wants, by the day, at a very modest rate. Provided that they accumulate they are content. . . . Is there land from a ferme for sale? They [the fermiers] purchase it [land] at any price, so that now, only they can survive.[116]

On the eve of the Flour War, the situation described above had already developed in that village, and the two fermiers targeted fit the description. One fermier, Charles Benoist, leased a ferme from the Feuillants that

113. "Procès-verbal (8 août 1776)," AD Oise, B non coté, maréchaussée de Beauvais, 1776.

114. On the increasing frequency of eruptions of harvest strikes or "bacchanals" in these regions, see Jean-Marc Moriceau, "Les 'Baccanales' ou grèves de moissonneurs en pays de France (second moitié du XVIIIe siècle)," *Mouvements populaires*, pp. 421–33, as well as Maurice Dommanget, "Les Grèves de moissonneurs du Valois sous la Révolution," *AHRF* 1 (1924): 507–44; and Octave Festy, *L'Agriculture pendant la Révolution française. Les Conditions de production et de récolte des céréales* (Paris, 1947), pp. 290–338.

115. That caution is necessary in using the cahiers to represent any one group's opinion goes without saying. Nevertheless, they remain useful sources for sampling opinion in certain contexts.

116. "Cahier de doléances de Baillet," in M. J. Mavidal and M. E. Laurent, *Archives parlementaires de 1787 à 1869, première série (1787 à 1799)*, vol. 4 (1879; reprint, Paris, 1969), pp. 332–33.

included 242 arpents of arable land, 12 arpents of pastureland, and the tithe, a ferme belonging to the Prince de Conti that consisted of 162 arpents of arable land, 22 arpents of pastureland, and the right to collect the *champart* on 90 arpents. He also leased a total of 71 arpents of arable land as well as more pastureland and the *dîmes novales* from other proprietors. He himself owned a mere 2 arpents of arable land and leased a house to a neighbor. His son, Pierre Charles Benoist, leased the seigneurial ferme of Fayel in the parish. The third largest taxpayer in the village, Etienne Benard, did not live there. He was actually the largest fermier and taxpayer in the neighboring village of Moisselles.[117]

Similar protests against the behavior of landed proprietors and fermiers echoed throughout the *pays de grande culture* in 1789. Many demanded limits either on the number of fermes or on the amount of land any one individual could lease. Some of these blamed the fermiers for the drive to accumulate; others pointed to the behavior of seigneurs or other landed proprietors. For example, the inhabitants of Angervilliers announced that "it ought to be prohibited for all laboureurs and *meuniers* to take more than one exploitation in ferme or mill . . . [and] for seigneurs to destroy fermes that form diverse habitations in order to consolidate them as one."[118] Cahiers from this region also frequently objected strongly to large-scale cultivators engaging in the grain and flour trade, including milling, beyond selling their own produce. This grievance was sometimes coupled with demands that the Crown enforce traditional subsistence regulations prohibiting sales from granaries and requiring public marketplace sales. Thus, the inhabitants from Angervilliers also demanded that "laboureurs and all other cultivators be excluded from this [grain] trade." The cahier of Magny-en-Vexin, in the heart of the great *pays de grande culture* and a town that had experienced a massive type 2 riot in 1775, explained:

117. "Lettre (3 mai)," AD Oise, B 1583ter; "Rôle de la taille, Baillet, 1774," AN, Z1G 360a. In 1775 Baillet had 32 households: Jacques Dupâquier, *Paroisses et communes de France. Dictionnaire d'histoire administrative et démographique, Région parisienne* (Paris, 1974), p. 463. "Rôle de la taille, Moisselles, 1774," AN, Z1G 360b.

118. Cahier of Angervilliers, Mavidal, *Archives parlementaires*, 4:296. Similar demands are found in the cahiers of Belloy-en-France (ibid., p. 353), Bouffemont (p. 367), Choisy-le-Roi (p. 436), Clichy-en-Aulnay (p. 446), Dammartin near Meaux (p. 484), Deuil (p. 487), La Ferté-sous-Jouarre (p. 636), Fresne (p. 570), Gonesse (p. 584), Goussainville (p. 589), Groslay (p. 596), Jouy-le-Moutier (pp. 623–25), Limours (p. 647), Montsoult (p. 738), Reuil-en-Brie (5:61), Sevran (ibid., p. 117), Triel (p. 143), Villepinte (p. 205), Villiers-sur-Marne (p. 216), and Boisemont (Marc Bouloiseau and Philippe Boudin eds., *Cahiers de doléances du Tiers Etat du bailliage d'Andely* [Rouen, 1974], p. 58).

We are far from disapproving of the encouragements that are accorded those who engage in agriculture; but we think that these encouragements need to be modified and combined in such a way that they do not give too much advantage to the cultivators over the people. It would be good, perhaps, in view of the habitually excessive prices of grain and livestock and the extreme dearth of bread and meat at this time, to proscribe, in the case of grain and bread, the new system in indefinite freedom of commerce in grain and reinstate the former laws that prohibited fermiers and laboureurs from selling the grain from their harvests anywhere other than the *halles* and markets.[119]

The inhabitants of Herblay, Conflans-Sainte-Honorine, Dammartin, Gonesse, and Jouy-le-Moutier issued similar protests.[120]

The Revolution exposed further hostilities toward surplus-producers, both proprietors and their fermiers. In July 1789, riots erupted around the town of Mantes that focused on fermiers and laboureurs who were suspected of hoarding grain. Two from the village of Rosny fled following accusations against them because they feared attack. They were declared *émigrés*.[121] In June 1790 an official reported from Craonne, a market town located between Laon and Reims, that he had heard people saying "they had destroyed the clergy and the nobility, [and now] it was necessary to destroy the laboureurs and the maréchaussée."[122] The Revolution would cast the subsistence question in concrete, formal, political and social terms. As critics of the period refined distinctions between "political economy" (the market economy) and "popular political economy" (the moral economy) and politicized their content, the common people became potential *sans culottes*.[123] Merchants

---

119. "Cahier de la ville de Magny-en-Vexin-françois," in Jacques Dupâquier, *Ainsi commença la Révolution . . . Chaumont*, pp. 365–66.

120. See Mavidal, *Archives parlementaires*, 4:604, 458, 484, 585, and 624, respectively.

121. Henri Dinet, "La Grande Peur du Beauvaisis et du Valois, juillet 1789," *Paris et Ile-de-France* 23–24 (1972–73): 241.

122. Georges Dumas, "Emotions populaires en 1789–90 dans le Laonnais et la Thiérache," in *Actes du 101e Congrès national des sociétés savantes, Lille, 1976* (Paris, 1978), 2:95–110. Dumas also relates a story from April 1789 when authorities discovered pamphlets distributed in Laon and Crécy that spoke of "the just punishment of a laboureur" who had refused grain to a widow with eleven children (one not yet weaned) and was two days later discovered dead not far from his farm. The tract further reported that, after checking into his affairs, some 4,000 sacks of grain were discovered hidden in a quarry. Although surely a fictitious story, it reflected the level of hostility these powerful, surplus-producing fermiers and laboureurs inspired among many people in the Paris Basin.

123. We need further research on the role grain warfare played in the making of popular political

and surplus producers became potential *aristocrates*. The *armées révolution-naires* described by Richard Cobb were empowered to engage in widespread searches and requisitions from the granaries of cultivators as they battled the subsistence crisis of 1793.[124] Of course, not all fermiers provoked violent hostility in 1775 or during the Revolutionary period,[125] and not all rioters or writers of cahiers assailed either seigneurialism or agricultural or commercial capitalism—but many did, and their positions are an important feature of the evolution of eighteenth-century popular opinion through the Flour War and on into the Revolution.

The magnitude of rioting in the countryside in 1775, coupled with the overwhelmingly wage-laboring, male composition of the rural crowds, may have made these riots appear more threatening to the government than previous movements. To Louis XVI's ministry, which was intent on imple-menting massive changes in the process of provisioning in particular and mobilizing the country's resources for greater wealth in general, the Flour War appeared to signal danger. As long as the *taxation populaire* remained the domain of mothers and unruly women (who, as Métra pointed out, could be very violent and dangerous), or even fathers and sons of the traditional common people, and limited itself to attacks on bakers' shops, incursions into granaries in market towns, and the *entrave*, they were vexatious—and sometimes worse—to those who had to subdue them, but they were also familiar. Once men entered the arena in large numbers and flooded into the countryside that produced the lifeblood of the capital, official perceptions changed. The presence of men whose gender roles were not restricted to the private sphere (no matter how poor or vulnerable they were), whose public actions embraced the political sphere, and whose public

---

consciousness in the pre-Revolutionary period. The Flour War suggests that the debates over provisioning policies, national interest, and sovereignty had not yet become a matter of open debate among the common people of Paris or of the provinces. The pre-Revolutionary and Revolutionary crises indicate, however, that at some point the types of disaffection from local authorities in place that characterized food rioting of earlier periods had developed further into disillusionment and dissatisfaction with national authority. We need a more intensive examination of the period between 1775 and 1789, and even beyond, to learn how the common people of Paris and the provinces got caught up in the confrontations that dominated more elite circles.

124. *The People's Armies*, trans. M. Elliot (New Haven, 1987; Paris, 1961–63). Cobb also describes what he called "ultra-revolutionary municipalities" (Presles, Taverny, Jagny, Ecouis, Lyons-la-Forêt) that favored violent action against fermiers (p. 275). See also the fate of the estate manager for the Saulx-Tavanes studied by Robert Forster, *The House of Saulx-Tavanes: Versailles and Burgundy, 1700–1830* (Baltimore, 1970).

125. On certain issues during the Revolution, fermiers were embraced as allies; see, e.g., Jessenne, *Pouvoir*, pp. 49–89. But even Jessenne points out that where there had been tension between fermiers and people before the Revolution, they rarely allied during it.

action had always attracted severe retaliation may have appeared further to politicize the movement.

Thus, the Flour War—examined in the light of previous subsistence movements and in its own context in the Paris Basin—manifested the effects of the transformations at work within Ancien Régime France. Those who formed the rank-and-file of the Flour War's battalions came more frequently from the lower ranks of the common people—those who had already experienced the social effects of proletarianization and protoindustrialization were also those who suffered soonest from high prices—than the rioters who were their predecessors. The growing numbers of men who had undergone this debilitating experience more frequently joined with women to protest their own and their families' dependence and vulnerability, and they turned more and more of their hostility against the targets in which lodged the provocative combination of traditional privilege and emerging large-scale commercial agriculture. The pattern of victims assailed in the countryside shows that the rioters did not choose their targets at random, but rather attacked the citadels of power—the power of expansionist, profit-maximizing landholders, the power of the Ancien Régime seigneurial system, and most infuriating, the two combined. In fact, recourse to this type of riot increased after 1775. Whereas before 1775 only 4.2 percent of all riots whose type is known belonged to this category of behavior, after 1775 some 20.4 percent were this type 4 riot.[126] By their choice of targets, and by their adaptation of the weapons of the past, the people signaled their perception of an evolving, insecure future.

126. Of the riots after 1775, I have been able to determine the "type" for 59.8 percent. Of these, 21.4 percent were type 1 riots (compared with 20.3 percent for the period before 1775), 10.2 percent were type 2 riots (compared with 10.7 percent), and 41.8 percent were type 3 riots (down from 53.6 percent in the period before 1775). The decline in type 3 riots and the rise in type 4 riots constitute the only significant changes between the periods.

CONCLUSION

In time, calm returned to the Flour War's battlegrounds. As the grain rose in the fields—a good and plentiful crop this time—and harvest time approached, prices finally fell and the repression subsided. By the end of the summer of 1775, France looked much as it had before. Even most of those arrested gradually drifted back to resume their lives, leaving only a handful in the state's custody or wandering strange lands while their sentences of banishment ran out. As a traditional food riot, the Flour War had run its traditional course, joining previous popular movements in the collective memory of the people. Yet traditional did not mean unchanging.

The Flour War reflected the larger processes of transition within Ancien Régime society by containing within itself changes of both scale and scope. By locating it in the specific historical conjuncture of the development of capitalism in the context of still-dynamic feudal structures, the centralization of the state and its shifting subsistence policies, social changes that included a widening economic and cultural gap between the haves and have-nots, and the ongoing process of adjusting relations of power to meet all this, we can see how it compared with previous and subsequent food riots and how it fit into the larger sphere of the evolution of French society. The Flour War manifested modalities of behavior and participation that coincided with the nature of development in the Paris Basin by 1775.

The marketplace continued to serve as the nexus of collective action in 1775, just as it had in 1630, but its centrality diminished as the structure of the provisioning trade changed. As merchants and producers bypassed the *halle* to sell directly from private granaries scattered throughout towns or on farms, food rioters likewise diversified their activities. Flour War rioters still stopped barges and carts transporting grain and flour along the provisioning routes of the Paris Basin, but they also engaged in frequent preemptive *entraves* that commandeered grain as it rested in storage room and granary. Urban consumers continued to dominate the provisioning process by demanding marketplace sales, requisitioning the stocks of cultivators, and closing city gates to rural consumers; however, rural consumers had begun to battle this urban imperialism by, among other things, requisitioning for themselves the stocks of the surplus-producing rural cultivators.

The common people *(menu peuple)* formed the overwhelming majority of rioters and leaders of the Flour War, just as they had over the previous century and a half. But this was a more proletarianized, more economically dependent segment of the common people than had existed to make food riots in the seventeenth and early eighteenth centuries. Elites—urban and rural property-owners and local notables—could still be found to take the more vulnerable consumer's side during the Flour War, but ever more had turned against the common people out of real fear for their property or, more abstractly, to embrace the principles of Physiocracy. Women still played central roles in food riots, especially in marketplace disturbances, but men increased and expanded their participation, not simply in the marketplace but also in the country confrontations—those hundreds of incidents in the farms of large-scale cultivators and the tenant farmers of the privileged—where they formed the most numerous and dynamic group.

The year 1775 thus witnessed a still largely traditional marketplace food riot dominated by women of the common people, on the one hand, as well as a growing rural component dominated by wage-laboring and marginal peasant men, on the other hand. The more familiar type of marketplace behavior and participation occurred most frequently outside the surplus-grain-producing *pays de grande culture* in the parts of the Paris Basin that imported grain or fed the consumers with local products. The countryside behavior and participation characterized the regions most intensely developed for commercial agriculture. In between these two types of behavior lay greater variety of participation.

These variations in behavior and participation resulted from variations in the communities that subsistence crises could mobilize, and these communities resulted from specific historical developments. Indeed, subsistence crises simultaneously called forth multiple communities of different but intersecting constructions. Although all those who rioted—as well as some merchants, producers, and authorities who supported the crowd—adhered more or less strongly to the vision of a collective responsibility for public welfare that included ensuring that everyone had sufficient and accessible food (the "moral economy of the crowd"), the catalyzing forces behind riot participation, as well as the social networks activated for collective action, varied considerably. Motives ranged from outright need, to personal advancement, to personal vendettas, to a general hatred of the bastions of Ancien Régime power in its many forms. When they took collective action, food rioters also drew on multiple overlapping social networks forged in concrete contexts. Bonds derived from historical experiences (such as patronage), geographical/neighborhood relations, occupation, and gender formed the most cohesive material from which riots were forged. In 1775, women and men tended to form separate networks in which occupation and neighborhood supplied the secondary but still powerful relationship.

The particular construction of the community or communities that confronted the subsistence crisis of 1775 varied considerably and depended on the nature of the relationship between the dominant and the dominated, as well as that between the dominant or the dominated themselves. In some places, common people and local notables—including seigneurs, their tenant farmers, and local officials—resolved the crisis without tumult when those who controlled the grain or its products functioned in classic paternalist roles to alleviate popular distress through charity or mediation. In other places, violence erupted when local notables abdicated what the people considered their collective responsibility in order to defend the interests of private property. In still other places, local officials and notables turned against each other, or the common people fragmented into opposing camps. While peculiarities of personalities and personal relations certainly played their roles in some types of behavior, the course of economic and social development in the Paris Basin, as well as the dictates of royal policy, had by 1775 made peaceful resolution of the paternalist type an increasingly unlikely outcome.

In pre-Revolutionary France, food rioters played numerous political roles. The Flour War constituted an episode in the political construction of a society adjusting to transformations. The riots of 1775, like those of the 1760s, delivered a trenchant critique of liberalization and opened royal policy to public scrutiny. But the public in 1775 did not directly include the

people, although their riots helped to focus attention of ministers, Parlements, agricultural societies, chambers of commerce, intellectuals, and local
administrators who examined and debated the proper role of the state in the
economy in general and the grain trade in particular.[1] The 1760s and 1770s
witnessed a formidable flow of pamphlets, articles, and treatises on the
subject of physiocratic reform.[2] The period stretching from Turgot's accession
as controller general to the Flour War rocked in a flood of debate. The issue
of liberalization crossed intellectual and political boundaries. It polarized
the philosophes and alienated other potential friends of the Enlightenment.
While its supporters included Dupont de Nemours, Condorcet, Abbé
Morellet, and Mirabeau, resistance to free trade united Diderot, Grimm,
Abbé Galiani, and Necker. Voltaire vacillated over the issue but largely
supported liberalization. Turgot, of course, although never actually a Physi-
ocrat himself, symbolized the cause in the 1770s.

Liberalization also resurrected the specter of conflict between members of
the Parlements and the monarch.[3] Still covetous and careful of their newly
restored powers after their unhappy encounters with Maupeou's reforms, the
Parlements of Paris and Rouen hesitated before the free-trade judgment.
Clearly torn over the issue, the Parisian court registered the legislation only
reluctantly. It accompanied its ratification with a statement imploring the
king to look after the "daily subsistence" of his subjects, an exhortation for
action that was anathema to the spirit as well as the letter of the judgment.
The Paris magistrates protested more aggressively during the Flour War itself,
when they discovered that Turgot had ordered the prévôtal courts to exercise
summary justice in the prosecution of rioters. The king was ultimately forced
to resort to a *lit de justice* to enforce compliance.[4]

The Rouen Parlement showed itself even more reluctant. During the first
liberal experiment, the magistrates had swung from support to open hostility

1. The most important contribution to royal policy on the subsistence issue before Louis XVI's
reign is Steven Kaplan, *Bread, Politics, and Political Economy in the Reign of Louis XV*, 2 vols. (The
Hague, 1976).

2. See Georges Weulersse, *La Physiocratie sous les ministères de Turgot et de Necker (1774–1781)*
(Paris, 1950), pp. 3–35; Kaplan, *Bread*, 1:97–124, 2:590–612; Elizabeth Fox-Genovese, *The Origins
of Physiocracy: Economic Revolution and Social Order in Eighteenth-Century France* (Ithaca, N.Y.,
1976), pp. 64–67.

3. See Kaplan, *Bread*, 2:410–17, 513–15, 520–26; Edgar Faure, *La Disgrâce de Turgot* (Paris,
1961), pp. 223–24; Bailey Stone, *The Parlement of Paris, 1774–1789* (Chapel Hill, N.C., 1981),
pp. 130–33.

4. See Gustave Schelle, ed., *Oeuvres de Turgot*, 4:420–26; Jules Flammermont, ed., *Les
Remonstrances du Parlement de Paris au XVIIIe siècle* (Paris, 1888–98), 3:267–73; "Blés-Emeute
(1775)," Papiers du Président de Lamoignon, BN, ms. français 6877.

to free trade. In 1774–75 they clung to their last stance. The court accompanied its delayed ratification of the judgment with a modification that undermined the reform. The Rouenais magistrates announced that they expected the "police within its jurisdiction to continue, as in the past, to assure that the markets were sufficiently provisioned with grain." The Conseil d'Etat annulled the stipulation soon after its publication.

Both Parlements, stinging from their earlier humiliation by Maupeou, still managed to find ways to demonstrate their resistance to liberalization and to pronounce their special concern for public welfare. Although they buckled to royal will by registering his judgment, they assumed a wait-and-see posture that permitted them to disassociate themselves from royal policy without appearing to obstruct it. When Turgot denied the courts jurisdiction over the prosecution of rioters after the Flour War, he removed an opportunity for the magistrates to bludgeon the government with the repercussions of its legislation. But he also saved them from having to compromise their avowed support for the little people by wielding the arm of justice against them. After all, the magistrates were in an ambiguous position. Hostile to popular disorder under any circumstances, significant landed proprietors in their own right, and in this case potential proprietors of farms and grain raided during the Flour War, they could not have looked lightly on such flagrant attacks on property and order.

From their vantage point above the fray, the courts could look compassionately at the connection between misery and revolt and between liberalization and economic dislocation. They could point to the Flour War as symptomatic of the incompatibility of free trade and public welfare. On 4 May, in its protest over its loss of jurisdiction to the prévôtal courts, the Parlement of Paris supplicated the king "to take measures, inspired by his prudence and love for his subjects, to lower the price of grain and bread to a level proportionate to the needs of the people."[5] The Flour War, like the episodes of the 1760s and early 1770s before it, thus served as a basis for a critique of national policy. On 6 May the Parlement promised "never to stop representing [to the king] the needs of his subjects and soliciting from him all the care possible."[6] As the Parlement of Paris proclaimed less than a year after the rioting:

> A popular movement becomes a popular riot, and then the instruments of suppression must come into play to restore law and order,

5. Flammermont, *Les Remonstrances*, 3:268–69.
6. Ibid., pp. 272–73.

a law and order that would always be best guaranteed by the constant and vigilant authority of the law.

It was, Sire, because they had weighed these drawbacks that our fathers multiplied precautionary measures in the interior of our cities; they regarded need as the primary force moving all men. . . . One does not reason about necessity, for it involves one's own existence.[7]

In 1775 Turgot stood at the center of controversy, for liberalization had become a national issue of tremendous political importance, and the resulting politicization and nationalization of the subsistence question was a phenomenon for which the royal government was largely responsible. Subsistence crises increasingly resonated on a national scale. Louis XVI even considered reducing the costs of his coronation ceremony at Reims and other royal celebrations to help "those of my subjects who were victims of the seditious rioters."[8] The Flour War stood as one part of an ongoing process that increasingly subjected royal policy to public scrutiny, on the subsistence issue or a growing number of other concerns. That process would accelerate in the next decade and a half.

But behavior in 1775 did not only demonstrate a clash of two world views—one the popular "moral economy" and the other the up-and-coming physiocratic vision of laissez faire—or even a struggle between those who had grain (the powerful elite) and those who did not (the powerless masses). More important for those outside the bastions of "high politics," subsistence crises also tested relations of authority and power by testing membership in the community, a situation that applied to elites and common people alike. When rioters signaled to local authorities, to merchants in the marketplace, to fermiers and laboureurs in the countryside, or to seigneurs (secular and ecclesiastical alike) that again the time had come to shoulder their collective responsibilities, they tested the nature of local power relations. Recourse to violence exposed the asymmetry of relations and drove the holders of power to rely on overt force to maintain their positions, to find new ground on which to stand, and to seek new groups as allies.

Because study of food riots like the Flour War so effectively enlarges our understanding of such complex facets of past societies, the thirty-year-old

7. Ibid., pp. 300–301; also cited in Stone, *Parlement of Paris*, p. 134.
8. "Lettre de Louis XVI au Duc de la Vrillière (31 mai)." He was ultimately dissuaded. "Lettre de M. le Marquis de Dreux (23 juin)" and "Lettre de M. de la Michodière (23 juin)," AN, H2* 1876.

project of studying them, inspired by Rudé, Cobb, Thompson, and others, continues. Not only do food riots attract the interest of those who are preoccupied with the history of popular "events," they also link concerns with the history of *mentalités*, economic development, social change, and politics. They lend themselves to comparative study, for many other countries in Europe and as far away as Japan have experienced similar convulsions.[9] Yet, as I have attempted to show for France, food riots were also products of specific historical developments, national as well as local, which merit more detailed analysis for the light they can shed on how people in a particular time and place lived and responded to the world around them.

Many phenomena, of course, remain unexplained; many questions remain unanswered, or only partially answered. These include, for example, questions about the incidence of food rioting, the relationship between food rioting and state formation, or the linkages between food rioting and the creation of popular political consciousness on the eve of and during the Revolutionary period.

First, we need further study of the causes underlying the increasing frequency of subsistence disturbances from the end of the eighteenth century through the Revolutionary period. The team headed by Jean Nicolas and Guy Lemarchand documented 652 riots between 1760 and 1789, and John Markoff identified more than 1,200 between 1788 and 1793.[10] I have argued that the general elements of the "moral economy" prevailed among common people in Early Modern France (and I believe into the nineteenth century), as it had among the English rioters studied by E. P. Thompson. But this cultural umbrella only establishes the context for food rioting. Shared "moral economic" assumptions did not detonate food riots. Rather, clashes between different approaches to the grain trade and subsistence crises did. My work suggests that changing socioeconomic and political structures helped create a context that increased the probability of subsistence rioting. Furthermore, not only did the number of food consumers increase over the

9. Such a comparative study for France, Great Britain, and Germany is currently under way and funded in part by a Council for European Studies Research Planning Group grant that involves my own further research on France, John Bohstedt's contributions for Great Britain, and Manfred Gailus's work on Germany. On Japan, see James W. White, "Rational Rioters: Leaders, Followers, and Popular Protest in Early Modern Japan," *Economic Development and Cultural Change*, Jan. 1989, pp. 35–69.

10. Guy Lemarchand, "Troubles populaires au XVIIIe siècle et conscience de classe: Une Préface à la Révolution française," *AHRF* 279 (Jan.–Mar. 1990): 34–35; John Markoff, "When and How Did the Countryside Revolt? A Statistical Study of Revolutionary France, 1788–1793" (Paper presented to the Western Society for French History, Reno, 1991).

course of the century—consumers who were sensitive to fluctuations in the price of all necessities and especially grain—but the trade also itself changed. More and more grain passed not through the marketplace but instead directly into the hands of large-scale middlemen.[11] The king's commitment to market regulation vacillated frequently, and changes in local intervention occurred often.

Other factors, however, may have affected the frequency and geography of rioting. British historian R. B. Outhwaite has suggested that food rioting might also be an example of "learned" as much as "spontaneous" behavior. By "learned behavior," he does not mean some response dictated from above, but rather information passed on via channels of commerce and communication—a type of "contagion" spread not only over space but also across time.[12] This may help to explain why some places became veritable hotbeds of food rioting. For example, Caen experienced food rioting nine times between 1631 (one of the earliest recorded eruptions anywhere in France) and 1725, Marseille witnessed seven outbreaks between 1709 and 1789 (with six eruptions in the second half of the century), Rouen generated twelve between 1693 and 1784 (with ten after mid-century), Toulouse saw nine, and such towns as Vernon (in Normandy), Troyes, and Nevers experienced six.[13] News of the success of rioting in one place clearly encouraged eruptions elsewhere and became part of collective memory. Thus, we need further research on the role of improved and more heavily utilized transportation and communication networks in facilitating the spread of rioting, while clashes over moral economic assumptions and changing social, economic, and political relations (which also benefited from the same improvements) established the context.

A second question involves the relationship between grain warfare and state formation. As we have seen, the king increasingly associated himself and his role with the subsistence question. Moreover, the subsistence issue increasingly called forth a response from the state at the national as well as local level. Earlier food riots engaged authority locally. Local elites relied on

11. Although the people and some authorities believed strongly that this resulted in a reduction of grain for sale at the marketplace, this has yet to be shown. It may, in fact, be impossible to document, because the vagaries of quantities of sales in individual markets depended on many things, including changing seigneurial obligations and challenges from other markets.

12. R. B. Outhwaite, *Dearth, Public Policy, and Social Disturbance in England, 1550–1800* (London, 1991), p. 53.

13. There is a potential bias in reporting here. Other towns may have experienced even more riots but been neglected by historians. Nevertheless, this does not negate the fact that there were repeated incidences of rioting.

negotiation, the *milice bourgeoise*, and the maréchaussée to resolve local subsistence crises.[14] Yet just as royal intervention increasingly elevated the subsistence issue to a national concern, so too did food rioting focus national repression. After the 1747 riots in Toulouse, royal troops "became an important factor in the pacification of the urban populace."[15] The Flour War not only witnessed widespread rioting throughout the Paris Basin but also brought massive repression that relied heavily on royal troops. The deployment of 25,000 troops accompanied the arrest, interrogation, and sentencing of hundreds of suspects. Troops remained stationed in the towns of the Paris regions until November to enforce the king's peace. All this constituted state intervention on a significant scale, since troops never billeted anywhere without provoking other tensions.

We need to know more about how this process of state intervention into both the policies of provisioning and the management of provisioning crises resonated at both the national and local levels. The deployment of troops— also used during the antitax rebellions of the seventeenth century—signified not only royal power but also local weakness and mounting disorder from below. Local elites desperately requested army assistance to suppress unrest, but they also recognized that the presence of troops threatened local autonomy. Food riots may therefore have played a crucial role in furthering and shaping absolutism in the late seventeenth and eighteenth centuries.

Third, we need to know more about how grain warfare resonated in the pre-Revolutionary crisis and what role it played in the making of popular political consciousness. As we have seen, in 1775, some rioters clearly associated the king with the subsistence issue, while many others did not (or at least did not leave a written record). The subsistence question in the mind of the common people, was linked not only to the conduct of the grain trade but also to the contours of grain production, property rights, and power relations. But they continued to cast these largely in a local context. In 1789, in the midst of a serious subsistence crisis, cahier after cahier declared subsistence a paramount national concern. By the Revolutionary period, the common people had come to interpellate frequently not just

14. Indeed, Robert Schneider suggests that food rioting caused such towns as Toulouse to augment the size and expand the powers of local militia. See Schneider, *Public Life in Toulouse, 1463–1789: From Municipal Republic to Cosmopolitan City* (Ithaca, N.Y., 1989), pp. 318–20, and a personal communication of October 1991. See also Gregory W. Monahan, "Lyon in the Crisis of 1709: Royal Absolutism, Administrative Innovation, and Regional Politics," *FSH* 16 (Fall 1990): 833–48.

15. Schneider, *Public Life in Toulouse*, p. 321.

local authority but also ministerial, Parlementary, and even royal authority
(and eventually the Revolutionary governments themselves).

We still only vaguely understand the ways in which this transformation in
popular political consciousness took place. The Flour War suggests that the
debates over provisioning policies, national interest, and sovereignty had
not yet become a matter of open debate among the common people of Paris
or of the provinces. The pre-Revolutionary and Revolutionary crises indicate, however, that at some point the types of disaffection from local
authorities in place that characterized food rioting of earlier periods had
developed further into disillusionment and dissatisfaction with national
authority. Further study of the period between 1775 and 1789, and even
beyond, may better explain how the common people got caught up in the
confrontations that dominated more elite circles.

Moreover, food rioting contributed to creating a new conception of
property. Moral economic assumptions accepted and supported the existence
of property rights, but qualified those rights when they clashed with what
they saw as a superseding right to accessible, affordable subsistence. Over
time, those with property in grain and its products defended more overtly
and aggressively a less malleable vision of absolute private property that
denied social claims on grain regardless of the circumstances. Subsistence
rioting contributed greatly to the emergence of increasing numbers of
defectors from the moral economic position who eschewed even the trap-
pings of paternalist responsibilities. This process of defining absolute private
property rights was lengthy, took place in many arenas, and contributed to
defining property rights in particular and bourgeois class-consciousness in
general.

Such a combination of conclusions, together with an agenda for further
study, itself constitutes one of the logical outcomes of research in such
fruitful areas as subsistence crises and their attendant eruptions. These
turbulences exposed relations of power in their multiple, Ancien Régime
forms and created the context for forging or consolidating other such
relations in response to changes observed or suspected. Thus, through the
Flour War, for example, we can see that by the late eighteenth century the
pace of change in France had accelerated, with multiple consequences. On
the surface, the Flour War had ended in time-honored resolutions, but not
for long. Much more was to come, and soon.

By the time of the subsistence explosions of 1789, no one could predict
the course or outcome of popular rioting. Social tensions had not diminished
after 1775, the economic crisis of 1787–89 exceeded that of 1774–75 and

was far more widespread, and the national concerns involving debating and writing the *cahiers de doléances* and electing deputies to the Estates General had crystallized many issues. Some food riots became tangled in local politics of the pre-Revolutionary and early Revolutionary periods; many had become suffused with overt political concerns. Some Revolutionary food riots took antiseigneurial tones; others took a far more anticapitalist direction. In almost all cases, and increasingly so after 1789, the subsistence issue—still, as always, a burning local issue—carried national significance, now in the voices of the common people as well as elites. Food riots were not immutable, regressive popular rituals. Although they drew heavily on popular traditions of behavior, they were creative and adaptive. The Flour War showed how people modified behavior to create new strategies in response to changes in their world. The Revolution was to show that the process did not end in 1775.

APPENDIX 1
OCCUPATIONS OF ARRESTED RIOTERS

Rioter Occupations by Category: 548 total (455 men, 93 women)

Cat. 1: Unskilled Day-Laborers: 78 total (14.2 percent)
Among women: 4 *journaliers*, 8 *manouvriers*, 1 *servante*.
Among men: 1 *domestique*, 4 *journaliers*, 60 *manouvriers*.

Cat. 2: Semiskilled Laborers and Dependant Skilled Laborers: 88 total (16.1 percent)
Among women: 1 *compagnon/journalier*, 3 *fileuses de coton*, 1 *manouvrier/fripier*, 1 *garçon maréchal*, 1 *manouvrier/marchand de vaches*, 1 *scieur-de-pierres* (see Savary, *Dictionnaire de Commerce*, who claims that their status is more like *manouvriers* than *scieurs*), 1 *ouvrier/tailleur/pauvre*, 2 *manouvriers/vignerons*, 1 *porte-faix*.
Among men: 2 *batteurs-en-grange*, 1 *journalier/bedeau*, 1 *manouvrier/berger*, 1 *compagnon cordier*, 1 *compagnon cordonnier*, 4 *compagnons de la rivière*, 3 *compagnons maçons*, 1 *compagnon maréchal-ferrant*, 1 *compagnon menuisier*, 1 *compagnon salpêtrier*, 3 *compagnons scieurs-de-long*, 6 *compagnons sergers*, 1 *compagnon tanneur*, 1 *compagnon tisserand*, 6 *chartiers* employed by others, 1 *débardeur*, 1 *fils bûcheron* (13 years old), 1 *fils tabletier* (16 years old), 1 *garçon d'écurie*, 4 *garçons jardiniers*, 1 *garçon maréchal-ferrant*, 1 *garçon menuisier*, 1 *garçon taillandier*, 1

garçon vigneron, 1 *journalier/fileur*, 1 *journalier/tabletier*, 1 *journalier/vigneron*, 1 *manouvrier/batteur-en-grange*, 1 *manouvrier/evantailliste*, 1 *manouvrier/marchand d'harengs*, 1 *manouvrier/maçon*, 1 *manouvrier/scieur-de-long*, 1 *manouvrier/tabletier*, 1 *manouvrier/tambourinier*, 1 *manouvrier/terrassier*, 5 *ouvriers en laine*, 1 *ouvrier/ compagnon serger*, 1 *porte-sac*, 9 *porte-faix*, 1 *scieur-de-long* (employed in large shop), 1 *soldat*, 1 *terrassier*.

Cat. 3: Independent Artisans and Skilled Craftspeople: 80 total (14.6 percent)

Among women: 1 *boucher*, 1 *brasseur*, 1 *charron*, 1 *chaudronnier*, 3 *cordonniers*, 6 *tabletiers*, 1 *tailleur de pierre*, 1 *taillandier*, 2 *tisserands*, 1 *tonnelier*, 1 *scieur-de-long*.

Among men: 3 *bouchers*, 1 *bûcheron/terrassier*, 2 *bûcherons*, 2 *carriers-en-plâtre*, 2 *carriers*, 2 *chaudronniers*, 1 *cordonnier en vieux*, 6 *cordonniers*, 1 *couvreur en chaume*, 1 *fontenier*, 1 *maître perruquier*, 1 *maçon en plâtre*, 1 *maçon/cabaretier*, 1 *maçon/couvreur*, 7 *maçons*, 5 *maréchaux-ferrants*, 1 *menuisier*, 1 *paveur*, 1 *rémouleur*, 2 *sabotiers*, 4 *scieurs-de-long*, 4 *tabletiers*, 2 *tailleurs*, 5 *tisserands*, 2 *tonneliers*, 2 *tourneurs*.

Cat. 4: Merchants/Service: 30 total (5.5 percent)

Among women: 1 *coquetier*, 1 *fripier*, 1 *marchand de chevaux*, 1 *marchand de chevaux/cabaretier*, 1 *marchand de fagots*, 1 *marchand mercier*, 1 *voiturier*.

Among men: 1 *chiffonier*, 3 *coquetiers*, 1 *épicier*, 2 *fripiers*, 1 *marchand de boucles*, 1 *marchand d'eau de vie*, 1 *marchand de gallets*, 1 *marchand de poudre à tuer des rats*, 3 *marchands de vaches*, 1 *marchand de volaille*, 1 *maquignon*, 1 *pêcheur*, 1 *fripier/tailleur*, 4 *voituriers*.

Cat. 5: Innkeepers/Publicans: 9 total (1.6 percent)

Among women: 1 *aubergiste*, 1 *cabaretier*.

Among men: 4 *cabaretiers*, 1 *cabaretier/carrier*, 1 *cabaretier/charron*, 1 *cabaretier/ charpenteur*.

Cat. 6: Vine-Growers: 144 total (26.3 percent)

Among women: 16 *vignerons* arrested in Pontoise; 7 *vignerons* arrested elsewhere.

Among men: 73 *vignerons*, 2 *fils vignerons*, and 1 *vigneron/arpenteur* arrested in Pontoise; 48 *vignerons*, 2 *vignerons/cabaretiers*, 1 *vigneron/tisserand*, and 1 *vigneron/voiturier* arrested elsewhere.

Cat. 7: Rural Propertied Groups (except vine-growers): 7 total (1.3 percent)

Among women: 1 *fruitier/épicier*.

Among men: 1 *haricotier*, 2 *jardiniers*, 1 *laboureur*, 2 *laboureurs/voituriers*.

Cat. 8: Officials/Notables: 32 total (5.8 percent)

Among women: 1 *garde de chasse*, 1 *huissier*, 1 *maître d'école*.

Among men: 1 *commis des fermes abonnataires des droits d'inspection des boucheries*, 1 *conseiller du roi*, 7 *curés*, 1 *doyen des notaires et procureurs/lieutenant général de police*, 1 *garde messier*, 4 *gardes de chasse*, 1 *huissier*, 1 *maire*, 1 *maître d'école*, 1 *maître d'école/greffier*, 1 *notaire*, 1 *practicien*, 1 *procureur fiscal*, 1 *sergent au bailliage et duché de* Beaumont-du Gatinais, 2 *syndics*, 1 *syndic/manouvrier*, 1 *syndic/laboureur*, 1 *syndic/vannier*, 1 *syndic/vigneron*.

Cat. 9: Grain/Flour Merchants/Bakers/Millers (including employees): 17 total (3.1 percent)

Among women: 0.

Among men: 1 *ancien meunier*, 1 *ancien farinier*, 1 *blatier*, 3 *boulangers*, 1 *cabaretier/boulanger/charcutier*, 1 *facteur/measureur*, 8 *garçon meuniers*, 1 *meunier*.

Cat. 10: Others: 8 total (1.5 percent)

Among women: 1 *veuve d'ancien officier*, 1 *femme de suisse des tailles*.

Among men: 1 *canayeur*, 1 *marinier*, 1 *marleur*, 1 *menlier*, 1 *placier*, 1 *negociant* (from Dunkerque).

Cat. 11: Unknown: 55 total (10.0 percent)

Among women: 12.

Among men: 43.

APPENDIX 2
OCCUPATIONS OF RIOT LEADERS

Leader Occupations by Category: 86 total (70 men, 16 women)

Cat. 1: Unskilled Day-Laborers: 10 total (11.6 percent)
  Among women: 0.
  Among men: 8 *manouvriers*, 2 *journaliers*.

Cat. 2: Semiskilled Laborers and Dependent Skilled Laborers: 29 total (33.7 percent)
  Among women: 1 *compagnon maçon*, 1 *manouvrier/marchand de vaches*, 2 *fileuses*.
  Among men: 4 *compagnons de la rivière*, 4 *compagnons sergers*, 2 *compagnons maçons*, 1 *garçon jardinier*, 1 *garçon maréchal ferrant*, 1 *manouvrier/bûcheron*, 1 *manouvrier/tabletier*, 1 *manouvrier/tambourinier*, 4 *ouvriers en laine*, 5 *portefaix*, 1 *tabletier/garçon écurie/journalier*.

Cat. 3: Independent Artisans and Skilled Craftspeople: 13 total (16.3 percent)
  Among women: 1 *dentellière/ancien maître d'école*.
  Among men: 1 *boucher*, 1 *carrier-en-plâtre*, 2 *cordonniers*, 1 *maçon*, 2 *maréchaux-ferrants*, 2 *sabotiers*, 1 *tabletier*, 1 *tailleur*, 2 *tisserands*.

Cat. 4: Merchants/Service: 6 total (7 percent)
   Among women: 1 *coquetier*, 1 *fripier*, 1 *marchand de fagots*.
   Among men: 1 *chiffonnier*, 1 *coquetier*, 1 *marchand de boucles*.

Cat. 5: Innkeepers/Publicans: 3 total (3.5 percent)
   Among women: 0.
   Among men: 1 *cabaretier*, 1 *cabaretier/ancien boulanger*, 1 *cabaretier/vigneron*.

Cat. 6: Vignerons: 6 total (7 percent)
   Among women: 4 *vignerons*.
   Among men: 2 *vignerons*.

Cat. 7: Other Propertied Groups (e.g., *vignerons*): 0

Cat. 8: Officials/Notables: 5 total (5.8 percent)
   Among women: 1 *ancien garde de chasse*.
   Among men: 1 *commis*, 1 *garde de chasse*, 1 *syndic/manouvrier*, 1 *syndic/vannier*.

Cat. 9: Grain/Flour Merchants/Bakers/Millers (including employees): 3 total (3.5 percent)
   Among women: 0.
   Among men: 3 *garçons meuniers*.

Cat. 10: Other: 1 total (1.2 percent)
   Among women: 0.
   Among men: 1 *canayer*.

Cat. 11: Unknown: 9 total (10.5 percent)
   Among women: 2.
   Among men: 7.

APPENDIX 3
TYPE OF ACTION AND OCCUPATION

	Occupations	Types 1 & 2	Type 3	Type 4
1.	Unskilled day-laborers	21 M. (8.6%)	2 M. (11.8%)	32 M. (25.2%)
		7 W. (9.5%)	2 W. (28.6%)	3 W. (33.3%)
2.	Semiskilled & dependent	51 M. (20.9%)	0 M. (0.0%)	24 M. (18.9%)
	skilled day-laborers	10 W. (13.5%)	0 W. (0.0%)	1 W. (11.1%)
3.	Artisans/independent crafts	28 M. (11.5%)	6 M. (35.3%)	19 M. (15.0%)
	(except milling, baking,	16 W. (21.6%)	2 W. (28.6%)	0 W. (0.0%)
	etc.)			
4.	Merchants/service (except	10 M. (4.1%)	5 M. (29.4%)	6 M. (4.7%)
	grain/flour merchants, etc.)	6 W. (8.1%)	0 W. (0.0%)	0 W. (0.0%)
5.	Innkeepers/publicans	3 M. (1.2%)	0 M. (0.0%)	3 M. (2.4%)
		2 W. (2.7%)	0 W. (0.0%)	0 W. (0.0%)
6.	Vine-growers	73 M. (29.9%)	1 M. (5.9%)	24 M. (18.9%)
		16 W. (21.6%)	0 W. (0.0%)	1 W. (11.1%)
	Pontoise	22 M. (9.0%)		
	Elsewhere	6 W. (8.1%)		
7.	Rural "propertied" groups	3 M. (1.2%)	1 M. (5.9%)	1 M. (0.8%)
	(except vine-growers)	0 W. (0.0%)	1 W. (14.3%)	0 W. (0.0%)
8.	Officials/notables	8 M. (3.3%)	0 M. (0.0%)	8 M. (6.2%)
		3 W. (4.1%)	0 W. (0.0%)	0 W. (0.0%)
9.	Grain/flour traders bakers/	14 M. (5.3%)	2 M. (11.8%)	2 M. (1.6%)
	millers (including	0 W. (0.0%)	0 W. (0.0%)	0 W. (0.0%)
	their workers)			
10.	Others	3 M. (1.2%)	0 M. (0.0%)	2 M. (1.6%)
		2 W. (2.7%)	0 W. (0.0%)	0 W. (0.0%)
11.	Unknown	8 M. (3.3%)	0 M. (0.0%)	6 M. (4.7%)
		6 W. (8.1%)	2 W. (28.6%)	4 W. (44.4%)
Totals		244 M. (99.5%)	17 M. (100.1%)	127 M. (100.0%)
		74 W. (100.0%)	7 W. (100.1%)	9 W. (99.9%)
		318 TOTAL	24 TOTAL	136 TOTAL

This appendix correlates the number and percentage of men (M) and women (W) arrested and their occupations (by category) with the type of action in which they participated. A total of 478 men and women participated in one of the four types of action described in Chapter 4. Seventy other people were involved in other forms of actions, such as failure to make restitution (but there was no information about where the original action occurred) or misfeasance and malfeasance by local notables.

BIBLIOGRAPHY

UNPUBLISHED PRIMARY SOURCES

Departmental Archives

I consulted thirteen departmental archives (listed below). Series B (Cours et juridictions) and Series C (Administrations provincials) formed the backbone of my sources in these archives. Series B contains the arrest and interrogation records compiled by the maréchaussée and executed by the courts, the testimonies of witnesses and victims (*informations* and *dépositions*), the *procès-verbaux* of the police, and various other decisions having to do with the repression. Series C contains administrative correspondence between all levels of Ancien Régime officialdom (royal and local), tax records of the *taille* and the *vingtième* as well as other taxes, and responses to *enquêtes* conducted by the controller general and intendants. In several archives I also consulted sources in Series J (which contained seigneurial records) and Series G and H (ecclesiastical records). Detailed citations are in the notes for each chapter. The thirteen departmental archives consulted are:

> Archives départementales de l'Aisne (Laon)
> Archives départementales de l'Aube (Troyes)

Archives départementales de Calvados (Caen)
Archives départementales de l'Eure (Evreux)
Archives départementales de l'Eure-et-Loir (Chartres)
Archives départementales de Marne (Châlons-sur-Marne)
Archives départementales de l'Oise (Beauvais)
Archives départementales de l'Orne (Alençon)
Archives départementales de Seine-et-Marne (Melun)
Archives départementales de Seine-Maritime (Rouen)
Archives départementales de Somme (Amiens)
Archives départementales de Yonne (Auxerre)
Archives départementales des Yvelines (Versailles)

Archives Nationales

Series E: Arrêts du Conseil du Roi: Reign de Louis XVI
Series F: Especially F10, Agriculture; F11, Subsistances; and F12, Commerce et Industrie
Series H: Administrations locales et comptabilités diverses: Especially H*2, Délibérations de Bureau de la Ville de Paris; H2, Correspondance avec le Ministre
Series K: Monuments historiques: Especially Ville de Paris
Series O: Maison du Roi: Especially O*, Lettres du Ministre de la Maison du Roi
Series Y: Châtelet de Paris; Brouillon des Archives de la Bastille; Prévôté de l'Ile-de-France; papiers des commissaires de police
Series Z: Juridictions spéciales et ordinaires. Especially Z1C, Connétablie et Maréchaussée de France; Z1G, Rôles de la Taille pour l'Election de Paris

Archives de la Préfecture de Police

Series AB: Registres de la Province, Registres de la Conciergerie, Registres du Grand Châtelet

Bibliothèque Nationale

Collection Joly de Fleury: Collection of administrative correspondence. Especially vol. 1159 (for year 1775).
Fonds français 6680–6687: Hardy, Simeon-Proper. *Mes Loisirs, ou Journal des événements tel qu'il parviennent à ma connaissance (1764–1789)*, 8 vols. Especially vols. 6681–6682.

Fonds français 6877–79: Personal papers of President Chrétien François II de Lamoignon de Basville.

Bibliothèque de l'Arsenal

Archives de la Bastille: Correspondance, Interrogatoires.

Bibliothèque municipale de Beauvais

Collection Bucquet: Especially vol. 82 on the Beauvaisis in 1775.

PRINTED PRIMARY SOURCES

Almanach royal, année M DCC LXXV présenté à Sa Majesté. Paris: Le Breton, 1775.

L'Ami du peuple français ou mémoire addressé à M. Turgot contrôleur des finances (par le fils d'un laboureur). Paris: Editions d'histoire sociale, 1976.

Bachaumont, Louis Petit de. *Mémoires secrets pour servir à l'histoire de la République des lettres en France depuis 1762 jusqu'à nos jours, ou Journal d'un observateur*, 30 vols. London: J. Adamson, 1780–86.

Boislisle, Arthur Michel de, ed. *Correspondance des contrôleurs généraux des finances avec les intendants des provinces*, 3 vols. Paris: Imprimerie nationale, 1874–97.

Bouloiseau, Marc, ed. *Cahiers de doléances du Tiers Etat du Bailliage de Rouen pour les Etats généraux de 1789*. Paris and Rouen: PUF and Imprimerie administrative de la Seine-Maritime, 1957, 1960.

Bouloiseau, Marc, and Philippe Boudin, eds. *Cahiers de doléances du Tiers Etat du Bailliage d'Andely*. Rouen: N.p., 1974.

Bouloiseau, Marc, and Bernard Chéronnet, eds. *Cahiers de doléances du Tiers Etat du Bailliage de Gisors pour les Etats généraux de 1789*. Paris: Bibliothèque nationale, 1971.

Brette, Armand, ed. *Recueil de documents relatifs à la convocation des Etats généraux de 1789*, 4 vols. Paris: Imprimerie nationale, 1894–1915.

Charpentier. *La Bastille dévoilée*, 9 vols. Paris: Desenne, 1789.

La Chronique villageoise de Varreddes. Une Document sur la vie rurale des XVIIe et XVIIIe siècles, ed. J.-M. Desbordes. Paris: Editions de l'Ecole, n.d.

Couard, E., and F. Lorin, eds. *Bailliage royal de Monfort en 1789*, vol. 16, *Mémoires de la Société archéologique de Rambouillet*. Versailles: Aubert, 1903.

Delamarre, Nicolas. *Traité de la police*, 4 vols., 2nd ed. Amsterdam, 1729.

Des Essarts, Nicolas-Toussaint Lemoyne. *Dictionnaire universel de police*, 7 vols. Paris: Moutard, 1786–1790.

Diderot, Denis, et al. *Encyclopédie, ou Dictionnaire raisonné des sciences, des arts et des metiers*, 45 vols., new ed. Geneva: Pellet, 1777–79.

Dufort, Jean-Nicolas, comte de Cheverny. *Mémoires sur les règnes de Louis XV et Louis XVI et sur la révolution*, ed. Robert de Crevecoeur, 2 vols. Paris: E. Plon, Nourrit & Cie, 1886.

Dumay, Gabriel, ed. *Une Emeute à Dijon en 1775, suivie d'une ode à Monseigneur d'Apchon*. Dijon: Darantière, 1886.

Dupâquier, Jacques. *Ainsi commença la Révolution . . . Campagne électorale et cahiers de doléances de 1789 dans les Bailliages de Chaumont-en-Vexin et Magny-en-Vexin.* Pontoise: Société historique et archéologique de Pontoise, du Val-d'Oise et du Vexin, 1989.

———. *Ainsi commença la Révolution . . . Campagne électorale et cahiers de doléances de 1789 dans le Bailliage de Pontoise.* Pontoise: Société historique et archéologique de Pontoise, du Val-d'Oise et du Vexin, 1990.

Flammermont, Jules, ed. *Les Remonstrances du Parlement de Paris au XVIIIe siècle,* 3 vols. Paris: Imprimerie nationale, 1888–98.

Georgel, J.-F., abbé. *Mémoires pour servir à l'histoire des événemens de la fin du dix-huitième siècle,* 6 vols. Paris: A. Eymery, 1817–18.

Isambert, François André, et al., eds. *Recueil général des anciennes lois françaises depuis l'an 420 jusqu'à la révolution de 1789,* 29 vols. Paris: Belin-LePrieur, 1822–33.

Laurent, Gustave. *Cahiers de doléances pour les Etats généraux de 1789,* vol. 1, *Bailliage de Châlons-sur-Marne;* vol. 4, *Bailliage de Reims.* Epernay: Henri Villers, 1906; Reims: Matot-Braine, 1930.

Lenoir, Jean-Charles-Pierre. "Essai sur la guerre des farines: Le Lieutenant de police J.-P. Lenoir, la guerre des farines et l'approvisionnement de Paris à la veille de la Révolution," ed. Robert Darnton. RHMC 16 (Oct.–Dec. 1969): 611–24.

———. "The Memoirs of Lenoir, lieutenant of police of Paris, 1774–1785," ed. Robert Darnton. *English Historical Review* 85 (July 1970): 532–59.

Le Parquier, E., ed. *Cahiers de doléances des paroisses du Bailliage de Neufchâtel-en-Bray, secondaire du Bailliage de Caux (1789).* Rouen: Cagniard, 1908.

Linguet, Simon-Nicolas-Henri. *Canaux navigables, ou Développement des avantages qui résulteraient de l'exécution de plusieurs projets en ce genre pour la Picardie, l'Artois, la Bourgogne, la Champagne, la Bretagne.* Paris: L. Cellot, 1769.

Lorain, Ch. *Les Subsistances en céréales dans le district de Chaumont de 1788 à l'An V: Documents publiés,* 2 vols. Chaumont: R. Cavaniol, 1911.

Mallet, Ernest, ed. *Les Elections du Bailliage secondaire de Pontoise en 1789 comprenant: . . . Les Cahiers des assemblées des corporations de la ville de Pontoise, des communautés et paroisses du ressort.* Pontoise: Bureau de la société historique, 1919.

Marmontel, Jean-François. *Mémoires de Marmontel,* ed. Maurice Tourneux, 3 vols. Paris: Librairie des bibliophiles, 1891.

Mavidal, M. J., and M. E. Laurent, eds. *Archives parlementaires de 1787 à 1860,* vol. 4, *Etats généraux—cahiers des sénéchaussées et bailliages.* 1879. Reprint, Nendeln/Liechtenstein: Klaus, 1969.

Mercier, Louis-Sébastien. *Le Tableau de Paris,* 12 vols. Amsterdam: N.p., 1782–88.

Métra, François. *Correspondance secrète, politique et littéraire, ou mémoires pour servir à l'histoire des cours, des sociétés et de la littérature en France depuis la mort de Louis XV,* 18 vols. London: J. Adamson, 1787–90.

Moreau, Jacob-Nicolas. *Mes Souvenirs,* ed. Camille Hermelin, 2 vols. Paris: E. Plon, Nourrit & Cie, 1898–1901.

Morellet, André, abbé. *Analyse de l'ouvrage intitulé: "De la législation et du commerce des grains."* Paris: Pissot, 1775.

Nougaret, P.-J.-B. *Anecdotes du règne de Louis XVI (1774–1776).* Paris: J.-F. Bastien, 1776.

Nouvelles éphémérides économiques, ou bibliothèque raisonnée de l'histoire, de la morale, et de la politique. Paris, 1774–76.

Pidansat de Mairobert, Mathieu-François. *Journal historique de la révolution opérée dans la constitution de la monarchie françoise,* 7 vols. London: N.p., 1774–76.

Porée, Charles, ed. *Cahiers de doléances du Bailliage de Sens pour les Etats généraux de 1789.* Auxerre: Imprimerie coopérative ouvrière, 1908.

Restif de la Bretonne, Nicolas-Edme. *Les Nuits de Paris,* ed. Henri Bachelin. Paris: Editions du Trianon, 1930.

Ségur, Louis Philippe, comte de. *Mémoires, ou souvenirs et anecdotes,* 2 vols. Paris: A. Eymery, 1827.

Soulavie, Jean-Louis. *Mémoires historiques et politiques sur le règne de Louis XVI,* 6 vols. Paris: Treuttel & Wurtx, 1801.

Terray, Abbé. *Mémoires de l'abbé Terray, contrôleur-général de finance avec une relation de l'émeute arrivée à Paris en 1775,* ed. Jean-Baptiste-Louis Coquereau. London and Paris, 1776.

Thénard, M. *Bailliages de Versailles et de Meudon. Les Cahiers des paroisses.* Versailles: E. Aubert, 1889.

Turgot, Anne-Robert-Jacques. *Oeuvres de Turgot et documents le concernant,* ed. Gustave Schelle, 5 vols. Glashutten im Taunus: Detlev Auvermann KG, 1972.

Véri, Joseph-Alphonse, abbé de. *Journal de l'abbé de Véri,* ed. Baron Jehan de Witte, 2 vols. Paris: J. Tallandier, 1928–30.

Vernier, J.-J., ed. *Cahiers de doléances du Bailliage de Troyes et du Bailliage de Bar-sur-Seine pour les Etats généraux de 1789,* 3 vols. Troyes: P. Nouel, 1909–10.

Young, Arthur. *Travels in France During the Years 1787, 1788, and 1789,* ed. Jeffry Kaplow. Garden City, N.Y.: Doubleday, 1969.

BIBLIOGRAPHY OF STUDIES OF FRENCH SUBSISTENCE MOVEMENTS

Beauroy, Jacques. "The Pre-Revolutionary Crises in Bergerac, 1770–1789." In *Proceedings of the First Annual Meeting of the Western Society for French History, March 1974,* pp. 75–97.

Bercé, Yves-Marie. *Revolt and Revolution in Early Modern Europe: An Essay on the History of Political Violence,* trans. J. Bergin. New York: St. Martin's Press, 1987.

Blin, Léon. "La Face administrative d'une crise frumentaire en Bourgogne, 1747–1749." *Annales de Bourgogne* 189 (Jan.–Mar. 1976): 5–42.

———. "Notes sur une disette de grains en Bourgogne (1770–1771)." In *Actes du 93e Congrès national des sociétés savantes, Tours, 1968,* 1:245–66. Paris: BN, 1971.

Bloch, Camille. "Les Femmes et la Révolution à Orléans." *La Révolution française* 43 (1902): 49–67.

Boislisle, A.-M. de. *Correspondance des contrôleurs généraux des finances avec les intendants des provinces,* 3 vols. Paris: Imprimerie nationale, 1879–97.

———. "Le Grand Hiver et la disette de 1709." *Revue des questions historiques* 73 (1903): 442–506; 74 (1903): 486–542.

Bondois, P.-M. "La Misère sous Louis XIV. La Disette de 1662." *Revue d'histoire économique et sociale* 12 (1924): 53–118.

Bourderon, H. "La Lutte contre la vie cher dans la généralité de Languedoc au XVIIIe siècle." *Annales du Midi* 25–28 (1954): 155–70.

———. "Recherches sur les mouvements populaires dans la généralité de Languedoc au XVIIIe siècle." In *Actes du 78e Congrès national des sociétés savantes, Toulouse, 1953.* Paris: Imprimerie nationale, 1954.

Boussinesq, Georges, and Gustave Laurent. *Histoire de Reims.* 1933. Reims: Matot-Braine, 1980.

Boutier, Jean. *Campagnes en émoi. Révoltes et révolutions en Bas-Limousin, 1789–1800.* Treignac: Editions "Les Monédières," 1987.

———. "Jacqueries en pays croquant. Les Révoltes paysannes en Aquitaine (décembre 1789–mars 1790)." *AESC* 34 (July–Aug. 1979): 760–86.

Bricourt, M., M. Lachiver, and J. Queruel. "La Crise de subsistance des années 1740 dans le ressort du Parlement de Paris." *Annales de démographie historique (1974):* 281–333.

Caillard, Michel. "Recherches sur les soulèvements populaires en Basse Normandie (1620–1640) et spécialement sur la Révolte des Nu-Pieds." In *A Travers la Normandie des XVIIe et XVIIIe siècles,* pp. 23–152. Cahiers des Annales de Normandie, no. 3. Caen, 1963.

Cameron, Iain A. *Crime and Repression in the Auvergne and the Guyenne, 1720–1790.* Cambridge: Cambridge University Press, 1981.

Caramon, P. "La Disette des grains et les émeutes populaires en 1773 dans la généralité de Bordeaux." *Revue historique de Bordeaux et du département de la Gironde* 3 (1910): 297–319.

Cardénal, Louis de. "Les Subsistances dans le département de la Dordogne, 1789–an IV." *La Révolution française* 82 (1929): 217–54.

Castan, Nicole. *Les Criminels de Lanquedoc. Les Exigences d'ordre et les voies du ressentiment dans une société pré-révolutionnaire (1750–1790).* Toulouse: Association des Publications de l'Université de Toulouse–Le Mirail, 1980.

———. "Emotions populaires en Languedoc au XVIIIe siècle." In *Actes du 96e Congrès national des sociétés savantes, Toulouse, 1971,* pp. 91–108. Paris: Bibliothèque nationale, 1971.

Castan, Yves. *Honnêteté et relations sociales en Languedoc (1715–1788).* Paris: Plon, 1974.

Chambois, Em.-L. "Emeute populaire à Laval relativement à la cherté des grains, 1725–1726." *La Province du Maine* 10 (1902): 226–34.

Cobb, Richard. "Les Disettes de l'an II et de l'an III dans le district de Mantes et la vallée de la basse Seine." *Paris et Ile-de-France* 3 (1951): 227–51.

———. *The Police and the People: French Popular Protest, 1789–1820.* London: Oxford University Press, 1970.

———. *Terreur et subsistance, 1793–1795.* Paris: Clavreuil, 1964.

Courant, L. "Crises agraires en Anjou à la fin du Grand Siècle." *L'Anjou historique,* 1954: 15–33.

Crozet, René. *Histoire de Champagne.* Paris: Boivin & Cie, 1933.

———. *Histoire de l'Orléanais.* Paris: Boivin & Cie, 1936.

Davies, Alun. "The Origins of the French Peasant Revolution of 1789." *History* 49 (Feb. 1964): 24–41.

Désert, Gabriel, ed. *Histoire de Caen.* Toulouse: Privat, 1981.

Desmarest, Charles. *Le Commerce des grains dans la Généralité de Rouen à la fin de l'Ancien Régime.* Paris: Jouve & Cie, 1926.

Deyon, Pierre. *Amiens, capitale provinciale. Etude sur la société urbaine au XVIIe siècle.* Paris: Mouton, 1967.

Dinet, Henri. "L'Année 1789 en Champagne." *AHRF* 55 (1983): 570–95.

———. "La Grande Peur du Beauvaisis et du Valois, juillet 1789." *Paris et Ile-de-France* 23–24 (1972–73): 199–388.

———. "La Grande Peur en Hurepoix." *Paris et Ile-de-France* 18–19 (1967–68): 99–204.

———. "Les Peurs de 1789 dans la région parisienne." *AHRF* 50 (1978): 34–44.

Dumas, François. *La Généralité de Tours au XVIIIe siècle. Administration de l'intendant du Cluzel (1766–1783).* Paris: Hachette, 1894.

Dumas, Georges. "Emotions populaires en 1789–1790 dans le Laonnais et la Thiérache." In *Actes du 101e Congrès national des sociétés savantes, Lille, 1976,* pp. 95–110. Paris: CTHS, 1978.

Endres, André. "Une Emeute de subsistance à Meaux en 1790." In *Actes du 86e Congrès national des sociétés savantes, Montpellier, 1961,* pp. 475–82. Paris: Imprimerie nationale, 1962.

Evrard, F. "Les Paysans du mâconnais et les brigandages de juillet, 1789." *Annales de Bourgogne* 19 (1947): 7–121.

Farge, Arlette, and André Zysberg. "Les Théâtres de la violence à Paris au XVIIIe siècle." *AESC* 5 (Sept.–Oct. 1979): 984–1015.

Frayssenge, Jacques, and Nicole Lemaître. "Les Emotions populaire en Rouergue au XVIIIe siècle." In *Mouvements populaires et conscience sociale,* ed. J. Nicolas, pp. 371–81. Paris: Maloine, 1985.

Gauthier, Florence, and Guy-Robert Ikni. "Le Mouvement paysan en Picardie: Meneurs, practices, maturation et signification historique d'un programme (1775–1794)." In *La Guerre du blé au XVIIIe siècle. La Critique populaire contre le libéralisme économique au XVIIIe siècle,* ed. F. Gauthier and G.-R. Ikni, pp. 187–203. Paris: Editions de la Passion, 1988.

Godechot, Jacques. "En Languedoc et Gascogne au XVIIIe siècle: Les Paysans et les femmes contre le pouvoir." In *Mouvements populaires et conscience sociale,* ed. J. Nicolas, pp. 383–90. Paris: Maloine, 1985.

Gouda, Frances. "Women, Subsistence, and Survival: Some Observations About Mutuality and Morality." Paper presented before the Social Science History Association, St. Louis, Missouri, October 1986.

Guéneau, L. *L'Organisation du travail (industrie et commerce) à Nevers aux XVIIe et XVIIIe siècles (1660–1790).* Paris: Hachette, 1919.

Hours, Henri. "Emeutes et émotions populaires dans les campagnes du Lyonnais au 18e siècle." *Cahiers d'histoire* 9 (1964): 137–53.

Hufton, Olwen. "Social Conflict and the Grain Supply in Eighteenth-Century France." *JIH* 14 (Autumn 1983): 303–31.

———. "Women and the Family Economy in Eighteenth-Century France." *FHS* 9 (Spring 1975): 1–22.

Hunt, David. "The People and Pierre Dolivier: Popular Uprisings in the Seine-et-Oise Department 1791–1792." *FHS* 11 (Fall 1979): 184–214.

Ikni, Guy-Robert. "L'Arrêt des bateaux de grains sur l'Oise et l'Aisne en février 1792." *Annales historiques compiègnoises modernes et contemporaines* 5 (Jan. 1979): 13–36.

Jacquin, Henri. "Le Ravitaillement de Saint-Jean-de-Losne au XVIIIe siècle." *Annales de Bourgogne* 183 (July–Sept. 1974): 129–46.

Janin, Edouard. *Histoire de Montluçon d'après les documents inédits.* 1904. Reprint, Marseille: Laffitte, 1975.

Jones, Peter. *The Peasantry in the French Revolution.* Cambridge: Cambridge University Press, 1988.

Kaplan, Steven L. *Bread, Politics, and Political Economy in the Reign of Louis XV,* 2 vols. The Hague: M. Nijhoff, 1976.

Lantier, Maurice. "La Crise de subsistances en 1789 à Saint-Lô." *Annales de Normandie* 25 (Mar. 1975): 13–31.

Laurent, Gustave. *Reims et la région reimoise à la veille de la Révolution.* Reims: Matot-Braine, 1930.

Lebrun, François. "Les Soulèvements populaires à Angers aux XVIIe et XVIIIe siècles." In *Actes du 90e Congrès national des sociétés savantes, Nice, 1965,* pp. 119–40. Paris: Bibliothèque nationale, 1966.

Le Goff, T.J.A. *Vannes and Its Region: A Study of Town and Country in Eighteenth-Century France*. Oxford: Clarendon Press, 1981.

Leguai, André. "Les 'Emotions' et séditions populaires dans la généralité de Moulins aux XVIIe et XVIIIe siècles." *Revue d'histoire économique et sociale* 43 (1965): 45–64.

Lehoreau, René. *Cérémonial de l'Eglise d'Angers, 1672–1727*, ed. François Lebrun. Paris: C. Klincksieck, 1967.

Lemarchand, Guy. "Les Crises économiques et atmosphère sociale en milieu urbain sous Louis XIV." *RHMC* 14 (July–Sept. 1967): 244–65.

———. *La Fin du Féodalisme dans le Pays de Caux, conjoncture économique et démographique et structure sociale dans une région de grande culture, 1640–1795*. Paris: Editions du CTHS, 1989.

———. "Les Troubles de subsistance dans la généralité de Rouen (seconde moitié du XVIIIe siècle)." *AHRF* 35 (Oct.–Dec. 1963): 401–27.

———. "Troubles populaires au XVIIIe siècle et conscience de class: Une Préface à la Révolution française." *AHRF* 279 (Jan.–Mar. 1990): 32–48.

Le Roy Ladurie, Emmanuel. "Rural Revolts and Protest Movements in France from 1675 to 1788." *Studies in Eighteenth-Century Culture* 5 (1976): 423–52.

Letaconnoux, Joseph. *Les Subsistances et commerce des grains en Bretagne au XVIIIe siècle*. Rennes: Oberthur, 1909.

LHéritier, Michel, ed. *Les Débuts de la Révolution à Bordeaux d'après les tablettes manuscrites de Pierre Bernadau*. Paris: Société de l'histoire de la Révolution française, 1919.

Ljublinski, Vladimir S. *La Guerre des farines: Contribution à l'histoire de la lutte des classes en France à la veille de la Révolution*, trans. F. Adiba and J. Radiquet. Grenoble: Presses Universitaires de Grenoble, 1979.

Lorain, Ch. *Les Subsistances en céréales dans le district de Chaumont de 1788 à l'an V: Documents publiés*, 2 vols. Chaumont: R. Cavaniol, 1911.

Maillard, Brigitte. "Une Emeute de subsistance à Tours au XVIIIe siècle." *Annales de Bretagne et des Pays de l'ouest* 92 (1985): 27–43.

Marion, Marcel. "Une Famine en Guyenne (1747–48)." *Revue historique* 46 (May–Aug. 1891): 241–87.

Marjolin, Robert. "Troubles provoqués en France par la disette de 1816–1817." *RHM* 8 (1933): 423–60.

Marzaux, Serge. "La Révolte des femmes en 1709 à Vaison: Crime, Punition, Pardon." In *Actes du 107e Congrès national des sociétés savantes, Brest, 1982*, pp. 305–11. Paris: CTHS, 1984.

Miller, Judith A. "Politics and Urban Provisioning Crisis: Bakers, Police, and Parlements in France, 1750–1793." *JMH* 64 (June 1992): 227–62.

Monahan, W. Gregory. "Lyon in the Crisis of 1709: Royal Absolutism, Administrative Innovation, and Regional Politics." *FHS* 16 (Fall 1990): 833–48.

Mourlot, F. *La Fin de l'Ancien Régime dans la Généralité de Caen (1787–1790)*. Paris: Société de l'histoire de la Révolution française, 1913.

Nicolas, Jean. "Les Emotions dans l'ordinateur, table ronde." In *Troubles populaires en France aux XVIIe et XVIIIe siècles*. Forthcoming.

———. "Pour une enquête sur les émotions populaires au XVIIIe siècle." *AHRF* 45 (Jan.–Mar. 1973): 593–607.

———. "Pouvoir et contestation en Savoie au XVIIIe siècle. Aux sources d'une culture populaire." In *Culture et pouvoir dans les Etats de Savoie du XVIIe siècle à la Révolution: Actes du colloque d'Annecy-Chambéry-Turin, 1982*, pp. 231–52. Geneva: Slatkine, 1985.

Paris, André. "La Crise de 1709 dans le Bailliage de Montfort-L'Amaury. Le Marché des grains vu à travers le contrôle de l'administration royale." In *Actes du 101e Congrès national des sociétés savantes, Lille, 1976*, pp. 199–222. Paris: CTHS, 1978.

Pillorget, René. "Essai d'une typologie des mouvements insurrectionnels ruraux survenus en Provence de 1596 à 1715." In *Actes du 92e Congrès national des sociétés savantes, Strasbourg, 1967*, pp. 359–82. Paris: Bibliothèque nationale, 1970.

———. *Les Mouvements insurrectionnels de Provence entre 1596 et 1715.* Paris: A. Pedone, 1975.

———. "Les Mouvements insurrectionnels de Provence (1715–1788)." In *Mouvements populaires et conscience sociale*, ed. J. Nicolas, pp. 351–59. Paris: Maloine, 1985.

Pillorget-Rouanet, Suzanne. "Une Crise de colère des paysans d'Arles. Les Emeutes frumentaires des 2 et 3 janvier, 1752." In *Actes du 92e Congrès national des sociétés savantes, Strasbourg, 1967*, pp. 383–91. Paris: Bibliothèque nationale, 1970.

Poitrineau, Abel. "Le Détonateur économio-fiscal et la charge des rancoeurs catégorielles profondes, lors des explosions de la colère populaire en Auvergne au XVIIIe siècle." In *Mouvements populaires et conscience sociale*, ed. J. Nicolas, pp. 361–69. Paris: Maloine, 1985.

Post, John. *Food Shortage, Climatic Variability, and Epidemic Disease in Preindustrial Europe: The Mortality Peak in the Early 1740s.* Ithaca, N.Y.: Cornell University Press, 1985.

———. *The Last Great Subsistence Crisis in the Western World.* Baltimore: Johns Hopkins University Press, 1977.

Reddy, William M. *The Rise of Market Culture: The Textile Industry and French Society, 1750–1900.* Cambridge: Cambridge University Press, 1984.

———. "The Textile Trade and the Language of the Crowd at Rouen, 1752–1781." *Past and Present* 74 (Feb. 1977): 62–89.

Ricommard, Jean. *La Lieutenance générale de police à Troyes au XVIIIe siècle.* Paris: Hachette, 1934.

Rocher, Jean-Pierre. "Une Emeute frumentaire à Saint-Fargeau (Yonne) en 1829." In *Actes du 92e Congrès national des sociétés savantes, Strasbourg, 1967*, pp. 393–415. Paris: Bibliothèque nationale, 1970.

Root, Hilton. "Politiques frumentaires et violence collective en Europe modern." *AESC* 45 (Jan.–Feb. 1990): 167–89.

Rose, R. B. "Eighteenth-Century Price Riots, the French Revolution, and the Jacobin Maximum." *International Review of Social History* 4 (1959): 432–45.

———. "The French Revolution and the Grain Supply: Nationalization Pamphlets in the John Rylands Library." *Bulletin of the John Rylands Library, Manchester* 39 (1956–57): 171–87.

Rudé, George. *The Crowd in History: A Study of Popular Disturbances in France and England, 1730–1848*, rev. ed. London: Lawrence & Wishart, 1981.

———. "La Taxation populaire de mai 1775 à Paris et dans la région parisienne." *AHRF* 143 (Apr.–June 1956): 139–79.

———. "La Taxation populaire de mai 1775 en Picardie, en Normandie, et dans le Beauvaisis." *AHRF* 165 (July–Sept. 1961): 305–26.

Ruff, Julius. *Crime, Justice, and Public Order in Old Regime France: The Sénéchaussée of Libourne and Bazas, 1696–1789.* London: Croom Helm, 1984.

Saint-Germain, Jacques. *La Vie quotidienne en France à la fin du grand siècle.* Paris: Hachette, 1965.

Saint-Jacob, Pierre de. *Les Paysans de la Bourgogne du Nord au dernier siècle de l'Ancien Régime.* Paris: Société les Belles Lettres, 1960.

Schneider, Robert. *Public Life in Toulouse, 1463–1789: From Municipal Republic to Cosmopolitan City.* Ithaca, N.Y.: Cornell University Press, 1989.

Sée, H. "Les Troubles agraires dans le Bas-Maine en juillet, 1789." *AHRF* 2 (1925): 528–37.

Tilly, Charles. *The Contentious French: Four Centuries of Popular Struggle.* Cambridge, Mass.: Belknap Press of Harvard University Press, 1986.

———. "Routine Conflicts and Peasant Rebellions in Seventeenth-Century France." In *Power and Protest in the Countryside: Studies of Rural Unrest in Asia, Europe, and Latin America,* ed. R. P. Weller and S. E. Guggenheim, pp. 13–41. Durham, N.C.: Duke University Press Policy Studies, 1982.

Tilly, Louise A. "Food Entitlement, Famine, and Conflict." *JIH* 14 (Autumn 1983): 333–49.

———. "The Food Riot as a Form of Political Conflict in France." *JIH* 2 (1971): 23–57.

Usher, Abbot Payson. *The History of the Grain Trade in France, 1400–1700.* Cambridge, Mass.: Harvard University Press, 1913.

Vovelle, Michel. *De la Cave au Grenier. Une Itinéraire en Provence au XVIIIe siècle. De l'Histoire social à l'histoire des mentalités.* Quebec: Serge Fleury, 1980.

———. "Les Taxations populaires de fevrier–mars et novembre–décembre 1792 dans la Beauce et sur ces confins." In *Ville et campagne au 18e siècle: Chartres et la Beauce,* pp. 230–76. Paris: Editions sociales, 1980.

———. "Les Troubles sociaux en Provence (1750–1792)." In *Actes du 93e Congrès national des sociétés savantes, Tours, 1768,* 3:523–72. Paris: BN, 1971.

Weulersse, Georges. *La Physiocratie à la fin du règne de Louis XV (1770–1774).* Paris: PUF 1959.

———. *La Physiocratie sous les ministères de Turgot et de Necker (1774–1781).* Paris: PUF, 1950.

SECONDARY SOURCES

Abel, Wilhelm. *Crises agraires en Europe (XIIIe-XXe siècles).* Paris: Flammarion, 1973.

Abolition de la "féodalité" dans le monde occidentale. Actes du Colloque international de Toulouse, 1968, 2 vols. Paris: Bibliothèque nationale, 1971.

Adams, Thomas M. *Bureaucrats and Beggars: French Social Policy in the Age of Enlightenment.* New York: Oxford University Press, 1990.

Afanassiev, George. *Le Commerce des céréales en France au XVIIIe siècle,* trans. P. Boyer. Paris: A. Picard, 1894.

———. *Tableau des mesures pour les grains qui étaient en usage en France au XVIIIe siècle.* Odessa: "Odessky Wiestnik," 1891.

Agulhon, Maurice. *Penitents et Franc-Maçons de l'ancienne Provence. Essai sur la sociabilité méridionale.* Paris: Editions Fayard, 1968.

———. *The Republic in the Village: The People of the Var from the French Revolution to the Second Republic,* trans. J. Lloyd. Cambridge and Paris: Cambridge University Press and Editions de la Maison des Sciences de l'Homme, 1982.

Airiau, Jean. *L'Opposition aux physiocrats à la fin de l'ancien régime.* Paris: Pichon & Durand-Auzias, 1965.

Alavi, Hamza. "Peasant Classes and Primordial Loyalties." *Journal of Peasant Studies* 1 (1973): 43–59.

Amin, Samir, and Kostas Vergopoulos. *La Question paysanne et le capitalisme*, 2nd ed. Paris: Anthropos, 1977.

Antoine, Michel, and H.-F. Buffet. *Guide des recherches dans les fonds judiciaires de l'ancien régime*. Paris: Imprimerie nationale, 1958.

Applewhite, Harriet B., and Darline G. Levy, eds. *Women and Politics in the Age of Democratic Revolution*. Ann Arbor: University of Michigan Press, 1990.

Arbellot, Guy. "La Grande Mutation des routes de France au milieu du XVIIIe siècle." *AESC* 29 (May–June 1973): 765–91.

Ardascheff, Paul. *Les Intendants de province sous Louis XVI*, trans. L. Jousserandot. Paris: F. Alcan, 1909.

Aulard, François Victor Alphonse. *La Révolution française et le régime féodal*. Paris: F. Alcan, 1919.

Babeau, A. *La Vie rurale dans l'ancienne France*. Paris: Perrin & Cie, 1885.

———. *Le Village sous l'Ancien Régime*. Paris: Perrin & Cie, 1915.

Babeau, Henry. *Les Assemblées générales des communautés d'habitants en France du XIIIe à la Révolution*. Paris: A. Rousseau, 1893.

Bahu, A. "Les Paysans de la région de Clermont de l'Oise à la fin de l'Ancien Régime." *AHRF* 14 (1937): 193–214.

Bailey, F. G., ed. *Gifts and Poison: The Politics of Reputation*. New York: Schocken Books, 1971.

Baker, Keith Michel. "French Political Thought at the Accession of Louis XVI." *JMH* 50 (1970): 279–303.

Balandier, Georges. *Political Anthropology*, trans. A. M. Sheridan Smith. New York: Pantheon Books, 1970.

Bardet, Jean-Pierre. *Rouen aux XVIIe et XVIIIe siècles. Les Mutations d'un espace social*, 2 vols. Paris: Société d'Edition d'Enseignement Supérieur, 1983.

Barrows, Susanna. *Distorting Mirrors: Visions of the Crowd in Late Nineteenth-Century France*. New Haven: Yale University Press, 1981.

Baulant, Micheline. "Groupes mobiles dans une société sédentaire. La Société rurale autour de Meaux aux XVIIe et XVIIIe siècles." In *Les Marginaux et les exclus dans l'histoire*, présenté par B. Vincent, pp. 78–121. Cahiers Jussieu No. 5. Paris: Université de Paris 7, 1979.

———. "Niveau de vie des paysans autour de Meaux en 1700 et 1750." *AESC* 32 (May–June 1975): 505–18.

———. "Le Prix des grain à Paris de 1431–1788." *AESC* 23 (May–June 1968): 520–40.

Béaur, G. "Le Centième denier et les mouvements de propriété. Deux Exemples beaucerons, (1761–1790)." *AESC* 33 (1976): 1010–33.

———. *Le Marché foncier à la veille de la Révolution. Les Mouvements de propriété beaucerons dans les régions de Maintenon et de Janville de 1761 à 1790*. Paris: Editions de l'Ecole des Hautes Etudes en Sciences Sociales, 1984.

Beloff, Max. *Public Order and Popular Disturbances, 1660–1714*. Oxford: Oxford University Press, 1938.

Bercé, Yves-Marie. *Croquants et Nu-pieds. Les Soulèvements paysans en France au XIXe siècle*. Paris: Gallimard, 1974.

———. *Fête et révolte. Des Mentalités populaires du XVIe au XVIIIe siècle*. Paris: Hachette, 1976.

———. *Histoire des croquants. Etude des soulèvements populaires au XVII siècle dans le sud-ouest de la France*, 2 vols. Paris and Geneva: Droz, 1974.

———. *History of Peasant Revolts: The Social Origins of Rebellion in Early Modern France*, trans. A. Whitmore. Ithaca, N.Y.: Cornell University Press, 1990.

————. *Revolt and Revolution in Early Modern Europe: An Essay on the History of Political Violence*, trans. J. Bergin. New York: St. Martin's Press, 1987.

Berger, Patrice. "French Administration in the Famine of 1693." *European Studies Review* 8 (1978): 101–27.

Bernard, R. "Une Emeute dans le Valois en 1775." *Mémoirs de la Société d'histoire et d'archéologie de Senlis*, 1930, pp. 35–148.

Binet, Pierre. *La Réglementation du marché de blé en France au XVIIIe siècle et à l'époque contemporaine*. Paris: Librairie sociale et économique, 1939.

Biollay, Leon. *Etudes économiques sur le XVIIIe siècle. Le Pacte de famine. L'Administration du commerce*. Paris: Guillaumin & Cie, 1885.

Bloch, Camille. *L'Assistance et l'état en France à la veille de la Révolution*. Paris: Picard, 1908.

————. *Le Commerce des grains dans la généralité d'Orléans (1768), d'après la correspondance inédite de l'intendant Cypierre*. Orléans: H. Herluison, 1898.

Bloch, Marc. *French Rural History: An Essay on Its Basic Characteristics*, trans. J. Sondheimer. Berkeley and Los Angeles: University of California Press, 1966.

————. *The Ile-de-France: The Country Around Paris*, trans. J. E. Anderson. Ithaca, N.Y.: Cornell University Press, 1966.

————. "La Lutte pour l'individualisme agraire dans la France du XVIIIe siècle." *Annales d'histoire économique et sociale* 2 (1930): 329–83, 511–56.

Bluche, François. *Le Magistrats du Parlement de Paris au XVIIIe siècle*, rev. ed. Paris: Editions Economica, 1986.

————. "L'Origine des magistrats du Parlement de Paris au XVIIIe siècle." *Paris et Ile-de-France* 5–6 (1953–54): 9–412.

Boehler, Jean-Michel. "Communauté villageoise et contrastes sociaux. Laboureurs et manouvriers dans la campagne strasbourgeoise de la fin du XVIIe au début du XIXe siècle." *Etudes rurales* 63–64 (July–Dec. 1976): 93–116.

Bohstedt, John. "Gender, Household, and Community Politics: Women in English Riots, 1790–1810." *Past and Present* 120 (Aug. 1988): 88–122.

————. "The Moral Economy and the Discipline of Context." In *Nahrungsmangel, Hunger und Protest in Deutschland, ca. 1770–1950*. Forthcoming, ed. M. Gailus and H. Volkman. Opladen: Westdeutschen, 1993.

————. *Riots and Community Politics in England and Wales, 1790–1810*. Cambridge, Mass.: Harvard University Press, 1983.

Bois, Paul. *Paysans de l'Ouest. Des Structures économiques et sociales aux options politiques depuis l'époque révolutionnaire dans la Sarthe*. Le Mans: M. Vilaire, 1960.

Booth, Alan. "Food Riots in the North-West of England, 1790–1801." *Past and Present* 77 (Nov. 1977): 84–107.

Bord, Gustave. *Histoire du blé en France. Le Pacte de famine, histoire, légende*. Paris: A. Sauton, 1887.

Bordes, Maurice. *L'Administration provinciale et municipale en France au XVIIIe siècle*. Paris: SEDES, 1972.

————. *La Réforme municipale du contrôleur général Laverdy et son application (1764–1771)*. Toulouse: La Faculté des Lettres et Sciences humaines de Toulouse, 1968.

Bosher, J. F. *French Finances, 1770–1795: From Business to Bureaucracy*. Cambridge: Cambridge University Press, 1970.

Bouchard, Gerard. *Le Village immobile. Sennely-en-Sologne au XVIIIe siècle*. Paris: Plon, 1972.

Bouis, R. "A Propos de la 'Guerre des Farines.' " *AHRF* (Oct.–Dec. 1958): 74–83.

Bourde, André J. *Agronomie et agronomes en France au XVIIIe siècle*, 3 vols. Paris: SEVPEN, 1967.

Bourdieu, Pierre. *Outline of a Theory of Practice*, trans. R. Nice. Cambridge: Cambridge University Press, 1977.

Boussinesq, Georges, and Gustave Laurent. *Histoire de Reims depuis les origines jusqu'à nos jours*, 2 vols. Reims: Matot-Braine, 1932; 2nd ed., 1980.

Bouton, Cynthia A. " 'L'Economie morale' et la guerre des farines de 1775." In *La Guerre du blé au XVIIIe siècle. La Critique populaire contre le libéralisme économique au XVIIIe siècle*, ed. G.-R. Ikni and F. Gauthier, pp. 93–110. Montreuil: Editions de la Passion, 1988.

———. "Gendered Behavior in Subsistence Riots: The Flour War of 1775," *JSH* 23 (Summer 1990): 735–54.

Boyreau, Joseph. *Le Village en France au XVIIIe siècle*. Paris: CDU, 1955.

Braudel, Ferdinand, and Ernest Labrousse, eds. *Histoire économique et sociale de la France*, vol. 2, *Des derniers temps de l'âge seigneurial aux préludes de l'âge industriel (1660–1789)*. Paris: PUF, 1970.

Brenner, Robert. "Agrarian Class Structure and Economic Development in Pre-Industrial Europe." *Past and Present* 70 (Feb. 1976): 30–75.

Brossard de Ruville. *Histoire de la ville des Andelys*, 2 vols. Les Andelys: Delcroix, 1863–64.

Brulé, J. D. "Trois communes de la Basse-Vallée de l'Oise: Cergy, Jouy-le-Moutier, Vauréal à la fin de l'Ancien Régime." *Mémoires de la Société historique et archéologique de Pontoise, du Val-D'Oise et du Vexin* 60 (1966): 25–44.

Bruley, E. "Nobles et paysans picards à la fin de l'Ancien Régime." *Revue d'histoire moderne et contemporaine* 16 (Oct.–Dec. 1969): 606–10.

Brunet, Claude. *Une Communauté rurale au XVIIIe siècle. Le Plessis-Gassot (Seine-et-Oise)*. Paris: Imprimerie nationale, 1964.

Brunet, Pierre. *Structures agraires et économie rurale des plateaux tertiaires entre la Seine et Oise*. Caen: Société d'Impressions Caron & Cie, 1960.

Cahen, Léon. "L'Approvisionnement en pain de Paris au XVIIIe siècle et la question de la boulangerie." *Revue d'histoire économique et sociale* 14 (1926): 458–72.

———. "Ce qu'enseigne un péage du XVIIIe siècle. La Seine entre Rouen et Paris." *Annales d'histoire économique et sociale* 12 (Oct. 1931): 486–518.

———. "L'Idée de lutte des classes au XVIIIe siècle." *Revue de synthèse historique* 12 (1906): 44–56.

———. "Le Pacte de famine et les spéculations sur les blés." *Revue historique* 152 (May–June 1926): 32–43.

Caillard, Michel, et al. *A Travers la Normandie des XVIIe et XVIIIe siècles*. Caen: Cahiers des Annales de Normandie, no. 3, 1963.

Calhoun, C. J. "Community: Toward a Variable Conceptualization for Comparative Research." *Social History* 5 (Jan. 1980): 105–30.

———. "History, Anthropology, and the Study of Communities: Some Problems in Macfarlane's Proposal." *Social History* 3 (Oct. 1978): 363–74.

———. *The Question of Class Struggle: Social Foundations of Popular Radicalism During the Industrial Revolution*. Chicago: University of Chicago Press, 1982.

Cameron, Iain A. *Crime and Repression in the Auvergne and the Guyenne, 1720-1790*. Cambridge: Cambridge University Press, 1981.

Caraman, P. "La Disette des grains et les émeutes populaires en 1773 dans la généralité de Bordeaux." *Revue historique de Bordeaux* 3 (1910): 297–319.

Castan, Nicole. "La Criminalité familiale dans le ressort du Parlement de Toulouse (1690–1730)." In A. Abbaiteci et al., *Crime et criminalité en France sous l'Ancien Régime*, pp. 91–108. Paris: Armand Colin, 1971.

————. *Les Criminels de Languedoc. Les Exigences d'ordre et les voies du ressentiment dans une société pré-révolutionnaire (1750–1790)*. Toulouse: Association des publications de l'Université de Toulouse–Le Mirail, 1980.

————. *Justice et répression en Languedoc à l'époque des lumières*. Paris: Flammarion, 1980.

Castan, Yves. "Attitudes et motivations dans les conflits entre seigneurs et communautés devant le Parlement de Toulouse au XVIIIe siècle." In *Villes de l'Europe méditerranéenne et de l'Europe occidentale du Moyen Age au XIX siècle*, pp. 233–39. Nice: Les Belles Lettres, 1969.

————. *Honnêteté et relations sociales en Languedoc (1715–1780)*. Paris: Plon, 1974.

————. "Mentalités rurale et urbaine à la fin de l'Ancien Régime dans le ressort du Parlement de Toulouse d'après les sacs à procès criminels (1730–1790)." In A. Abbiateci et al., *Crime et criminalité en France sous l'Ancien Régime*, pp. 109–86. Paris: Armand Colin, 1971.

Chaline, Olivier. "Le Juge et le pain. Parlement et politique d'approvisionnement en 1788–89, d'après les papiers du Procureur Général de Rouen." *Annales de Normandie* 39 (Mar. 1989): 21–35.

Charlesworth, A., and A. J. Randall. "Comment: Morals, Markets, and the English Crowd in 1766." *Past and Present* 114 (Feb. 1987): 200–213.

Charlesworth, Andrew, ed. *An Atlas of Rural Protest in Britain, 1548–1900*. Philadelphia: University of Pennsylvania Press, 1983.

Chartier, Roger, Marie-Madeleine Compère, and Dominique Julia. *L'Education en France du XVIe au XVIIIe siècles*. Paris: SEDES, 1976.

Chaussinand-Nogaret, G. "Capital et structure sociale sous l'Ancien Régime." *AESC* 23 (1970): 463–76.

Chevalier, Louis. *Classes labourieuses et classes dangereuses*. Paris: LGF, 1978.

Clarke, J., C. Critcher, and R. Johnson, eds. *Working-Class Culture: Studies in History and Theory*. New York: St. Martin's Press, 1979.

Coats, A. W. "Contrary Moralities: Plebs, Paternalists, and Political Economists." *Past and Present* 54 (Feb. 1972): 130–33.

Cobb, Richard. *Paris and Its Provinces, 1792–1802*. Oxford: Oxford University Press, 1975.

————. *The People's Armies*, trans. M. Elliot. New Haven: Yale University Press, 1987.

————. *The Police and the People: French Popular Protest, 1789–1820*. Oxford: Oxford University Press, 1970.

————. *Terreur et Subsistances, 1793–1795*. Paris: Clavreuil, 1964.

Cobban, Alfred. *The Social Interpretation of the French Revolution*. Cambridge: Cambridge University Press, 1964.

Collins, James. "The Economic Role of Women in Seventeenth-Century France." *FHS* 16 (Fall 1989): 436–70.

————. "Geographical and Social Mobility in Early Modern France." *JSH* 24 (Spring 1991): 563–77.

Comte de Luçay. *Angy-en-Beauvaisis. Son histoire, ses privilèges, sa prévôté royale*. Senlis: E. Payen, 1876.

Coornaert, Emile. *Les Corporations en France avant 1789*, 2nd ed. Paris: Les Editions Ouvrières, 1968.

Crozet, René. *Histoire de Champagne*. Paris: Boivin & Cie, 1933.

Dakin, Douglas. *Turgot and the Ancien Régime in France*. London: Methuen, 1939.

Dallas, Gregory. *The Imperfect Peasant Economy: The Loire Country, 1800–1914*. Cambridge: Cambridge University Press, 1982.

Danière, A. "Feudal Incomes and Demand Elasticity for Bread in Late Eighteenth-Century France." *Journal of Economic History* 18 (1958): 317–44.

Darras, Eugène. *Les Seigneurs-Châtelains de l'Isle-Adam (1014–1814)*. Persan: N.p., 1939.

Daumard, Adeline. "Une référence pour l'étude des sociétés urbaines aux XVIIIe et XIXe siècles. Projet de code socio-professionnel." *RHMC* 10 (July–Sept. 1963): 184–210.

———. *Structures et relations sociales à Paris au milieu du 18e siècle*. Paris: A. Colin, 1961.

Daumard, Adeline, and François Furet. "Les Archives notariales et la Méchanographie." *AESC* 3 (1959): 676–93.

Davies, Alun. "The Origins of the French Peasant Revolution of 1789." *History* 49 (Feb. 1964): 24–41.

Davis, Natalie Zemon. *Society and Culture in Early Modern France*. Stanford, Calif.: Stanford University Press, 1965.

Deck, Suzanne. "Les Muncipalités en Haute-Normandie." *Annales de Normandie* 10 (1960): 207–27, 317–29; 11 (1961): 279–300; 12 (1961): 77–92, 151–67, 213–34.

Deconinck, Jean-Marie. *Bruno d'Agay, intendant de Picardie (1771–1790)*. Amiens: CRDP, n.d.

Defresne, A., and F. Evrard. *Les Subsistances dans le district de Versailles de 1788 à l'an V*, 2 vols. Rennes: Oberthur, 1921.

Demangeon, Albert. *La Picardie et les régions voisines: Artois, Cambrésis, Beauvaisis*. 4th ed. Paris: Guenegaud, 1974.

Desgraves, Louis. *Les Subdélégations et les subdélégués de la généralité de Bordeaux aux XVIIIe siècle*. Toulouse: E. Privat, 1954.

Desjardins, Gustave. *Le Beauvaisis, le Valois, le Vexin français et le Noyonnais en 1789*. Beauvais: D. Père, 1869.

Desmarest, Charles. *Le Commerce des grains dans la généralité de Rouen à la fin de l'Ancien Régime*. Paris: Jouve & Cie, 1926.

Dewald, Jonathan. *Pont-St.-Pierre, 1398–1789: Lordship, Community, and Capitalism in Early Modern France*. Berkeley and Los Angeles: University of California Press, 1987.

Deyon, Pierre. *Amiens, capitale provinciale. Etudes sur la société urbaine au XVIIe siècle*. Paris: Mouton, 1967.

———. "Mentalités populaires: Un Sondage à Amiens au XVIIe siècle." *AESC* 17 (1962): 448–58.

———. "Le Mouvement de la production textile à Amiens au XVIIIe siècle." *Revue du Nord* 44 (Apr.–June 1962): 201–12.

———. "Quelques remarques sur l'évolution du régime seigneurial en Picardie, XVIe–XVIIIe siècles." *RHMC* 8 (Oct.–Dec. 1961): 271–80.

Dion, Roger. *Essai sur la formation du paysage rural français*. Tours: Arrault & Cie, 1934.

Dommanget, Maurice. "Les Grèves des moissonneurs du Valois sous la Révolution." *AHRF*, n.s. 1 (1924): 507–44.

Dontenwill, S. "Rapports ville-campagne et espace économique microrégional: Charlieu et son plât-pays au XVIIIe siècle." In *Villes et campagnes, XVe–XX siècles. IIIe Rencontre franco-suisses*, pp. 145–73. Lyons, 1977.

Doyle, William. "The Parlements of France and the Breakdown of the Old Régime, 1771–1788." *French Historical Studies* 6 (Fall 1970): 415–58.

———. "Was There an Aristocratic Reaction in Pre-Revolutionary France?" *Past and Present* 57 (Nov. 1972): 97–123.

Duby, Georges, and Armand Wallon, eds. *Histoire de la France rurale*, vol. 2, *L'Age classique, 1340–1789*. Paris: Editions Seuil, 1975.

Dumas, F. *La Généralité de Tours au XVIIIe siècle. Administration de l'intendant du Cluzel (1766–1783)*. Paris: Hachette, 1894.

Dupâquier, Jacques. "Les Caractères originaux de l'histoire démographique au 18e siècle." *RHMC* 33 (1976): 193–202.

——. "Etude de la propriété et de la société rurale d'après les terriers." In *Actes du 89e Congrès national des Sociétés savantes, Lyons, 1964*, pp. 259–70. Paris: Imprimerie nationale, 1965.

——. *La Propriété et l'exploitation foncière à la fin de l'Ancien Régime dans le Gâtinais septentrional.* Paris: PUF, 1956.

——. "Des rôles de taille à l'histoire de la société rurale à la fin de l'Ancien Régime." In *Actes du 88e Congrès national des sociétés savantes, Clermont-Ferrand, 1963.* Paris: Imprimerie nationale, 1964.

——. "La Situation de l'agriculture dans le Vexin français (fin du XVIIIe et début du XIXe) d'après les enquêtes agricoles." In *Actes du 89e Congrès national des Sociétés savantes, Lyon, 1964*, pp. 321–45. Paris: Imprimerie nationale, 1965.

——. "Structures sociales et cahiers de doléances. L'Exemple du Vexin français." *AHRF* 194 (Oct.–Dec. 1968): 434–54.

Dupâquier, J., M. Lachiver, and J. Meuvret. *Mercuriales du pays de France et du Vexin français (1640–1792).* Paris: SEVPEN, 1968.

Dupâquier, J., et al. *Paroisses et communes de France. Dictionnaire d'histoire administrative et démographique, Région parisienne.* Paris: Editions du CNRS, 1974.

Dupront, Alphonse. "Cahiers de doléances et mentalités collectives." In *Actes du 89e Congrès national des Sociétés savantes, Lyons, 1964*, pp. 375–77. Paris: Imprimerie nationale, 1965.

——. "Problèmes et méthodes d'une histoire de la psychologie collective." *AESC* 26 (1961): 3–11.

Durham, Mary Jay. "The Sans-Jupons' Crusade for Liberalization During the French Revolution." Ph.D. dissertation, Washington University, 1972.

Echeverria, Durand. *The Maupeou Revolution: A Study in the History of Libertarianism, France, 1770–1774.* Baton Rouge: Louisiana State University Press, 1985.

Eckstein, Susan, ed. *Power and Popular Protest: Latin American Social Movements.* Berkeley and Los Angeles: University of California Press, 1989.

Egret, Jean. *Louis XV et l'opposition parlementaire (1715–1774).* Paris: Armand Colin, 1970.

Evrard, Fernand. "Les Grandes Fermes entre Paris et la Beauce." *Annales de géographie* 32 (1923): 210–25.

Fairchilds, Cissie. *Poverty and Charity in Aix-en-Provence, 1640–1789.* Baltimore: Johns Hopkins University Press, 1976.

Farge, Arlette. *Delinquance et criminalité. Le Vol d'aliments à Paris au XVIIIe siècle.* Paris: Plon, 1974.

——. *La Vie fragile. Violence, pouvoirs et solidarités à Paris au XVIIIe siècle.* Paris: Hachette, 1986.

Faure, Edgar. *La Disgrâce de Turgot.* Paris: Gallimard, 1961.

Festy, Octave. *L'Agriculture pendant la Révolution française. Les Conditions de production et de récolte de céréales. Etude d'histoire économique, 1789–1795.* Paris: Gallimard, 1947.

Fitch, Nancy. "Rural Violence and Peasant Politics in Central France, 1789–1794." Paper presented before the Western Society for French History, Santa Barbara, California, 1990.

Flinn, Michael W. *The European Demographic System, 1500–1820.* Baltimore: Johns Hopkins University Press, 1981.

Floquet, Amable-Pierre. *Histoire du Parlement de Normandie*, 7 vols. Rouen: E. Frère, 1840–42.

Fogelson, Raymond, and Richard Adams, eds. *The Anthropology of Power: Ethnographic Studies from Asia, Oceania, and the New World.* New York: Academic Press, 1977.

Fontenay, Michel. "Paysans et marchands ruraux de la vallée de l'Essones dans la seconde moitié du XVIIe siècle." *Paris et Ile-de-France* 9 (1957–58): 157–282.

Forrest, Alan. *The French Revolution and the Poor.* New York: St. Martin's Press, 1981.

Forster, Robert. *The House of Saulx-Tavanes: Versailles and Burgundy, 1700–1830.* Baltimore: Johns Hopkins University Press, 1970.

———. *Merchants, Landlords, Magistrates: The Dupont Family in Eighteenth-Century France.* Baltimore: Johns Hopkins University Press, 1980.

———. *The Nobility of Toulouse in the Eighteenth Century.* Baltimore: Johns Hopkins University Press, 1960.

———. "Obstacles to Agricultural Growth in Eighteenth-Century France." *American Historical Review* 75 (1970): 1600–1615.

———. "The Provincial Noble: A Reappraisal." *American Historical Review* 68 (Apr. 1963): 681–91.

———. "The 'World' Between Seigneur and Peasant." In *Studies in Eighteenth-Century Culture*, ed. R. Rosbottom, 5:401–22. Madison: University of Wisconsin Press, 1976.

Forster, Robert, and Orest Ranum, eds. *Deviants and the Abandoned in French Society.* Baltimore: Johns Hopkins University Press, 1978.

Fossard, Albert. *Le Prieurie de Saint-Leu-d'Esserent.* Paris: Réveil, 1934.

Foster, G. M. "Peasants and the Image of Limited Good." *American Anthropologist* 67 (1965): 293–315.

Foucault, Michel. *Discipline and Punish: The Birth of the Prison*, trans. A. Sheridan. New York: Vintage Books, 1977.

Fox-Genovese, Elizabeth. "The Many Faces of Moral Economy: A Contribution to a Debate." *Past and Present* 58 (Feb. 1973): 161–68.

———. *The Origins of Physiocracy: Economic Revolution and Social Order in Eighteenth-Century France.* Ithaca, N.Y.: Cornell University Press, 1976.

Fox-Genovese, Elizabeth, and Eugene Genovese. "On the Social History of the French Revolution: New Methods, Old Ideologies." In *Fruits of Merchant Capital: Slavery and Bourgeois Property in the Rise and Expansion of Capitalism*, pp. 213–48. New York: Oxford University Press, 1983.

Friedl, Ernestine. "The Position of Women: Appearance and Reality." *Anthropological Quarterly* 40 (July 1967): 97–108.

Fritz, Gérard. *L'Idée de peuple en France du XVIIe au XIXe siècle.* Strasbourg: Presses universitaires de Strasbourg, 1988.

Funck-Brentano, F. *Lettres de cachet.* Paris: Imprimerie nationale, 1903.

Furet, François. "Ancien Régime et Révolution: Réinterpretations." *AESC* 29 (1974): 3–5.

———. *Penser la Révolution française.* Paris: Gallimard, 1978.

———. "Pour une définition des classes inférieures à l'époque moderne." *AESC* 8 (1963): 459–74.

Gabé, Hector. "Le Cadre institutionel de la vie à Nogent-sur-Marne sous l'Ancien Régime." *Paris et Ile-de-France* 38 (1987): 87–120.

Gailus, Manfred. "Food Riots in Germany in the Late 1840s." *Past and Present.* Forthcoming.

———. *Strasse und Brot. Sozialer Protest in den deutschen Staaten unter besonderer Berucksichtigung Preussens, 1847–1849.* Göttingen: Vandenhoeck & Ruprecht, 1990.

Ganiage, Jean. *Le Beauvaisis au XVIII siècle. La Campagne*. Paris: Editions de l'INED, 1988.

Garrioch, David. *Neighborhood and Community in Paris, 1740–1790*. Cambridge: Cambridge University Press, 1986.

Gauthier, Florence. "Formes d'évolution du système agraire communautaire picard (fin du XVIIIe–début du XIXe siècles)." *AHRF* 240 (Apr.–June 1980): 181–204.

———. *La Voie paysanne dans la Révolution française. L'Exemple picard*. Paris: F. Maspero, 1976.

Gauthier, Florence, and Guy-Robert Ikni, eds. *La Guerre du blé au XVIIIe siècle. La Critique populaire contre le libéralisme économique au XVIIIe siècle*. Montreuil: Editions de la Passion, 1988.

Gazier, A. "La Guerre des Farines (Mai 1775)." *Paris et Ile-de-France* 6 (1879): 1–23.

Geertz, Clifford. *The Interpretation of Cultures*. New York: Basic Books, 1973.

Gegot, Jean-Claude. "Etude par sondage de la criminalité dans le bailliage de Falaise (XVIIe–XVIIIe siècles). Criminalité diffuse ou société criminelle?" *Annales de Normandie* 16 (1966): 103–64.

Gillis, John. "Peasant, Plebeian, and Proletarian Marriage in Britain, 1600–1900." In *Proletarianization and Family History*, ed. David Levine, pp. 87–128. Orlando: Academic Press, 1984.

Gindin, Claude. "Le Pain de Gonesse à la fin du XVIIe siècle." *RHMC* 19 (July–Sept. 1972): 414–33.

Girard, René. *L'Abbé Terray et la liberté du commerce des grains, 1769–1774*. Paris: PUF, 1924.

Girod, P.-E. "Les Subsistances en Bourgogne et particulièrement à Dijon à la fin du XVIIIe siècle (1774–1789)." *Revue bourguignonne de l'enseignement supérieur* 16 (1906): i–xxiii, 1–145.

Glasson, E. "Communaux et communautés dans l'ancien droit française." *Revue historique de droit français et étranger*, 1891, pp. 446–79.

Godechot, Jacques, and S. Moncassin. "Structures et relations sociales à Toulouse en 1749 et en 1785." *AHRF* 37 (1965): 129–69.

Godelier, Maurice. *The Mental and the Material: Thought, Economy, and Society*, trans. M. Thom. London: Verso, 1986.

Goldsmith, James L. "The Agrarian History of Preindustrial France: Where Do We Go from Here?" *Journal of European Economic History* 13 (Spring 1984): 175–200.

Gomont, H. "La Guerre des farines." *Journel des économistes* 10 (Feb. 1845): 279–89.

Goubert, Pierre. *L'Ancien Régime*, vol. 2, *Les Pouvoirs*. Paris: Armand Colin, 1973.

———. *The Ancien Régime: French Society, 1600–1750*, trans. Steve Cox. New York: Harper & Row, 1974.

———. *Beauvais et le Beauvaisis de 1600 à 1730. Contribution à l'histoire sociale de la France du XVIIe siècle*, 2 vols. Paris: SEVPEN, 1960.

———. "The French Peasantry of the Seventeenth Century." *Past and Present* 10 (Nov. 1956): 55–78.

———. "Les Techniques agricoles dans les pays picards aux XVIIe et XVIIIe siècles." *Revue d'histoire économique et sociale* 35 (1957): 24–40.

Gouda, Frances. "Women, Subsistence, and Survival: Some Observations About Mutuality and Morality." Paper presented at the Social Science History Association, St. Louis, Missouri, October 1986.

Gouesse, J. M. *Documents de l'histoire de la Normandie*. Paris, 1972.

Goujard, Philippe. *Abolition de la "Féodalité" dans le pays de Bray (1789–1793)*. Paris: Bibliothèque nationale, 1979.

Goulard, R. "Une Episode de la 'Guerre des Farines' dans la Brie (1775)." *Le Vieux Saint-Maur. Bulletin de la Société historique et archéologique de Saint-Maur-des-Fosses et des localités avoisinantes,* 2nd ser., 8 (May 1931): 107–9.

Goy, Jacques, and Emmanuel Le Roy Ladurie, eds. *Prestations paysannes, dîmes, rente foncière et mouvement de la production agricole à l'époque préindustrielle,* 2 vols. Paris: Mouton, 1982.

Graham, Ruth. "Loaves and Liberty: Women in the French Revolution." In *Becoming Visible: Women in European History,* ed. R. Bridenthal and C. Koonz, pp. 236–54. Boston: Houghton Mifflin, 1977.

Grantham, George. "Jean Meuvret and the Subsistence Problem in Early Modern France." *JEH* 49 (Mar. 1989): 184–200.

Gras, Christian, and George Livet, eds. *Régions et régionalisme en France du XVIIIe siècle à nos jours.* Paris: PUF, 1977.

Gressier, James, et al. *Pontoise: 2000 ans d'histoire.* Pontoise: Paris, 1973.

Gruder, Vivian R. *The Royal Provincial Intendants: A Governing Elite in Eighteenth-Century France.* Ithaca, N.Y.: Cornell University Press, 1968.

Gruttner, Michael. "Working-Class Crime and the Labour Movement: Pilfering in the Hamburg Docks, 1888–1923." In *The German Working Class, 1888–1933: The Politics of Everyday Life,* ed. R. J. Evans, pp. 54–79. London: Croom Helm, 1982.

Gueneau, Louis. *L'Organisation du travail à Nevers aux XVIIe et XVIIIe siècles (1660–1790).* Paris: Hachette, 1919.

Gueroult, Jean. *Rôles de la taille de l'élection de Paris.* Paris: Archives nationales, 1981.

Gullickson, Gay L. "The Sexual Division of Labor in Cottage Industry and Agriculture in the Pays de Caux: Auffay, 1750–1850." *FHS* 12 (Fall 1981): 177–99.

———. *Spinners and Weavers of Auffay: Rural Industry and the Sexual Division of Labor in a French Village, 1750–1850.* Cambridge: Cambridge University Press, 1986.

Gutton, Jean-Pierre. *La Sociabilité villageoise dans l'ancienne France. Solidarités et voisinages du XVIe au XVIIIe siècle.* Paris: Hachette, 1979.

———. *La Société et les pauvres. L'Exemple de la généralité de Lyon, 1534–1789.* Paris: Les Belles Lettres, 1971.

Hanagan, Michael, and C. Stephenson, eds. *Confrontation, Class Consciousness, and the Labor Process: Studies in Proletarian Class Formation.* Westport, Conn.: Greenwood Press, 1986.

Hanley, Sarah. "Engendering the State: Family Formation and State Building in Early Modern France." *FHS* 16 (Spring 1989): 4–27.

———. "Family and State in Early Modern France: The Marriage Pact." In *Connecting Spheres: Women in the Western World, 1500–Present,* ed. M. Boxer and J. Quataert, pp. 53–63. Oxford: Oxford University Press, 1987.

———. *Le Lit de Justice of the Kings of France: Constitutional Ideology in Legend, Ritual, and Discourse.* Princeton: Princeton University Press, 1983.

Hardy, G. "L'Administration des paroisses du XVIIIe siècle. Les Reparations de bâtiments ecclésiastiques." *RHMC* 15 (1911): 5–23.

Harrison, Mark. "The Ordering of the Urban Environment: Time, Work, and the Occurrence of Crowds, 1790–1835." *Past and Present* 110 (1986): 134–68.

Hay, Douglas, et al. *Albion's Fatal Tree: Crime and Society in Eighteenth-Century England.* New York: Pantheon Books, 1975.

Hervieu, Bertrand. " 'Le Pouvoir au Village:' Difficultés et perspectives d'une recherche." *Etudes rurales* 63–64 (1976): 15–30.

L'Histoire sociale, sources et méthodes. Colloque de l'Ecole Normale supérieure de Saint-Cloud, 15–16 mai 1965. Paris: PUF, 1967.

Hobsbawm, Eric. "Peasants and Politics." *Journal of Peasant Studies* 1 (Oct. 1973): 3–22.
————. *Primitive Rebels: Studies in Archaic Forms of Social Movement in the Nineteenth and Twentieth Centuries.* New York: Norton, 1959.
Hoffman, Philip T. "Land Rents and Agricultural Productivity: The Paris Basin, 1460–1789." *JEH* 51 (Dec. 1991): 771–805.
————. "Social History and Agricultural Productivity: The Paris Basin, 1450–1800." Social Science Working Paper 742, California Institute of Technology, 1990.
Holton, Robert. "The Crowd in History: Some Problems of Theory and Method." *Social History* 3 (May 1978): 219–33.
Huard, Raymond. "Existe-t-il une politique populaire?" *Mouvements populaires et conscience sociale, XVIe–XIXe siècles,* ed. J. Nicolas, pp. 57–68. Paris: Maloine, 1985.
Hufton, Olwen H. "Attitudes Toward Authority in Eighteenth-Century Languedoc." *Social History* 3 (Oct. 1978): 281–302.
————. "Le Paysan et la loi en France au XVIIIe siècle." *AESC* 38 (May–June 1983): 679–701.
————. *The Poor in Eighteenth-Century France, 1750–1789.* Oxford: Clarendon Press, 1974.
————. "The Seigneur and the Rural Community in Eighteenth-Century France: The Seigneurial Reaction. A Reappraisal." *Transactions of the Royal Historical Society* 29 (1979): 21–39.
————. "Towards an Understanding of the Poor in Eighteenth-Century France." In *French Government and Society, 1500–1850: Essays in Memory of Alfred Cobban,* ed. J. F. Bosher, pp. 145–65. London: Athlone Press, 1973.
————. "Women and the Family Economy in Eighteenth-Century France." *FHS* 9 (Spring 1975): 1–22.
————. "Women in Revolution, 1789–1796." *Past and Present* 53 (Nov. 1971): 90–108.
Hunt, David. "Peasant Politics in the French Revolution." *Social History* 9 (Oct. 1984): 277–300.
Hunt, Lynn A. "Local Elites at the End of the Old Regime: Troyes and Reims, 1750–1789." *FHS* 9 (Spring 1976): 379–99.
————, ed. *The New Cultural History.* Berkeley and Los Angeles: University of California Press, 1989.
Hutt, M. G. "The 'Curés' and the Third Estate: The Ideas of Reform in the Pamphlets of the French Lower Clergy." *Journal of Ecclesiastical History* 8 (1957): 74–92.
Hyslop, Beatrice F. *L'Apanage de Philippe-Egalité, duc d'Orléans (1785–1791).* Paris: Société des Etudes Robespierristes, 1965.
————. *A Guide to the General Cahiers of 1789.* New York: Octagon Books, 1968.
Ikni, Guy-Robert. "La Critique paysanne radicale et le libéralisme économique pendant la Révolution française. Droit social, économie rurale ou économie politique populaire?" In *La Révolution française et le monde rural,* pp. 507–20. Paris: CTHS, 1989.
————. "La Guerre des farines. Mise au point et nouvelles recherches." *Bulletin de la Commission d'histoire économique et sociale de la Révolution française,* 1980–81, pp. 57–84.
Ikni, Guy-Robert, J. D. de La Rochefoucauld, and C. Wolikow. *Le duc de La Rochefoucauld-Liancourt.* Paris: Perrin, 1980.
Jacquart, Jean. "L'Administration locale en Ile-de-France des origines à la Révolution: Jalons pour une recherche." *Paris et Ile-de-France* 38 (1987): 3–6.
————. *La Crise rurale en Ile-de-France, 1550–1670.* Paris: Armand Colin, 1974.
————. "Quelques aspects de la communauté d'habitants dans la région parisienne au XVIIe siècle." *Revue d'histoire de droit français et étranger* 45 (1967): 718–20.

Jessenne, Jean-Pierre. *Pouvoir au village et Révolution: Artois, 1760–1848*. Lille: Presses Universitaire de Lille, 1987.

————. "Le Pouvoir des fermiers dans les villages d'Artois (1770–1848)." *AESC* 38 (May–June 1983): 702–34.

Johnson, Douglas, ed. *French Society and the Revolution*. Cambridge: Cambridge University Press, 1976.

Johnson, Richard. "Thompson, Genovese, and Social Humanist History." *History Workshop* 6 (1978): 79–100.

Jones, Colin. *Charity and "Bienfaisance": The Treatment of the Poor in the Montpellier Region, 1740–1815*. Cambridge: Cambridge University Press, 1982.

Jones, David J. V. *Before Rebecca: Popular Protests in Wales, 1793–1835*. London: Allen Lane, 1973.

Jones, Peter. *The Peasantry in the French Revolution*. Cambridge: Cambridge University Press, 1988.

————. *Politics and Rural Society: The Southern Massif Central, c. 1750–1880*. Cambridge: Cambridge University Press, 1985.

Julia, Dominique. "La Clergé paroissiale dans le diocèse de Reims à la fin du XVIIIe siècle." *RHMC* 13 (1966): 195–216.

————. "L'Enseignement primaire dans le diocèse de Reims à la fin de l'Ancien Régime." In *Actes du 95e Congrès national des Sociétés savantes, Reims, 1970*, pp. 395–415. Paris: Bibliothèque nationale, 1974.

Kaplan, Steven L. *Bread, Politics, and Political Economy in the Reign of Louis XV*, 2 vols. The Hague: M. Nijhoff, 1976.

————. *The Famine Plot Persuasion in Eighteenth-Century France*. Philadelphia: American Philosophical Society, 1982.

————. "Lean Years, Fat Years: The 'Community' Granary System and the Search for Abundance in Eighteenth-Century France." *FHS* 10 (Fall 1977): 197–230.

————. *Provisioning Paris: Merchants and Millers in the Grain and Flour Trade During the Eighteenth Century*. Ithaca, N.Y.: Cornell University Press, 1984.

Kaplow, Jeffry. *The Names of Kings: The Parisian Laboring Poor in the Eighteenth Century*. New York: Basic Books, 1972.

Krantz, Frederick, ed. *History from Below: Studies in Popular Protest and Popular Ideology*. London: Basil Blackwell, 1988.

Kriedte, Peter, Hans Medick, Jurgen Schlumbohm, eds. *Industrialization Before Industrialization: Rural Industry in the Genesis of Capitalism*, trans. B. Schempp. Cambridge: Cambridge University Press, 1981.

Labrousse, Ernest. *La Crise de l'économie française à la fin de l'Ancien Régime et au début de la Révolution*. Paris: PUF, 1944.

————. *Esquisse du mouvement des prix et des revenues en France au XVIIIe siècle*. Paris: Daloz, 1933.

Lachiver, Marcel. *Vin, vigne, et vignerons en région parisienne du XVIIe au XIXe siècles*. Pontoise: Société historique et archéologique de Pontoise, du Val-D'Oise et du Vexin, 1982.

Landes, Joan. *Women and the Public Sphere in the Age of the French Revolution*. Ithaca, N.Y.: Cornell University Press, 1988.

Landsberger, Henry A., ed. *Rural Protest: Peasant Movements and Social Change*. London: Macmillan, 1974.

Larrière, C. "L'Analyse physiocratique des rapports entre la ville et le campagne." *Etudes rurales* 49–50 (Jan.–June 1973): 42–68.

Laurent, Gustave. *Reims et la région reimoise à la veille de la Révolution*. Reims: Matot-Braine, 1930.

Lebeau, Edouard. "L'Affaire des blés dans la Brie en 1775 (épisode de la Guerre des farines)." *Revue de la Société historique de Villiers-sur-Marne et de la Brie française* 1 (Dec. 1962): 21–24.

Lefebvre, Georges. *Documents sur l'histoire des subsistances dans le district de Bergues*. Lille: C. Robbe, 1914–21.

———. *Etudes Orléanaises*, vol. 1, *Contribution à l'étude des structures sociales à la fin du XVIIIe siècle*. Paris: Commission d'histoire économique et sociale de la Révolution, 1962.

———. *Etudes sur la Révolution française*. Paris: PUF, 1954.

———. *The Great Fear of 1789: Rural Panic in Revolutionary France*, trans. J. White. New York: Vintage Books, 1973.

———. *Questions agraires au temps de la Terreur*. La Roche-sur-Yon: H. Potier, 1954.

Le Goff, T. J. A. "An Eighteenth-Century Grain Merchant: Ignace Advisse Desruisseaux." In *French Government and Society, 1500–1850: Essays in Memory of Alfred Cobban*, ed. J. F. Bosher, pp. 92–122. London: Athlone Press, 1973.

———. *Vannes and Its Region: A Study of Town and Country in Eighteenth-Century France*. Oxford: Clarendon Press, 1981.

Lemaire, Robert. *Paroisses et communes de France. Dictionnaire d'histoire administrative et démographique: Oise*. Paris: Ecole des Hautes Etudes en Sciences Sociales, 1976.

Lemarchand, Guy. "La Féodalité et la Révolution française. Seigneurie et communauté paysanne, 1780–1799." *AHRF* 52 (Oct.–Dec. 1980): 536–58.

———. *La Fin du féodalisme dans le pays de Caux. Conjoncture économique et démographique et structure sociale dans une région de grande culture, 1640–1795*. Paris: CTHS, 1989.

———. "Les monastères de Haute-Normandie au XVIIIe siècle." *AHRF* 179 (Jan.–Mar. 1965): 1–28.

Le Mée, René. "Population agglomerée, population éparse au début du XIXe siècle." *Annales de démographie historique*, 1971, pp. 467–93.

Lemercier, P. *Les Justices seigneuriales de la région parisienne de 1580 à 1789*. Paris: Editions Domat-Montchristen, F. Loviton, 1933.

Le Parquier, M. E. "Un Essai d'organisation municipale à Rouen du XVIIIe siècle. Le règlement pour l'administration de la Ville de Rouen du 15 juin 1767." *Précis analytique des travaux de l'Académie des sciences, belles-lettres et arts de Rouen*, 1933, pp. 123–40.

Le Roy, Gabriel. *Les Maires de Melun et le pouvoir municipal avant 1789*. Meaux: A. LeBlondel, 1875.

Le Roy Ladurie, Emmanuel. "L'Aménorhee de famine (XVIIe–XX siècles)." *AESC* 24 (1969): 1589–1601.

———. *Les Paysans du Lanquedoc*, 2 vols. Paris: Mouton, 1966.

———. "Pour une modèle de l'économie rurale française au XVIIIe siècle." *Cahiers d'histoire* 19 (1974): 1–27.

Letaconnoux, Joseph. "La Question des subsistances et du commerce des grains en France au XVIIIe siècle." *RHM* 8 (1906–7): 409–45.

———. *Les Subsistances et commerce des grains en Bretagne au XVIIIe siècle*. Rennes: Oberthur, 1909.

———. "Les Transports en France au XVIIIe siècle." *RHMC* 11 (1908–9): 97–114, 268–92.

Lethuillier, Jean-Pierre. "Les Structures socio-professionelles à Falaise à la fin du XVIIIe siècle." *Revue d'histoire économique et social* 55 (1977): 42–69.

Levine, David, ed. *Proletarianization and Family History*. Orlando: Academic Press, 1984.

Levy, Darline Gay, and Harriet B. Applewhite. "Women of the Popular Classes in Revolutionary Paris, 1789–1795." In *Women, War, and Revolution,* ed. C. R. Berkin and C. M. Lovett, pp. 9–36. New York: Holmes & Meier, 1980.

Levy, Darline Gay, Harriet B. Applewhite, and Mary Durham Johnson, eds. *Women in Revolutionary Paris, 1789–1795.* Urbana: University of Illinois Press, 1979.

Ljublinski, Vladimir S. *La Guerre des Farines. Contribution à l'histoire de la lutte des classes en France à la veille de la Révolution,* trans. F. Adiba and J. Radiquet. Grenoble: Presses Universitaires de Grenoble, 1979.

———. "Voltaire et la guerre des farines. *AHRF* 31 (1959): 127–45.

Logue, Kenneth J. *Popular Disturbances in Scotland, 1780–1815.* Edinburgh: J. Donald, 1979.

Louchitsky, Jean. "Régime agraire et populations agricoles dans les environs de Paris à la veille de la Révolution." *RHM* 8 (1933): 97–142.

Lucas, Colin. "The Crowd and Politics Between Ancien Regime and Revolution in France." *JMH* 60 (Sept. 1988): 421–57.

Macfarlane, Alan. *The Origins of English Individualism: The Family, Property, and Social Transition.* Oxford: Basil Blackwell, 1978.

Margadant, Ted W. *French Peasants in Revolt: The Insurrection of 1851.* Princeton: Princeton University Press, 1979.

Margairaz, Dominique. *Foires et marchés dans la France préindustrielle.* Paris: l'Ecole des Hautes Etudes en Sciences sociales, 1988.

Margolis, Diane R. "Considering Women's Experience: A Reformulation of Power Theory." *Theory and Society* 18 (1989): 387–416.

Marion, Marcel. *Dictionnaire des Institutions de la France au XVIIe et XVIIIe siècles.* 1923. Reprint, Paris: A. & J. Picard, 1979.

Marjolin, R. "Troubles provoqués en France par la disette de 1816–1817." *RHM* 8 (1933): 423–60.

Markoff, John. "Contexts and Forms of Rural Revolt: France 1789." *Journal of Conflict Resolution* 30 (June 1986): 253–89.

———. "Peasant Grievances and Peasant Insurrection: France in 1789." *JMH* 62 (Sept. 1990): 445–76.

———. "Peasant Protest: The Claims of Lord, Church, and State in the *Cahiers de doléances* of 1789." *Comparatives Studies in History and Society* 32 (July 1990): 413–54.

———. "The Social Geography of Rural Revolt at the Beginning of the French Revolution." *American Sociological Review* 50 (Dec. 1985): 761–81.

———. "When and How Did the Countryside Revolt? A Statistical Study of Revolutionary France, 1788–1793." Paper presented before the Western Society for French History, Reno, Nevada, 1991.

Marque, J.-P. *Institution municipale et groupes sociaux. Gray, petite ville de province (1690–1790).* Paris: Les Belles Lettres, 1979.

Massé, P. "Disette et mendicité en Poitou, XVIIIe–XIXe siècles." *L'Actualité de l'histoire* 27 (1959): 1–11.

Mazière, Léon. "Du Gouvernement et de l'administration de la commune de Noyon. Attribution des magistrats municipaux." *Comptes rendus et mémoires du Comité archéologique et historique de Noyon* 10 (1893): 207–414.

McPhail, Clark. *The Myth of the Madding Crowd.* New York: Aldine de Gruyter, 1991.

McPhee, Peter. "The French Revolution, Peasants, and Capitalism." *AHA* 94 (Dec. 1989): 1265–80.

Medick, Hans. "Plebeian Culture in the Transition to Capitalism." In *Culture, Ideology,* and Politics: Essays for Eric Hobsbawm, pp. 84–112. London: Routledge & Kegan Paul, 1982.

Meek, R. L. The Economics of Physiocracy. Cambridge, Mass.: Harvard University Press, 1963.

Mendras, Henri. Sociétés paysannes. Eléments pour une théorie de la paysannerie. Paris: Armand Colin, 1976.

Merrick, Jeffrey W. The Desacralization of the French Monarchy in the Eighteenth Century. Baton Rouge: Louisiana State University Press, 1990.

Merriman, John M., ed. Consciousness and Class Experience in Nineteenth-Century Europe. New York: Holmes & Meier, 1979.

Meuvret, Jean. Etudes d'histoire économique. Paris: Armand Colin, 1971.

———. Le Problème des subsistances à l'époque de Louis XIV, vol. 1, La Production des céréales dans la France du XVIIe et du XVIIIe siècle; vol. 2, La Production des céréales et la société rurale; vol. 3, Le Commerce des grains et la conjoncture. Paris: Armand Colin, 1977, 1987, 1988.

Meyer, Edmond. Histoire de la ville de Vernon et de son ancienne châtellenie, 2 vols. Les Andelys: Delcroix, 1874–76.

Miller, Judith. "Politics and Urban Provisioning Crisis: Bakers, Police, and Parlements in France, 1750–1793." JMH 64 (June 1992): 227–62.

———. "The Pragmatic Economy: Liberal Reforms and the Grain Trade in Upper Normandy, 1750–1789." Ph.D. disseration. Durham, N.C.: Duke University, 1987.

Mintz, Sidney. "The Rural Proletariat and the Problem of Rural Proletarian Consciousness." Journal of Peasant Studies 1 (Apr. 1974): 291–325.

Mireau, Emile. Une Province française au temps du Grand Roi: La Brie. Paris: Hachette, 1979.

Mitchell, Harvey. "The World Between the Literate and Oral Traditions in Eighteenth-Century France: Ecclesiastical Instructions and Popular Mentalities." Studies in Eighteenth-Century Culture 8 (1979): 33–67.

Moreau, Henri. "Le Rôle des subdélégués au XVIIIe siècle. Justice, police et affaires militaires." Annales de Bourgogne 29 (1957): 225–56.

Morel, Alan. "Pouvoir et idéologies au sien du village picard hier et aujourd'hui." AESC 30 (Jan.–Feb. 1975): 161–76.

Moriceau, Jean-Marc. "Les 'Baccanals' ou grèves de moissonneurs au nord de l'Ile-de-France." In Mouvements populaires et conscience sociale, XVIe–XIXe siècles, ed. J. Nicolas, pp. 420–34. Paris: Maloine, 1985.

———. "Mariages et foyers paysans aux XVIe et XVIIe siècles. L'Exemple des campagnes du sud de Paris." RHMC 28 (July 1981): 481–502.

———. "Un Système de protection sociale efficace. Exemple des vieux fermiers de l'Ile-de-France (XVIIe–début XIXe siècle)." Annales de démographie historique, 1985, pp. 127–44.

Moriceau, Jean-Marc, and Gilles Postel-Vinay. Ferme, Entreprise, Famille. Grande exploitation et changements agricoles, XVII–XIX siècles. Paris: Ecole des Hautes Etudes en Sciences Sociales, 1992.

Morineau, Michel E. "A la Halle de Charleville: Fourniture et prix des grains ou les mécanismes du marché (1647–1821)." In Actes du 95e Congrès national des Sociétés savantes, Reims, 1970, pp. 159–211. Paris: Bibliothèque nationale, 1974.

———. "Budgets populaires en France au dix-huitième siècle." Revue d'histoire économique et sociale 50 (1972): 203–37, 449–81.

———. Les Faux-semblants d'un démarrage économique. Agriculture et démographie en France au XVIIIe siècle. Paris: Armand Colin, 1970.

Moulin, Annie. *Les Paysans dans la société française de la Révolution à nos jours*. Paris: Editions du Seuil, 1988.

Mousnier, Roland. *The Institutions of France Under the Absolute Monarchy, 1598–1789*, 2 vols., trans. B. Pearce and A. Goldhammer. Chicago: University of Chicago Press, 1979, 1980.

———. *Peasant Uprisings in Seventeenth-Century France, Russia, and China*, trans. B. Pearce. New York: Harper & Row, 1970.

Muchembled, Robert. *Culture populaire et culture des élites dans la France moderne (XVe–XVIIIe siècles)*. Paris: Flammarion, 1978.

Neveux, Hugues, and Bernard Garnier. "Valeur de la terre, production agricole et marché urbain au milieu de XVIIIe siècle. L'Exemple de la Normandie entre la baie de Seine et la baie de Veys." In *Problèmes agraires et société rurale: Normandie et Europe du nord-ouest (XVIe–XIXe siècles)*, ed. G. Desert et al., pp. 43–99. Cahiers des Annales de Normandie, no. 11. Caen, 1979.

Nicolas, Jean. "Un Chantier toujours neuf." In *Mouvements populaires et conscience sociale, XVIe–XIXe siècle*, ed. J. Nicolas, pp. 13–21. Paris: Maloine, 1985.

Ortner, Sherry. "Theory in Anthropology Since the Sixties." *Comparative Studies in Society and History* 26 (1984): 126–66.

Outhwaite, R. B. "Dearth and Government Intervention in English Grain Markets, 1590–1700." *Economic History Review*, n.s., 34 (Aug. 1981): 389–406.

———. *Dearth, Public Policy, and Social Disturbance in England, 1550–1800*. London: Macmillan Education, 1991.

Paris, André. "Droits seigneuriaux, jachère et vaine pâture dans la région de Montfort-l'Amaury, XVIIIe–XIXe siècles." In *Ethnologie et histoire. Forces productives et problèmes de transition*. Paris: Editions sociales, 1975.

Payne, Harry C. "Pauvreté, Misère, and the Aims of Enlightened Economics." *Studies on Voltaire and the Eighteenth Century* 154 (1976): 1581–92.

———. *The Philosophes and the People*. New Haven: Yale University Press, 1976.

Peristiany, J. G., ed. *Honor and Shame: The Values of Mediterranean Society*. Chicago: University of Chicago Press, 1966.

Perrot, Jean-Claude. "Introduction à l'emploi des registres fiscaux en histoire sociale: L'Exemple de Caen au XVIIIe siècle." *Annales de Normandie*, 1966, 33–63.

Petit, Pierre. *Gournay-en-Bray. Pour conserver le souvenir du passé*. Gournay-en-Bray: Eclaireur Brayon, 1978.

Petrow, Eugène. "Les Communaux et les servitudes rurales au XVIIIe siècle." *AHRF* 15 (1938): 459–62.

Philipponneau, Michel. *La Vie rurale de la banlieue parisienne. Etude de géographie humaine*. Paris: Armand Colin, 1956.

Pillorget, René. *Les Mouvements insurrectionnels de Provence entre 1596 et 1715*. Paris: A. Pedone, 1975.

Plongeron, Bernard. *La Vie quotidienne du clergé français au XVIIIe siècle*. Paris: Hachette, 1974.

Popkin, Samuel. *The Rational Peasant: The Political Economy of Rural Society in Vietnam*. Berkeley and Los Angeles: University of California Press, 1979.

Porchnev, Boris. *Les Soulèvements populaires en France de 1623 à 1648*. Paris: SEVPEN, 1963.

Post, John D. *Food Shortage, Climatic Variability, and Epidemic Disease in Preindustrial Europe: The Mortality Peak in the Early 1740s*. Ithaca, N.Y.: Cornell University Press, 1985.

———. *The Last Great Subsistence Crisis in the Western World*. Baltimore: Johns Hopkins University Press, 1977.

Postel-Vinay, Gilles. *La Rente foncière dans le capitalisme agricole. L'Exemple du soissonnais.* Paris: Maspero, 1974.

Quinault, R., and J. Stevenson, eds. *Popular Protest and Public Order: Six Studies in British History, 1790–1920.* London: George Allen, Unwin, 1974.

Raeff, Marc. "The Well-Ordered Police State and the Development of Modernity in Seventeenth- and Eighteenth-Century Europe: An Attempt at a Comparative Approach." *AHR* 80 (Dec. 1975): 1221–43.

Ramsay, Clay. *The Ideology of the Great Fear: The Soissonnais in 1789.* Baltimore: Johns Hopkins University Press, 1992.

Reddy, William M. *The Rise of Market Culture: The Textile Trade and French Society, 1750–1900.* Cambridge: Cambridge University Press, 1984.

Redfield, Robert. *The Little Community: Peasant Society and Culture.* Chicago: University of Chicago Press, 1960.

Rey, Auguste. *Notes sur mon village. Syndics et municipalités à la fin de l'Ancien Régime.* Paris: H. Champion, 1891.

Ricommard, Jean. *La Lieutenance générale de police à Troyes au XVIIIe siècle.* Paris: Hachette, 1934.

———. "Les subdélégués des intendants aux XVIIe et XVIIIe siècles." *Information historique* 24 (Sept.–Oct. 1962): 139–48; (Nov.–Dec. 1962): 190–95; 25 (Jan.–Feb. 1963): 1–8.

Robin, Régine. *La Société française en 1789. Semur-en-Auxois.* Paris: Plon, 1970.

Roche, Daniel. *Le Peuple de Paris. Essai sur la culture populaire au XVIIIe siècle.* Paris: Aubier-Montaigne, 1981.

Roeder, Philip. "Legitimacy and Peasant Revolution: An Alternative to the Moral Economy." *Peasant Studies* 11 (Spring 1984): 149–68.

Rogers, John W. "The Opposition to the Physiocrats: A Study of Economic Thought and Policy in the Ancien Régime, 1750–1789." Ph.D. dissertation, Johns Hopkins University, 1971.

Rogers, Susan. "Female Forms of Power and the Myth of Male Dominance: A Model of Female/Male Interaction in Peasant Society." *American Ethnologist* 2 (Nov. 1975): 727–56.

———. "Women's Place: A Critical Review of Anthropological Theory." *Comparative Studies in Society and History* 20 (Jan. 1978): 123–62.

Root, Hilton L. *Peasants and King in Burgundy: Agrarian Foundations of French Absolutism.* Berkeley and Los Angeles: University of California Press, 1987.

———. "The Rural Community and the French Revolution." In *The French Revolution and the Creation of Modern Political Culture*, vol. 1, *The Politcal Culture of the Old Regime*, ed. K. Baker, pp. 141–53. Oxford: Pergamon Press, 1987.

Roover, Raymond de. "The Concept of the Just Price: Theory and Economic Politics." *Journal of Economic History* 18 (Dec. 1958): 418–34.

Roseberry, William. *Anthropologies and Histories: Essays in Culture, History, and Political Economy.* New Brunswick, N.J.: Rutgers University Press, 1989.

Rudé, George. *The Crowd in History: A Study of Popular Disturbances in France and England, 1730–1848.* 1964. Rev. ed. London: Lawrence & Wishart, 1981.

———. *The Crowd in the French Revolution.* Oxford: Oxford University Press, 1959.

———. *Ideology and Popular Protest.* New York: Pantheon Books, 1980.

———. *Protest and Punishment.* Oxford: Oxford University Press, 1978.

———. "La Taxation populaire de mai 1775 à Paris et dans la région parisienne." *AHRF* 143 (Apr.–June 1956): 139–79.

———. "La Taxation populaire de mai 1775 en Picardie, en Normandie et dans le Beauvaisis." *AHRF* 165 (July–Sept. 1961): 305–26.

————. "Urbanization and Popular Protest in Eighteenth-Century Europe." *Eighteenth-Century Life* 2 (Mar. 1976): 46–48.

Ruff, Julius. *Crime, Justice, and Public Order in Old Regime France: The Sénéchaussées of Libourne and Bazas, 1696–1789*. London: Croom Helm, 1984.

Sabean, David. *Power in the Blood: Popular Culture and Village Discourse in Early Modern Germany*. Cambridge: Cambridge University Press, 1984.

Sagnac, Philippe. "L'Agriculture et les classes sociales rurales en France au XVIIIe siècle." *Revue de synthèse historique* 12 (1906): 133–51.

Sahlins, Marshall. *Historical Metaphors and Mythical Realities: Structure in the Early History of the Sandwich Islands Kingdom*. Ann Arbor: University of Michigan Press, 1981.

Saint-Germain, Jacques. *La Vie quotidienne en France à la fin du grand siècle*. Paris: Hachette, 1965.

Saint-Jacob, Pierre de. "Etudes sur l'ancienne communauté rurale en Bourgogne. *Annales de Bourgogne* 13 (1941): 169–202; 15 (1943): 173–84; 18 (1946): 237–50; 25 (1953): 225–40.

————. *Les Paysans de la Bourgogne du Nord au dernier siècle de l'Ancien Régime*. Paris: Les Belles Lettres, 1960.

Samson, René. *La Guerre des Farines dans le Beauvaisis, 1775*. Beauvais: Centre départemental de documentation pédagogique, 1983.

Sars, Maxime de. *Lenoir: Lieutenant général de police, 1732–1807*. Paris: Hachette, 1948.

Schneider, Robert. *Public Life in Toulouse, 1463–1789: From Municipal Republic to Cosmopolitan City*. Ithaca, N.Y.: Cornell University Press, 1989.

Schwartz, Robert. *Policing the Poor in Eighteenth-Century France*. Chapel Hill: University of North Carolina Press, 1988.

Scott, James. "Everyday Forms of Peasant Resistance." *Journal of Peasant Studies* 13 (Jan. 1986): 5–35.

————. "Hegemony and the Peasantry." *Politics and Society* 7 (1977): 267–96.

————. *Moral Economy of the Peasant: Rebellion and Subsistence in Southeast Asia*. New Haven: Yale University Press, 1976.

————. *Weapons of the Weak: Everyday Forms of Peasant Resistance*. New Haven: Yale University Press, 1985.

Scott, Joan W. *Gender and the Politics of History*. New York: Columbia University Press, 1988.

Sée, Henri. *Economic and Social Conditions in France in the Eighteenth Century*, trans. E. H. Zeydel. New York: Cooper Square Publishers, 1968.

Segalen, Martine. *Mari et femme dans la société paysanne*. Paris: Flammarion, 1980.

Sen, Amartya. *Poverty and Famines: An Essay on Entitlement and Deprivation*. Oxford: Oxford University Press, 1981.

Seré-Depoin. *Trois catastrophes à Pontoise en 1788–1789. Etude administrative et de moeurs sous l'Ancien Régime*. Pontoise: A Seyés, 1880.

Sewell, William H. *Work and Revolution in France: The Language of Labor from the Old Regime to 1848*. Cambridge: Cambridge University Press, 1980.

Shanin, Teodor, ed. *Peasants and Peasant Societies: Selected Readings*, 2nd ed. London: Basil Blackwell, 1987.

Shepherd, Perry. *Turgot and the Six Edicts*. New York: AMS Press, 1903.

Sheppard, Thomas F. *Lourmarin in the Eighteenth Century: A Study of a French Village*. Baltimore: Johns Hopkins University Press, 1971.

Sider, Gerard. *Culture and Class in Anthropology and History: A Newfoundland Illustration*. Cambridge and Paris: Cambridge University Press and Editions de la Maison des Sciences de l'Homme, 1986.

Sion, Jules. *Les Paysans de la Normandie orientale. Pays de Caux, Bray, Vexin normand, vallée de la Seine.* Paris: Armand Colin, 1909.

Skocpol, Theda, ed. *Vision and Method in Historical Sociology.* Cambridge: Cambridge University Press, 1984.

Slack, Paul, ed. *Rebellion, Popular Protest, and the Social Order in Early Modern England.* Cambridge: Cambridge University Press, 1984.

Smelser, Neil J. *Theory of Collective Behavior.* New York: The Free Press, 1963.

Soboul, Albert. "La Communauté rurale (XVIIIe–XIXe siècles). Problèmes de base." *Revue de synthèse,* 1957, pp. 283–315.

———. *Contributions à l'histoire paysanne de la révolution française.* Paris: Editions sociales, 1977.

———. *La France à la veille de la Révolution.* Paris: SEDES, 1974.

———. "The French Rural Community in the Eighteenth Centuries." *Past and Present* 10 (1956): 78–95.

———. "Problèmes de la communauté rurale en France (XVIIIe–XIXe siècles)." In *Ethnologie et histoire. Forces productives et problèmes de transition.* Paris: Editions sociales, 1975.

———. *Problèmes paysans de la Révolution, 1789–1848.* Paris: Maspero, 1983.

———. *Les Sans-Culottes Parisiens en l'an II. Mouvement populaire et gouvernement révolutionnaire.* Paris: Clavreuil, 1958.

Sonenscher, Michael. *Work and Wages: Natural Law, Politics, and the Eighteenth-Century French Trades.* Cambridge: Cambridge University Press, 1989.

Stevenson, John. "The 'Moral Economy' of the English Crowd: Myth and Reality." In *Order and Disorder in Early Modern England,* ed. A. Fletcher and J. Stevenson, pp. 218–38. Cambridge: Cambridge University Press, 1985.

———. *Popular Disturbances in England, 1700–1870.* London: Longman, 1979.

Stone, Bailey. *The Parlement of Paris, 1774–1789.* Chapel Hill: University of North Carolina Press, 1981.

Sutherland, Donald. *France, 1789–1815: Revolution and Counterrevolution.* New York, Oxford: Oxford University Press, 1986.

Tackett, Timothy. "L'Histoire sociale du clergé diocésain pendant le XVIIIe siècle." *RHMC* 26 (1979): 198–234.

———. *Priest and Parish in Eighteenth-Century France: A Social and Political Study of the Cures in a Diocese of Dauphine, 1750–1791.* Princeton: Princeton University Press, 1977.

Tackett, Timothy, and Claude Langlois. "Ecclesiastical Structures and Clerical Geography on the Eve of the French Revolution." *FHS* 11 (Spring 1980): 352–70.

Tarle, E. V. *L'Industrie dans les campagnes en France à la fin de l'Ancien Régime.* Paris: E. Cornely, 1910.

Taylor, G. V. "Types of Capitalism in Eighteenth-Century France." *English Historical Review,* 79 (1964): 478–97.

Temple, Nora. "The Control and Exploitation of French Towns During the Ancien Régime." *History,* n.s., 51 (1966): 16–31.

Thomis, Malcolm I., and Jennifer Grimmett. *Women in Protest, 1800–1850.* London: Croom Helm, 1982.

Thompson, E. P. *Customs in Common.* London: Merlin Press, 1991.

———. "Eighteenth-Century English Society: Class Struggle Without Class?" *Social History* 3 (May 1978): 133–65.

———. "Folklore, Anthropology, and Social History." *Indian Historical Review* 3 (Jan. 1979): 247–66, as reprinted as a Studies in Labour History pamphlet (Sussex, 1979).

———. "The Moral Economy of the English Crowd in the Eighteenth Century." *Past and Present* 50 (1971): 76–136.

———. "Patrician Society, Plebeian Culture." *Journal of Social History* 7 (Summer 1974): 382–405.

———. *The Poverty of Theory and Other Essays.* London: Monthly Review Press, 1978.

———. " 'Rough Music': Le Charivari anglais." *AESC* 27 (1972): 285–312.

Tilly, Charles. *Big Structures, Large Processes, Huge Comparisons.* New York: Russell Sage Foundation, 1984.

———. *The Contentious French: Four Centuries of Popular Struggle.* Cambridge, Mass.: Belknap Press of Harvard University Press, 1986.

———. *From Mobilization to Revolution.* Reading, Mass.: Addison-Wesley, 1978.

———. "The Modernization of Political Conflict in France." In *Perspectives on Modernization: Essays in Memory of Ian Weinberg,* ed. E. B. Harvey. Toronto: University of Toronto Press, 1972.

———. "Proletarianization and Rural Collective Action in East Anglia and Elsewhere, 1500–1900." *Peasant Studies* 10 (Fall 1982): 5–34.

Tilly, Charles, ed. *The Formation of National States in Western Europe.* Princeton: Princeton University Press, 1975.

Tilly, Charles, Louise A. Tilly, and Richard Tilly. *The Rebellious Century, 1830–1930.* London: J. M. Dent & Sons, 1975.

Tilly, Louise A. "The Decline and Disappearance of the Classical Food Riot in France." New School for Social Research Working Paper No. 147, 1992.

———. "Food Entitlement, Famine, and Conflict." *JIH* 14 (1983): 333–49.

———. "The Food Riot as a Form of Political Conflict in France." *JIH* 2 (1971): 23–57.

Tilly, Louise A., and Joan W. Scott. *Women, Work, and Family.* Boston: Houghton Mifflin, 1978.

Tirat, J.-Y. "Problèmes de méthode en histoire sociale." *RHMC* 10 (July–Sept. 1963): 211–18.

Tocqueville, Alexis de. *The Old Regime and the French Revolution,* trans. S. Gilbert. New York: Doubleday, 1955.

Tönnies, Ferdinand. *Community and Society,* trans. J. Samples. 1887. New Brunswick, N.J.: Transaction Books, 1988.

Trou, Abbé. *Recherches historiques, archéologiques et biographiques sur la ville de Pontoise.* Pontoise: Dufey, 1841.

Tulippe, Omer. *L'Habitat rural en Seine-et-Oise. Essai de géographie du peuplement.* Paris: Librairie du Recueil Sirey, 1934.

Turner, Victor. *Drama, Fields, and Metaphors: Symbolic Action in Human Society.* Ithaca, N.Y.: Cornell University Press, 1974.

———. *The Ritual Process: Structure and Anti-Structure.* Ithaca, N.Y.: Cornell University Press, 1977.

Usher, Abbot P. *The History of the Grain Trade in France, 1400–1710.* Cambridge, Mass.: Harvard University Press, 1913.

Vaissière, Pierre de. *Les Curés de campagne de l'ancienne France.* Paris: Armand Colin, 1933.

Vardi, Liana. "Peasants and the Law: A Village Appeals to the French Royal Council, 1768–1791." *Social History* 13 (Oct. 1988): 295–313.

Venard, Marc. *Bourgeois et paysans au XVIIe siècle. Recherche sur le rôle des bourgeois parisiens dans la vie agricole au sud de Paris au XVII siècle.* Paris: SEVPEN, 1957.

———. "Une Classe rurale puissante au XVIIe siècle. Les Laboureurs au sud de Paris." *AESC* 10 (1955): 517–25.

Vidalenc, Jean. "La Crise de subsistances de 1817 dans la Seine-Inférieure." *Actes du 93e Congrès national des Sociétés savantes, Tours, 1968*, 1:297–350. Paris: Bibliothèque nationale, 1971.

Villes de l'Europe mediterranéenne et de l'Europe occidentale du moyen âge au XIXe siècle. Nice: Les Belles Lettres, 1969.

Villey, Edmond. "La Taxe du pain et les boulangers de la ville de Caen en 1776." *Revue d'économie politique* 2 (1888): 172–92.

Vincent, David. *Bread, Knowledge, and Freedom: A Study of Nineteenth-Century Working Class Autobiography.* London: Methuen, 1981.

Vovelle, Michel. *De la Cave au grenier. Un Itinéraire en Provence au XVIIIe siècle. De l'histoire sociale à l'histoire des mentalités.* Quebec: Comeditex & Serge Fleury, 1980.

———. *The Fall of the French Monarchy, 1787–1792*, trans. S. Burke. Cambridge: Cambridge University Press, 1984.

———. *Idéologies et mentalités.* Paris: Découvert, 1985.

———. "La Représentation populaire de la monarchie." In *The French Revolution and the Creation of Modern Political Culture*, vol. 1, *The Political Culture of the Old Regime*, ed. K. M. Baker. Elmsford, N.Y.: Pergamon Press, 1987.

———. *Ville et campagne au 18e siècle. Chartre et la Beauce.* Paris: Editions sociales, 1980.

Vovelle, Michel, and Daniel Roche. "Bourgeois, rentiers, propriétaires: Elements pour la définition d'une categorie sociale à la fin du 18e siècle." In *Actes du 84e Congrès national des Sociétés savantes, Dijon, 1959*, pp. 419–52. Paris: Imprimerie nationale, 1960.

Walter, Gerard. *Histoire des paysans de France.* Paris: Flammarion, 1963.

Walter, John, and Keith Wrightson. "Dearth and the Social Order in Early Modern England." *Past and Present* 71 (May 1976): 22–42.

Weber, Herman. "Le Sacre de Louis XVI." In *Le Règne de Louis XVI et la guerre d'indépendance américaine, Actes du colloque international de Sorèze, 1976*, pp. 11–22. Dourgne, 1977.

Weller, R. P., and S. E. Guggenheim, eds. *Power and Protest in the Countryside: Studies of Rural Unrest in Asia, Europe, and Latin America.* Durham, N.C.: Duke University Press Policy Studies, 1982.

Wells, Roger A. E. "The Development of the English Rural Proletariat and Social Protest, 1700–1850." *Journal of Peasant Studies* 6 (Jan. 1979): 115–39.

———. *Wretched Faces: Famine in Wartime England, 1793–1801.* New York: St. Martin's Press, 1988.

Weulersse, Georges. *La Physiocratie à la fin du règne de Louis XV (1770–1774).* Paris: PUF, 1959.

———. *La Physiocratie sous les ministères de Turgot et de Necker (1774–1781).* Paris: PUF, 1950.

Wilentz, Sean, ed. *Rites of Power: Symbolism, Ritual, and Politics Since the Middle Ages.* Philadelphia: University of Pennsylvania Press, 1985.

Williams, Dale E. "Morals, Markets, and the English Crowd in 1766." *Past and Present* 104 (Aug. 1984): 56–73.

———. "Were 'Hunger' Rioters Really Hungry? Some Demographic Evidence." *Past and Present* 71 (May 1976): 70–75.

Wolf, Eric. "The Vicissitudes of the Closed Corporate Peasant Community." *American Ethnologist* 13 (May 1986): 325–29.

Woods, Robert. "Individuals in the Rioting Crowd: A New Approach." *JIH* 14 (1983): 1–24.

Wuthnow, Robert. *Communities of Discourse: Ideology and Social Structure in the Reforma-
    tion, the Enlightenment, and European Socialism.* Cambridge: Cambridge University
    Press, 1989.
Zink, Anne. *Azereix: La Vie d'une communauté rurale à la fin du XVIII siècle.* Paris: J.
    Touzot, 1969.
Zunz, Olivier, ed. *Reliving the Past: The Worlds of Social History.* Chapel Hill: University
    of North Carolina Press, 1985.
Zupko, Ronald E. *French Weights and Measures Before the Revolution: A Dictionary of
    Provincial and Local Units.* Bloomington: Indiana University Press, 1978.

INDEX